EATON'S

THE TRANS-CANADA STORE

BRUCE ALLEN KOPYTEK

THE
History
PRESS

Published by The History Press
Charleston, SC 29403
www.historypress.net

Cover images: Front: images of Timothy Eaton, Round Room, Montreal Store, Gordie Howe and Winnipeg Store courtesy of Eaton Fonds; Canada map and image of Queen Street Store from the collection of the author. Back: images of the Yorkdale Store, Montréal map/ guide, "Eaton People" from the collection of the author; Eaton Carte Comptable courtesy of Martin Pelletier; Eaton's of Canada credit card courtesy of Scott Nimmo.

First published 2014

Manufactured in the United States

ISBN 978.1.62619.219.5

Library of Congress CIP data applied for.

Notice: The information in this book is true and complete to the best of our knowledge. It is offered without guarantee on the part of the author or The History Press. The author and The History Press disclaim all liability in connection with the use of this book.

Dedicated to my late father, Walter John Kopytek, who by planning magnificent annual car trips for his family, gave me a love of travel and enriched me with a world of positive memories that can never be forgotten.

Thanks, Dad!

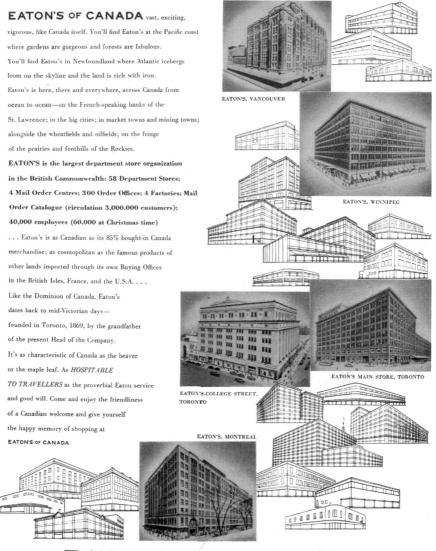

EATON'S OF CANADA vast, exciting, vigorous, like Canada itself. You'll find Eaton's at the Pacific coast where gardens are gorgeous and forests are fabulous. You'll find Eaton's in Newfoundland where Atlantic icebergs loom on the skyline and the land is rich with iron. Eaton's is here, there and everywhere, across Canada from ocean to ocean—on the French-speaking banks of the St. Lawrence; in the big cities; in market towns and mining towns; alongside the wheatfields and oilfields; on the fringe of the prairies and foothills of the Rockies.

EATON'S is the largest department store organization in the British Commonwealth: 58 Department Stores; 4 Mail Order Centres; 300 Order Offices; 4 Factories; Mail Order Catalogue (circulation 3,000,000 customers); 40,000 employees (60,000 at Christmas time)

... Eaton's is as Canadian as its 85% bought-in Canada merchandise; as cosmopolitan as the famous products of other lands imported through its own Buying Offices in the British Isles, France, and the U.S.A. ... Like the Dominion of Canada, Eaton's dates back to mid-Victorian days—founded in Toronto, 1869, by the grandfather of the present Head of the Company. It's as characteristic of Canada as the beaver or the maple leaf. As *HOSPITABLE TO TRAVELLERS* as the proverbial Eaton service and good will. Come and enjoy the friendliness of a Canadian welcome and give yourself the happy memory of shopping at **EATON'S OF CANADA**

EATON'S, VANCOUVER

EATON'S, WINNIPEG

EATON'S-COLLEGE STREET, TORONTO

EATON'S MAIN STORE, TORONTO

EATON'S, MONTREAL

EATON'S OF CANADA
LARGEST DEPARTMENT-STORE ORGANIZATION IN THE BRITISH COMMONWEALTH

A 1950s Eaton's of Canada advertisement portraying the company as "vast, exciting, vigorous" and operating from British Columbia on the Pacific Ocean to Newfoundland in the east—*A Mari Usque ad Mare. Collection of the author.*

Contents

CONTENTS

Acknowledgements

To tell the story of the T. Eaton Co. Limited is a task that literally stretches from coast to coast, just like the "Trans-Canada Store" itself. As a result, I was aided by many, many Canadians whose knowledge and enthusiasm for the topic equaled, and in many cases exceeded, my own. Their help ensured the accuracy and quality of the work, and it is no cliché to say that without fervent collaborators, no such book could ever be written.

Foremost among these has been the staff of the magnificent Archives of Ontario, located on the campus of York University in Toronto. Not only were Elena Bartucci, Serge Paquet, Patricia Lawton and Garin Kirwan helpful to this stranger (who was full of special requests and complicated questions!), but their sheer enthusiasm and willingness to be of every assistance was also, in a word, breathtaking. My experience leads me to believe that these qualities are viral at the institution, because the whole staff is, without fail, professional, helpful, kind and brimming over with all of the good qualities that humanity assumes. I offer special thanks to Elena for taking the time to negotiate a reasonable settlement to a parking ticket that I got while having a bad day on-site!

I am also fundamentally indebted to Fredrik Eaton, OC, O.Ont., who was very agreeable to the idea of yet another book about the history of his family's retail store and generously shared a book from his library for my use. Gay Raybould, Mr. Eaton's assistant, is to be commended for deftly managing the correspondence between two very busy people.

In addition, the experience of researching and writing this book has led me to believe that Canada's librarians and archivists are exemplary in their skill and service, whether in person or over long distances. My gratitude goes out to George R. French of the Corner Brook Museum and Archives; Garry D. Shutlak of the Nova Scotia Archives; Patricia of the Spring Garden Road Library of the Halifax Public Libraries; Kristen Morton of the Moncton Museum and Archives; Patricia Scoffield of the Peterborough Public Library; Ivars Kops of the Burlington Public Library; Karen Ball-Pyatt of the Kitchener Public Library; Sandra Enskat of the St. Catharines Public Library; Margaret Houghton and Jennifer McFadden of the Hamilton Public Library; Denise Kirk of the Brantford Public Library; Kate McCullough of the Chatham Public Library; Pat Reid and Kirsten Bertrand of the Greater Sudbury Public Library; Rhoda Berger of the North Bay Public Library; Gordon Stonehouse of the Teck Centennial Library in Kirkland Lake; Kevin Meraglia of the Sault Ste. Marie Public Library; the reference Staff of the Thunder Bay Public Library; Elaine Kozakovich of the Saskatoon Public Library; May P. Chan of the Regina Public Library; Dana Turgeon of the City of Regina Archives; Barb Gillard of the Calgary Public Library; Shelley Ross of the Medicine Hat Public Library; Angie Mills of the Stanley E. Milner Library of Edmonton; Joe Haigh of the New Westminster Public Library; Patti Wotherspoon, Barbara Webb and Kate Russel of the Vancouver Public Library; and Stephen Ruttan of the Greater Victoria Public Library. Everyone listed here responded with sincere interest in my quest for information and made my job as a researcher much, much easier than it (frightfully) might have been.

Professor Franco A. Fava of the University of Turin contacted me and indicated that we had a shared interest in the history of commerce. His encouragement and support have led to a newfound friendship and desire for cooperation on future projects, including involvement with his planned online Museum of European Commerce (MECC).

A number of individuals took up my search for Eaton's history by giving of their own precious time. Among these, I am indebted to Ross Crockford of Victoria for providing me with information about Eaton's in the town of his residence and for showing me how valuable social media can be as a research tool. In this respect, the Vintage Victoria, Vintage Moncton and Vintage Charlottetown (Ian Scott) FaceBook pages were surprisingly helpful. Catherine Hennessey of Charlottetown generously shared her own research with me, simply for the asking. Darrell Bateman kindly allowed me to use his unique photos of Eaton's stores in British Columbia. Historian John Rhodes generously helped with facts about Chatham, Ontario's long-gone Eaton operation. Guy Van Buekenhout transmitted his parents' Eaton stories over a long distance, and Scott Nimmo was kind enough to send charge card images from his collection that grace this book. Hubert and Leona Smith of New Brunswick even helped me reconstruct the old Moncton Eaton's over the phone!

During the research phase of this book's preparation, I met Kelly Mathews of Toronto, who is a fount of knowledge about Eaton Hall, and the tour of the property that she conducted for my wife and me was splendid and profoundly informative. Kelly also introduced me to her dear and charming "Nana," Olga Gudz, who shared her own story with me so entertainingly. I am also grateful to Kelly, who said that her Nana would enjoy my "accent," for teaching me the proper pronunciation of Omemee, Lady Eaton's birthplace. (That's "Oh, Mimi," by the way.)

A number of journalists indulged my requests for stories and information from Canadians who regularly listen to their radio programs or read their articles. As a result, I made contact with many of the people who were so keen to register their memories of working or shopping at Eaton's. Among them are Vanessa Blanch of CBC Radio Moncton, Alan Cochrane and Brent Mazerolle of the *Moncton Times and Transcript*, Jeff Mahoney of the *Hamilton Spectator* and Diane Crocker of the *Western Star*.

It would take a book in and of itself to thank all those who spoke with me about their Eaton's experience. Readers will find their names attached to the quotes they provided, and it will be clear to both readers and the contributors themselves that their recollections make this book come alive and put a human face on an enormous institution. My contact with all of these Canadians was certainly one of the great joys of taking on this book project.

Often lost and unrecognized in the process of producing a book such as this one is the work of the copy editor. In this case, the work of Ryan Finn in monitoring and improving the raw product I produced was of high order and greatly appreciated.

As always, my family members have been both a help and an inspiration, but special gratitude, affection and appreciation are, as ever, due to my wife, Carole, who, by her nature, is a partner in all I attempt to accomplish. During the time of my research, she has been colleague, assistant, proofreader and literally a second voice when my own head can't find a way through. Add to that her loving attention to my needs, and it's easy to see why I am a lucky man indeed. Finally, I should thank our cat and companion, Bella, who always stays up late with me while I write—although I am never quite certain that it isn't really just for her midnight snack.

Prologue

A Mari Usque Ad Mare

How compelling it can be when the process of research reveals bits and pieces of information that might otherwise go unnoticed. In the study and examination of history—and, in particular, the history of a certain place, organization or person—mere inquiry can be simply thought-provoking. In certain instances, however, when the time and topic are just right, scrutiny inevitably engages the mind in a riveting and engrossingly intimate way. By way of example, the Canadian coat of arms, seen from an innocuous distance, simply looks like many other heraldic symbols, especially those associated with the British Isles.

Digging a little deeper into the symbolism of the coat of arms, it is easy to recognize the crown and the Royal Crest (a lion holding a red maple leaf), or the escutcheon, also known as a shield, divided into sections representing England (three golden lions on a red background), Scotland (the red lion rampant), Ireland (the harp of Mara) and France (the fleur-de-lis). Elsewhere, the Union Jack and the flag of royal France appear, as do suggestive botanical symbols: the Tudor rose, the shamrock, the thistle and the lily.

Yet it is the motto on the coat of arms that invites even further examination and provides a link to the story of the T. Eaton Co. Limited, one of Canada's greatest commercial organizations and arguably the most outstanding of its homegrown department stores. The Latin phrase *A mari usque ad mare* ("from sea to sea") not only suggests the vast and beautiful nature of Canada itself but also provides a link to this fascinating part of the county's history.

The Royal Coat of Arms of Canada. *Collection of the author.*

Confederation formed the Dominion of Canada in 1867, joining Ontario and Québec with Nova Scotia and New Brunswick into one federal nation. Queen Victoria gave royal assent to the British North America Act of 1867 and proclaimed the Dominion of Canada as of July 1 of that year. Eventually, Manitoba (1870), British Columbia (1871), Prince Edward Island (1873) and Alberta and Saskatchewan (1905) joined the Confederation, in time forming the country with which we are now familiar, a land of sweeping beauty possessed of a gracious citizenry with an astonishing history.

It was British Columbia's conditional requirement to join the Confederation—that the country build a railroad from coast to coast—that, in many ways, truly bound Canada together, making a distinctive nation out of a group of former colonies. The first railway to meet the westernmost province's requirement—albeit with political, financial and logistical difficulty—was the Canadian Pacific Railway (CPR), which was incorporated in 1881. By 1885, the line through Canada's Rocky Mountains had been completed, and in the next year, the CPR operated its first transcontinental through passenger service.

Canada was ultimately crossed by two major railways; the other was the Canadian National (CNR), formed from several financially troubled private lines (including the Grand Trunk Railway in Québec and Ontario and the Intercolonial Railway in the Maritime Provinces) into a truly national rail transportation system. Both the CPR and CNR prospered in competition with each other, and famous trains such as the Dominion, the Continental Limited, the Canadian, the International Limited and the Ocean Limited became Canadian travel icons; they were certainly noted for the luxury of their accommodations, but many of them also carried inexpensive sleeping car accommodation—the so-called colonist cars that brought waves of immigrants and settlers to the more remote parts of the country. The Canadian coat of arms also hints at this bit of history—on a ribbon woven through and behind the whole composition is a secondary motto, *Desiderantes meliorem patriam*, which translates as "desiring a better country." Although the United States had much more aggregate trackage than Canada, no railroad south of the Canadian border could claim truly transcontinental status like the two Canadian giants that daily connected one end of the sprawling nation to the other and served all points in between.

As if that weren't enough, the railways created another uniquely Canadian institution: the grand Château-Hotel. The Canadian Pacific Railway took the lead in developing hotels to complement its rail lines and, under the leadership of President Cornelius Van Horne, began a chain of magnificent hostelries that were to the hospitality industry what the railway itself was to transportation: nothing less than a magnificent achievement. The great idea began, as so many do, humbly, with Van Horne building chalets in the stunning mountain terrain of Western Canada. However, when he was shown the unique hot springs deep in the Rockies, west of Calgary, he hired New York architect Bruce Price to design a hotel in the style reminiscent of a French château to cater to guests who would come there by rail, famously saying that "those hot springs…are worth more than a million dollars."

From the time it opened in 1888, and through several reconstructions, the Banff Springs Hotel became a one-of-a-kind destination in a one-of-a-kind setting. Later, Price designed the Place Viger in Montréal and the iconic Château Frontenac in 1893, on a bluff overlooking the mighty St. Lawrence River and the old town of Québec below. Soon, similar grand hotels popped up all over the place, and Canada had yet another unique coast-to-coast institution to add to its attractions. The CNR—through its precursor, the

Grand Trunk Pacific Railway—got in on the game, too, and built its own chain of railway hotels, including the majestic Château Laurier in Ottawa, Canada's capital.

It should also be noted that the CPR—with its rail lines, luxurious trains, castle-like hotels and the great "Empress" steamships that crossed both the Atlantic and Pacific Oceans—once called itself "the world's greatest transportation system." Later, it added an airline, which along with the national flag-carrier, Air Canada, was truly Canadian, transcontinental and even international in character.

Eaton's, too, was firmly and consistently Canadian from the day of its inception, just two years after Confederation created a nation where once only colonies existed. In many ways, the company's growth mirrored that of Canada itself. In 1937, Eaton's announced a huge, two-day sale in Toronto, naming it the "Trans-Canada Sale," but it wasn't until 1955, after it had achieved the distinction of having retail stores in every province, that the sale took on a deeper meaning, reflecting the true nature of the T. Eaton Co. as the "Trans-Canada Store." Venerable competitor the Hudson's Bay Company may have been older, but for much of its history, it operated primarily in Western Canada and didn't really operate as a true department store organization until the late 1800s. The Robert Simpson Co. Limited may have been a glamorous and worthy competitor, but it was small in comparison to Eaton's.

Most large Canadian cities boasted an Eaton's store in the centre of their downtown shopping core, and if they didn't, there was the ever-present *Eaton's Catalogue*. In many cases, the stores were notable buildings designed by fine Canadian architects on behalf of the retailer, and they fit Canada's interesting and historic urban areas to a "T." From the magnificent railway terminals in big cities like Toronto and Vancouver to the historic and welcoming hotels that were ambassadors of Canadian hospitality, the great representative stores of Eaton's could be added, whether they were the classic variety such as the Montréal store on St. Catherine Street or the one-of-a-kind Art Deco masterpiece that was the 1930 Eaton's–College Street.

If it wasn't the stores themselves, it was the merchandise, or more specifically the confidence in stylish, fine-quality stocks backed by the "Satisfaction Guaranteed or Money Refunded" assurance that was the hallmark of any Eaton's shopping excursion. Add to that the experience itself: not just shopping, but an opportunity to purchase almost anything under one roof (especially mind-boggling in the big stores) and to enjoy myriad in-house services, crowned by fine restaurants that were

No other sale in all Canada causes such a flurry of excitement as EATON'S Trans-Canada Sale! It's the biggest sale effort of Canada's largest retail organization—and it's a two-day event in EATON Stores all across Canada! Planning for EATON'S Trans-Canada Sale began months ago . . . with the facilities of the entire EATON buying organization, both in Canada and abroad, being used to secure merchandise in huge quantities to sell in EATON Stores from Halifax to Vancouver. Our Comparison Shoppers have been busy for weeks comparing for value! Our Research Bureau has been available for checking on quality! Every effort has been made to make this the greatest Trans-Canada sale EATON'S has ever presented!

Over 250 specially planned money-saving values! Watch Trans-Canada Sale price tickets on every floor of EATON'S-Main Store, EATON'S-College Street and EATON'S Annex, on Monday and Tuesday! While all Trans-Canada Sale items were planned for a two-day selling, we cannot guarantee that quantities will last both days. So please shop early Monday to avoid disappointment.

Telephone Order Service Opens Monday at 8 a.m. Dial TR. 5111

No other Sale in Canada equals the Trans-Canada Sale because no other organization has the vast quantity buying power here and abroad that is provided by EATON stores from coast to coast

Eaton's Trans-Canada Sale became a highly anticipated biannual event. When Eaton's management unwisely discontinued it in the early 1990s, the store's days were already numbered. *From an ad, collection of the author.*

often Canadian landmarks themselves. It has been said often and likely wouldn't need repeating if it didn't set the tone for the story so well: Eaton's was more than a store.

To this day, those who remember it still mourn its passing as if an old friend had died. June Sagness wrote about her experiences fourteen years after Eaton's disappeared from Canada:

> *I remember going to Eaton's Queen Street Store with my older sister & my mom at Christmas. We went downtown to see Santa and then went for a ride on the train that went all around Toy Land, at the end of the ride we got a Punkinhead Book and a present (usually a book, game or puzzle). My mother used to say that T. Eaton Company had the biggest selection of dolls in Toronto (my sister and I always got a doll for Christmas); I still have some of them. It was always a treat to go to the Annex and have soft chocolate ice cream or an ice cream sandwich and watch the ladies making the waffles. It was such fun to go shopping and hide from my mom in amongst the clothes. It wasn't fun for her to find two kids amongst the clothes, but later I used to take my little boys down so they could enjoy the store like I did as a child. Such things can never be forgotten.*

It wasn't just customers, though. Eaton's staff was truly the human element that made the store come alive. Eaton's retail executives and those who worked under them created its public image, and the store staff was truly the company's ambassador to the Canadians, and visitors, who took Eaton's to their own hearts. Eaton's was, for many years, Canada's largest commercial employer, and those on its payroll styled themselves as "Eatonians." As such, they were loyal employees and fulfilled an ideal of customer service outlined by Timothy Eaton himself. June Rysinski, of Thunder Bay, Ontario, remembers her dad as an example of the quintessential Eatonian:

> *My father, Victor Tuomi, worked for twenty-nine years specializing in men's suits. He retired at age sixty-five in 1983. The place where he worked was near and dear to his heart. Eaton's became his second home and family. All I could think of were memories of him running around the department with his measuring tape around his neck and flashy ties—always ready to suit up one of his customers. No matter how bad a suit looked on you when you tried it on, Vic would measure it up to fit like a glove! When they wanted to look their best, customers knew to see Vic. He had a huge clientele and cared dearly about his customers. My father was a true professional. It wasn't just a job for him…it was his vocation. He put his heart and soul into everything he did for his customers and was a loyal, dedicated employee of Eaton's.*

June's memories of Eaton's and of her father's employment are many and varied, but among her favourites are going to the store to see her father dressed in a vintage costume, along with his colleagues in the Port Arthur store, celebrating Canada's 1967 centennial in style. When Vic achieved twenty-five years with Eaton's, becoming a member of the "Quarter Century Club," he was treated like a celebrity and received a diamond ring for his service to Eaton's. "He wore that ring with such pride and never took it off. He even wore it while gardening. Even though his hands got covered in mud, I can still see the image of that diamond shining through all the dirt!"

Perhaps Lori Stiles-Thurrott, who began working at Highfield Square in Moncton, New Brunswick, in 1983, summed it up best, saying, "[W]ith seventeen years there, I will always consider myself an Eatonian."

Not only was it a nationwide staple of Canadian commerce, but it also offered a richly unique experience to Canadians. No other store featured a world-class performing arts venue in its hometown. No other store was operated by the founding family for so long. No other store grew up

Victor Toumi, a human "fixture" of the Port Arthur Eaton store, shown with his characteristic tape measure in the men's shop of the store where he served for more than twenty-nine years. *Courtesy of June Rysinski.*

alongside, and become associated with, Canada like Eaton's, and no other store boasted a Knight Bachelor as its president, aided by his wife, Lady Eaton. Eaton's, undeniably, was an inseparable part of what made Canada the uncommon nation that it is.

This book tells the story of the T. Eaton Co. and how it grew to become the "Trans-Canada Store." As an author, I am loath to devote space to writing in the first person, but I find it necessary because readers will inevitably want to know why the subject matter inspired such a text, especially when the author is a foreigner and, at first glance, appears unrelated. The question as to why an American would take such an interest in a Canadian topic will surely arise as readers turn these pages. The answer is succinct: I grew up on the shores of the Great Lakes, and my family considered Canada and

Canadians to be our good neighbours. It was always clear that we loved it a great deal. Canada was, for us, as a family, an opportunity to escape from our routine and enter a world where things were just a little different. Niagara Falls was a favoured and nearby destination and travelling to Montréal to visit Expo '67 was the proverbial "icing on the cake" for a family with such an inquisitive nature, especially regarding a fascination with out-of-the-way and exotic places.

The language of Canada's citizens was different, and the influence of the old cultures on the other side of the Atlantic (to which we belonged) was that much more tangible. The natural beauty of Canada needs no recommendation; for a family who loved to travel in North America, Canada was the ultimate destination. Growing up, it seemed that these journeys were not so much long automobile rides but rather the unfolding of a stunning scenic and cultural wonderland right before our very eyes. Our parents' desire to give us a firsthand learning experience took us to the Maritimes, Ottawa, Montréal and Toronto. Riding the great Comet roller coaster at Ontario's Crystal Beach was as frequent a pastime as if the place were nearby. We didn't just "see the world" at Expo '67—we visited the shrine of Ste-Anne de Beaupré to pray and worship together and experienced the natural beauty that Canada offered at every turn. The varied scenes of my mother trying to order us (in English) a snack of *patates frites* at a roadside stand in Québec or of my parents so happily dancing one summer evening to the silky sounds of Guy Lombardo tunes on the shores of Lake Ontario at the Canadian National Exhibition have been indelibly etched in my memory for years.

Eaton's played a role in these vacations because of my mother's love of shopping and my dad's desire to explore new places. As a result, I was privileged to experience the venerable Queen Street store in Toronto before it was replaced by the contemporary Eaton Centre. The enormous Montréal store likewise was a favourite. Eaton's became a household name in our home in the United States as well, and when the 1980s brought Eaton's to nearby Sarnia, Ontario, I acquired two snappy wool suits from the store as I embarked on my career as an architect. My affection for Eaton's built up over many years and consisted of many experiences, all of them positive.

In the charmed life with which I have been blessed, I have, like others, known tragedy as well. Often, when at a loss for words, simple consolations have always proven by experience to be the best, and when a dear relative or friend has passed on, I have been frequently reminded that the world seems very tangibly poorer and just a little less humane without the one whose loss hurts so much. Canada is a beautiful nation with an astounding history and

Toronto society women shopping in the *soignée* Ensemble Shop on the first floor of Eaton's landmark College Street store. Not for Eaton's the bargain racks and concrete floors of today's "big box" retailers—nothing but space, light, comfort and attentive service to the needs of the customer. *Archives of Ontario: T. Eaton Fonds F229. Used with the permission of Sears Canada Ltd.*

has so much to recommend it, but a Canada without Eaton's will never seem completely whole to those who knew this superlative institution and how it played a pivotal role in the lives of Canadians—and even this American as well.

The history of Eaton's, then, might be seen as a mere epitaph, and yet because of the store's icon status, it inevitably turns out to be so much more than just that. The tale is fueled by remembrance and as such should evoke great nostalgia in all those who experienced the store, whether they were customers or employees. To everyone else, let it be an inspiration to the value of thoughtful and creative ideas and their practical application as shown by Timothy Eaton's worthy and uplifting example: Eaton's, the "Trans-Canada Store."

Ballymena

Trust in the Lord and do good and verily thou shalt be fed.
—Timothy Eaton

R ising spectacularly from the Ulster countryside in the far northeastern corner of the Emerald Isle, Mount Slemish dominates the landscape and casts its shadow over the town of Ballymena to its west. Majestic beauty notwithstanding, the extinct volcano, properly called *Slieve Mish*, is known the world over as the location of St. Patrick's toils as a captive before he returned to his home in Roman Britain, where he went on to study Christianity. The beloved saint's renown as the "Apostle of Ireland" derives from his later return to the land of his captivity as a Christian missionary, where his works, such as his use of the shamrock to illustrate the concept of the Holy Trinity to the locals, whom he sought to convert, gained him prominence as the patron saint of Ireland. His worldwide cult-like status is celebrated with both religious fervor and secular gusto to this day.

The young Roman, born around AD 387, was, according to his own words, taken captive by Irish raiders and brought to Ireland as a slave. Although Christianity had come to be embraced by the Roman empire at this time, and though Patrick's family were indeed active members of the church, the sixteen-year-old had grown up without embracing the Christian faith in any particular way. In captivity, he was made to work as a shepherd on the gentle inclines of Slemish, just below the steep, rocky slopes that reach dramatically for the blue Irish sky above. It was in this inspirational natural environment that young Patrick (or *Pádraig* in Gaelic) turned to prayer during his work and found his true calling. According to his *Confessio* (one of his two extant written documents), he came to recognize God's mercy, and his devotions led to a vision predicting his return home to fully embrace his faith and religious calling.

Almost 1,500 years later, another young man toiled in the shadow of Slemish and combined his acceptance of hard work with the convictions of strong Christian faith, eventually propelling him to world fame as well. Today, even though the store bearing his name exists no more, a commemorative "blue plaque" placed by the Ulster History Circle on the house in which he lived draws attention to the fact that Timothy Eaton was a man of worldwide stature, one who came from this humble place in the wild landscape of Ireland.

The Eaton family arrived in County Antrim in the 1620s from Scotland as tenant farmers, "imported" by the powerful Adair family during the Plantation of Ulster. Scottish families such as the Eatons were English-speaking Presbyterians who became known as Anglo-Irish, or more specifically, in this case, as Scotch-Irish. These hardworking people, although they adhered to their Calvinistic Protestant faith and remembered their Scottish ancestry, eventually identified as Irish as well.

Timothy Eaton's parents, John (1784–1834) and Margaret Craig Eaton (1796–1848), were Ulster natives who produced a family of nine children (Robert, born 1816; Eliza Jane, born 1819; Mary Ann, born 1821; Margaret, born 1824; John, born 1827; Nancy, born 1829; Sarah, born 1831; James, born 1832, and Timothy, born 1834) while farming on their land at Clogher, just north of the market town of Ballymena on the River Braid. Their property, at thirty-two Irish acres (roughly fifty-two acres), could be ranked in the top 3 percent of Irish farms at the time, according to size. Flax and, to a lesser degree, potatoes and grain were the crops raised there during Timothy's lifetime. Despite these indications of wealth, the fact that such a farm could likely not employ all of the Eaton children, as well as the Great Famine, which occurred from 1845 to 1852, led the family's offspring to seek employment in other professions and far-away locations.

When Timothy was born in March 1834, his mother had already been a widow for two months. He attended the so-called national schools of the day but did not show great promise as a student; in fact, his unusual grammar and mixture of numbers and words in his writings became characteristic of him, even at the height of his achievement, such as a note to be found in Eaton's archives stating, "I done 2 much Selling not to no a thing or to."

The farm at Clogher, near Ballymena, Northern Ireland, where Timothy Eaton was born, and the commemorative "Blue Plaque" later affixed to it. *Archives of Ontario: T. Eaton Fonds F229. Used with the permission of Sears Canada Ltd.*

Perhaps because of his lackluster school performance, and the terrible famine that had Ireland in its grip at the time, his mother had him apprenticed at age thirteen to a shopkeeper cousin in Portglenone, a small town on the important River Bann, which flowed from the uplands in southeastern Ulster through Lough Neagh and out to the North Sea near the town of Coleraine. Because of its length, the Bann played a role in the industrialization of Ireland and made Portglenone a significant, though small, settlement on the river. Margaret Eaton's cousin, Mr. Smith, operated the most prominent shop in Portglenone, and as was the custom of the day, Margaret set down a bond of £100 there to ensure her son's apprenticeship, with the money to be returned after the obligatory five-year period was over.

The nine-mile distance between Clogher and Portglenone being too far for Timothy to commute, so to speak, the young man customarily slept in the store (under a counter, as legend would have it), and he regularly returned home to Clogher on Sundays to attend church services. It was said that Timothy never dared to even look up to ask Smith for a ride to church, as the shopkeeper's carriage clattered by him on his Sunday treks towards home, because he knew that he would never receive even acknowledgement, let alone the courtesy of a ride.

Although the young Eaton's mind didn't excel at schoolwork, he did devour all he saw and experienced in Smith's store, and indeed, this experience, combined with his strong Christian faith, caused him to see, analyze and question the world around him; as a result, he developed an intuition that would drive his thought processes for the rest of his life. His work hours were long, almost ridiculously so when seen from a twenty-first-century point of view; he worked fourteen hours per day (from 5:00 a.m. until 7:00 p.m.) on weekdays and nineteen (from 5:00 a.m. until midnight) on Saturday. One of his responsibilities was to serve a cup of whisky as a courtesy to farmer-customers on their way to market in the morning and again on the way home at the end of the day.

From these experiences, he questioned the value of such lengthy workdays and came to detest the use of alcohol under the guise of hospitality (as it was surely proffered) in order to make the farmers more likely to part with their money at Smith's business. Much like St. Patrick, Timothy used his work experience to discern and plan his future—so much so that by the end of his apprenticeship in 1854, his dreams and visions of a future were simply too big for Portglenone, Ballymena or even Ireland itself. His very own Christian faith led him, according to a description in Eaton's *Golden Jubilee Book* of 1919, to "believe that the world and that all therein is, was made to increase the welfare of the individual man, and to perfect the human race."

Timothy's mother, Margaret, passed away in 1848, and two of Timothy's brothers had already left Ireland for the promise of a better life in Canada. Twenty-year-old Timothy collected the £100 owed him, along with the customary new suit of clothing and a watch, and took the arduous month-long journey, under sail, to Canada in 1854. It is thought that he first spent time with his Aunt Agnes Craig Reid's family in Georgetown, Ontario, in the Halton Hills northwest of Toronto, and took a job as a store clerk in nearby Glen Williams. With money earned from his work there, he relocated with his brother James to Kirkton, due north of London, Ontario, which was, at the time, no more than a clearing in the woods. Here they purchased a small general store, operating from a log cabin that served local farmers. Although it was somewhat remote from the tracks themselves, he was likely encouraged at the time by the progress of the Grand Trunk Railway, which was being

Opposite: Comparison view of Timothy Eaton's first workplace in Portglenone. *Top*: View from the early nineteenth century. *Bottom*: The shop as it exists today. *Archives of Ontario: T. Eaton Fonds F229. Used with the permission of Sears Canada Ltd.*

built to connect Montréal and Toronto with Sarnia at the Michigan border and across that state to Chicago. The Grand Trunk's effect on Ontario at the time was to encourage inland economic development along its route, when Canada's economic growth had previously concentrated itself along the St. Lawrence River and on the banks of the Great Lakes.

The "J. & T. Eaton" store became a hub of the small community, especially after it incorporated a post office and James Eaton was appointed postmaster, with a lucrative mail contract to his credit as well. Timothy Eaton minded the store, and just as at Portglenone, he analyzed the business conditions he faced and, in a formative moment, isolated the three discouragements of bartering, bargaining and credit that limited the success of his business, even though the store was reasonably prosperous.

Timothy became aware that a merchant under the conditions present in Kirkton was burdened by trying to set prices in an environment where—again according to his store's 1919 *Golden Jubilee* publication—"Money was even rarer than virtue in those times." The small store's customers were most often local farmers, who brought produce, animals and other goods in to barter for the things they needed. The shop owner was thus forced to evaluate not only the quality and marketability of the goods offered but also their ultimate value when compared against his stock. It was understandably difficult to run a for-profit business with so many unpredictable variables.

The situation was further complicated by the accepted process of bargaining in stores, which was an old custom derived from early marketplaces in Europe that came to the New World intact, causing the rise in popularity of the phrase *Caveat emptor* ("Let the buyer beware"). Prices for goods were not marked on items or announced by signs in stores of the era; it was customary for the shopkeeper to quote a higher price than he recognized as producing a fair profit, not only because he knew that the bargaining process would ultimately lower the amount he received for the goods but also because a less-skilled bargainer could be "taken" for a higher price and greater profit. As a result, women and children of the day seldom did any shopping. Furthermore, the combination of bartering and bargaining made for an excruciatingly long shopping experience, one that surely gave little pleasure to merchant or client alike.

The third difficulty was the accepted (and prevalent) practice of buying on credit. Contemporary retailing seldom involved cash, due not just to its scarcity but also to the fact that farmers, hunters and other income producers in rural Ontario did not receive regular wages; rather, they were paid when they had goods to sell—for example, after the fall harvest. The credit system was the only way to conduct business under such circumstances. The idea of promoting cash selling is often erroneously credited solely to Timothy Eaton; in reality, most merchants would have preferred to have cash in hand after any sale, but under the circumstances, such transactions were very thin on the ground.

One problem with the credit practices of the day was that there were no safeguards in place that merchants could use to make their businesses less vulnerable to the shortcomings of the system. Most shopkeepers encouraged customers to pay their accounts in full at the end of the year, but in reality, few were able to do so. In the process, merchants had to carry the cost of goods sold over long periods of time, and they themselves had difficulties paying creditors, most often goods wholesalers from larger towns such as London and Hamilton. In his own letters to his brothers, Eaton bemoaned the shortcomings of the prevalent credit system time and again.

Timothy Eaton, again using his powers of analysis, began to develop a vision of a time and place where he could effect change in the habits of the marketplace, thereby lessening the trials faced by a merchant. It is also reasonable to assume, given the evolving journey of his faith, that he likely believed that the transformation about which he fantasized would benefit not just himself but his customers too, building a more amicable commercial environment for anyone involved in the process.

Regarding faith, during their time in Kirkton, Timothy and his brother James became active in local Presbyterian church affairs, with Timothy serving as Sabbath schoolteacher towards the end of his stay in the village. The Kirkton school served both Methodists and Presbyterians but provided separate teaching for the differing beliefs. In late 1858, Timothy attended a Methodist revival in Kirkton and subsequently made the decision to turn away from the dour Calvinistic faith of his ancestors, which held that one's course through life, and a person's ultimate salvation, was predestined by God. Timothy, who was not nearly finished with all he hoped to achieve, was deeply inspired by the Wesleyan revival. The Methodist belief that Christian service and love for one's neighbour led to union with God and ultimate salvation surely ignited his desire to grow his business, which (albeit much later) adopted the slogan "The Greatest Good to the Greatest Number."

In 1857, Canada's economy suffered a recession, but within two years, the Grand Trunk Railway, though flirting with bankruptcy, connected Sarnia to Québec through nearby St. Marys, where James had joined his brother Robert in a business venture that struggled due to the economy. As the railway traffic built up, though, St. Marys acquired a commercial energy that propelled it out of the recession. In late 1860, Timothy left Kirkton and established a bakery business in St. Marys that lasted only a few months before a May 1861 advertisement announced the establishment of a new T. Eaton store on the town's Queen Street, offering dry goods "cheap and for cash."

Portrait of Timothy Eaton in middle age. *Archives of Ontario: T. Eaton Fonds F229. Used with the permission of Sears Canada Ltd.*

The business in St. Marys took root and prospered, and although he tried, Timothy Eaton was not fully able to exorcise the demons of bartering, bargaining and credit from his life's work. During this period, the burgeoning store witnessed the Confederation of 1867, which created the Dominion of Canada, and, significantly, the marriage of Timothy to Margaret Beattie (1841–1933), a high-spirited, dark-haired girl from nearby Woodstock, which took place in May 1862. The couple had met at a church picnic a year earlier. Margaret, who was not just a wife but a de facto business partner, bore Timothy three children during their years in St. Marys: Edward Young, born 1863; Josephine Smith, born 1865, and Margaret Beattie, born 1867. Thus the couple settled down into a happy and fairly prosperous life on the banks of the north branch of the Thames River.

Yet for all his success, Timothy's ongoing analysis of his situation, and his vision for the future, made him realize that his business goals could never be realized in the small town of St. Marys. It was, at the time, more obvious than ever that that the pattern of Canada's and Ontario's future economic development had been set. London became a major railroad junction, and York, now known as Toronto, which had served as the capital of Upper Canada since 1796, took on the same role for the province of Ontario and was developing as a large city in its own right. It also became clear that his ambition to rid his business of bartering, bargaining and credit was better suited to the big city than the small town, no matter how successful he already was.

Toronto the Good

We are made 2 work—and as long as the Lord give me a continuation of health
& energy—I am determined to work & work with a will.
—Timothy Eaton

In 1869, Timothy Eaton moved to Toronto, on the banks of Lake Ontario, and on December 9 of that year, an announcement appeared in the *Toronto Globe* calling attention to a new dry goods business, successor firm to the store of James Jennings at 178 Yonge Street. Conspicuous in the ad itself are the words, "We propose to sell our goods for CASH ONLY—In selling goods, to have only one price." The retail revolution that Timothy brought with him from Ireland had begun.

The new beginning was not without fits and starts. Timothy had first tried his hand at a small wholesale business near Front Street but found that intensive competition from established wholesalers made doing such business virtually impossible given the small scale of his affairs. He considered the grocery business but was advised that his aversion to selling "licquors" would be a fatal flaw in his plan.

At the time, the Britannia House, a retail business on the southwest corner of Yonge and Queen Streets—where the beautiful sandstone edifice built by the Robert Simpson Co. Limited today houses the Hudson's Bay Company's Toronto flagship—was up for sale, owing to the proprietor James Jennings's desire to expand his interest in his wholesale business and exit retail altogether. Eaton paid $6,500 to acquire the stock and operation of the business and gave it his own name. The location, although it did produce traffic, was remote from East King Street, where most of the "better" shops clustered and attracted the cream of Toronto's shoppers. Although the new venture was moderately successful from the start, Eaton still had to put his inquisitive mind to work in order to attract the trade he needed and have the desired effect on the retail market. The *Toronto Star* of 1933 remembered, "The first Eaton store had no carriage lines. The Eaton business was not founded for the fashionables…Yonge Street was the thoroughfare for pedestrians. The carriages still drove along King Street."

The Toronto market was vastly different from what anyone would experience today—or even fifty or one hundred years ago. The relationship between merchant and customer was tangled up in the retail custom of the day, and the problems of long-term credit and price bargaining were still prominent factors built into any transaction. Customers, if well dressed and well mannered, might be treated cordially, and even the bargaining phase could be glossed over with genteel language, but varying degrees of mutual disrespect and underlying distrust characterized the day's commerce. For instance, it was not unusual that if a customer, after examining merchandise, made no indication that he or she intended to actually make a purchase, he or she would be firmly but politely asked to leave. And the eventual resolution of customers' accounts was no better in Toronto than it was elsewhere, in spite of the growing city's increasing wealth and vast (for the day) population of people with newly earned cash to spend.

After the sale, the real meaning of *Caveat emptor* became apparent, especially if the goods proved defective or not as described by sales clerks or advertising. Customers were simply stuck with the merchandise, and retailers wouldn't even speak about returns or exchanges. In Timothy Eaton's eyes, archaic, unwieldy and, according to his deeply ingrained faith, immoral business practices were not just wrong; rather, they were an impediment to business growth and a better merchant/customer relationship that fulfilled one of his fundamental goals: "The Greatest Good to the Greatest Number."

Timothy found yet another fly in the ointment regarding the customary store hours in Toronto, a city whose population jumped by 15 percent in his first two years in business. Selling was conducted from 8:00 a.m. to 10:00 p.m. on weekdays and from 8:00 a.m. to midnight on Saturdays. Business was never conducted on Sunday in the city, which over the years developed a nickname as "Toronto the Good" due to its collective piety. To Timothy Eaton, the practice of keeping such long store hours was hypocritical because of the burden it placed on the employees of the store, whose free time was almost completely restricted to the Sabbath day.

In T. Eaton & Co.'s opening advertisement, Timothy addressed a few of these issues. The adoption of a one-price policy, clearly marked, was a radical departure from the norm. Although it would seem odd to *not* have to bargain, customers eventually realized the fairness of the practice—previously, it was impossible for a buyer to know if he or she paid fairly for an item. Furthermore, when, through the power of advertising, customers saw the outstanding prices for which T. Eaton & Co. was willing to sell goods, genuine enthusiasm for his store began to take hold among the public.

His policy of selling only for cash was less startling—many retailers in the Toronto of the day accepted and even preferred cash payments—but no one dared reject the system of long-term credit buying, which was standard procedure in stores. T. Eaton & Co. held fast to the policy, sometimes explaining to customers how the cash-only system allowed the store to offer the best prices for goods in handbills and through its sales personnel. According to a store legend, Margaret Eaton selected some merchandise needed at home one day and asked the clerk to have her husband pay for it out of his account. She was politely rebuked by her subordinate, who kindly explained to her that he was bound to deny any sale on credit that was against the store's stated policy.

With his set-in-stone opening policies, Timothy dealt a deathblow to the aspects of retailing that he could change at the time, and he soon turned his mind to working on the others. His detractors were many—competitors wondered aloud how he could make money at the out-of-the-way location, how he could sell goods so cheaply and why anyone would be his customer if he or she had to drag cash to his store just to make a purchase. They ridiculed him as "a faddist, crazy reformer, idealist and fanatic" and reserved acute scorn for the human interest he took in his customers and employees. The growing stream of people who came in the little store to view the goods on offer, simply and directly displayed, gave Eaton, who would later be called a "man with a complicated simplicity of character," the courage to stay true to his convictions, as well as an optimistic faith in his own ideas.

Indeed, success was not immediate, although the store's popularity grew steadily. Within five years, the sales floor was expanded towards the back by forty feet, and a year after that, the second floor (previously an apartment) was added to the sales space. Margaret Eaton, whose talents and personality made her a fine domestic manager, regularly visited the store and lent the

NEW DRY GOODS BUSINESS !

T. EATON & Co.,

Have purchased from Mr. JAMES JENNINGS his

ENTIRE STOCK OF DRY GOODS,

At a very considerable reduction from the cost price, which amounts to several thousand dollars, every dollar of which they propose to give to those customers who may favour them with their patronage.

With excellent facilities for the importation of their Goods from the British and Foreign Markets, they hope to secure a moderate share of public patronage. Nothing will be wanting on their part to secure this end, by the constant exercise of energy and attention to the wants of their customers.

They propose to keep a well-assorted Stock throughout the year in all

STAPLE HABERDASHERY

AND OTHER GOODS.

SOUND GOODS, GOOD STYLES AND GOOD VALUE,

Will be points that will always have their attention. In the meantime, they propose to offer from the present Stock, by way of clearing it off rapidly, and making way for their Spring Imports, the following inducements :—

Over 4,000 yds. WINCEYS from 5c per yd.
Over 13,000 yds. FANCY DRESS GOODS, newest styles from 10c per yd.

MOURNING GOODS, STAPLES AND FLANNELS,

Will be given at the same rates. A large lot of new

Velveteen and other Jackets,

VELVET BONNETS, HATS,

And all Millinery Goods, at EXACTLY HALF the market price.

We propose to sell our goods for CASH ONLY —In selling goods, to have only one price.

We invite an examination of our Stock —and to all we offer our best services

T. EATON & CO.

Left: Two drawings of the original T. Eaton & Co. store at 178 Yonge Street. The only existing photo of the premises shows it after it was vacated by Timothy Eaton and taken over by competitor Robert Simpson. *Archives of Ontario: T. Eaton Fonds F229. Used with the permission of Sears Canada Ltd.*

Right: December 8, 1869 ad in the *Toronto Globe* announcing the opening of T. Eaton & Co. *Archives of Ontario: T. Eaton Fonds F229. Used with the permission of Sears Canada Ltd.*

helping hand of her input to her husband, all the more valuable since the store was set up to be welcoming and homelike and its employees members of an extended family. That she was active in her husband's business is illustrated by an anecdote conveyed in Eaton's 1919 *Golden Jubilee* book:

In 1877 the second floor of the store was obtained and laid out as a showroom for millinery and mantles. It was opened with a formal display which lasted for several days, the only fly in the ointment as far as the milliners and mantle makers were concerned being the lack of hand-mirrors. "We couldn't persuade Mr. Eaton that they were necessary," said one who was on the staff in those vital days. "He couldn't understand that a woman wants to see if the back of her hat is becoming." We were forced to enlist the sympathy of Mrs. Eaton, and beg her to use her influence on our behalf. She always showed a gracious interest in the employees—and the mirrors were installed: two of them!

Earlier, Margaret had become familiar with the business by trimming hats for Timothy to sell, and her character seems to indicate that Timothy Eaton was as good a judge of a potential spouse as he was of people in general; his own qualities drew others of talent and exceptional character to him as well, and this helped him build a loyal workforce while he was alive.

Meanwhile, according to his mantra ("Prosper—fair days and foul"), Timothy bore his disappointments and continued to work towards the dreams he had for himself and his store. He began to advertise that "no one will be importuned to buy" at Eaton's, meaning that customers were welcome to come in and browse on a regular basis, simply to see what the store had to offer. This was the age of the great international exhibitions in Paris, London and elsewhere, and retailers were keen on developing on their premises the atmosphere of an exciting bazaar of merchandise; this meshed perfectly with the age, which was characterized by growth, urbanization and a general increase in wealth.

To address the difficulties he found with local wholesalers, who clustered around Front Street in Toronto, he broke his custom of spending the hours between 9:00 a.m. and 12:00 p.m. doing business with them by taking regular buying trips to Europe, where he could procure quality goods for sale at better prices, especially given a good reputation for paying promptly on the credit he was extended. Thus, Eaton not only eliminated the middleman in these cases but also became the sole arbiter of quality regarding the goods he offered. Customers benefitted as Timothy increased his profit potential, and the competition he provided lowered prices overall, as one merchant after another sought to attract customers by keeping up with his example.

Dramatically, during a period of business expansion, the working hours of Eaton's staff were reduced to nine hours a day, or from 10:00 a.m. to 6:00 p.m. on weekdays, and further improvements in conditions were yet to

Timothy Eaton
1834-1907

Margaret Eaton
1841-1933

THE **T. EATON C**O LIMITED
TORONTO   CANADA

Portraits of Timothy and Margaret Eaton taken later in life. *Archives of Ontario: T. Eaton Fonds F229. Used with the permission of Sears Canada Ltd.*

come. The disdain that his fellow merchants displayed towards his ideas, and his application of them in the marketplace, turned to bewilderment when they realized that he made even more money *in spite of* reducing his opening hours. Not surprising, though, from hindsight—Timothy Eaton was, after all, the man who tipped the horse-drawn trolley drivers of the day quite handsomely to announce, "Queen Street, all out for Eaton's store!" when he strove to draw attention to his premises and attract customers away from the King Street retail centre of the day.

Most importantly, though, Timothy reacted to the new situation he himself brought about. The increased competition meant that he needed to remain diligent and strive for supremacy in the marketplace. When he put out fabric selling for three and a half cents per yard, his competitors could easily match or even undersell him and often did. Noting that the customers were not as loyal to him as he would like, given the primacy of price in their minds, he devised an audacious solution and advertised it to the public for the first time in 1870: "Goods Satisfactory or Money Refunded"—a policy, slogan and way of doing business that endeared the Eaton store to its customers and cloaked the Eaton name with a sense of honesty, integrity and good will that were, in reality, simply a reflection of Timothy Eaton's character, which he imposed on the institution he led. When referring to the advantages that his policy provided to the public and the reliability that characterized his business, Eaton further claimed that even a "child can safely shop in this store."

Timothy Eaton could not control some of the disappointments of the era, however, although surely his faith played a role in the way they were settled in his mind. Timothy and Margaret came to occupy a house at 4 Orde Street near downtown Toronto, and he joined the Elm Street Methodist Church downtown. Aside from pressures of business, the family lived at this location in pleasant circumstances, but tragedy was not unknown to them. Their fourth child and the first to be born in Toronto, Kathleen (born 1869), died at the age of eleven months. Timothy Wilson (born 1873) passed away from a case of bronchitis at ten months, and their last child, George (born 1882), died of a tragic drowning accident at the age of two. In addition, Margaret delivered a stillborn baby in 1872. Of the children born in Toronto, only two—William Fletcher (born 1874) and John Craig (born 1876)—lived to see adulthood. In an 1874 letter to his brother James, as found in the Eaton Archives, Timothy states, "Our little Timothy W. fell asleep in Jesus—after 3 days suffering with Cold Bronkitis [sic] took him off…the cloud seems to hang heavily—we are endeavouring to trust in God."

When the Elm Street Methodist Church could not hold its growing congregation, Timothy offered assistance to the group, which ultimately formed Trinity Methodist Church on Bloor Street at Spadina Avenue, where he became an active member; he even moved his family to a comfortable new home at 182 Lowther Avenue nearby. In times of success, his dedication to his faith took root and grew just like his store.

The popularity of Eaton's store was such that in 1883, Timothy forsook the landlocked building on the corner of Yonge and Queen Streets and moved to new quarters at 190–196 Yonge Street to the north of the old location. Eaton purchased three units of the Page Block (built in 1856), also known as the London House. Again, Timothy's wisdom was questioned when he proposed to demolish the fairly new buildings and then spend

The original Page Block on Yonge Street. The portion purchased by T. Eaton & Co. is shown shaded in grey. *Archives of Ontario: T. Eaton Fonds F22. Used with the permission of Sears Canada Ltd.*

his hard-earned profits to produce what fellow businessmen considered a potential white elephant. In the event, negative commentary was silenced after the scaffolding on the new structure came down, revealing a modern, purpose-built store with a lofty street floor and enormous plate glass windows, perfect for the display of merchandise. Customer approval quickly followed, and with the new building, Eaton's ceased to be merely one of a number of dry goods establishments in Toronto and instead became a department store, setting out on an expansion that would see it eventually cover most of the block bounded by Yonge, Queen, James and Albert Streets. For the next forty-one years, additions, expansions and improvements followed one after another until the store emerged as the familiar emporium that came to be a choice anchor in downtown Toronto—a store that to citizens of and visitors to the "Meeting Place on the Lake" evolved to represent the best in Canadian retailing.

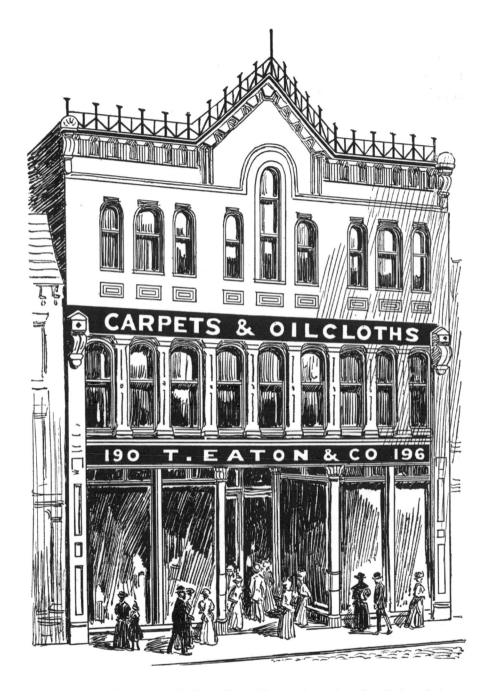

T. Eaton & Co.'s first store at 190 Yonge Street. Note the large plate glass display windows, an innovation at the time (1882). *Archives of Ontario: T. Eaton Fonds F229. Used with the permission of Sears Canada Ltd.*

In 1885, Eaton's installed its first telephone, and one year later, an adjacent 184-foot-deep property fronting on Queen Street was acquired, allowing an expansion that gave it an L-shaped form. The imposing, large-windowed façade of the new wing had a 31-foot frontage and a major entrance on Queen Street. With the addition, the store got its first passenger elevator, and due to its innovation (it was among the first in Toronto at the time), it was not well patronized by worrisome customers until fully dressed mannequins were placed in it to convince potential users that the device was safe! In the same year, Timothy Eaton initiated a Saturday afternoon closing for the months of July and August for the benefit of employees. To counter the loss of sales from the closing, he also instituted a Friday Bargain Day during the closure, after witnessing female customers clamoring over a half-price clearance of "odd lines" on an upper floor. Friday Bargain Day offset the shorter Saturday hours and helped turn Eaton's stock by moving odds and ends and broken lines.

The later years of the nineteenth century were characterized by a flurry of activity and expansion on all accounts. The store's mail-order business grew, and by 1886, Eaton's was employing 150 people. Space needs were such that the first of several new sections of the store was built facing James Street in 1889, giving the store a T-shaped configuration. The firm's growth was not without its detractors, mostly smaller shops that felt that the big

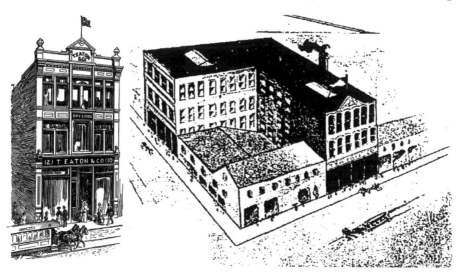

Composite view of the first Queen Street addition (left) to the store and an overall view from a newspaper article, showing the extent of Eaton's at the time (1886). *Collection of the author.*

store's magnanimity—which they, due to size, could not match—put their own concerns at a disadvantage. Wholesale firms, too, resented Eaton's buying directly in Europe, effectively shutting them out of a portion of his business. In 1890, an area of the upper floors of the adjacent building at 198 Yonge Street was taken over for the manufacture of undergarments, at the time known as whitewear.

The idea that Eaton's could manufacture its own goods for sale—which ultimately became an enormous operation covering nineteen acres in Toronto, factories in other locations and the employment of thousands of people—began, like many innovations at the store, almost as an afterthought. And yet again the story is, perhaps more importantly, a telling indication of Eaton's power of analysis and openness to new ideas as they presented themselves to him, and Eaton himself had now become known to his employees as "the Governor":

> *One morning he walked into the window-blind department and found the manager of it making a great noise; a most unusual noise. In fact the young man was operating a sewing machine. "Mr. D—, what are you doing?" "Well, sir, we are behind in deliveries and I can't get deliveries fast enough from the makers, so I thought I could catch up a bit by making a few blinds myself." "Oh! So you can. But your time is too valuable to be spent at a sewing machine. Get two machines. Put a girl at each of them. A girl can sew better than you can."*

James Street Extensions 1889

Albert Street 1893

The 1889 and 1893 additions to Eaton's gave the store an entrance on each street bordering the block occupied by the main store. In the centre is a view of the interior light well, a feature of the store at the time. *Collection of the author.*

According to the story, as recounted in Eaton's 1919 *Golden Jubilee* narrative, that sewing machine was the actual foundation stone of a vast manufacturing operation that produced thousands of commodities and spread to Hamilton, Oshawa and Guelph, Ontario, as well as to Saint John, New Brunswick, and Montréal, Québec, and its first superintendent was the former manager who had the initiative to procure the machine itself. Other experiments—in opening a furniture department, acquiring a store-owned farm and opening in-store restaurants—began under similar circumstances. The same book goes on to sum up Timothy Eaton's position by the 1880s:

> *By the time he was fifty years of age, Timothy Eaton had proved that mere success in his business is only an incident in a man's life's work. His success was phenomenal. He had built his business on a bed-rock of sound principles, and the pillars of the structure were the people whom he had made his associates in the work. Any appraiser classing him among the top row of "self-made successful men" and letting it go at that would have missed the vital secret of the man's life. The great business that Timothy Eaton had at the age of fifty was not the greatest of all of his assets. It was only the instrument on which he played. The greatest asset he ever had was his own personal character, out of which even at middle age, he could have re-created the business if he had ever been faced with a calamity that swept it away.*

By 1891, 6:00 p.m. closure on Saturdays had become permanent, and one year later, Timothy Eaton acquired a dairy farm in Islington, as much for his love of nature as to supply the store's soda fountain (in the recently erected James Street section) with cream. When there was surplus production of dairy products during the winter, a manager suggested that the store serve oyster stew for ten cents per bowl. An area of the basement was set aside to serve the stew, and the popularity of the offering was such that desserts and drinks (strictly non-alcoholic) were soon added as accompaniments. Before long, larger and better-ventilated quarters were found on an upper floor. From such simple beginnings came a full-fledged restaurant operation that included the fifth-floor Cafeteria and Grill Room, a "Quick Lunch Room" in the basement and further dining facilities set aside for the convenience of employees and managers.

Similarly, a store manager's upcoming marriage, and his subsequent need to furnish a new house, led to a proposal to open a house-furnishings department; the selling of holiday nuts and candies was likewise the basis for the eventual opening of a grocery department in the Eaton store. The number of departments grew accordingly, and in 1891, the store's name was changed to the T. Eaton Co. Limited when it became a limited stock company. In spite of the change, it continued to operate as a family-owned firm due to the fact that more than 80 percent of the store's stock was always held by the Eaton family; financial reports remained a closely guarded secret, often referred to as the best-kept secret in Canada.

Not surprisingly, the store began to acquire the sense of a dynastic commercial empire as Timothy and Margaret's son Edward Young Eaton joined the firm in 1880 at the age of seventeen. Before long, he had risen to the position of the Governor's assistant and ultimately first vice-president of the firm. E.Y., as he was known, made a profound contribution to his father's business, initiating the opening of foreign buying offices in London in 1893 and Paris in 1898 and convincing his skeptical father that the technical innovation of an extensive pneumatic tube cash delivery system would aid in all phases of the store's business. He took personal responsibility for improving the store's delivery service, which began under his direction in 1877, and his design for the distinctive commercial blue, fire red and arctic white livery, albeit with modification over the years, became a familiar sight throughout Canadian cities. Timothy Eaton's wisdom in training his son as a successor is illustrated by the following anecdote:

> [At his] *Muskoka retreat, Mr. Eaton received a prepaid telegram from his son Edward, Vice-President, and in charge of the Private Offices during his father's absence. The telegram advised him that a certain buyer was anxious to make a return trip to Europe, and the Vice-President was interested in what Mr. Eaton thought of it. There was no answer. The message was repeated, and again prepaid—still more urgently, and still no reply. A third message was sent by Edward, this time collect—and the answer came back in two words: "See Edward."*

In her autobiography, Timothy's daughter-in-law, Flora McCrea Eaton, later known as Lady Eaton, spoke with reverence about the Governor, saying, "One of the matters of great joy and thankfulness for me is the realization that Timothy Eaton lived long enough to see how well and truly he had laid the foundations of his business." She added, "I have spent... my life being grateful that it was given me to sit at the great man's feet and learn...I realized that it was Timothy Eaton who had taught me to weigh matters and make a decision, no matter how difficult it might be." Lady

Eaton also recounted, with obvious relish, the following story about the man who fathered her husband, Sir John Craig Eaton:

> *One Saturday…Mr. Eaton stopped the young man who was wheeling his chair and said "Go tell Rogerson I want to see him," pointing to the Department Manager's office. The young man came back and with more truthfulness than tact said, "Sir, Mr. Rogerson is asleep." Mr. Eaton's only remark was, "Very well, let us go on," but years later Mr. Rogerson told me the aftermath. "On Monday morning," he said, "I was called to the Governor's office. I went in and said 'Good morning, sir.' The Governor looked up and said 'Good Morning, Rogerson. Rogerson, do you know you were asleep on Saturday afternoon a week before Easter?' 'Yes, sir.' 'Why were you asleep?' 'Because, sir, I knew there were six better men than me out in the department.' 'Oh. Thank you, Rogerson. That's all.'" "So," Mr. Rogerson recalled with a broad smile, "I left, feeling that that was over and done with. But on Tuesday morning I got another summons to the Governor's office, and when I went in he said to me, 'Good morning, Rogerson. Rogerson, go out and get me thirty men like those six you say you have on your millinery floor.' The Governor had called my bluff!"*

The Toronto flagship acquired frontage on each of the streets bounding the block when it opened a five-storey addition on Albert Street in 1893. Soon, the James Street frontage was expanded, and the store's façade on Yonge Street was doubled in width. In 1896, the year an *Eaton's Catalogue* proclaimed it as "Canada's Greatest Store," the Queen Street wing was expanded and rebuilt to a height of four floors, and a newly built four-storey building was acquired on the corner of James and Albert Streets. Eaton's had come to fill a majority of the block. The same catalogue outlined the store's growth, announcing:

> *The record here is one of continuous improvement and growth. Look at the facts:*
> *Store area in 1883—24,544 square feet*
> *Store area in 1889—120,304 square feet*
> *Store area in 1896—293,538 square feet*
> *In 1883—over 275 employees*
> *In 1886—over 600 employees*
> *In 1896—over 1,500 employees*

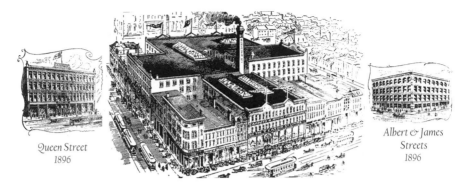

Queen Street
1896

Albert & James
Streets
1896

By the time the store expanded in 1896, it had begun to dominate the block. *Archives of Ontario: T. Eaton Fonds F229. Used with the permission of Sears Canada Ltd.*

Although dedicated to his store and the goals he set for it, Timothy Eaton was not a workaholic, a fact illustrated by his love of nature, his appreciation for the benefits of recreation and his love of horses and horsemanship in particular. He and Margaret bought property in Muskoka, north of Toronto, where they built their summer home, which they named Ravenscrag. The Eatons made frequent use of the beautiful property, and while there, Timothy took special pleasure in cruising on his steam yacht, *Wanda*, although when it was outrun by a neighbour's craft, he replaced it with a newer and more powerful one, the *Wanda II*.

Conversely, although Timothy Eaton had little interest in the arts and scarcely ever attended theatrical performances, these were areas in which his wife took great interest. In 1906, near the end of his life, the Governor donated the funds to build the Margaret Eaton School of Literature and Expression, whose principal, Emma Scott Raff, to whom Margaret had served as patron, famously said that she sought to educate the young woman "not so much…who can stand on her head and perform with her feet, but the student who can stand on her feet and perform with her head." Housed in a beautiful stone building reminiscent of a Greek temple and designed by Canadian architect W.R. Mead, the school was located on present-day Bay Street near Bloor but has since been demolished.

In 1899, while driving his coach out to the Islington farm, Eaton's horses ran away, and in the ensuing accident, the Governor suffered a fractured hip, which greatly limited his mobility. A second, similar incident further weakened him, and the fairly rapid decline and ultimate death of his diabetic son (and heir apparent), Edward, from Bright's (kidney) disease in 1900 may have, in spite of Timothy's long and deeply held Christian faith, affected him emotionally as well. During his late years, physical infirmity notwithstanding, the Governor was able to travel to the opening of Eaton's big new store in Winnipeg (where he held his grandson, Timothy Craig Eaton, on his lap while in his wheelchair) and also enjoyed a motoring trip of the British Isles with Margaret in 1906. In fact, that year he replaced his horse carriage with a deluxe new Packard automobile, built in Detroit, Michigan, and not long afterwards replaced it with an even bigger and more powerful model. He also commissioned a private railway car, the "Eatonia," which was built to make the family's long-distance travel more comfortable and reliable. When, during these years, Eaton's youngest son, John Craig Eaton, was being groomed as the store's future head, the young man personally saw to his father's comfort at the store during the period of his infirmity, even driving the Governor home in the afternoon on the days when he was too tired to be of effective use at work.

Certainly an event that captured the imagination of all of Canada, let alone Eaton's, was the visit of the Duke and Duchess of Cornwall and York, later George V and Queen Mary, in 1901. The royal pair had commenced on a seven-month tour of British colonies aboard the HMS *Ophir* in April of that year, reserving four weeks in September and October to visit Québec,

By the turn of the century, Eaton's was an imposing store indeed. The Mail Order building was across Albert Street, and the stables and delivery building can be seen beyond the corner of James and Albert Streets. *Archives of Ontario: T. Eaton Fonds F229. Used with the permission of Sears Canada Ltd.*

Ontario, the Maritimes and Newfoundland. As was true of all such visits, it caused a sensation in Toronto, the likes of which had not been seen since the Duke's father, the Duke of Connaught (later Edward VII), made a visit to Canada in 1860. The streets of Canada were ablaze with bunting, and innumerable Union Jacks and the Canadian flag of the day were strung above every major thoroughfare to welcome the royals, while great masses of people came out in their best clothes, hoping to catch a glimpse of the man who would soon be their king, along with his wife and life's partner. Eaton's, too, took part, beginning its oft-repeated tradition of elaborately decorating the store as a welcoming gesture whenever the royal family came to visit, although the store itself was still growing, changing and expanding. In 1901, large semicircular buntings of red, white and blue fabric, ringed with flags, adorned the Yonge Street façade, and a giant sign announced, "God Bless the Royal Party." Even a statue of Queen Victoria, the Duke's mother, stood in the main entrance archway, above the crowds.

During this period, Timothy Eaton slackened his cash-only policy via the establishment of Deposit Accounts, commonly referred to as "D.A.s." A forerunner of today's debit cards, the D.A. allowed customers to put money on deposit with Eaton's, and a shopper's account was debited accordingly as purchases were made. Eaton's cash liquidity was obviously an advantage in this setup, but the company generously paid a good rate of interest on unused funds to the depositor for the privilege.

On a cold January day in 1907, John Craig Eaton called his wife to ask if she were available to serve tea to the Governor at his office, a ritual that she normally fulfilled with pleasure. A talented singer, she was in the midst of a vocal lesson, according to *Memory's Wall*, and was somewhat reluctant to come, but her husband persisted, saying, "You'll never be sorry if you come now." She quickly recognized that her father-in-law was unwell at the time, and he returned home for rest, for he had developed a fever. The family, assured by doctors that they were doing all they could for the Governor, resigned themselves to fulfill an obligation to journey to Ottawa to attend a performance given by students of the Margaret Eaton School at a drama competition, but Flora remained at the Governor's bedside. A few days later, on January 31, with his lungs filled with fluid and his dear "Florrie" by his side, Timothy Eaton passed away, before his wife and son were able to return to be with him. He did, though, leave Florrie with one final instruction for his son, who was to go on to lead the empire he created: "Take good care of mother. Always be good to mother. She's grand."

Eaton's celebrated the visit of the Duke of Connaught (who became King Edward VII) in 1901 with elaborate decorations. *Archives of Ontario: T. Eaton Fonds F229. Used with the permission of Sears Canada Ltd.*

The store was closed upon notice of his passing for an appropriate period of mourning, and the flags that typically snapped valiantly in the wind above his store were lowered to half-staff in respect; at the time, around nine thousand people worked for the T. Eaton Co. in Toronto, Winnipeg and the various locations of the company's factories. Timothy Eaton's obituary, on the front page of the *Toronto Globe*, dated February 1, 1907, summarized the varied achievements of the man, of whom the paper said:

> *There is hardly a name in Canada, in fact, so well-known to the people at large as that of Mr. Timothy Eaton. Mr. Eaton stood out pre-eminently in the Dominion as the typical merchant prince, or, more truly perhaps, so enormous and varied were the interests that sprung up under his name, the typical captain of industry. By no one has the ideal of the departmental store been brought to greater perfection.*

The mayor of Toronto was quoted, after a necessarily lengthy summary of all that the Governor had accomplished, as saying that Eaton "was a man of high personal character, possessed of remarkable administrative and executive genius, firm and determined, but of a kindly and genial manner." His former pastor, Reverend Dr. W.F. Potts, noted that he "was a man as remarkable in his career as his character…one of the foremost commercial organizers. He had his peculiarities, which did not meet the approval of everybody, but on the whole, he was an earnest Christian man." Reverend Potts also recounted the time Eaton asked him to deliver a sermon "on the subject of shorter hours for shop girls…[He] was the first merchant in Canada in shortening the hours of those working for him." Tribute after tribute filled two columns on the fourth page of the newspaper, not to mention the editorials that were written on the occasion of his funeral. Timothy Eaton is interred in the striking Greek Revival Eaton mausoleum at Mount Pleasant Cemetery in Toronto.

Just as it was said that the Timothy Eaton's dreams were often too big to be contained in any one place, the progress of his store had reached a momentum that could not be halted by his own death. The store that carried his name continued to go from strength to strength under those he groomed to take it over once he had passed from this earth. In thirty-eight years, the little shop had become a great business, expanding far beyond its original confines, and indeed beyond the walls of its stores, to every corner of Canada through one of its most beloved innovations: *Eaton's Catalogue*.

The Book of Timothy

Let hope predominate but do not be visionary.
—Timothy Eaton

The birth of an esteemed Canadian icon happened almost as an afterthought. Yet *Eaton's Catalogue,* even if the great metropolitan stores and all of Timothy Eaton's dramatic history itself had never existed, would still be of one of the largest and most fascinating retail institutions ever to do business. Known as the "Homesteader's Bible," the catalogue was the first (and often the only) wide-ranging retail option for those who settled the vast and beautiful lands of the Canadian west or those who lived in isolated rural communities north and east of the large urban areas where Eaton's stores reigned supreme. Although it is still joked that "many an Eaton's catalogue spent the last days of its usefulness in the outhouse," it could arguably be called one of the implements that built twentieth-century Canada, and its cultural contribution is illustrated by the references to it in two beloved pieces of Canadian literature.

Both examples illustrate how the catalogue was woven into the fabric of Canadian life. In the fourth chapter of Lucy Maud Montgomery's *Anne's House of Dreams,* the 1917 sequel to her classic novel *Anne of Green Gables,* Mrs. Rachel Lynde, Anne's opinionated neighbour, expresses her negative feelings for department stores and their catalogues as a root of evil after Anne's friend Diana extolls the beauty of her wedding day, saying, "You couldn't have had a finer one if you'd ordered it from Eaton's."

In Roch Carrier's short story *The Hockey Sweater* (*Le Chandail de Hockey* in French), made into a memorable short film in 1980, the subject is the embarrassment felt by the young protagonist, a fan (like all Québec boys of the time) of the Montréal Canadiens and its star player, Maurice Richard. His mother, who struggles with English, orders him a new hockey jersey by letter to Eaton's. To his horror, the sweater bears the colours and logo of the archrival Toronto Maple Leafs, and he is forced to wear it and bear the scorn of his friends (and his priest, who is the referee!) because his mother refuses to return it and "offend Monsieur Eaton." Carrier's story also confirms the legend that old Eaton's catalogues made excellent shin-guards (held in place by stockings) for young hockey players whose families couldn't afford proper protective equipment!

In 1884, the Toronto Industrial Exhibition, a forerunner of today's Canadian National Exhibition (CNE), was held at Exhibition Place on the banks of Lake Ontario. Ever intent to capitalize on current events, Eaton's produced a thirty-two-page pink-toned booklet to distribute at the fair to advertise the breadth of its stock and the prices at which various items listed were sold. Almost to everyone's surprise, orders swarmed in, not just from Toronto but from across the country; the booklets went home with visitors and were shown to friends and neighbours, who were obviously attracted by the offerings and had perhaps heard of the store's reputation. One saleswoman was, from the start, dedicated to receiving and fulfilling the orders, although a boy was enlisted to help her with the packing of parcels for delivery.

The next year, a forty-eight-page booklet was issued, and soon requests came into the store for catalogues from people who had been showed them by travellers to the exposition. Soon the catalogues described and illustrated features of the store itself to familiarize readers with aspects of the company that they couldn't experience from so far away. The one desk and makeshift shelves used by the pair of workers on a disused mezzanine soon blossomed into a whole department on the second floor of the store. The fall/winter 1886–87 catalogue informed out-of-towners that all orders

are entrusted to a staff of young ladies, wholly independent of our regular selling force, who have been carefully selected for their painstaking dispositions and excellent judgment in matters of dress, thus eminently qualifying them to occupy the positions with which they are entrusted. These lady clerks go, letter in hand, from counter to counter until the entire order is filled, and give distant purchasers the benefit of a thorough knowledge of the most advanced fashions which constant attention only can cause one to acquire.

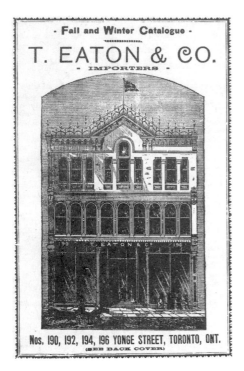

- Fall and Winter Catalogue -

T. EATON & CO.

- IMPORTERS -

Nos. 190, 192, 194, 196 YONGE STREET, TORONTO, ONT.
(SEE BACK COVER)

The cover of Eaton's first mail-order catalogue, in reality a pamphlet distributed to visitors of the 1884 Toronto Industrial Exhibition. *Archives of Ontario: T. Eaton Fonds F229. Used with the permission of Sears Canada Ltd.*

The service described reinforced the integrity and expertise of Eaton's, but over the years, catalogue orders were handled with the same personal care and correspondence that was characteristic of the greatest of retail organizations, which strove to emphasize the human aspect of their operations. When a postal strike halted letters to the Moncton mail-order office, clerks complained that during their absence, they "missed the letters from people, often the chatty ones from the Maritime provinces," and famous stories, like one about the letter asking "Mrs. Eaton or a member of her family to try it [a piece of vocal music] over on the melodeon" as a seal of approval, were legion. Once on record, a farm wife sent a basket of fresh plums "for Mrs. Eaton" to thank her for a purchase that gave great pleasure. The mail-order department was once surprised, if not shocked, to hear that an aboriginal native of Canada's far north expressed disappointment with his order, which the store assumed to be, and indeed fulfilled, as a parcel of women's apparel. Apparently, according to his note, he had been expecting a pretty wife, as illustrated in the catalogue, to go with them.

In another mail-order legend, the company sent out a catalogue to a regular customer after she had passed away. Her daughter, who was winding down her mother's affairs, sent the heavy book back with the tersest of one-word notes: "Dead!" Inadvertently, her name wasn't taken off the catalogue mailing list, and when the next one went out, the executor doubled her effort, writing, "Still dead!"

On a happier note, nonagenarian Reverend Kenneth Bernard Clarkson, who was born in tiny Stoughton, Saskatchewan, and served in Goose Bay, Labrador, as a Royal Air Force radio operator during World War II, is happy to report that the toy steam engine that he gleefully received from *Eaton's Catalogue* when he was five years old has been with him all of his life and still works. "The catalogue was the main thing back then," he said. "It and the Eaton's stores, from the various towns I've lived in across Canada, served me well all of my life and I miss them all terribly." He added that he married later in life at the age of forty-four in 1966; needless to say that his sweetheart's engagement ring came from the catalogue and is still right where it belongs: on his wife Ada's finger!

> *I'm sure you are not surprised when I tell you that when I married the lady who would be my wife for all these years, I bought her engagement and wedding rings from Eaton's. Incidentally, she still has among her treasures an Eaton Beauty Doll that she bought as a little girl. Our first TV set, a Viking model from Eaton's, is now replaced by an up-to-date colour one, but it still works! As does the typewriter I bought when I started university in 1950, and which is being used to type this letter.*

Often, the early catalogues illustrated the growing Toronto store and adjacent buildings on their covers, and to celebrate the store's Golden Jubilee in 1919, the mail-order department held a competition, inviting artists to submit works to grace the cover of the fall and winter 1919–20 editions. Curtice O. Westland of Toronto was selected as the winner by the Canadian Society of Graphic Art, and his cover design, entitled *Dreams that Have Come True*, shows two smartly clad Victorian-era couples peering over the skyline of 1860s Toronto, with Timothy Eaton's first store sitting squarely in the centre. Above them rise clouds housing dreamlike representations of all of the major buildings that Eaton's had recently erected across Canada.

Arch-rival Simpson's entered the mail-order business ten years after Eaton's, giving rise to competition for out-of-town dollars, but once established, Eaton's mail-order department went from milestone to milestone. In 1903, it moved out of the main store building to its own newly built headquarters across Albert Street in Toronto. As of this move, clerks no longer circulated through the store, "shopping" for out-of-town customers, but rather wrote vouchers for store clerks to fill; merchandise was transferred via tunnel to a shipping room in the new premises. In 1907, the store elaborated the "Goods Satisfactory or Money Refunded" policy for mail-order shoppers by offering to pay the return charges on any unsatisfactory merchandise, a further enticement to buy.

A collage of various familiar Eaton's catalogue covers. In the centre is the 1919 Golden Jubilee catalogue, with cover artwork entitled *Dreams that Have Come True. Collection of the author.*

Because of the amount of mail-order business done in the west, in Québec and in the Maritimes, Eaton's opened a mail-order facility along with its 1905 store in Winnipeg and followed it with similar facilities in Saskatoon in 1916, Regina in 1918 and in Moncton, New Brunswick, in 1920. While Eaton's became a major employer wherever it went, in Moncton, it was said that because it was a major rail junction and the location of the repair and maintenance operations of the Intercolonial (later CN) railway shops, "a person either worked for CN or Eaton's." As a mail-order hub for all of Eastern Canada, the Moncton building was of tremendous importance, and many of the city's residents have, or have had handed down to them, captivating memories.

Joseph D. LeBlanc was a member of Moncton's sizeable French Canadian population and has an intimate connection with the building that Eaton's built to serve its Maritime mail-order customers. His father, Jean LeBlanc, worked on the building when it was being remodeled in the mid-1950s and regularly took a bus home for lunch, along with his colleague Leonard Bourque. Bus schedules being what they were, the two men slid down the building's façade on ropes rather than use the slow elevators. The awaiting bus drivers would wager on who would win the race to the ground.

LeBlanc recounted the most dramatic part of his father's story:

> *They were working on the roof dismantling the staging which they had used for the construction work. My father didn't realize that part of the staging had already been dismantled, so when he hit it, the part that he was working on let go and he fell 4 stories below, landing on a platform that was used to stop the bricks from falling on the people below. He survived the fall, but had a lot of broken bones. The doctors later told him that had he was extremely lucky to be alive. Half an inch one way, he would have broken his neck and half an inch the other way he would have broken his spine. In telling his story after the accident, he said that, he didn't have time to pray, but thought of the Blessed Virgin and that's what saved him. For the next few years, there was a lot of rehab, and a lot of pain. Later, we moved to Massachusetts and my parents had 2 more children, but the Eaton building remained a part of our family history, which we will never forget.*

Linda Roach of Moncton remembered, as an employee of the *Eaton's Catalogue* return desk, that one day *the wife of a well-known news anchor returned three long gowns which she had used over Christmas and New Year's. I looked at the dresses with no tags, which were clearly worn, and they even had deodorant stains on them. I started to advise the customer that we could not accept this merchandise due to their condition. One of my co-workers quickly pulled me aside and said "Linda, you cannot do that—take back the dresses and give her back her money. The customer is always right, we don't argue with them. We accept the return because we guaranteed customer satisfaction. Never refuse a return." And that's the way it was. The customer was always right... period. When I graduated from high school and left Eaton's the ladies in catalogue sales gave me a silver charm for my charm bracelet with the Eaton's logo and the date on it. I still have it and when I look at it I always have wonderful memories of my three years in a great place. Eaton's was a place where I was treated with respect, given responsibility, and I felt my contribution was important.*

Another employee (this time anonymous) recounted the day that a stove and refrigerator had been set out on the loading dock for pickup by a certain Mr. Smart. A customer arrived while a junior employee was on duty during a manager's coffee break and, claiming that he was the purchaser, had the appliances loaded into his vehicle. A short time later, the real Mr. Smart arrived looking for the goods he had ordered. Eaton's, obviously, "swallowed the loss, but the junior employee never lived down the embarrassment of failing to check the bogus customer's identification or ask for the receipt!" Training practices were hastily stepped up afterwards.

An idea of the unusual situations imposed on mail-order employees was provided by Marilyn Matthews, who was working as a catalogue sales employee in 1969:

One day we had a phone call from a lady living outside the city with her list of items. One of my colleagues had spent a while on the phone with her as she listed off numerous items...I think it took my friend nearly an hour before she realized this lady must have been suffering from dementia. The final order totaled over a million dollars. Needless to say we didn't process the order but did a follow up call to her the next day to determine the seriousness of her request. The customer cancelled her order. But she said she had fun making the list from the new catalogue. It also gave us a laugh telling the story among ourselves.

These anecdotes illustrate the human side of the catalogue giant, which in 1909 became a separate entity, with its own distinct stock of merchandise separate from the retail stores. Outgrowing its Albert Street headquarters, the operation moved into a former Eaton factory on Louisa Street north of the main Toronto store, and the old premises was converted to a showroom for catalogue merchandise. Soon, freestanding merchandise order offices appeared in many Canadian cities, and by 1964, they had developed into showrooms displaying the items that could be had through the catalogue. These offices, including the catalogue order desks in the stores themselves, rose to a maximum number of more than three hundred and even increased beyond that when the company closed stores in small cities in the 1960s and replaced them with familiar blue- and white-fronted order offices.

Three other institutions, which served the retail stores as well, developed because of the popularity and success of *Eaton's Catalogue*. Eaton's Research Bureau, with its laboratory, scientists and testing experts, was established under Sir John Craig Eaton's leadership in 1916 in order to minimize the risk inherent in the "Good Satisfactory or Money Refunded" policy and to support Timothy Eaton's early insistence that Eaton's advertisements, and even the word of salespersons, must be accurate and honest at all times when describing merchandise.

The Research Bureau, at its peak, conducted more than twenty thousand tests per year on merchandise and developed detailed product specifications based on the results. A natural counterpart to the Research Bureau was the Comparison Office, which sent out specialists to make sure Eaton's prices were in line with the competition. As a result, both of these operations supported buyers in the search for quality goods for the store or catalogue and set the standards that Eaton's vast manufacturing operation was bound to attain as well.

The acreage north of the Queen Street flagship developed into a unique warehouse and manufacturing district; had it not been demolished in the 1970s, it would be considered an industrial heritage site of the highest order today, unlike anything else in Canada. Beginning in 1897, a new delivery shed and stables were built on the block bounded by James, Albert, Bay and Louisa Streets. Eventually, property was acquired across Albert Street from the main store for the new Mail Order Building, which was completed in 1902. Manufacturing moved to the north side of Louisa Street with the construction of the so-called Factory #2, which eventually came to house the mail-order operation, especially after the tall, twelve-storey factories were built surrounding the ancient Trinity Church and its eponymous square nearby. The small, atmospheric church around which these huge factories developed was designed by architect H.B. Lane and built in 1847. It was endowed by Mary Lambert Swale of Settle, England, who requested that her name never be made public, but her generous gift to the Anglican Church and the people of Toronto was later revealed.

The final elements of the factory complex were the garage buildings, which were added to the existing delivery shed and stables block in 1911;

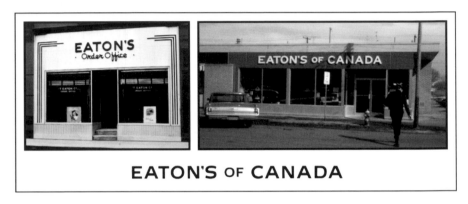

Examples of Eaton's order offices across Canada. *Archives of Ontario: T. Eaton Fonds F229. Used with the permission of Sears Canada Ltd.*

An overall view of the Eaton property in 1912, focusing on the factories. The tall Downey's Lane building at Terauley Street had yet to be constructed. *Archives of Ontario: T. Eaton Fonds F229. Used with the permission of Sears Canada Ltd.*

a warehouse (1910) on the Bay Street frontage of the same street; and the aforementioned Terauley Street factories, which enclosed Trinity Square with sheer, vertical walls around its southern, western and northern sides after 1919. A system of tunnels, referred to as "underground subways," connected this remarkable complex, which Eaton's promotional materials of the day described as the exact antithesis of "unsanitary places and toil-driven people" implied by the word *factory*. Features like smoke-proof stairways, large windows, drinking fountains and an on-site hospital were provided within for the well-being of workers, whose hours of labour were reduced in parallel with those of retail employees.

To pay for these amenities and improvements, the factories, by producing output solely for Eaton's own stores, eliminated expenditures related to sales, bookkeeping and marketing to outside customers. The Eaton factories in Toronto produced men's, women's and children's apparel along with textiles, garments made of fur, school books, drugs and toiletries and furniture, and the buildings that housed them were designed to be as flexible as possible as new needs arose in the future.

Eaton house brand names, often produced in these factories, soon became icons all over Canada and included Haddon Hall home furnishings; Birkdale men's wear; BabyFair, Bonnie Brae and Mountie children's wear; and women's fashions and shoes sold under the BelleFair, Gleneaton and Featherweight names. Several catch-all house brands included TECO, mostly used for housewares and home heating equipment, and the famous

Eatonia, a name that graced a large variety of items from men's and women's fashions to rugs and fabrics. Other items that earned renown for their quality and innovation included Eaton's TruLine sporting goods, Glider brand bicycles and Viking appliances and home entertainment equipment.

The factory operation grew beyond Toronto with the opening of a short-lived textile plant in Oshawa, Ontario, in 1903; a further plant in Montréal, Québec, in 1909; and a knitwear operation in Hamilton, Ontario, in 1916. The company, after being its customer for a number of years, bought the Guelph Stove Company in Guelph, Ontario, in 1919 and built

Atmospheric drawing of Trinity Square, showing the diminutive Church of the Holy Trinity surrounded by the tall Eaton factories, built in 1916. *Collection of the author.*

an entirely new factory to house its operations ten years later. Smaller factories, such as the Bloor Street plant, also of 1916, specialized in other items, in this case embroidery.

A third institution that supported Eaton's catalogue operation was the store's global buying organization, which in itself became a legend of sorts. With buying offices from Europe and the British Isles to Japan, and buyers and managers in Canada itself, it was said that "the sun never sets on Eaton's empire." There was a day when, if a Canadian wondered about a foreign destination, advice would be given to speak to an Eaton's buyer because "they've been all over." Fellow employees sought out tales of the exotic locales visited by buyers or firsthand accounts of historical events they may have witnessed in the line of duty.

Stories abound about the adventures of Eaton buyers—how a buyer in Sweden was arrested and charged with burning down a hotel, until it was realized that he was an almost exact double for the real criminal; how buyers raced to get merchandise out of Europe on the eve of World War II; or how stewards on the great transatlantic liners knew Eaton buyers by name because of the frequency of their crossings. Other stories are neither amusing nor heroic but rather decidedly tragic: an Eaton's buyer was killed in the cataclysmic Tokyo earthquake of 1923, one went down with the *Titanic* (although several arrived at the dock late and missed the ill-fated sailing) and three died when the Cunard Liner *Lusitania* was torpedoed during World War I.

Timothy Eaton himself often travelled to Britain to do the store's buying, but as the company grew, it became obvious that his long absences for that purpose were counterproductive. After Timothy Eaton's son Edward encouraged the opening of buying offices in London and Paris, his brother John broadened the list of outposts by adding offices in Manchester and New York in 1911; Zürich, Switzerland a year later; and Belfast and Leicester in 1913. In Japan, the ill-fated Yokohama office was opened in 1918, as was one in Kobe in 1919.

Each of these offices had its own specialty and reason for existence within the great retail empire. The London office bought books, tweeds, toys and sporting goods, as well as famous British products like Staffordshire pottery and Sheffield cutlery. Not surprisingly, Manchester specialized in textiles for the Canadian market, while Leicester bought knitwear and hosiery and Belfast funneled the finest in Irish linens to Eaton's.

The Paris office dealt in fashion, but the staff was also required to regularly attend the opera or travel to places like the French Riviera or the *soignée* seaside resort of Deauville just to observe what the fashionable were wearing and report the information back to Canada. The Zürich office was a veritable gateway to the products of Germany and eastern Europe and was supplanted by a Frankfurt buying office in later years. Japanese offices began by helping Eaton's procure the finest in Asian silks and embroideries but later expanded their list of expertise to include toys, transistor radios and plastics from growing Asian markets. Not surprisingly, the New York office dealt mainly with ready-to-wear items.

Eaton's first female buyer to go abroad, Margaret Stephenson, did so in 1890, and two years later, Timothy Eaton dispatched a female manager to London to dress down a local buyer accused of acquiring "abominable stuff" for the store. After World War II, even more women joined the ranks of buyers, and they gained an envied reputation as drivers of a hard bargain as well.

The catalogue itself grew along with the store. The first French-language catalogue was issued in 1910, but regular issues in French did not become common until after the store became established in Montréal in 1927. After World War II, non-English-speaking immigrants to Canada helped learn not just the language but the culture of their new home by reading their coveted *Eaton's Catalogues*, long after its status as the "Homesteader's Bible" had worn off. At its zenith, 17 million copies of six editions per

Illustration showing the massive size of the Eaton factories surrounding Trinity Square. *Collection of the author.*

year were issued in English and French, using up 2,500 tonnes of paper and 300,000 pounds of ink just for the major Spring/Summer and Fall/Winter editions alone.

Surprisingly, in 1966, the company reduced the size of the catalogue from 9¾ by 12 inches to 8 by 11 inches. The size change was not accomplished in order to save on paper, ink or shipping costs but rather was a ploy to get *Eaton's Catalogue* on the top of the pile of other such books that might accumulate in a typical Canadian's home, given the increased competition brought on by Simpsons-Sears or other players that challenged Eaton's supremacy in the market.

An amusing incident occurred in 1967, when Eaton's, which paid extra compensation to lingerie

A page from Eaton's French-language fall and winter 1967 catalogue showed off the snappy, youthful fashion style desired by Canadian customers of the day. *Collection of the author.*

models who posed in catalogue photos "for their embarrassment," decided to airbrush the navels off of models shown wearing the latest in underwear or two-piece bathing suits. The attempt at modesty backfired when letters criticizing the appearance of the models flooded in, and the practice was quietly discontinued. In other areas, the catalogue carried on Eaton's tradition of honest advertising without hyperbole, going to great lengths to properly (and honestly) describe the characteristics of merchandise for catalogue readers and buyers.

The production of the catalogue employed a staff of about 130 Canadians, who researched, sketched, photographed and did the layouts required to produce the catalogue, which could contain fifteen thousand items, and was often called "Canada's Favourite Book." As it gained acceptance, and was supported by the customer-friendly policies that Timothy Eaton and his successors developed, *Eaton's Catalogue* opened up enormous potential for the Toronto firm—serving the customers of the great Canadian west.

Go West, Yonge Man!

John, do you think five floors will do?
—Timothy Eaton

From the time it opened in 1905, Eaton's Winnipeg store has held a special place in the company. Long before Eaton's ever dreamed of having stores from coast to coast across Canada, the Winnipeg store, lovingly known as "the Big Store" to residents of Canada's "Chicago of the North," was a pioneer itself and paved the path for future expansion. What's more, its phenomenal success was illustrated by the fact that it dominated the retail trade in Winnipeg like no other store could, and it was widely recognized as one of the most profitable department stores in North America—one that for many years had the highest market share of any such place of business on the continent.

While the tremendous success of Eaton's mail-order service across Canada gave the store access to customers in remote places, that very fact illustrated a functional problem. Deliveries were growing, but the means of delivering them had not attained the capacity or technology to improve the long wait time for merchandise to which customers, particularly those on the prairies or in coastal areas, had been accustomed. The situation began to change in 1885 with the completion of the Canadian Pacific Railway, Canada's first transcontinental line. Accordingly, the store's management, still headed by Timothy Eaton, began to discuss the creation of a large mail-order facility in the west that could stock goods in bulk and deliver them more quickly to the west, in particular the newly created provinces of Alberta and Saskatchewan.

John Craig Eaton, then being trained and groomed to succeed his father, advocated for a combined retail and mail-order facility in Winnipeg, which had become a major rail junction and the town through which any train (i.e., person, animal or piece of merchandise) had to pass on its westbound journey. What's more, Winnipeg was growing rapidly, and American retailers like Montgomery Ward were taking notice and could easily capture the market if Eaton's didn't take action. An experimental exhibition of Eaton's merchandise and policies was mounted at the 1899 Winnipeg Industrial Exhibition to "test the waters" for a store in the west.

Afterwards, planning for the Winnipeg store began in earnest, and John and Flora Eaton took a trip via train to Winnipeg in order to secure a site for it early in 1904. She wrote in *Memory's Wall*:

"Official" portrait of the Winnipeg store of the T. Eaton & Co. The Donald Street Annex and the Mail Order can be seen on the left. *Archives of Ontario: T. Eaton Fonds F229. Used with the permission of Sears Canada Ltd.*

Jack's cousin, R.Y. Eaton, met us in Winnipeg, and on that very first day, I learned about Winnipeg mud. It was of a gluey consistency, dirty yellow in colour, and the carriage wheels would sink into holes six or eight inches deep. The splashes of it that settled on our boots and clothes were most difficult to remove, and always left a permanent stain. Jack and I spent a good part of our days driving about to look at possible sites, and I still have a clear picture in my memory of the muddy streets, board sidewalks, little houses of new lumber, and the generally sprawled, busy, disorganized look of a city in its birth throes.

A site was chosen on Portage Avenue, remote from the existing shopping district on Main Street, where small local shops conducted business and where the august Hudson's Bay Company had a store. No sooner had the property—490 by 266 feet in size and bounded by Portage Avenue, Hargrave Street, Graham Avenue and Donald Street—been acquired than criticism began to be voiced. It was Toronto all over again: the store was too far out; it would be too large and Eaton's policies themselves would never be accepted in the west.

Yet the groundbreaking occurred on July 27, 1904, for a six-storey building of "Chicago style" construction, with a sturdy steel frame onto which were hung enclosing curtain walls of brick and Bedford stone. The architect chosen was local Winnipegger John Woodman, and it was forecast that the store would open in one year, to coincide with the 1905 Winnipeg Industrial Exhibition in order to take advantage of the projected influx of visitors to the fair.

From this time, John Craig Eaton took sole responsibility for the new Winnipeg operation. A wrench was thrown into the progress, according to his wife, when E.R. Wood, a noted financier and friend of Timothy Eaton, returned from the construction site and told the older man that "[t]here's a hole in the ground there so big that it will never be needed during your lifetime or mine." A worried Timothy decided to proceed with the store but asked his son if he thought it workable to reduce the height of the store by one floor to five stories. According to Eaton's 100th Anniversary book, *The Store that Timothy Built*, the older Eaton may have had no clear knowledge of the store's location on the edge of town at the time, but "for Jack to stake his business reputation on such a location—as he made it plain he was doing—was like a man betting his entire bankroll on a horse he'd only seen munching oats in the stable."

They needn't have worried. From the day it opened its doors on July 15, 1905, it was a tremendous success, and Winnipeg took Eaton's to its heart like no other store. On its first day of actual business, it welcomed fifty thousand customers, on the fringes of a town with a population of only seventy-seven thousand. Two weeks after the opening, the original staff of 700 was increased to 1,250, and plans were made to "add back" the deleted sixth floor.

The original staff consisted of 450 locals, bolstered by 250 Toronto employees, referred to, according to different sources, as "the Originals," "the Pioneers" or "the Vanguard," who were enticed to relocate to Winnipeg in order to bring experience to the new store. The company offered to return them to Toronto and reinstate their original jobs if, after one year, they didn't wish to remain, but according to store publicity, "fewer than a dozen" chose to do so. In the 1969 centennial edition of *Eaton Quarterly*, the memoirs of three members of "the Vanguard" were printed:

> *Mrs. Jean Drynan, who met her husband in Winnipeg, recalled the early days when she worked in the Catalogue and received orders for bustles and high-button shoes. She also remembers the 10-hour workday with one hour for lunch, six days a week. Reginald Harvey, who worked in alterations and Ladies' Ready-to-Wear, recalled stocking ladies' flannelette nightgowns for 95 cents and cotton combinations at the same price. Sweaters were a big seller, fetching prices from 95 cents and going all the way up to $40. Mrs. Martha McNeil wasn't too impressed with her first glimpse of Winnipeg. "In some spots, the streets were ankle deep in mud and we had to lift our skirts high to keep the hems from getting dirty," she said.*

Some of the employees from Toronto, particularly the women, were not happy with the boarding houses and dormitories that had been provided for them in the still-young town. Circulating about and making inquiries, they found that Winnipeggers welcomed them open-heartedly into their homes when hearing that they were from Eaton's, and they also rented them much more satisfactory accommodations.

The opening ceremony was attended by the Eaton family and was, in fact, just one of many events that put them in close contact with their customers; they eventually gained celebrity status in the country, being called the "closest thing Canada has to royalty." Yet before this phenomenon took root, the event was merely a typical grand opening celebration. After a luncheon for dignitaries in the store's restaurant, Timothy Eaton held John and Flora's young son, Timothy Craig Eaton, on his lap and descended to the main floor in one of the new store's elevators. The Governor then guided his grandson's finger to the button that announced the opening of the new store to the public. Curtains hiding the contents of the large display windows slowly drew back, and a young boy who was the first person to dash through the enormous store's doorway received the princely sum of five dollars from Timothy Eaton himself.

Once inside, visitors saw a classic, simple interior designed to focus their attention on the merchandise, with structural columns and beams exposed to view and a pressed-tin ceiling embossed with Eaton's "Diamond-E" logo of the day. A sensation was caused by the floral decorations and merchandise displays, not to mention a vast array of goods of a quantity and quality previously unseen in a city like Winnipeg. Escalators, lighting and a state-of-the-art sprinkler system fed from the building's own water source were innovations that likewise captured the imagination of first-day sightseers.

From today's perspective, when Canada is phasing out use of the penny, the exact opposite of this policy gave cause for an oft-repeated anecdote about the Winnipeg opening. Western Canada did not use the penny, then derisively known as a "copper," because of its low value, and stores set prices in multiples of five cents or simply rounded up or down to accommodate the fact that the nickel was the smallest unit of currency in use. Many department stores had begun to price merchandise at prices such as $1.97, $2.98 or $3.99 in order to indicate merchandise that was on clearance, sold as a special purchase or simply on sale. Rather than revise its pricing schedule, the store procured a hoard of pennies and instituted their use from day one in Winnipeg. If a customer refused the copper change, they were directed to drop it into charity boxes that had been set up in the store. Before long, Eaton's policy helped the lowly copper penny work its way into Western Canada!

When the new Winnipeg store formally opened for business two days later, on Monday, it was thronged with shoppers and did a brisk business, no doubt enhanced by the then traditional *Eaton's Daily Store News* newspaper advertisements that described the bounty to be found at "the Big Store."

Since thirty-two horses and the required number of delivery carts had been shipped to Winnipeg in advance of the opening, a delivery service, as complete and well managed as its counterpart in Toronto, could take customers' purchases to their homes. The beautifully groomed Hackney horses and elegant livery of the delivery wagons became familiar to Winnipeggers, and the sight of the whole fleet departing, parade-like, down the city's streets in the morning became, within time, something of a tourist attraction and a source of pride for the store. In fact, the horses themselves were exhibited at fairs, and some were even known by name to the public. Delivery by horse-cart was being phased out when World War II forced a comeback, and the high-stepping Hackneys were still to be seen as late as 1950.

As a result of the continuous sales growth of Eaton's in Winnipeg, the store's facilities had to be expanded again and again. When the store opened, it had a full frontage on Portage Avenue, but it only extended about halfway back towards the opposite end of the block. In 1906, a full sixth floor was added on top of this section, and one year later, a six-storey wing, in the same style, was extended back to Graham Avenue. In two years, it was necessary to add a seventh floor, as well as a two-storey portion in the centre of the block, over an existing basement section. Finally, in 1910, the eighth floor was added, and the building was extended by a wing on Hargrave Street. By the time of this addition, Eaton's covered the whole block.

In 1927, the store building was enhanced at ground level with a new front of Tyndall stone, and the forty-two display windows received new glass and handsome bronze frames. The *Financial Post* of September 30,

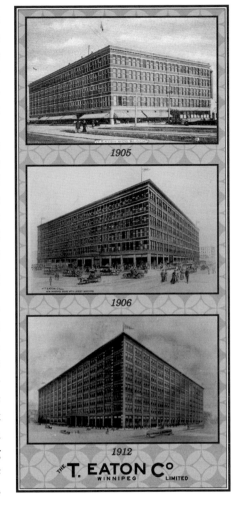

A study of the growth of the Winnipeg store from its construction through 1912, when it grew incrementally from five to eight stories. *Archives of Ontario: T. Eaton Fonds F229. Used with the permission of Sears Canada Ltd.*

1927, reported on the changes, informing readers that "marble and stone to the top of the first storey has been substituted for brick" and opining that "the ensemble is now very much more ornate than was the case in the past." Advances in glass technology allowed the elimination of a central vertical mullion that divided the show windows and obscured the elaborate displays created by the store's display staff. Following the standards set by Timothy Eaton in Toronto, the display windows' curtains were drawn after midnight on Saturday and were not opened until the start of business the next Monday.

Success also fueled the expansion of the Winnipeg mail-order operation. The store opened heavy goods warehouses in Saskatoon and Regina in 1916 and 1917, respectively, as an aid to the efficient distribution of these items to customers and to take pressure off the Winnipeg facilities, which were located on the upper floors of the store block. In 1917, though, the nine-storey Mail Order Building No. 1 was built on the Donald Street side of newly acquired property to the south of the main store, extending to St. Mary's Avenue. In 1921, the facility was effectively doubled by the construction of Mail Order Building No. 2, which fronted Hargrave Street on the same block. The identical wings were joined by tunnels and bridges, but the space between them was soon filled in as well. The Mail Order Buildings were designed in a commercial style matching the store, and along with later structures along with the store's retail annexes on Donald and Hargrave Streets, the power plant and garage building formed a unique commercial ensemble dedicated to Eaton's business.

"The Mail Order," as these buildings were called, featured spacious showrooms on the ground floors, and older Winnipeg residents will remember that, since the catalogue merchandise was warehoused on the floors above, clerks on roller skates could quickly retrieve items for the customer's inspection.

Eaton's had developed a grocery business and opened "Foodaterias" and "Groceterias" all over Canada. With the coming of grocery chains in the 1930s, Eaton's food stores became less popular and were closed as the company focused on its department store and catalogue business. In Winnipeg, however, the store's large Foodateria became Winnipeg's premier grocery store. Eaton's overcame the potential difficulties of downtown grocery shopping in the automobile age; when a multi-storey "Carpark" for customers opened in 1957, an underground link was established by which a grocery order could be conveyed to the garage for convenient auto pickup.

The popularity of the Foodateria wasn't just about convenience, though. It offered enormous selections of well-priced food items and was augmented by a third-floor gourmet department, a cake counter and what was claimed to be the world's longest meat counter. A special service known as the "Hostess Shop" offered Grill Room products to go and would even cook dishes in customers' own serving dishes if they were brought in ahead of time.

The Winnipeg Mail Order, located behind the retail store. *Archives of Ontario: T. Eaton Fonds F229. Used with the permission of Sears Canada Ltd.*

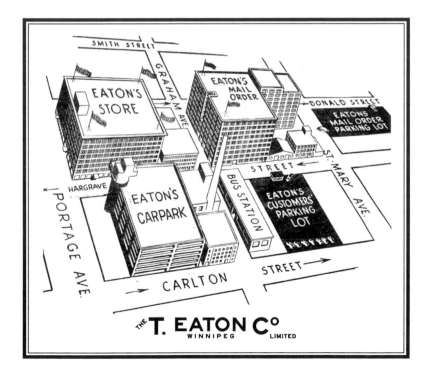

Eaton's huge complex in Winnipeg spanned several city blocks. *Collection of the author.*

The Winnipeg store's main-floor clock, like those in many department stores, became a favourite meeting place, as did the second bronze Timothy Eaton statue installed on the occasion of the company's Golden Jubilee in 1919. The restaurants, too, were favourites and offered many styles of dining according to customer's needs. The top of the line was the deluxe Grill Room on the fifth floor, an elegant room beamed and paneled in oak, accented by stained-glass panels and lit by chandeliers of wrought iron. Here, entertained by a string quartet, ladies and businessmen could enjoy Eaton's famous oyster stew or the Winnipeg Eaton specialty of toasted asparagus and cheese rolls, served with house-made Thousand Island dressing. Like many department stores, Eaton's is remembered for its chicken pot pie, but the version served in the Winnipeg Grill Room was unique: it included no potatoes in its recipe.

The memories of accountant Michael Kulczycki, a lifelong resident of Winnipeg, confirm that the Grill Room was undoubtedly among the best and most sought-after restaurants in the city. He gladly remembered "[g]oing with my grandmother almost every Saturday to the Grill Room on the 5th floor to have the Roast Baron of Beef or the Turkey dinners with all the trimmings. What a great meal!"

Other restaurants over time included the adjacent Valley Room cafeteria, the 1969 "Char Bar" specializing in hamburgers and an Art Deco coffee bar on the third floor that was replaced in later years by a new restaurant named Euphoria. The store's basement also had a quick lunch counter and several snack bars to entice customers to stay and partake of the store's culinary excellence, and many did just that.

Beyond the food, sometimes spectacular events attracted customers to the store. During the well-known Manitoba Bonspiel curling tournament, Eaton's held its own "Bonspiel Fair," featuring entertainment and demonstrations on every floor of the store. As would be expected from a store offering the best in designer fashions in its fourth-floor Ensemble Shop and Town House, it put on elaborate fashion shows and events, such as the 1964 "Boulevard International" import fair. All of this kept the store feeling fresh, unique and very "with it," especially in the swinging '60s and '70s. The seventh-floor Assembly Hall was the venue for many happenings and was also used free of charge by Winnipeg charity organizations for meetings or luncheons.

On the occasion of the Winnipeg store's fiftieth anniversary in 1955, the *Winnipeg Free Press* waxed:

For 50 years now Eaton's Winnipeg store has been many things to many people. To a wide-eyed child, it's the magic of the Santa Claus Parade, the tufted whimsy of a Punkinhead doll. To a 10-year old freckled frontiersman, it's the Davy Crockett Trading Post. To young lovers, it's a rendezvous spot beside Timothy's bronze statue. To a young matron, it's the city's most dazzling fashion shows with European haute couture. To a western farmer on the town, it's all the boots and overalls and oil burners alive to the sight and touch that once lay in print in Eaton's fat slick mail order catalogue. To Winnipeggers—it's part of the landscape, part of the way of life. To visitors—it's a rubber-necking attraction that claims priority attention over the Legislative Buildings or Assiniboine Park.

Eaton's specialized in becoming involved in community affairs, but the events surrounding three local disasters showed how much the store had become a part of Winnipeg itself over the years. In the spring of 1950, the Red River broke its banks and inundated one-eighth of the city, causing the dislocation of more than 100,000 people. Eaton's lent assistance by hosting a flood relief centre in the Hargrave annex and by feeding relief workers for the duration of the emergency. (At the time, Eaton's Valley Room cafeteria alone served more than ten thousand meals per day.) The store

The original Hargrave Street annex of the store. *Archives of Ontario: T. Eaton Fonds F229. Used with the permission of Sears Canada Ltd.*

also used its facilities to assist employees whose homes were threatened by the rising waters.

Deliverymen picked up furniture from employees' houses and brought it to the Mail Order, where it was stored safely, or they helped the owners move their items to safe upper floors. In all, 225 families were served in this way by Eaton's.

At the time of the flood, Eaton's was out of the line of danger, located safely on high ground. By contrast, in 1954, when the capacious Time Building across the street was destroyed by a massive fire that started in a faulty neon sign above a tenant's shop, Eaton's was literally at disaster's doorstep. All told, the blaze completely destroyed three nearby buildings and seriously damaged two others. The Big Store, just 150 feet away, would surely have been among these, and the blaze even more devastating than it was, if not for the heroic efforts of Eaton's fire brigade and facilities personnel who got out of bed upon hearing Eaton's siren to come downtown and help when they were informed about the peril facing their place of employment. Eaton's own water supply had to be used to create a water curtain along the store's Portage Avenue façades. To accomplish this saving feat, employees had to hang over the building's parapet, while co-workers grasped their ankles, in order to spray water down the walls and prevent the conflagration's sparks from igniting Eaton's as well. Serious damage in the form of broken windows and melted metal window frames occurred, but the building and its contents were saved from destruction.

In March 1966, a morning snowfall of fourteen inches accompanied by fifty-mile-per-hour winds became a paralyzing blizzard that stranded 1,100 employees and almost 400 customers in the store, unable to get home; 30 employees formed a planning committee to direct the work needed to house people overnight, guaranteeing their comfort and safety, while still protecting Eaton's facilities and merchandise. Entertainment, in the form of televisions and refreshments, were provided in the Grill Room, while the Valley Room cafeteria served dinner to the refugees, as well as breakfast the next morning. The furniture departments were used as a makeshift dorm. After providing this emergency housing for one night, Eaton's served as headquarters for, and donated support services to, "Operation Snowbound," a longer-term effort that assisted the elderly in town who were seriously affected by the blizzard.

The T. Eaton Co. has often been criticized for coming late to suburban shopping centres. The negative appraisals may have been founded in fact, but in Winnipeg, where one store dominated trade as Eaton's did, it

Eaton's Brandon store in later years. The label scar of the earlier "Eaton's of Canada" logo can be clearly seen on the building's façade. *Archives of Ontario: T. Eaton Fonds F229. Used with the permission of Sears Canada Ltd.*

was clearly difficult for management to see the need for more locations around town. Eaton's opened a TECO store and Groceteria in nearby Brandon in March 1928. It was eventually converted to a full-line Eaton's store in 1939 and modernized and rebuilt in September 1956. The seventy-seven-thousand-square-foot branch anchored the Rosser Avenue shopping district and came to be appreciated as a touch of the big city in Brandon, providing both a place to shop as well as major and respected source of employment.

Back in Winnipeg, Eaton's addressed the increasing use of the automobile by shoppers when it opened a large garage across Hargrave Street from the store. The "Carpark," as it was known, also connected the store with a bridge over the street for convenience and protection from Winnipeg's often-brutal weather. Likewise, Eaton's built a huge outlying "Service Building" at Wellington Avenue and Berry Street in 1961. Near the entrance to Winnipeg's airport, it provided warehousing space for heavy home furnishings, as well as a catalogue showroom, and took pressure off space in the downtown Eaton's campus; the Service Building had to be doubled in size in 1967.

The profound affection of Winnipeggers for "the Big Store" is rooted in millions of memories of shopping trips, special lunches, Christmastimes and the impromptu episodes for which the store provided a characterful backdrop. Meghan Nieman's vivid memories of events that took place over forty years ago, while charmingly detailed and specific to her own history, probably echo countless shopping trips made by countless customers over the venerable store's lifetime:

Every Saturday I would make a plan to meet my grandmother after my class at the Royal Winnipeg Ballet, and meet her in front of the Timothy Eaton statue, where I would rub his foot for good luck and look at the rows and rows of names listed on the plaques commemorating the World Wars.

The first thing we would do was to go to the information booth on the main floor to look at the movie page of the Free Press. After we had chosen what movie to see late in the afternoon, we would head up to the Hair Salon (there were elevator attendants in my early childhood), where my nana would have Vickie do her hair. I remember Vickie as being very elegant—red hair sprayed into a fantastic sweep and full-length dresses which were really sophisticated to the eyes of a young girl! While my nana got her hair done, I would roam around the store with the few dollars she had given me. The toy department on the 8th floor was, of course, a favourite, but I also liked books, children's clothes, and records.

After my nana had sat under the hairdryer and read her movie magazine, we headed over to the Char Bar, where I would admire the feature of the day which was always sitting on a plate under a clear plastic dome as you came in. Perfectly scooped mashed potatoes were usually involved. Winnie almost always waited on us, and I usually got fries with gravy and a milkshake.

Sometimes we would splash out and go to the Grill Room, which was truly the most elegant place I could conceive of. I remember the waiting room out front with its wood-panelled walls and the wedding cake shop to the right. And when you got in to the main room and looked up, it never ceased to amaze me how high the ceilings were and how lovely they were with their beams and plaster relief work. Like Winnie in the Char Bar, these women wore uniforms with little hats, and they raced back and forth to the kitchen at the back of the room with great speed. I believe we ordered asparagus cheese rolls and tea every time.

After we did some shopping, we would head over to the cinema—the Metropolitan, the Odeon, or the Garrick—to see our movie. These places were palaces to me, too. Despite the fact they had been chopped up and altered by then, you could still see vestiges of the beautiful plaster work around and above you. My nana used to tell me about the days when they were vaudeville theatres, and how her brothers had performed there.

There was always a bus home from around Eaton's at the end of the day. Sometimes we would wait in between the doors at one of the entrances. The big old store kept us warm a little longer before we went out into the cold night.

When I think of my dear grandmother, Eaton's is often the backdrop and to this day, memories of Eaton's still keep me warm!

When it came time to address the store's needs in the suburbs of Winnipeg, Eaton's went ahead with a large, 190,000-square-foot branch in 1968 at the Polo Park shopping centre, where a Simpsons-Sears store had already been anchoring the centre for nine years. Nonetheless, an advertising section in the *Winnipeg Free Press*, issued in advance of the store's May 2 opening, announced that the $5 million store was "a new and especially pleasurable experience…planned for the shopper—her comfort and her convenience" and that on all three of its levels, and in its Garden Court restaurant, it "offers a richly rewarding experience for all members of the family."

Eaton's joined another, earlier Simpsons-Sears store at the six-year-old Garden City Shopping Centre in West Kildonan on August 10, 1976. The one-floor store was roughly half the size of Polo Park but nonetheless included a Garden Room restaurant. Eaton's advertising gave a hint of what customers could expect when they crossed the new branch's threshold:

Eaton's Polo Park store was a handsome composition of light brick with deep recesses, corner windows and a precast-concrete coping. *Archives of Ontario: T. Eaton Fonds F229. Used with the permission of Sears Canada Ltd.*

Welcome to Winnipeg's most beautiful new store, Eaton's Garden City. An exciting store with the accent on fashions to wear, fashions for the home, fashions for living. A friendly store with those special Eaton Services that make life easier for you. And those concerned Eaton people that make shopping pleasanter. A beautiful store with a country-casual atmosphere. Warm cedar paneling, soft lighting, lots of green and growing things. A natural look, a welcoming look. Your kind of store—Eaton's Garden City. We've all the specialty shops you love—Timothy E., The Trimmers, No. 1, Young World, Abstract Shop and Kitchen Country. We've Eaton's Travel and an Attractions Ticket Office. And our Garden Terrace where the food is great, the mood relaxed and friendly. All waiting for you now at Eaton's Garden City.

In spite of it all, though, the Garden City branch had difficulty competing, and consumer preference seemed to remain with the existing stores. In fairness, though, it was up for comparison with the Big Store on Portage Avenue and the popular Polo Park branch, both of which were among the very best-performing stores company-wide.

A view of Eaton's, the "Big Store," in its twilight years. *Archives of Ontario: T. Eaton Fonds F229. Used with the permission of Sears Canada Ltd.*

Garden City

St. Vital

EATON'S Winnipeg

By 1979, Eaton's had opened two more branch stores in the Winnipeg area. *Archives of Ontario: T. Eaton Fonds F229. Used with the permission of Sears Canada Ltd.*

In October 1979, a big new store at St. Vital joined the other branches. The very modernity and fashion thrust of the spacious, splashy store, described by Eaton's during the theatrically themed grand opening as "a store produced in the Style of the 80s, for you, the customer of the 80s. St. Vital has everything modern and new combined with the same old friendly service you've always enjoyed when shopping at Eaton's."

Amid all of the chrome, mirrors and plush carpeting, the old store on Portage Avenue may have seemed hopelessly antiquated and belonging to another era. However, a 1970s-era visitor's guide to Winnipeg printed by

Eaton's reminded readers that "[i]t's the little shops that make Eaton's just a little different." Picturing the Abstract Shop, Action 5, the Pine Room and other specialty boutiques for which Eaton's had become famous, it also recommended the time-honoured Grill Room, saying that the "favourite rendezvous for Winnipeggers and visitors" was a place to "relax—enjoy the quiet surroundings" in the great store, described by the guide matter-of-factly as "[t]he exciting way to one-stop shopping." With its 835,000 square feet of retail space in the main building, annexes and catalogue showroom, it remained for many years Eaton's venerable western flag-bearer in Winnipeg, just as it had since 1905.

Sir John and the Lady

Business itself must evolve the men who are to direct its affairs.
—Timothy Eaton

After Edward Young Eaton passed away in 1900, Timothy Eaton looked to his youngest son, John Craig Eaton, to be the new heir apparent who would rule the empire he founded. To describe the T. Eaton Co. as a "realm" at the dawn of the twentieth century is apt; the family business had spread across Canada, and there was, in Timothy Eaton's mind, much more to be conquered. What's more, under the right leadership, the horizon was, from his point of view, practically limitless.

At first glance, the carefree, affable "Jack" (as he was known) was in many ways the antithesis of his quiet, reserved and stern father. Where Timothy wouldn't have a thing to do with alcohol or tobacco (nor would his stores), Jack drank liberally and enjoyed a good cigar. Yet Jack shared his father's aptitude for business and took on a leadership role in the company as to the manner born. He loved adventure, and all things mechanical intrigued him. In fact, a popular anecdote, recounted in author Augustus Bridle's article on the then-titled Sir John Craig Eaton, for the store's *Golden Jubilee* book, revealed that at six years old, the boy revelled in participating in his father's business:

> [A] *vivid extract from the life of Sir John carries back to the Christmas season of 1882…Fair in the middle of the store—a very different Store*

from that of 1919, there was for one week a large box more or less full of spinning tops. Beside the box stood a curly-haired six-year-old spinning the tops on a plate on the lid of the box. Every top he spun was music to that boy, and every time he spun one, he reached out his hand for somebody's quarter, said "Thank You!" and handed over the top to be parceled.

Thus it was that Jack familiarized himself with operations, spending weekends working in the parcel department, and he later became a frequent visitor the store's power plant, where workers indulgently allowed the young man to stoke, oil and clean the machinery that was the store's lifeblood. He later worked in the wages office, in sales and as a floor-walker. Perhaps knowing that E.Y.'s life might be cut short by diabetes, Timothy Eaton abruptly sent Jack on a worldwide tour in 1895 (he had to borrow luggage on the spot), before he reached the age of twenty, and under the guidance of experienced Eaton buyers.

When he became a director of the T. Eaton Co. in 1905, he had something more than mere business experience; he had already developed great affection for his dad's enterprise, its innovations and its people, and he came to see them all as inseparable from his own family, and indeed his way of life. From Timothy Eaton, he learned firsthand how his father used his own character to build relationships and how thoughtful analysis of any situation could be used to arrive at decisions that would serve the company and his family well. Being rewarded with a vice-presidency of the firm, and with his success in Winnipeg behind him, Jack was more than prepared to assume the reins after the sad memories of Timothy Eaton's 1907 death retreated into the past.

Luck was with him as well. When his parents thought that the energetic young man's out-of-the-office lifestyle of booze, cigars and night life might be improved by professional treatment, they checked him into Rotherham House, a small, private hospital in Toronto. He met and quickly became smitten with Flora McCrea, a nurse-in-training at the time. She had come to Rotherham House after serving at Toronto General Hospital, where, after a three-month probationary period, she was told that she wasn't "fitted to be a nurse."

Flora McCrea came from the tiny town of Omemee, northeast of Toronto near Peterborough, and was one of eight children of an established cabinetmaker. Years later, at the prodding of her grandchildren, she wrote down her memoirs, and the result was the best-selling book *Memory's Wall*, published in 1956. Anyone with an interest in history should be glad that she

Sir John Craig Eaton
1876-1922

Lady Flora McCrea Eaton
1880-1970

Official portraits of Sir John and Lady Eaton. *Archives of Ontario: T. Eaton Fonds F229. Used with the permission of Sears Canada Ltd.*

took her family's advice, for the book offers not only gripping insight into the Eaton story from an eyewitness but also a charming and detailed portrait of life in her era; though not without sadness and difficulty, hers was a charmed life that comes alive in her own words.

She described the rigors of life in a small, rural Ontario town in the late 1800s. Her striking description of the shared family work of acquiring the staples of life—and, in the case of food, preparing for the cold winter—creates a vivid contrast with modern life and parallels the history of the famous family of which she would become a member.

She became friendly with the twenty-four-year-old Jack, who took her on rides in his Winton phaeton automobile, one of the first in Canada (it sported the license plate "No.1," which was later memorialized in one of Eaton's most famous shops-within-a-store, the No. 1 Shop, selling contemporary fashions). After meeting his parents and visiting their Lowther Avenue home, she was informed by the hospital's director that Jack was interested in proposing to her and that Timothy and Margaret Eaton "were most pleased with his decision." Soon after, the couple travelled to Flora's home to ask for her father's approval, and after a March engagement, they were married in Omemee on May 8, 1901.

Her writing is also an insight into her husband's character, as well as her own personal journey through life; she admitted that she, along with her father, wondered if it might not be too difficult for a girl of twenty like her to become a member of a wealthy family accustomed to a life of luxury. In the end, she decided that the graciousness showed her by the Eatons and similarities of the two families would carry the day:

> *Our parents had much in common, but the Eatons were wealthy while the McCreas were just comfortable. My mother used to say, "Money is the root of all evil, but it could be a very useful root," meaning that it could grow in the direction of good. This was an implication that I have never tried to forget.*

Their wealth grew fabulously as Eaton's became a household name, and the Eaton family acquired status as well, no doubt to the good-looking Jack's public reputation as much as the store profits that allowed them a richly luxurious lifestyle, the type of which most people only dream of. After a month-long honeymoon at Ravenscrag, the couple returned to a wedding gift from Jack's parents: a fully furnished house on Walmer Road in Toronto's developing Annex neighbourhood. It was at this address that the couple learned the subtle balance of a successful marriage partnership, and in *Memory's Wall* can be found the telling words, "Jack was strong-willed, and so was I; both of us quickly recognized this fact and set ourselves to learn to give-and-take…The fifty-fifty arrangement is not enough; sometimes it requires the whole 100 percent. The result, a continuing, happy marriage is well worth the effort."

Thus the material trappings of the Eaton family descended on a couple whose marital foundation was strong enough to withstand them, and indeed they lived their lives to the fullest in a state of great privilege. After his father's death, Jack took the reins of the flourishing department store and manufacturing business, and while maintaining his father's policies, he enriched it with his own vision as well. The ensuing success brought wealth piled on top of wealth and a lifestyle that matched it.

The young family of Sir John and Lady Eaton posed for a portrait shortly after the birth of their son John David in 1909. *Archives of Ontario: T. Eaton Fonds F229. Used with the permission of Sears Canada Ltd.*

They, with their firstborn son, Timothy Craig, took an extensive tour of Europe in 1907, departing on the first eastbound crossing of the ill-fated liner *Lusitania* and occupying its sumptuous Royal Suite. The voyage took them to England, France, Switzerland, Austria and Ireland, where they retraced the steps of Jack's father. Further travels abroad ensued before Jack, ever interested in the various methods of conveyance and new technologies, purchased a sailing yacht named *Tekla*, which was looked after by a crew of ten.

With the coming of their second son, John David, in October 1909, they bought a ten-acre property near friend and moneyed financier Sir Henry Pellatt's property, where he sought to build his dream home, Casa Loma.

The Eatons engaged architect Frank Wickson, of the firm of Wickson & Gregg, to design their own palatial Georgian mansion, which they called Ardwold, an Irish name aptly describing their estate as "a high, green hill." Two years later, Flora was off on another trip to Europe, where she rented a London home located across from Kensington Gardens, toured the Paris Opéra, had a glimpse of Austrian kaiser Franz-Josef and lunched at the still-famous Sacher Hotel in Vienna. In *Memory's Wall*, she recounted that "just to sit at a table in an open café,

A fine portrait of Ardwold, the home of Sir John Eaton. The cupola that provided panoramic views is clearly visible above the roof of the house. *Archives of Ontario: T. Eaton Fonds F229. Used with the permission of Sears Canada Ltd.*

The Great Hall of Ardwold, showing Sir John's organ and its console. *Archives of Ontario: T. Eaton Fonds F229. Used with the permission of Sears Canada Ltd.*

sipping Viennese Coffee and nibbling at their delicious pastries, while a string orchestra played Strauss somewhere near at hand, was for me a pleasurable experience."

Upon her return, Jack whisked her directly to Ardwold, which he had completed and furnished in her absence. Although John David, upon seeing the house, remarked, "I don't like this hotel...I want to go home!"

there really was much to admire in the mammoth residence, which featured fifty rooms, a swimming pool and a small hospital, with the whole thing surmounted by a cupola that served as an observation deck from which, on a fine day, the steam rising from Niagara Falls could be seen. Jack's pride and glory was the Aeolian organ that graced the vaulted grand hall, which was lined in Circassian walnut paneling. Flora described him as having "a special joy in all beautiful things," but he was fascinated with the organ's mechanical player mechanism and assembled a great collection of "operas, symphonies, overtures, and oratorio things" on recordings, which he played nightly after dinner.

The home became the scene of brilliant soirees to befit the setting, and it was soon augmented by three Rolls-Royces (named Bluebird, Yellowbird and Ladybird) and a 192-foot-long steam yacht named *Florence*, which the family sailed from New Jersey back to Toronto and a berth at the Royal Canadian Yacht Club. By the time the war in Europe loomed over the horizon, the couple had built Kawandag, a landmark, colonnaded vacation home, on property beside Lake Rosseau that they purchased in 1906. A third son, Edgar Allison, was born to the couple in 1911.

If this *embarras de richesse* were all that characterized John Craig and Flora Eaton, their lives would have gone down in history as simply wealthy, but what they contributed to the nation, to their employees and to the T. Eaton Co. made them legends worthy of the name. Following his father, who just before his death gave a gift of $50,000 (roughly $1,150,000 today) to the Toronto General Hospital, Jack gave the princely sum of $365,000 (which funded a surgical wing named in memory of Timothy Eaton) in 1909. This example of inherited and learned generosity and compassion (his father was known to have instructed his secretary to have a stock of $100 bills on hand to help employees when he learned of their difficult situations) was only one of his many throughout Canada.

When his mother, Margaret, expressed an interest in erecting a suitable monument in memory of her husband, John donated the property for and bankrolled the construction of a great church on St. Clair Avenue. The new congregation, however, proposed the name of the new Neo-Gothic house of worship on its own, and it has been known ever since as the Timothy Eaton Memorial Church.

In defence of his country's economic and, he himself might add, cultural sovereignty, John Craig Eaton opposed Liberal prime minister Henri Charles Wilfred Laurier's plans to enter into a reciprocity (free trade) agreement with the United States. Along with seventeen other prominent

The lakeside front of Kawandag, Sir John and Lady Eaton's summer home on Lake Rosseau in the Muskokas. *Archives of Ontario: T. Eaton Fonds F229. Used with the permission of Sears Canada Ltd.*

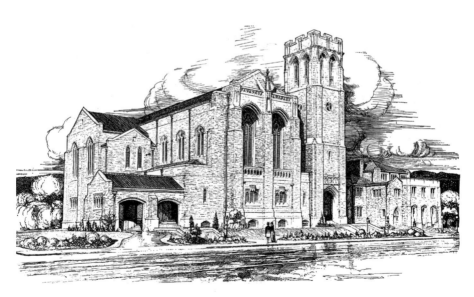

Official portrait drawing of the Timothy Eaton Memorial Church on St. Clair Avenue in Toronto. The edifice was given debt-free to the congregation by Sir John Eaton in December 1914. *Collection of the author.*

Toronto businessmen, who normally would have supported the prime minister, his signature appears on the Canadian National League's *Manifesto Against Reciprocity with the United States of America*. The document's item no. 10 states, "Believing as we do that Canadian nationality is now threatened with a more serious blow than any it has heretofore met with, and that all Canadians who place the interest of Canada before any party, or section, or any individual therein, should at this crisis state their views openly and fearlessly, we, who have hitherto supported the Liberal Party in Canada, subscribe to this statement." The activities of the League, and John Craig Eaton's support of it, changed not just the course of the election that ended Wilfrid Laurier's fifteen years as prime minister but Canada's direction as well. (Sixty-seven years later, the issue would come up again, a dozen years before the disappearance of the business that bore the Eaton family name.)

John Craig Eaton's most notable contributions were in defence of his country, a part of the British empire, during the cataclysm that was World War I. This brutal, bloody war, one of the first to incorporate modern

Overview of the T. Eaton & Co. properties in Toronto, circa 1910,. showing the first portion of its eight-storey main store on the corner of Yonge and Albert Streets. *Archives of Ontario: T. Eaton Fonds F229. Used with the permission of Sears Canada Ltd.*

technologies, affected Canada from the day it began on July 28, 1914, and John Craig Eaton was quick to see that any powers at his disposal were ready to help the Allies achieve victory.

Among his first actions in support of his nation's war effort was to call a meeting of Eaton's directors, who concurred with his suggestion that any war volunteer who worked for Eaton's would continue to receive a full salary if married, and one-half salary if single, for the duration of the war. Furthermore, in any war-related contracts undertaken by Eaton's (for uniforms and other goods the company might provide or produce), any profits would be returned to the government for the war effort. Contracts with German firms were terminated in retaliation for the aggression.

John Craig Eaton served on the organizing committee for the Patriotic Fund, whose mission was to look after soldiers' dependents and their welfare, and Eaton's employees contributed more than $600,000 towards the noble cause. He had the yacht *Florence* stripped of its luxuries and donated it to the war effort (it was later sunk off the coast of Trinidad), and he later pressed his new, Pullman-built all-steel private railway car "Eatonia II" into war service.

When he was made aware of a dangerous shortage of machine guns for the Canadian forces, John Craig Eaton gave a personal donation of $100,000 to equip the Eaton Machine Gun Battery, which saw service in France. Flora used her powers of organization, honed in the rigors of her rural upbringing, to see to the Patriotic Fund's goals; in her memoir, she documented the day when her husband was asked if he would receive a title in thanks for his war efforts. The surprised couple decided to answer in the affirmative because "the award was not only to Jack but also to the many people in the Store and associates who had given him assistance."

So it was in June 1915 that John Craig Eaton's name appeared on King George V's list of honours as a Knight Bachelor. The investiture ceremony was held that fall in Ottawa at Rideau Hall, the residence of Governor General HRH the Duke of Connaught (Prince Arthur, son of Queen Victoria and nephew of the king). Jack officially became Sir John Craig Eaton, and Flora, now Lady Eaton, described the day with great relish in *Memory's Wall*:

> *It was a wonderful moment for me when Jack's name was called. He walked up, knelt in front of the Duke of Connaught who touched him on each shoulder with his sword and uttered the ancient command beginning "Arise, Sir Knight…" I felt shivers up and down my spine and I could hardly restrain my tears—but they were tears of pride and happiness.*

After lunching with the Duke and Duchess and their daughter, Princess Patricia, the pair returned home to Toronto, where they received a "royal welcome" indeed, with beaming servants addressing them for the first time as "Sir John" and "My Lady." Even their children (now numbering four on the account of the recent birth of son Gilbert McCrea) took delight in "discarding the familiar 'Mummie' and 'Daddy' entirely, in order to greet us ceremoniously with our new titles."

Lady Eaton continued with her charitable service, remarking that "from time to time there was the sorrowful duty of calling at the house of a friend or relative, bereaved overnight by the telegraphed message from Ottawa, 'killed in action.'" More pleasant activities at Ardwold included fundraisers and impromptu entertaining of soldiers, some of whom merely dropped in for breakfast! She also served as patroness of the 109th Battalion of the Canadian Expeditionary Force, of Lindsay, Ontario, near her birthplace.

Towards the end of the war, in December 1917, a collision between the SS *Mont Blanc*, a cargo ship loaded with explosives, and another vessel resulted in an onboard fire that sparked the calamitous Halifax Explosion. Sir John was quick to respond to the horrible and tragic news of death and destruction wrought by the tragedy. He had a boxcar loaded with supplies and used the "Eatonia II" to transport a team, including ten department heads, two doctors and the family's personal nurses, to Nova Scotia. Once there, Sir John put his talents of organization and business management together in order to distribute free aid to the victims for a period of one week. An anecdote related in *The Store that Timothy Built* singles out one episode from the expedition that went largely unpublicized at the time:

> *One man, exhausted and freezing in the bitter weather, appeared at 4 a.m., and apologized for coming so late: He'd just finished digging his wife and four children from the ruin of their home. They were dead of course, but if he could just have something to keep himself warm, he'd be most grateful… "I never saw Sir John cry before," said H.S. Thornton, one of the Eaton team, later. "He was almost dead with exhaustion himself, but he spent an hour outfitting that poor, sad man."*

At the war's end, Sir John and Lady Eaton shared their fellow Canadians' feelings of relief and joy, even though the family suffered losses itself. Sir John's cousin Thomas Alden Eaton died at age thirty-four while serving as a lieutenant in the Canadian infantry in France, and his sister, Josephine, and her daughter, Iris, were returning from Europe on the *Lusitania* in 1915 when it was torpedoed and sunk off the coast of Ireland. Josephine was dragged onto an overturned lifeboat, but Iris, then twenty, drowned, as did three Eaton buyers on the same voyage. Putting aside tragedy, Lady Eaton recalled Armistice Day in *Memory's Wall*:

> *Everywhere in the streets of Toronto the people went mad with joy; church bells rang; crowds sang and capered in the streets. Jack and I walked around downtown in a heady feeling of elation…It was a night to stay up, and out! At five o'clock in the morning we went into the store and up to the lunchroom, and when the first chef came on duty he found me cooking bacon and eggs and buttering a mound of toast.*

The store, its operation and its employees were not forgotten during the war or the years leading up to it. Although it was announced in 1904, the construction of a new, eight-storey commercial building on the corner of Yonge and Albert Streets was not started until just after Timothy Eaton's death in 1907 and was completed in 1909. Additions to the annex block, for garages, continued from 1907 until 1913, when a ten-storey building was added to the ensemble at the northwest corner of James and Albert Streets, known as Eaton's House Furnishings Annex. Upon its opening in January 1913, an *Eaton's Daily Store News* advertisement announced that inauguration of the building, whose basement and first five floors contained furniture for any room of the house, "will be formally opened by the inauguration of The Great February Sale of Furniture" and that the building was connected to the main store by subway.

The tall factories surrounding Trinity Square were completed during the war years, during which manufacturing personnel made up about half of the T. Eaton Co.'s twenty-two-thousand-strong staff at the time. Rumours also persisted, and denials issued, that Eaton's was planning to build a structure a number of blocks to the north at Carlton Street. In fact, the company had been busy acquiring property in the block bounded by Yonge, Hayter, Bay and College Streets, but it was not revealed until later that Sir John nixed a plan to build the College Street store until the Allies had won the war. Another rumour, that the store was up for sale, perhaps to American interests, was quashed after he made his famous 1920 remark (at a dinner for department managers in the store's Grill Room) that "[t]here is not enough money in the whole world to buy my father's name." In fact, Eaton's business had practically tripled during the war years.

Eaton's Annex began life as the Furniture Building in 1913 but housed a budget store operation after the construction of Eaton's–College Street in 1930. *Archives of Ontario: T. Eaton Fonds F229. Used with the permission of Sears Canada Ltd.*

Shortly thereafter, Eaton's acquired the five-storey property of the Adams Furniture Co. at the corner of Queen and James Streets, which dovetailed nicely with the rest of the complex of older buildings. However, the differing floor levels made the whole Queen Street store a hodgepodge of levels and archways leading from one structure to the other. With this latest acquisition, the business practically filled the block, except for the four-storey building at the corner of Yonge and Queen Streets, commonly referred to as the Woolworth Block, and a few storefronts to the north of it. Surprisingly, the

Woolworth building, with its façade partially restored and partially covered with modern aluminum cladding, is the only structure on the block to survive to the present day.

Elsewhere, the aforementioned Regina and Saskatoon warehouses were augmented by the construction of a Maritimes mail-order distribution centre in Moncton, New Brunswick, in 1919, and even the number of foreign buying offices grew.

Despite the war and a 1912 strike—the latter handled in fairly heavy-handed fashion by the company, which led to resentment of its policies towards employees as "paternalistic"—Sir John, with the encouragement of Lady Eaton, continued his father's benevolent treatment of staff. The participants in the relief effort in Halifax received silver pins with the letters "E.W.S." inscribed on them, denoting "Eaton Welfare Service" and noting "Halifax Relief, December 1917" on the back. From these initials, Lady Eaton formed the Eaton Women's Society to provide assistance and mentoring to the young women, often from out of town like herself, who came to the big city to work at Eaton's.

Her husband's interest in physical culture meshed with the benevolent attitude towards workers when the company established the Eaton Young Men's Country Club at Scarborough and the Shadow Lake Camp for Girls in Stouffville, Ontario. These were both places where Eaton's employees could enjoy a week's camping vacation, with associated activities such as swimming and horseback riding, for a reasonable fee in line with their salaries. Later, Girls' and Boys' Clubs were organized in town for their children's benefit, and employees were encouraged to join Eaton's teams in intramural sports activities.

Before Timothy Eaton's death, the store took another step in 1904 towards shortening working hours by closing at five o'clock, and his son further shortened the store's hours by opening one half hour later than previously, at 8:30 a.m. In Eaton's Golden Jubilee year of 1919, Jack and Flora welcomed a baby girl into their family, Florence Mary, but for customers and employees, the big news was the planned celebrations for the fiftieth anniversary of the founding of the colossal enterprise. On December 31, 1918, an ad began with the words, "A New Year and a New Era" and ended with the reminder that "Our Jubilee Year is happily also the first year of Peace. May the New Year be for one and all the beginning of a New Era of the best kind of progress—an Era of Service based on mutual Good-will."

Signed by Sir John, the announcement also carried the news that the store would close thereafter at 1:00 p.m. on Saturdays, except during July and

For decades, a favourite meeting place in Eaton's Queen Street store was the enormous bronze statue of the Governor. A similar statue graced the Winnipeg store, too. *Archives of Ontario: T. Eaton Fonds F229. Used with the permission of Sears Canada Ltd.*

August, when it would close all day for the benefit of employees, thus taking a step further towards his father's dream of a five-day workweek. As a result of the new hours, and the pressure put on the store during shortened opening times, the traditional "Friday Bargain Day" was moved to Thursday.

January 2, 1919, was the beginning of a year-long celebration, which got off to a fine start when Margaret Eaton, accompanied by her son John, opened the store with a solid gold key and received a floral tribute. Following official reception by the company's directors, the pair passed row after row of admiring employees. An orchestra played from a balcony, and a special chorus sang the hymn "Praise God from Whom all Blessings Flow" before the party toured the store from top to bottom (including the furniture building). To close, "O Canada" and "God Save the King" were sung by the same forces when the group returned to the main floor. The whole event, described in the *Golden Jubilee Book* as representing "the bigness of the achievement, the significance of the progress of fifty years, and the innate forcefulness of the originator of it all," was brought to a close by three cheers for Sir John and what he had achieved as successor to the great merchant.

As the year went on, the Jubilee celebrations continued. A Quarter Century Club was founded for long-serving employees, who received the gift of a watch in commemoration (which four years later was augmented by six weeks' vacation with pay). Aside from more private celebrations held for management at Ardwold and in the store, a massive celebration was held on June 24, 1919, for almost half of the Eaton workforce in the Toronto Armory. At the event, Sir John was presented with a bound volume of the names of twelve thousand Eaton employees who had collectively donated $20,000 to benefit the Toronto Hospital for Sick children and to endow a cot at the hospital in his name.

Eaton's remembered its employees who died in World War I with a prominently displayed bronze tablet. *Archives of Ontario: T. Eaton Fonds F229. Used with the permission of Sears Canada Ltd.*

On the actual anniversary of the store's opening, December 8, 1919, a gift to Margaret Eaton from grateful employees was unveiled in a pre-opening ceremony. Ivor Lewis, an employee of the advertising department, had sculpted an enormous likeness of Timothy Eaton, which, because of its size and ten-ton weight, had to be cast at a foundry in New Jersey. According to newspaper reports, Margaret Eaton openly wept as the seated likeness of her husband executed in bronze was revealed to throngs of cheering employees.

On December 11, 1919, a similar event, though not attended by Mrs. Eaton, inaugurated an identical statue in "the Big Store" in Winnipeg. Over the years, both statues became known to dispense prosperity and good luck to those who rubbed their extended left feet; as a result, the toe of Timothy's left boot always appeared shinier than the right.

For customers, Eaton's constructed an indoor "Jubilee Park" on the first floor of the furniture building for the duration of the Jubilee. Replete with a waterfall, a lagoon for boat rides, hammocks, swings and resting places, the park featured an "outdoor café" where sodas and ice cream could be had while admiring "bright lights suspended from above in pink, blue, green, red, gold and amethyst."

Towards the end of the year, an immense banquet was held for 1,800 employees who returned safely from the Great War, in the same building. The *Toronto Globe* article of December 22, 1919, in describing the Saturday night affair in which "from 6:30 o'clock when the men gathered, until Big Ben announced the arrival of Sunday, officers and employees of the company made merry," referred to Sir John as "their King" and Margaret Eaton as "Queen Mother," while Lady Eaton's entrance was met with a rousing chorus of "For She's a Jolly Good Fellow." Later, 49 Eaton veterans who were decorated for valour received bejeweled medals for their service, and all others received gold medals, which, like the others, were inscribed with the Latin words *Vincit omnia veritas* ("Truth conquers all") and an inscription reminding them that the token was "Presented by Sir John Eaton, as a mark of appreciation of service in the Great War, 1914–1918."

Amid the merrymaking and repeated cheers, a moment of silence was observed for the 238 Eatonians who perished in the conflict. Almost one year later, in November 1920, another gathering was held by veterans, in the auditorium of the furniture building, in order to formally present Sir John and Lady Eaton with a bronze plaque thanking them for making "easier their going, their fighting, and their return" from the war. The newspaper article describing the event revealed that during the war years, Eaton's paid out more than $2.2 million in salaries to 3,327 employees who served their country in those difficult years. Later, an immense bronze memorial would be erected in the store to pay homage to the dedicated employees and Canadian patriots who gave their lives to the war effort, and it is significant to note that twenty-eight pages of the store's *Golden Jubilee Book* were used to list the names of all those who enlisted.

With the troubles of war, and the celebrations of a company milestone behind them, the Eaton family looked forward to a happy future. Sir John and Lady Eaton made the acquaintance of noted Canadian singer Edward Johnson, who encouraged her to take to the stage with him and sing for the benefit of charity. On the morning of a dress rehearsal concert given for Conservatory students, Lady Eaton's youngest son, Gilbert, was rushed to the hospital and operated on for appendicitis. She maintained her composure, and the formal concert was a great success and resulted in Edward Johnson becoming a lifelong friend of the Eaton family.

In 1921, Sir John and Lady Eaton travelled to England, where they rented a house in London before visiting St. Moritz to relax amid the breathtaking Alpine scenery and to take in the fresh mountain air of Switzerland. On the trip back, they stayed at the fabled Ritz Hotel in London and encountered both Sergei Diaghilev and Charlie Chaplin before sailing home on the Canadian Pacific steamship *Empress of Scotland*.

According to Lady Eaton, the memories of this trip and the months afterwards were clouded in fog by what transpired starting in January 1922. Sir John travelled to Montréal to attend a board meeting of the Canadian Pacific Railway, of which he was a director. While there, he contracted influenza and returned home by train for rest and treatment. A family doctor appraised his condition, warning Lady Eaton that "it is serious." The seven weeks of illness suffered by Sir John before he passed away were referred to in *Memory's Wall* as "the long, losing battle," and she, along with the children, Jack's mother and the loyal Ardwold staff maintained a constant, loving vigil until the end came on March 30, 1922. Sir John Craig Eaton was forty-six years of age, and for such a young man, he had accomplished so much with what he was given; others would have to see to the progress of his father's company.

According to newspaper reports, the streets outside the Timothy Eaton Memorial Church were clogged with crowds totalling fifty thousand people who could not get into the crowded sanctuary for the April 3 funeral service, in spite of "days of storm and sleet." Under a headline stating, "Deep Sorrow Enshrouds His Native City as Last Touching Tribute of Fellowmen Is Paid to Memory of Sir John C. Eaton," a lengthy description of the funeral mentioned an "unprecedented display of sympathy and affection" and reported that a "solid wall of humanity" formed along the funeral route from the church to the Eaton Mausoleum at Mount Pleasant Cemetery, adding that "every foot of the entire distance was dense with humanity."

For Lady Eaton and the immediate family, while the shock of their beloved Jack's loss was softened by this outpouring of emotion for "one widely loved, great in life, great in death," as the *Globe and Mail* described him, their private grief would take time to heal. She revealed in *Memory's Wall*: "As for me, while I was conscious of all the kindness and sympathy that flowed in from the great and small, all over the world, inwardly I felt like a stone...I wished I could have rushed away into the woods and hidden like a suffering animal. But no one can run away from life or death."

Eaton's, the store her husband guided through unprecedented growth and prosperity, could not run away, either, for its own momentum was too great and Lady Eaton herself too full of the force of life to give up her public role as a Canadian leader. She would go on to accomplish much more after her husband's passing and live to see her son take the reins of the great store once held so nobly by Sir John.

Regency Style

*This company is proud of the fact that in its progress through the years it has
been able to keep pace with the inspiring development of the city, and, indeed with
that of this great country as a whole.*
—Robert Young Eaton

With the death of Sir John Eaton, the T. Eaton Co. began a journey
through an intriguing period that encompassed the expanding
wealth and *joie de vivre* of the Roaring Twenties, the privations of the
Great Depression and the onset of World War II. His will stipulated
that his shares in the T. Eaton Co. Limited and—due to his having
owned 8,890 out of 10,000 of them—its control would transfer to the
one son (or daughter) deemed best suited to the task by the trustees of
his estate. However, the inheritance could not occur until his youngest
son had achieved the age of twenty-seven—or, given the birth dates of
his children, not before 1942. Eaton's board of directors installed the
Irish-born Robert Young Eaton, Sir John's contemporary and cousin, as
president. His hand would direct the company as a regent until an heir
to Sir John appeared, or for the next twenty years.

Robert Young Eaton was born near Ballymena at a small place called
Killyree in 1875; his father was John Eaton, who had remained on the Auld
Sod after his uncle Timothy left for the New World. In 1897, Timothy
Eaton visited his Irish birthplace and family in County Antrim and met his
nephew, whom he encouraged to take up a life of commerce as opposed to

the civil service career to which the young man aspired. Accordingly, he relocated to London and took a job in the company's office there, and he spent his evenings in the pursuit of a Bachelor of Arts degree at the University of London. He rose through the company and had a stint in the Paris buying office before moving to Toronto in 1902. By 1907, he was working alongside Sir John Eaton as a member of the board of directors and a first vice-president of the firm. Like Sir John, he married a small-town girl, Hazel Ireland, who was studying in Toronto before the couple tied the knot in 1911 in her native Carberry, Manitoba.

A tall, severe and balding man, Robert took on the nickname "R.Y." and was quite the antithesis of the jovial Sir John. He developed a reputation as a severe and direct leader, who often wrote long missives to his employees rather than confront them directly, but his considerable abilities—which,

Robert Young Eaton
1875-1956

™ T. EATON C? LIMITED
TORONTO   CANADA

Robert Young Eaton led the store after the untimely death of Sir John Eaton. Under his guidance, Eaton's experienced remarkable growth throughout Canada. *Archives of Ontario: T. Eaton Fonds F229. Used with the permission of Sears Canada Ltd.*

after all, were recognized by his uncle at an early age—let him put his mark on the store and steer it through both calm and rough waters alike. Furthermore, he led it towards a great expansionary period that saw the T. Eaton Co. achieve remarkable growth and begin to establish itself far beyond its original locations.

The 1920s were a period of consumerism, and the sales potential of Eaton's stores rose even higher with the advent of new technologies for selling. At the time, many department stores reconstructed their premises, replacing ancient, cobbled-together buildings, built or acquired haphazardly, and the preferred mode was the Chicago style of commercial building, introduced and perfected in the eponymous Midwestern American city. Eaton's had already begun a similar process in 1909 when it completed an addition to its store on newly acquired property at the corner of Yonge and Albert Streets. In the last days of 1922, the store announced that it would be rebuilding the oldest section of the store that Timothy Eaton built in 1883, and it issued a sketch showing a uniform, eight-storey façade on Yonge Street. After demolition of the outmoded buildings commenced in February 1923, the new structure, designed by Toronto firm Sproatt and Rolph, rose quickly on the site. It consisted of two basements, and its parapet rose 115 feet above Yonge Street.

In typical fashion, no gala opening was held, but the store did announce department relocations and new features in its *Eaton's Daily Store News* ads as the new building was occupied floor by floor and joined up with the existing facilities. The Queen Street frontage was modernized as well. When it was completed in 1924, the main store of the T. Eaton Co. assumed a form that it was to have for the next half century.

After her husband's death, Lady Eaton remained on Eaton's board of directors, as she waited out the years until one of her sons would follow in Sir John Eaton's footsteps. She made an annual tour of Eaton's stores,

The last addition to the Queen Street store was an extension of the earlier eight-storey building, which replaced the original 1883 structure at 190 Yonge Street and gave the store a tall, uniform frontage on Yonge Street. *Archives of Ontario: T. Eaton Fonds F229. Used with the permission of Sears Canada Ltd.*

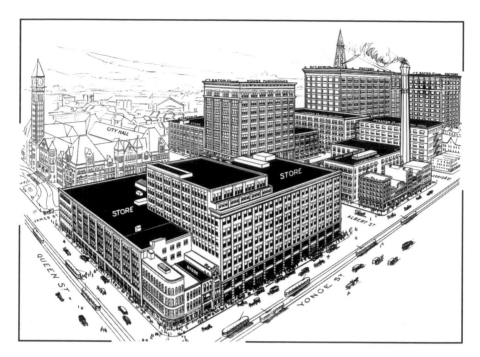

By 1924, the physical plant of Eaton's in downtown Toronto had reached the familiar form that it would have for the next fifty years. Note the ninth-floor addition that housed the Georgian Room restaurant. The small storefront between Woolworths (on the corner of Yonge and Queen Streets) and the main Eaton building housed the 186 Shop, a specialty shop for men. *Archives of Ontario: T. Eaton Fonds F229. Used with the permission of Sears Canada Ltd.*

travelled extensively to Europe, continued her charitable works and, due to her interest in food, guided the operations of Eaton's restaurants. With her sons Timothy and John David in England studying, Lady Eaton spent part of the year travelling, and it was in France, while renting a villa in Cannes in 1924, that she adopted a daughter, Evlyn Rose, half a year younger than Florence.

Later, Lady Eaton purchased a home, the *Villa Natalia*, in Fiesole, outside Florence, where she lived in the prewar years while visiting Europe. *Villa Natalia* was built for Queen Elizabeth of Romania, wife of King Carol I but more famous by her pen name Carmen Sylva, the subject of an atmospheric waltz composed by the famous Romanian composer Iosif Ivanovich. According to *Memory's Wall*, when Lady Eaton's sister, Anna, visited and expressed a concern that the villa might be cold at night, an American friend piped up and suggested that she "tell them that you want two priests in your bed." It was later revealed to the startled Anna that "priest" was the local term for a hot-water bottle, just as in England that essential item of equipment was known as a "pig."

On one of her journeys, she visited London department stores, whose world was turned upside down by Selfridge & Co., the department store brainchild of American merchant Harry Gordon Selfridge, who brought modern merchandising, display methods and store design to the Old World. After dining in the directors' room of one of London's big stores, she made the observation that, with the exquisite atmosphere and appointments, cultured service and elaborate food served on the best of china, she could never return the invitation at the store that bore her name because they were "clean and dull; there was no attempt at interesting decoration, and the dishes were of the railway-station type." The results of her experiences were encapsulated in her oft-quoted words from *Memory's Wall*:

> *I began to dream of something better. Toronto badly needed a new, good restaurant, and I was groping toward the kind that would attract women as well as businessmen...I presented my case to the Eaton Directors. I knew that what I wanted wouldn't be a cheap venture, but I strongly felt that it would be a profitable investment in the end. Alas, my suggestion was turned down; the plan was too costly, I was told, and actually wasn't "a business proposition." I said I was willing to accept the decision, but then added, "Now I would like to ask a favour. I want you to close down the restaurant we have, for I am ashamed of it."*

Later that afternoon, R.Y. paid her a visit at Ardwold to tell her that the board had reversed its decision and wanted her to go ahead with the plan. She engaged Violet Ryley, whom she had befriended years earlier. Ryley had gone on to serve as chief dietician for Canadian military hospitals during World War I, and Lady Eaton had once hired her to cross-train her staff at her first home in Toronto. According to Lady Eaton, "With this experience, supported by her excellent training, and her own organizing talent and good taste in everything, she was most definitely the person we needed as head of our new restaurant."

The design of the restaurant was entrusted to René Cera, an École des Beaux-Arts–trained architect who became head of the T. Eaton Co.'s design and engineering department. It was decided to locate the new Georgian Room high atop the Eaton's store, in a double-height penthouse designed expressly for the new undertaking. Its name came from the elaborate interior décor of soaring, marble column-supported ceilings with gilded plaster-

T. EATON C^O LIMITED

ADASKIN'S
ORCHESTRA
WILL
PLAY
DURING
LUNCHEON
AND
AFTERNOON
TEA
HOURS

FOR
GEORGIAN
ROOM
TAKE
SOUTH
YONGE
ST.
ELEVATORS

The Georgian Room

The New Restaurant and Tea Room on the Ninth Floor of the Store

OPENS TO EATON CUSTOMERS ON MONDAY, MARCH 10TH, 1924.

LOFTY AND COOL AS A CATHEDRAL, its floor of noiseless Italian stone, with classic pillars holding high its vaulted roof. Quietly luxurious as an English ballroom—grey panelled walls, tall windows curtained in blue brocade, courtly crystal chandeliers, and musicians' gallery overhanging the distant doorway. An inviting place to have luncheon or tea. Don't you think so?

SERVICE

An attendant to check wraps, overcoats, etc—to direct you, if you wish, to the comfortably equipped dressing-rooms for ladies and gentlemen.

The Head Waitress or one of her Captains to allot you a table, and a deft waitress in smart tan uniform to receive your order. Quick, expert service will be one of the first good reasons for satisfaction in lunching or taking tea in the Georgian Room.

APPOINTMENTS

Charming dishes—Haviland china banded with ochre and patterned with purple and blue. Fine linen woven in Ireland specially for the Georgian Room. Such nice silver —Colonial design. And black bud vases for the daffodils, snapdragons, marigolds—whatever the flower of the day.

FOOD

The best that experienced marketing can obtain and scientific skill can prepare.

Every item exactly as stated on the menu—absolutely no substitutes employed.

Vegetables cooked in new type of steaming basket.

Meats prepared under direction of highly trained chef.

Endless variety in salads seldom served in a restaurant—concocted from home recipes.

Desserts from best approved Household Science recipes.

BEHIND SCENES

A palatial kitchen, gleaming with white marble tiles, flooded with light from scores of windows, and so high of ceiling that steam and odors are lost in the vast space of its upper regions. Refrigerators that are marvels of convenience and hygienic equipment. A salad table topped by the great trays of chopped ice. The latest word in cooking ranges and serving tables. All the very acme of sanitary perfection.

A Bakery surrounded on two sides by windows—airy and light as a sun parlor, with electric oven and finest equipment.

A Laboratory to try out all new recipes and to aid in the search for most perfect methods of retaining nutriment and flavor in preparation of foods.

MANAGEMENT

Miss Ryley is manager of the new restaurant. During the War she was General Organizing Dietitian of Canadian Military Hospitals. Miss Ryley's standards are lofty as the Georgian Room itself. She has surrounded herself with talent of a high order. Her assistant manager and head of Laboratory hold degrees from University of Toronto, Household Science Course.

The Chef, trained in Europe, has had wide experience in famous New York hotels.

T. EATON C^O LIMITED

An advertisement calling the Georgian Room "lofty and cool as a cathedral" appeared in newspapers to entice customers to visit Eaton's groundbreaking new restaurant, the brainchild of Lady Eaton. *Archives of Ontario: T. Eaton Fonds F229. Used with the permission of Sears Canada Ltd.*

work, walnut paneling and oil-rubbed bronze-and-crystal chandeliers, all executed in Georgian style. The decorative scheme was further enhanced by custom-made Limoges china, a musician's gallery for entertainment and brocade tapestries on the walls. High Palladian windows on the west side of the room allowed an incomparable vista of Toronto, spreading out to the horizon beyond. The *Globe* reported:

> *Amid tall ferns and roses, and to the strains of music from the orchestra balcony, the Georgian Room…was formally opened yesterday morning at 11 o'clock. Tall oval windows, extending two stories, curtained in blue and gold, provided but one of the distinctive features of the large cream-panelled room, with its classic pillars, Italian stone floor, Wedgwood blue rugs and oxidized bronze crystal chandeliers. Patrons are met at the door by one of the captains-in-charge, and conducted to charmingly-set walnut tables and chairs upholstered in blue, where they are quickly and quietly served by trim waitresses in tan uniforms. Each table is attractively set with cream and blue china, Georgian silver service, and black bud vases, each containing a beautiful rose. Cooking is done by a European chef.*

With stately architecture, lavish materials and fine appointments, it is no surprise that the Georgian Room became one of the most popular and respected restaurants in Toronto. *Archives of Ontario: T. Eaton Fonds F229. Used with the permission of Sears Canada Ltd.*

Even when the room was modernized in the 1950s, still retaining its original form, it remained an icon. Competitor Simpson's, in its 1928 expansion, opened the Arcadian Court, a similarly monumental dining room that was a clear attempt to catch up to what Eaton's had accomplished on its ninth floor in 1924. Few who experienced the Georgian Room will forget the breathtaking impression that the rooftop ensemble created from the time the elevator doors slid open to reveal the suave, opulent atmosphere of the marvellously alluring dining room and the décor that gave it such élan. The food, served from adjacent kitchens and of a very high order indeed, rivaled that at local hotel dining rooms, and a number of the Georgian Room's specialties gained fame over time, like the signature chicken pot pie and red velvet cake, which became synonymous with Eaton's. From the moment the Georgian Room was revealed to the public, fine food service became a hallmark of Eaton's large stores all over Canada.

Later, in the 1920s, it became clear that while Eaton's store sales continued their upward swing, those of the catalogue had leveled off. The stagnation was caused by competition, like the Robert Simpson Co.'s catalogue operation, which had opened warehouses and stores in Halifax and Regina, and the fact that the population, with the rise in automobile ownership, had become more mobile. The pendulum shifted back to local retailers, who once both feared and loathed the negative effect that *Eaton's Catalogue* had on their business; now they could offer customers more fluid stock than a twice-yearly catalogue. Another change was the fact that the catalogue was increasingly used by city dwellers, who didn't have time to spend shopping. R.Y. subsequently initiated a great expansion of the company into a business that would serve all of Canada's major cities and stretch from coast to coast.

R.Y. Eaton also was possessed of exquisite taste and an abiding interest in the arts, both of which he brought to bear on the store. He shifted Eaton's focus away from the everyday and commonplace and sought to increase the store's prestige by introducing a higher proportion of luxury merchandise. It was during his era as president that the store opened a Fine Art Gallery, and he himself was on the board of governors of the Toronto Conservatory of Music, as well as served as president of the Art Gallery of Toronto from 1922 to 1940. R.Y. and his family lived lavishly at an enormous mansion in Toronto that he renamed Killyree after his birthplace in Northern Ireland and relaxed at an opulent vacation property on Georgian Bay called Ryestone. In spite his standing, wealth and a reputation for a stern and controlling personality, he was not above, on one occasion, leaving his family's Christmas Day celebrations to go to the store, pick up and deliver a food order, after he was informed by a phone call that the store neglected to deliver it as promised to a customer.

In the period from 1925 to 1929, Eaton's opened a number of TECO stores in smaller communities, expanded its Groceteria stores into twenty-seven Canadian cities and purchased existing department store businesses in Montréal (1925), Saskatoon and Hamilton (1927) and Edmonton and Halifax (1928). The store expanded its Saskatoon warehouse building in 1926 and, in the same year, converted the Regina warehouse into a full-service department store, albeit one that operated on Broad Street in the city's warehouse district rather than downtown. A newly built retail store opened adjacent to the 1920 Moncton Mail Order in 1927, and new stores came online in 1928 in Moose Jaw and Saskatoon, Saskatchewan. The year 1929 saw the opening of the firm's large Calgary store, and by the end of the decade, Eaton's retail savvy was familiar to western, Maritime and French-speaking Canada.

These early Eaton branches served not only the urban areas in which they were located but the surrounding rural communities as well. With large, comprehensive stores in place, Eaton's enticed farmers and dwellers of small towns into them by carrying merchandise that had appeal to all walks of life. Growing up in the 1930s, the experiences of Velma Van Buekenhout offer detailed insight into Canadian life during the R.Y. Eaton era:

I was raised on a farm south of Dysart, Saskatchewan, where I was born in 1932. This was during the depression, when there was little money to buy anything, except the essentials, and most of these were bought at Eaton's in Regina or ordered from the T. Eaton Co. mail order catalogue. My parents were Joe and Jean Mellnick; I had three brothers and three sisters, and I spent many happy and carefree years growing up on the farm. My parents worked very hard on that farm, and we always had a large garden, planted from seeds in packages from Eaton's. The store also sold many items that my dad would use on the farm, and they also sold hundred-pound cloth bags of flour and sugar. My mom would laboriously wash and bleach out the Eaton logo and other printing, so she could sew dresses for the girls and shirts for the boys. When she had extra bags, she made tea-towels, pillowcases, and tablecloths from them. All of these items looked nice and wore well, which helped our family a lot.

As a family, we would raise cattle, plant crops, and work in the garden, and our labor as children alongside our parents helped make ends meet. Eaton's helped us, too. My dad liked raising cattle, and took great pride in

*his herd. He bought most of his harnesses, bridles and just about everything
else from Eaton's. They had a large hardware department and a good
selection in the Eaton catalogue.*

Retail facilities in Ontario were expanded almost overnight when the T.
Eaton Co. announced the purchase of the Canadian Department Stores
Limited on May 2, 1928. The firm, formed in 1926, was in effect a merger
of twenty-one independent department stores in Ontario cities (along with
one in Montréal) that sought to improve their performance through such a
union. In the spring of 1927, an offering of Canadian Department Stores
Limited bonds was accompanied by a quote from the Canadian magazine
Saturday Night:

*It is reasonable to suppose that the centralized buying of merchandise
from large manufacturers and consolidated operation will increase the
net earnings. This will depend mainly on the experience and ability of
Mr. G.H. Rennie, President and General Manager, who had with the
Robert Simpson Company Ltd., a remarkably rapid rise to the position of
Assistant General Manager. He is off to an excellent start in his new task
in view of the fact that many of these stores are leaders in their particular
communities, and have all been established for a period averaging more than
44 years. Canadian Department Stores, Limited, the largest chain store
system in Canada, includes the following stores:*

Duncan Ferguson Co., Limited, Stratford
Dundas & Flavelle, Limited, Lindsay
The Ritchie Co., Limited, Belleville
E.J. Coles Co., Limited, Woodstock
The Chas. Austin Co., Limited, Chatham
A. Bristol & Son, Picton
The Robt. Wright Co., Limited, Brockville
H.H. Engel & Co., Limited, Hanover
Bryans, Limited, Sault Ste. Marie

Opposite and following pages: Eaton's purchased the Canadian Department Stores Limited in
1928, thereby acquiring branches in many cities throughout Ontario. *Archives of Ontario: T.
Eaton Fonds F229. Used with the permission of Sears Canada Ltd.*

Belleville, Ontario

Brantford, Ontario

Brockville, Ontario

Chatham, Ontario

Hanover, Ontario

Huntsville, Ontario

Lindsay, Ontario

Midland, Ontario

THE CANADIAN DEPARTMENT STORES LIMITED

Napanee, Ontario

North Bay, Ontario

Ottawa, Ontario

Pembroke, Ontario

Peterborough, Ontario

Picton, Ontario

Port Arthur, Ontario

St. Catharines, Ontario

THE CANADIAN DEPARTMENT STORES LIMITED

Sault Ste. Marie, Ontario

Stratford, Ontario

Sudbury, Ontario

Woodstock, Ontario

ᴛʜᴇCANADIAN DEPARTMENT STORESLIMITED

The Robinson Co., Limited, Napanee
Ogilvie-Lochead, Limited, Brantford
A.A. Fournier, Limited, Ottawa
Beamish & Smith, Limited, North Bay
Huntington's, Limited, Midland
The Cressman Co., Limited, Peterborough
Beamish and Adams, Huntsville
McLaren & Co., Limited, St. Catharines
I.L. Matthews & Co., Port Arthur
Letendre, Limited, Montréal, Que.
Stafford, Limited, Sudbury
Fenton & Smith, Pembroke
T.H. Pratt, Limited, Hamilton

However, in December 1927, the Canadian Department Stores Limited was placed into receivership after four separate petitions were received by the Bankruptcy Court from creditors after the chain was unable to meet its obligations. Throughout much of 1928, it operated in receivership as it tried to reorganize, until the creditors and receivers were summoned to a meeting in Toronto on March 23, during which an offer to purchase the struggling retailer was discussed. On May 2, 1928, it was revealed that the T. Eaton Co. Limited had purchased the chain for $4 million and would continue to operate the stores under the name of the Canadian Department Stores Limited. It was stated at that time that there would be no changes in the operation of the stores except for the "the adoption of Eaton policies of the guarantee of goods satisfactory or money refunded; cash dealing and the elimination of night shopping," according to an article in the *Globe*.

Of course, changes did occur over the years as the stores were integrated into the Eaton organization. As the company phased out TECO stores in Ontario, they were converted into the Canadian Department Stores nameplate; the operation was later extended into the Maritimes when Eaton's converted Groceteria or TECO stores as well. The Montréal operation survived for a time as a TECO store, but along with the superfluous Hamilton branch, it was eventually closed owing to the large Eaton's stores nearby.

The Canadian Department Stores operated as small-town branches of Eaton's, using the parent company's buying and marketing structure. As they adopted Eaton's policy and assortments, they became in reality Eaton's stores, albeit geared to small-town markets. By 1949, their names had been changed to Eaton's to reflect this fact. It is an interesting fact that the former A.A. Fournier store in Ottawa was for many years the only Eaton store in Canada's capital city, an oddity for a company that saw itself as Canada's premier department store firm.

Eaton's entered the Great Depression under R.Y.'s leadership as a highly profitable concern, known as the "Greatest Retail Organization in the British Empire." Yet the enormous debt brought on by its remarkable expansion in the 1920s reduced its profitability and weakened its ability to deal with the financial calamity that Canada faced after "Black Tuesday," October 29, 1929. Eaton's was forced to reduce staff, lower wages, cut employee discounts and lengthen work hours in order to weather the slowdown.

Prior to the crash, Eaton's took up a longstanding project to build a self-contained department store and office building that would house both the retail and administrative functions of the company in one giant complex. As Toronto's natural growth spread fanlike from its centre, its business district marched north along Yonge Street. Accordingly, in the years leading up to World War I, the company began to assemble the parcels of land needed to create its new, prestigious home. However, in spite of intense speculation in the press and frequent rumours about the "mystery department store," nothing came of it until later in the 1920s, when Eaton's had secured one whole city block at Yonge and College Streets for the construction of its dream store.

One persistent rumour in the Robert Young Eaton years was that Eaton's wanted to move up Yonge Street in order to isolate its competitor Simpson's as Toronto grew northward, but in reality, the store offered property adjacent to the College Street development to the Robert Simpson Co., so that both stores would benefit from a synergy at the new location. Simpson's, under its then-president, Sir Joseph Flavelle, rejected the offer and stayed at the corner of Yonge and Queen Streets, where it completed a large, stone-faced *Moderne*-style addition that expanded the store all the way to Bay Street.

When the official announcement came on November 14, 1928, the project was hailed by the *Globe* as "A Truly Vast Emporium!" The announcement also described a structure 675 feet tall and composed of a 3-million-square-foot department store with an additional 1.2 million square feet of office and service space in the tower soaring above it. Significantly, the newspaper story mentioned that the building would be built in phases, the first being about one-sixth the size of the total. When the depression came and the business was hard-hit, all Eaton's could do was complete the portion that had already been started and ultimately abandon the dream.

In March 1929, the company formed a wholly owned subsidiary, the T. Eaton Realty Co., which bought the stores' real estate holdings from the Eaton family before the market crashed, protecting their interests as property values dropped in the panic.

As the store cut back staff and wages to weather the economic hard times, it experienced controversy and negative press for the first time, brought about by H.H. Stevens, then Trade and Commerce Minister, who had been a conservative but joined the populist bandwagon in a bid to gain leadership of the party away from Prime Minister R.B. Bennett, who earlier had been his opponent. Stevens formed the Royal Commission on Price Spreads and Mass Buying, which accused big business of abuses that affected the common Canadian. A particular target of Stevens's commission was Eaton's, which held a large share of the retail market in Canada.

Called in front of the body, Eaton's was forced to reveal executive salaries and explain the difference between what it paid for goods and the prices at which they were sold. The company, which in the past had a reputation as the fairest of all fair-dealing businesses, was tarnished in the attack. Before long, though, Bennett withdrew his support for Stevens, and the commission folded. Stevens ultimately left the conservative party to form his own political organization, but he was not successful.

At the height of the controversy, the T. Eaton Co. Limited was investigated, and a detailed report was delivered to the commission on June 11, 1934, by W.L. Gordon, the body's auditor. The *Montréal Gazette* published an account of the report the next day. While the report was meant to show the unfairness of the company's executive salaries and bonuses, it would seem that these decreased with the depression, dropping from an average of $54,800 in Eaton's top year of 1929 to $33,900 in 1933. Sales of the company grew from $22,500,000 in the year of Timothy Eaton's death tenfold to $225,050,000 in 1929 but dropped to $132,500,000 in hard-hit 1933. The net profit for the company peaked at more than $8 million in 1929 and then dipped until losses of more than $2 million per year were suffered in 1932 and 1933.

Another target of the commission was the great wealth of the Eaton family. Here, the auditor had more concrete facts to report, revealing that the company paid dividends on the average of over $500,000 per year, 88.9 percent of which went to the estate of the late Sir John Craig Eaton. A one-time payment of almost $1 million was paid to the direct descendants of Timothy Eaton in 1929, and the family also benefitted from the transaction that founded the T. Eaton Realty Co. by a figure of $12 million.

From a historical point of view, the report is valuable in the way it provides a snapshot of the company at a point in time. According to the report, the T. Eaton Co. Limited was the holding company for a variety of other affiliated businesses. It operated thirteen large department stores, five mail-order distribution centres, thirty-two smaller department stores, fifty-seven Groceterias, forty freestanding mail-order offices, six factories, four major warehouses and nine overseas buying offices. Affiliated companies directly controlled by the Sir John Craig Eaton estate were the Eaton Knitting Co. Limited of Hamilton, Ontario; the International Realty Co. Limited of Toronto; and the T. Eaton Life Assurance Co. Limited, a general life insurance business conducted primarily for the benefit of Eaton employees.

Held by the T. Eaton Co. Limited were the T. Eaton Drug Co. Limited, the Eaton Delivery Co. Limited and the T. Eaton House Furnishing Limited, which were involved in the operation of the Toronto stores, and two small companies, the T. Eaton General Insurance Co. and Purchasers Finance Co. Limited, which served the business in insuring goods while in transit and financing deferred payments, which were only then being offered to customers. The Guelph Stove

Company Limited and the related Chromolox Company Limited were also subsidiaries of the holding company.

Other subsidiaries included the T. Eaton Realty Co. Limited, which in 1934 owned the main stores in Toronto, Winnipeg, Saskatoon, Hamilton, Regina, Calgary and Moncton, and the Canadian Department Stores Limited, operating twenty-one stores in Ontario, four in Nova Scotia and one in New Brunswick; the similarly named Canadian Stores Limited had responsibility for the Groceterias in the Maritimes.

The T. Eaton Co. Limited Montréal owned and operated the Montréal store, a clothing factory and a mail-order office, as well as one TECO store in Québec. The T. Eaton Co. Maritimes Limited operated the Moncton store and mail order; an overall and shirt factory in Saint John, New Brunswick; and the store and five Groceterias in Halifax, as well as a Groceteria in Dartmouth, Nova Scotia.

The year before the Stevens commission's hearings, Lady Eaton was staying in London at the *soigné* Hyde Park Hotel with members of her family when the Canadian High Commissioner asked her to accept an invitation to be presented to King George V and Queen Mary at court. She concurred, acquired the requisite finery and made her appearance, along with her niece Isobel Mulligan; she later described it with delight in her autobiography. After the pomp and circumstance of the face-to-face greeting with the king and queen at Buckingham Palace, the party came through to the supper-room, which "continued the impression of glittering splendor." She later lamented that "it is a pity that courts have been abandoned, and the much less formal outdoor ceremony of garden-party presentations substituted."

Eaton's, under R.Y., had been shaken by the events of the early 1930s but grew out of the depression years intact. A casualty of the scrutiny of Stevens's attacks was the company's openness. After the depression, the finances and organization of the T. Eaton Co. were closely guarded, and Eaton's became known as one of the most secretive corporations in Canada. In its recovery, though, the store placed renewed emphasis on value and began to modernize its facilities as the depression faded into memory. Some of the Canadian Department Store (CDS) branches, like those in Peterborough, North Bay and Sault Ste. Marie, were modernized and expanded, and traditions like the Santa Claus Parade went on as before, though the company, like Canada and its neighbour, the United States, emerged from the ordeal in a vastly changed state.

Canada rejoiced in the May 1937 coronation of King George VI, and as before, Eaton's continued its tradition of decorating the stores for the event.

The decorations for the 1937 coronation included elabourate displays over the store's main entrance on Yonge Street. *Archives of Ontario: T. Eaton Fonds F229. Used with the permission of Sears Canada Ltd.*

Union Jacks and royal banners hung from all of the store's façades, and the display department created a dramatic marquee over the main Yonge Street entrance featuring four horsemen and the inscription "Long May They Reign!" surmounted with a crown. In its traditional back-page ad in the Toronto newspapers, the store proclaimed:

> *Modern eyes are dazzled by the splendor of it. London is an enchanted city. The whole universe is enthralled by the colour and pomp that invest the Crowning of our King and Queen. Those jeweled Maharajahs coming out of the East to pay homage to their Emperor. That vast proud cavalcade from other dominions and territories of the far-flung Empire. Those princes and potentates from neighbouring nations. Those emissaries from great republics. Those travellers from every country and clime. Distance and diversity disappear amid the glory of England's throne…Ecstatic peal of chimes. Fanfare of trumpets. The Golden Coach rolls over the cobbles. The*

The Queen Street store was bedecked with flags and decorations on the occasion of the coronation of King George VI in 1937. *Archives of Ontario: T. Eaton Fonds F229. Used with the permission of Sears Canada Ltd.*

venerable Abbey blazes with coronets and regalia of Britain's centuries of coronations. In the solemn hush of the supreme moment stand those two whom destiny has cast into Earth's most majestic setting…And Eaton's joins with heart and voice as Canada shouts with one accord: God Save the King! Long May He Reign!

The Queen Street side of Eaton's in the late 1930s, decorated for the coronation of King George VI, with Toronto's city hall tower in the background. *Archives of Ontario: T. Eaton Fonds F229. Used with the permission of Sears Canada Ltd.*

When King George VI and his wife, Queen Elizabeth, returned for a royal tour in 1939, similar pomp and fanfare was undertaken by the store, especially owing to the fact that it was the first time that a reigning sovereign visited Canada.

Chez Eaton au Québec

*High prices or low prices does not make so much difference
with us here as nice goods.*
—Timothy Eaton

It was perhaps inevitable that Eaton's would come to Montréal, in the 1920s
Canada's largest and most dominant city. In the event, it was Eaton's first
example of expanding geographically through the purchase of an existing
business, and the store not only became the company's largest freestanding
retail outlet but also took on a chic, French-influenced atmosphere that was
all its own. What's more, Eaton's landed on St. Catherine Street in Montréal,
where, for many years, it went head to head with four other large department
stores that were already well-established in Montréal.

On March 20, 1925, the *Montreal Gazette* announced that the assets of
Goodwin's Limited, a St. Catherine Street department store that had been
in business for fourteen years, were acquired by the T. Eaton Co. Limited
for $5,294,425 in cash. The article predicted that the front portion of the
store would be demolished to create a new ten-storey store that would cost
$3 million and employ double the number of present staff.

The article gave a brief history of Eaton's, which had operated a factory
in Montréal since 1909, and a catalogue sales office as well, but it only briefly
went into the history of Goodwin's. The tortured chronicle of the premises
Eaton's chose isn't merely interesting—it gives a good indication of the
vicissitudes of the retail business in a booming city in a growing nation.

The department store business of S. Carsley Co. Limited was founded in Montréal two years after Eaton's, in 1871, and actually got into the mail-order business earlier than the big Toronto store. Carsley's occupied a large store on Notre Dame Street, between St-Jean and St-Pierre Streets, with a wing extending back to St-Jacques Street in the old city. As Montréal grew, the fashionable shopping area shifted from old Montréal and Notre Dame Street uptown to St. Catherine Street in the years leading up to the turn of the century.

Fully intending to occupy both locations, Carsley's purchased, in May 1906, the St. Catherine Street building then under lease to W.H. Scroggie Limited, a competing department store business begun in 1885. Under the terms of its lease, Scroggie's could remain at the location—which, after an 1892 expansion, consisted of two three-storey wings flanking a taller central portion—until April 1910. A dispute occurred between the two retailers that resulted in Samuel Carsley physically evicting Scroggie's (which had to scramble to find temporary quarters) in April 1909 before opening the new Carsley's Uptown on June 2, 1909.

Shortly thereafter, Carsley's store was purchased by the firm of A.E. Rae & Co. Limited, a Toronto whitewear manufacturer that wanted to expand into the retail business. Within a year, though, it became apparent to the management of Rae's that they had overextended themselves in purchasing the business and expanding the store and could not pay Carsley

In 1925, Eaton's took over the premises of Goodwin's Limited of Montréal and transformed the site into an enormous, nine-storey department store. *Archives of Ontario: T. Eaton Fonds F229. Used with the permission of Sears Canada Ltd.*

for the property they bought. Subsequently, Carsley sold the property to a partnership headed by noted financier J.W. McConnell, businessman Lorne McGibbon and retail executive W.H. Goodwin.

Goodwin, a former employee of Eaton's, had come to Toronto in 1905 and spent six years at the John Murphy Company Limited, a major St. Catherine Street retailer that ultimately became the Montréal store of the Robert Simpson Company. Leaving Murphy's, where he had attained the position of general manager, Goodwin set about making the new department store that he and his partners envisioned one of the city's finest. After another forced eviction, Goodwin's Limited opened on April 20, 1911, and the ad that accompanied the event proudly stated, "It is new. It is Grand. It is something that proud Montreal can well afford to be proud of. Its accommodations spell 'Beauty,' 'Comfort' and 'Real Service.'" The ad also drew attention to its second-floor French Room, which featured "a very large assemblage of Paris Frocks, Gowns, Robes, Gowns, and Dress Accessories—just unpacked."

W.H. Goodwin retired in 1924, and although Goodwin's had struggled in the years after its inception, it had become a popular and profitable store by the time Eaton's purchased it. Whatever the status of the existing store, Eaton's wasted no time in establishing itself as a retail force on St. Catherine Street. While Goodwin's continued to operate for several weeks, on April 14, 1925, newspaper ads appeared announcing the takeover of the store by the T. Eaton Co. of Montréal. A preceding letter from J.W. McConnell thanked consumers for their patronage of Goodwin's and introduced the Eaton name to Montréal, heretofore familiar there only through its catalogue. Eaton's introduced itself through the use of a quote made by Timothy Eaton fifty-five years earlier:

> *With excellent facilities for the importation of their goods from British and Foreign markets they hope to secure a moderate share of public patronage. Nothing will be wanting on their part to attain this end by the constant exercise of an energy and attention to the wants of their customers. They propose to carry a well-assorted stock throughout the year—Sound Goods, Good Styles, Good Value, will be points that will always have their attention. We invite an examination of our stock—and to all we offer our best services.*

In the following days, the public was informed of Eaton's unique features, like the Research Bureau, the famous "Goods Satisfactory or Money

Refunded" guarantee, the advantages of Eaton's cash-only policy or Eaton's D.A. (Deposit Account), while at the same time it explained to Montrealers that "it will be some time before the store is stocked according to our own high standards." In November, full-page advertisements announced that another Eaton tradition, the Santa Claus Parade, would come to Montréal.

Eaton's secured the services of the esteemed Montréal firm of Ross and MacDonald to design a new store to replace the collection of buildings on the site, and by November 1926, it was able to hold a pre-Christmas formal opening of the new premises. An ad for the opening proudly stated, "We have reason to believe that the promise made by the fine Architectural exterior of the Store will be amply fulfilled by the internal service." The exterior of the dignified new building was sheathed in stone with carved Neoclassical details, and its massive walls were broken into smaller recessed planes to minimize its great bulk. Large arches on the University and Victoria Street sides invited pedestrians into a luxurious, vaulted pedestrian arcade, lined with display windows.

Similar to Eaton's experience in Winnipeg twenty years earlier, it was found that the size of the store was not enough to handle the business, in spite of the depression. On January 3, 1930, Eaton's announced that construction had commenced on a three-floor expansion of the store, which would add five acres of floor space. The exterior design, again the work of Ross and MacDonald, according to an announcement, would harmonize with the existing building. A brief mention was made of the new restaurant that was to crown the top of the expanded store, but details of the space were not forthcoming. Construction continued through 1930, and the new floors were occupied by the end of 1931.

Many features of the store made Eaton's a favourite Montréal shopping destination and gave it a chic style and atmosphere all its own. Nothing, though, contributed to the Montréal store's unique quality as much as the celebrated ninth-floor restaurant, known locally in French as *Le 9e*. Opening on January 26, 1931, the restaurant was reminiscent of the French Art Deco dining room of the fabled 1927 transatlantic liner SS *Île-de-France* and was the work of French architect Jacques Carlu, who had recently collaborated

Opposite: Eaton's wasted no time rebuilding the Montréal premises to an elegant design, by noted Canadian architectural firm Ross and MacDonald, and eventually added five floors to it in 1931. *Archives of Ontario: T. Eaton Fonds F229. Used with the permission of Sears Canada Ltd.*

with Lady Eaton on the design of the Round Room restaurant in Eaton's new College Street store in Toronto.

That the Montréal restaurant paid homage to its counterpart on the SS *Île-de-France* was no surprise. The liner, which eschewed period interiors and as a result was hailed as a masterpiece of a new style (the *Style Paquebot*), was a favourite of Lady Eaton on her travels. In fact, the style was born in the buildings and exhibits of the *Exposition Internationale des Arts Décoratifs et Industriels Modernes*, held in Paris in 1925. Jacques Carlu became a prime exponent of the ensuing *Style Moderne* movement and later went on to design the Palais de Chaillot on the Trocadéro opposite the Eiffel Tower, an Art Deco stage setting if there ever was one. Years earlier, he worked on the design of the French liner's revolutionary interiors, and Lady Eaton's choice of him for her new Toronto and Montréal restaurants was a natural, given her desire to provide the public with high-profile spaces in which to see and be seen.

For Eaton's ninth-floor restaurant, Carlu designed a series of spaces that culminated in the basilica-like main dining room, which was set parallel to St. Catherine Street and was accessible from a foyer that looked out over the rooftops of Montréal and beyond to the St. Lawrence River. The foyer was flanked on each side by private dining rooms, the so-called Gold Room and Silver Room, which shared the view. The ceilings in these spaces were kept at a normal height to emphasize the drama of the lofty main dining room, which was entered from the middle of the room. Natural light poured into the room from opal-glass clerestory windows and ceiling-mounted light fixtures grilled with the then-new nickel alloy known as Monel. The corners of the thirty-five-foot-high space were curved, imparting a fluid yet unifying overall character, and the clerestory was supported by sixteen rectangular pilasters sheathed in polished *escalette breche* marble of variegated pink and grey colours. The coral-coloured soffit between the pilasters on the side walls were affixed with bas-reliefs, executed by the artist Denis Gélin, which depicted the art of eating and drinking. Raised seating areas occupied the ends of the room and continued under the lower ambulatories beyond the pilasters.

At each end of the room, two great illuminated alabaster urns rose up, flanking the steps to the raised seating areas. Similar urns were used in the Salon du Thé on the SS *Île-de-France*. Dramatic enough in themselves, these urns were merely a foil to the restaurant's twin focal points: marvellous and richly coloured murals painted by the architect's wife, Natacha (née Anne Pecker), housed in recesses in the tall vertical walls at either end of the long dining room.

When the Ninth Floor Restaurant opened in 1931, Eaton's enticed customers with an atmospheric drawing of the lofty Art Deco space. *From an ad, collection of the author.*

The whole ensemble created a unique environment that just begged for a crowd of people to fill and enliven it. In fact, it became tremendously popular with the public, who came as much for the food and fine, cultured service as they did to make an appearance in an overwhelmingly glamorous atmosphere, even if they were just shopping. Its charismatic mélange of style, luxurious materials and a dramatic use of volume stood in stark contrast to competitor Jas. A. Ogilvy's roughly contemporary (1929) Adam Dining Room and Tudor Hall on the other end of St. Catherine Street.

In 1989, in the twilight years of *Le 9e*, filmmaker Catherine Martin, under the auspices of the Office National du Film du Canada, crowned *Le 9e*'s reputation as a cultural landmark by examining its history and patrons for the documentary film *Les Dames du 9e*. The overwhelming impression given is one of wonder and celebration of the place that *Le 9e* occupied in the hearts of its regulars and employees over a period of almost sixty years. The restaurant had literally become integrated into the lives of generations of people, and in the film, a ninety-one-year-old customer named Madame Dagenais spoke about it with great emotion and described the meaning it held for her: "The Art Deco style was something completely new, and along with the size of the restaurant, as well as the elaborate table settings, it really left an impression on me. The waitresses were impeccable, and many of them stayed on for years, so we became familiar. I have taken enormous delight in this place throughout my long life!"

Due to the economic boom after World War II, the store found itself again short of space, and an expansion program carried out in the late 1950s brought Eaton's of Montréal to its ultimate form, filling the block bounded by St. Catherine Street, University Street, Boulevard de Maisonneuve and Victoria Street. When the addition, designed in a modern style by Montréal architect Grattan Thompson, was completed in 1960, the entire block rose to a height of nine stories for the first time, air conditioning was installed and a new shipping and receiving facility was created in the basement of the new section, with truck access provided by a ramp under Victoria Street from Eaton's parking lot. At this time, Eaton's of Montréal became the largest single store in the T. Eaton Co., at 1,052,000 square feet.

Over the years, Eaton's in Montréal gained a reputation for design and fashion leadership in spite of competition from notable sources such as Holt Renfrew, Ogilvy's and Eaton's next-door neighbour, the well-established Henry Morgan & Co. Limited. When Eaton's opened its new store in 1926, its inaugural ad touted its new third-floor "Vista of Specialty Shops," and by the 1960s, it had begun to introduce specialty shops into its merchandise mix as the result of the opinions of shoppers who liked Eaton's avant-garde advertising style but found that the store lacked the "intimacy and warmth" of smaller specialty shops such as those found on toney Sherbrooke Street nearby. Due to the success of the Montréal strategy, it was applied to

The soaring top-floor enclosure of the Ninth Floor Restaurant was more akin to a basilica than a restaurant, and it was indeed patterned after the dining room of the *Île-de-France*, one of the most popular ocean liners of the day. *Courtesy of Martin Pelletier.*

other large stores in the chain, and management took a fancy to promoting the Eaton's as "the Large Store with the Small Shops."

Shops like the New Orleans Townhouse; *La Boutique*; Coach House for women; Marco Polo for men; and *Place Elegante*, the *Table d'Hôte* and *La Maison Rustique* for home furnishings were among the special boutiques added to the regular Eaton offerings in Montréal. On the Main Floor, the store housed not just the chic College Shop but also a large book shop and an extensive gourmet shop, the most famous component of which was the fabled Blue Cake Counter.

Eaton's didn't have just a beauty shop for female customers but rather a fifth-floor *Salon Elysée*, and something as plain as a bath accessory shop was transformed into *Chez Elle*, befitting a city with a reputation for chic and beautiful women. It seemed that every nook and cranny of the store offered something special to customers, ranging from the everyday and mundane to the exotic and exclusive, together making Eaton's of Montréal one of the best examples of a large and varied metropolitan department store *par excellence*.

Much of the Montréal store's stellar performance was due in the 1950s and 1960s to the leadership of John Wallace "Jack" Eaton (1912–1990), Robert Young Eaton's son, who was by all accounts a superb merchant. After completing his education at Cambridge, Eaton served Canada with

In 1960, Eaton's in Montréal became the firm's largest store by the addition of an enormous modern extension to the back (north) of the original building. *Archives of Ontario: T. Eaton Fonds F229. Used with the permission of Sears Canada Ltd.*

distinction in World War II, ultimately commanding the Eighth New Brunswick Hussars. He returned to his employment at Eaton's after the war and transferred to the Montréal store in 1947. He eventually became a director of the T. Eaton Co. Limited of Montréal in 1950 and joined Eaton's board of directors in 1960. Notably, his brother, Captain Erskine Robert Eaton, paid the ultimate price for his country, losing his life in the ill-fated Dieppe Raid of August 1942.

Among Jack's achievements were the hiring and encouragement of the staff that bought for the store's all-important fashion boutiques, as well as those that created the innovative colour ads that appeared regularly among the pages of the *Montréal Gazette*, Canada's largest newspaper. Jack Eaton's skill in running the Montréal store was legendary—although the store more than doubled in size in 1960, its sales-per-square-foot numbers did not suffer in the expansion. Those figures, shown in a 1975 Eaton document comparing the performance of Eaton stores across Canada, tell the story. Sales per square foot hovered between $63 and $120 for most Eaton branches at the time, but the enormous store on St. Catherine Street produced a whopping $184 per square foot, bettering even the vaunted Winnipeg store at $168 and the time-honoured Queen Street store at $170.

In 1967, when Montréal hosted Expo 67, Eaton's participated as a representative host to guests to the city, who poured into the store from its newly opened subway entrances (on the recently renamed "Metro Level") and, according to Eaton's own publicity, "were bemused by the sheer élan of the store itself." At Expo 67, Eaton's produced four fashion shows in the fair's Hospitality Centre. Later, longtime store manager Adolphe Leduc admitted, "We made up our minds long ago that we would not only be the biggest store in Canada's greatest city, but the best store as well."

If Expo 67 wasn't enough, Eaton's offered its own import fairs to entice customers after the big exposition closed for good in October 1967. The next year saw "Scandinavian Adventure" open at the store on St. Catherine Street on September 26, 1968. Co-sponsored by Scandinavian Airlines System (SAS), the event began with five special fashion shows featuring the works of Danish designers Margit and Erik Brandt, modeled by none other than Miss Denmark herself, and men's fashions by Swedish designer Sighsten Herrgard. Elsewhere, Danish culinary delights were featured in the Fine Food Shop, SAS presented an exhibition of children's art and Danish Orrefors and Swedish Boda crystal were exhibited, along with Norwegian ski equipment. The Ninth Floor Restaurant offered Scandinavian menus, while a "Tivoli Gardens" eatery was set up on the fifth floor.

**SOFTENED
DETAILS
INFLUENCE
FASHION**

EATON'S

Spring harvests a new colour—pumpkin, a new season change that blossoms forth in costumes and accessories. Following the influence of softness, you'll see it appear in lush suedes, silks and airy wools. Keeping in the same family, flaxtones, buttery creams, putty shades have equal authority. Details carry on the theme: overblouses are an integral part of the suit and costume, softened with large poufed bows or deep cowls. Seaming is shapely, subtle, lengthening jackets and indicating waistlines. Skirts are slender or have gentle gathers. Exemplifying this feminine feeling, two highlights from Eaton's Spring Fashion Shows this week. Left to right. From Paris, black-and-flax wool tweed costume lined and overblouded in light pumpkin silk. 295.00. Cloche to match. 49.95. The tailleur, in fine cream wool, revealing a cafe au lait polka dot silk blouse. 89.95. Natural panama straw, swathed in pumpkin organza. 59.95. Putty shade glace kid gloves. 12.95. Watch Eaton's fashion pages for more news and be sure to see the St. Catherine Street windows.

T. EATON C?.

Eaton's of Montréal fashion advertisement from 1963, with a fanciful pointillist-style illustration by Eugenie Groh. *From an ad, collection of the author.*

For Eaton's 100th anniversary, the store threw a World Import Fair that really showed off the prowess of its buying, marketing and display staff. Goods from all over the world were featured, and a special "Grand Bazaar" was set up on the fifth floor. In addition to the obligatory fashion shows, full-size replicas of the Venus de Milo and Michelangelo's *Last Supper* were on display, along with an exhibition of contemporary French paintings, all marketed under the Expo-like slogan, "Come to Eaton's and see the World." Coming as it did between the Trans-Canada Sale in September and the all-important Christmas shopping season, the World Import Fair kept Montrealers coming to the department store just to be entertained.

Eaton's Montréal promotions were supported by truly artistic advertising that captured the spirit of the fashions being offered to the public, and throughout the '60s, when Eaton's gained the coveted back-page advertising space that had been occupied by competitor Morgan's ads for many years, it showed off its style and verve with illustrations that captured the spirit of the age. Primarily the work of store artists Eugenie Groh and Georgine Strathy, along with layout artist Jack Parker, the trend-setting ads took mere fashion illustration (itself an art form) and elevated it to the highest levels of applied art.

Martin Pelletier, a resident of Québec, said of Eaton's in the French-speaking province:

> *I'm a great fan of department stores, and I know enough about their history. For my part, I shopped a lot at Eaton's, mainly in the downtown Montréal store, when I lived in there. Eaton was my favourite store for years, and nothing has replaced Eaton's variety, always at the right price. The merchandise was always well presented. I used to love shopping in department stores, for the atmosphere, and also the promotional activities; it all gave us a sense of belonging with these stores that we just do not have now.*

Pelletier also remembered the architecture of Eaton's branch stores as being outstanding in the 1960s. While Henry Morgan & Co. Limited, Montréal's oldest department store, began locating branch stores throughout the area, beginning in 1950, Eaton's relied solely on its St. Catherine Street store until 1965, when it opened its first department store branch in Québec at the Fairview-Pointe Claire shopping centre, just west of Dorval airport on the Trans-Canada Highway. Eaton's described the novelty of the 142,000-square-foot store at its grand opening by proclaiming that

> *Like a perennial, Eaton's blossoms again—bigger, better, brighter. It's Eaton's Fairview-Pointe Clair—where everything's coming up Fashion-new, Fashion-right. A thrilling new world of Fashion! An exciting new way of shopping. From the moment you enter from Eaton's Court, where lush foliage, sparkling fountains and the soft temperature of 70 degrees brings the outdoors, indoors all year 'round. The focal point, the magnificent chandelier, a reproduction of an early French Canadian design, circa 1770,*

Eaton's modern branch in the Fairview Pointe Claire Shopping Centre was the work of pioneering retail architects John Graham and Company (top). The interior of the Fairview Pointe Claire store was different from what customers would experience in the downtown store—light, open, compact and reflecting its suburban location (bottom). *Archives of Ontario: T. Eaton Fonds F229. Used with the permission of Sears Canada Ltd.*

lights your way to this new adventure in modern shopping. Beautifully coordinated pastels, and décor of understated elegance reflect a feeling of freshness and sunshine. There's a warm welcome in the air, an atmosphere that is inviting with lasting appeal. And the fine customer services for which Eaton's is famous, are yours at Eaton's Fairview.

The *Montréal Gazette*—which called the store, designed by Seattle architect John Graham, "impressive"—noted that the building's simple massing was softened by elabourate landscaping featuring pines, birches and Vermont fieldstone. The landscaping covered the sloped ground, which allowed the store parking access to both of its levels, one of the first suburban department stores to be designed with this arrangement which helped equalize traffic on each floor. Special attention was paid to the store's own boutiques, like the glass-enclosed *La Terrasses* garden shop and *La Cuisine*, the rustic French Canadian–themed restaurant that overlooked the Eaton Court and was decorated with wooden ceiling beams, fieldstone, natural barn wood and "many fascinating antique accessories." The *Gazette* noted that customers would enjoy "traditionally fine Eaton fare…in an authentic French-Canadian atmosphere" at *La Cuisine* and emphasized the panoramic view, through a sixty-foot window, of the enclosed shopping centre as just one of the store's features that "add enjoyment to shopping at Fairview."

Three years later, a second, slightly larger (155,000 square feet) suburban store opened in the Ville d'Anjou north of Montréal, but it was of a very different design that became a model for other Eaton stores in Ontario and New Brunswick. This time, the store contracted with local Montréal firm Bolton, Elwood & Aimers, which created a simple rectangular building of light brick surmounted with a brown precast concrete coping. Entrances were denoted by triple recessed arches lined in precast concrete and filled in with decorative

In 1968, the Anjou store appeared as a follow-up to Fairview Pointe Claire and gave Eaton's its second suburban branch in Montréal. *Archives of Ontario: T. Eaton Fonds F229. Used with the permission of Sears Canada Ltd.*

vertical grilles, which were backlit at night. As at Fairview, the store's restaurant overlooked the Eaton's spacious mall entry court and was reminiscent of the new subway entrances to the downtown store created earlier by the same architects. The *Montréal Gazette* described the store's escalator placement, in which the escalators were separated to form an interior court, with glass-panel railings at the second-floor level and a deeply coffered ceiling above, from which hung a chandelier composed of amber glass globes.

Eaton's presence in Ottawa, the nation's capital, began in May 1928. With the purchase of the Canadian Department Stores Limited, Eaton's acquired the former business of A.A. Fournier Limited, on the northeast corner of Bank and Laurier Streets. The three-storey building was remodeled and brought up to the standards of the Eaton organization, and it was operated for twenty-one years before it was renamed as the T. Eaton Co. Ottawa Branch in July 1949. The small store was sold off in 1966, along with many others in Ontario that had been acquired in 1928.

In 1973, Eaton's reentered the Ottawa market by inaugurating a store in the Bayshore Shopping Centre, again located along the Trans-Canada Highway, this time in suburban Nepean. The large, 170,000-square-foot Eaton's branch was sheathed in warm-coloured brick and was distinguished by greenhouse entrances with massive, bronze-anodized canopies over the doorways. Despite the fact that it was in Ontario, albeit just across the Ottawa River from Québec, the store was managed for some time as a part of the Montréal division.

Several more stores were opened in the 1970s to serve the outlying areas of Montréal. A few weeks after the Bayshore opening, on the penultimate day of August, a 137,000-square-foot store opened at Cavendish Mall in Côte St-Luc, along with a similar but negligibly smaller branch at the Carrefour de L'Estrie in Sherbrooke, Québec. A distinctive, 193,000-square-foot branch serving the outlying areas north of the Island on Montréal is located at the Carrefour de Laval. Opened on March 28, 1974, the store's sloping walls, shallow arched "eyebrow" windows and recessed entries covered with knife-edge canopies were certainly influenced by the avant-garde architectural styles previewed at Expo 67, some seven years earlier.

On September 11, 1975, Eaton's entered the Québec City market for the first time with a store in Place Ste-Foy on Boulevard Laurier in the city's western outlying area. The simple, white brick exterior of the 126,000-square-foot store, the work of architectural firm Eliasoph & Berkowitz, somewhat masked the warm interior design, and its traditional mall entrance court was overlooked by a second-floor restaurant. The Québec market had many local competitors,

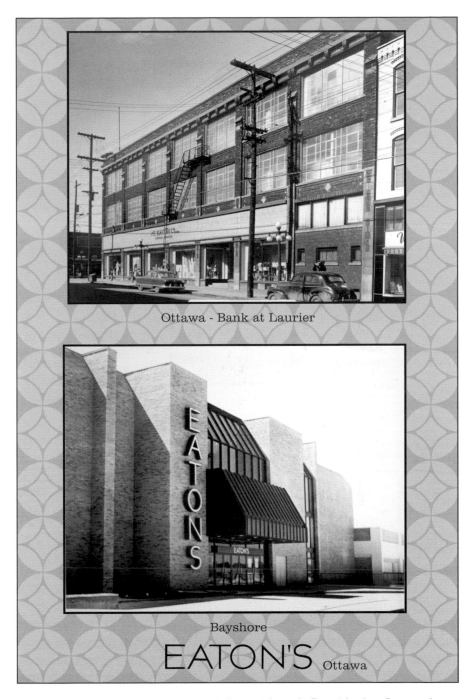

Ottawa - Bank at Laurier

Bayshore

EATON'S Ottawa

The 1973 opening of the Bayshore branch (bottom) brought Eaton's back to Ottawa after an eight-year absence. Its earlier store at Bank and Laurier Streets was acquired in 1928 as a part of the Canadian Department Stores deal. *Archives of Ontario: T. Eaton Fonds F229. Used with the permission of Sears Canada Ltd.*

Cavendish

Laval

Les Promenades St-Bruno

EATON Montréal

Eaton's continued to open branch stores in the suburbs of Montréal throughout the 1970s.
Pictured, from top to bottom, are stores at Cavendish Mall, Laval and Les Promenades St-Bruno. *Archives of Ontario: T. Eaton Fonds F229. Used with the permission of Sears Canada Ltd.*

Eaton's first store in Québec's capital was the rather severe-looking branch at Place Ste-Foy. The inset shows the store's more inviting mall entrance, overlooked by a restaurant on the store's second floor. *Archives of Ontario: T. Eaton Fonds F229. Used with the permission of Sears Canada Ltd.*

such as the traditional Compagnie Paquet and Syndicat de Québec stores or Le Maison Simons, which was a long-established fashion-oriented favourite. Chic Canadian retailer Holt Renfrew was founded in Québec City and maintained a store in the old quarter along with one it opened in 1965 at Place Ste-Foy. Eaton's, though, found success in Québec, and the store joined the competition in fulfilling the needs of the ancient city's shopping public. The last store of the 1970s in the Montréal suburban area, a 130,000-square-foot branch, opened on August 23, 1978, at Les Promenades Saint-Bruno in Saint-Bruno-de-Montarville. The store served the city's eastern suburbs and shared a design similar to the contemporary St. Vital store in the Winnipeg area, albeit with the Gallic touches so characteristic of Eaton's Montréal stores.

Eaton's has occasionally been criticized as an Anglophone interloper in Quebéc. However, Eaton's enduring popularity, its willingness to advertise in the French-language press and even its big store (Canada's biggest, in fact) at the busiest corner in town would seem to indicate that it sought earnestly to serve all residents of Québec as well as it did anywhere in Canada. Personal experience, along with the typical loyalty of employees, would tend to bear out this fact as well.

Françoise Borel, a native *Québecoise* who lives in France, recalled the experiences of her father, Jean Eloi, who was born in France in 1932 and immigrated to Canada as an adult. At Eaton's, he was not just offered an opportunity to work; his aptitude and personal ethic allowed him, surprisingly, to grow into a career in fashion at the store:

My father began working at Eaton's in 1958 as an electrician at the downtown store. He was in charge of the maintenance of elevators, escalators, and the mechanical and electrical systems. My mother convinced him to apply for the job because she was secretary to Mrs. Perdy, executive assistant for Mr. Jack Eaton, the store manager. Later, my mother left the company to not create conflicts of interest. A very sympathetic gentleman, Mr. Reynald Prince, a sales manager, offered him a position as a buyer for basement women's fashion. My father did not know much about it, but he was very eager to learn and grow, and, as a result his work was considered more than satisfactory. His considerate dealings with staff and the procurement office helped made him successful, and he found out that he had a flair for fashion. The basement was for Eaton's downtown a very important floor with its wide range of customer and a very accessible price range. On its opening in 1965, he was transferred to the Pointe-Claire store, where he was in charge of receiving and junior fashion. He then went back downtown as a buyer for the Young Montrealer Shop and then manager of the third floor. Later he managed the second floor and even though the economic crisis of the 1980s in Québec forced many staff cuts, he stayed on as manager of the shoe department. After becoming head of sales for eastern Canada, he worked on the sixth floor and his office was ultimately transferred to Laval, where he reconnected with his old friend Reynald Prince, who set his career in motion so many years earlier. My father retired in 1991 and passed away 20 years later.

Françoise herself remembers growing up with Eaton's in Montréal, saying, "Eaton was for me a fantastic store were you could buy wonderful merchandise, luxurious articles. The Fine Food Shop on the first floor was extraordinary; there was nothing at all like it in Montréal at the time. Fabulous food from France, excellent fresh meat, cheeses and on and on."

She added that special events at Eaton's of Montréal are a particularly fine memory for her. "There was the great Trans-Canada sale, twice a year, and I also remember my mother taking me to 'Goldrush Day.' It was a sale, and the staff were invited to wear old-fashioned costumes. Ladies were wearing long dresses and men in cowboy suits!" Her fondest memories surround Christmas

Portrait of Eaton's of Montréal employee Jean Eloi (left) and the store's sales management team dressed as the "Blues Brothers" (right) for a promotion. *Photos courtesy of Françoise Borel.*

with Eaton's in Montréal: "That was the major event of the year along with New Year. Eaton downtown had the most magic windows on rue Ste-Catherine for Christmas. As a child it made me dream of a magic world with Santa!"

Speaking of Eaton's relations with French-speaking Canada, Françoise recalled:

> *Yes, definitely, Eaton was in the heart of numerous Quebecois. Even if it was at its core an "English" store from Toronto. Eaton was always at the mercy of journalists when it was time to talk about Bill 101 and the use of English. My father had to go in the middle of the night in the early '70s, climb a ladder up the façade and remove the "s" from Eaton's to become Eaton. They were so afraid of bombs at that time.*

For many years, and in spite of competition from local and national competitors, the Montréal stores proudly carried the Eaton name in the predominately French-speaking province. When Québec's language law, known as Bill 101, was passed in 1977, the store did comply by shortening the name on its signs and in advertising from "Eaton's" to simply "Eaton" to reflect the official tongue of the province. Language and nomenclature notwithstanding, the people of Québec took to Eaton's as "their" store almost from the day it opened, and it was always considered to be the Eaton store with a stylish Gallic spirit.

Plains and Mountains

This company is proud of the fact that in its progress through the years it has been able to keep pace with the inspiring development of the city, and, indeed with that of this great country as a whole.
—Robert Young Eaton

In the 1920s, the T. Eaton Co. worked its way towards the craggy, majestic mountains that loomed up to the west over Canada's fertile prairies, and as ever, its mail-order operation led the way. With the stunning success of the retail and mail-order operation in Winnipeg, the company sought to expand its business westward as the population did the same.

The year 1927 was one of speculation about Eaton's. Throughout the fall of that year, newspapers were full of rumours about the possibility of Eaton's opening further retail facilities in the West. One prescient article in the *Financial Post* even set forth the idea that Eaton's was negotiating to purchase British Columbia's David Spencer Limited, thereby giving it a foothold in Vancouver. Even though the company denied them, the rumours of the day speculated that due to the automobile and other factors, the mail-order business remained stagnant, and according to another article in the *Financial Post*, "The big mail order house will open up a chain of stores in a dozen or more western towns which, while they will not carry the full departmental store stock will specialize in men's clothing, groceries, and furniture."

The article cited the store's recent expansion away from its Toronto headquarters, its experimentation with the smaller, limited-line TECO store format and its growing number of freestanding mail-order offices as examples of Eaton's attempts to conquer new markets. In concluding, the article mentioned that

> *The quiet, steady pushing out into new territories which the Eaton company is engineering without any heralding by trumpets is being watched with interest generally, and with uneasiness in some quarters. It is realized that the able management which has distinguished the company from its foundation, its policy of making haste slowly, its enormous ramifications…may well develop a situation that will revolutionize the retail trade of Canada.*

On February 7, 1916, Eaton's inaugurated a distribution warehouse in Saskatoon, the ten-year-old city on the banks of the South Saskatchewan River. Located at 209–211 Avenue D at Twenty-third Street, the warehouse (identified in newspaper reports as the former Stamco Building) included a showroom and an order office for Saskatoon customers. Two years later, on August 13, 1918, another warehouse opened to the southeast in the city of Regina. While both facilities did help accomplish the task of getting *Eaton's Catalogue* merchandise to customers faster, the Regina warehouse—a long, narrow two-storey brick building on Seventh Street in the city's warehouse district—included a heavy goods display. A catalogue sales office and showroom began to operate on the premises one year later. The year 1922 saw the addition of a Groceteria to the building, and later, men's and boys' clothing became available as well.

Traffic at the warehouse was brisk enough that a number of other lines were added, until by November 19, 1926, a full merchandise selection was on offer, and the warehouse was transformed into a department store. Despite its rather out-of-the-way location and humble beginnings, the store became very popular and competed successfully, giving downtown merchants like the R.H. Williams & Sons Co. Limited quite a run for the money. The Robert Simpson Co. Limited, anxious to gain a foothold in the west as well, operated a mail-order warehouse nearby and, in the 1930s, began operating a full-line department store on its building's first floor, until it bought the Williams store outright in 1946.

Maurice Van Buekenhout began work at Eaton's in March 1946, when he was seventeen and a half years old, noting that "it was supposed to be part-time but it lasted over forty years full-time until my retirement in May of 1992." From the time he started in Regina until 1963, the grocery operation formed a large part of the store's business:

In 1920, Eaton's opened a warehouse in Regina, Saskatchewan, but six years later, the building was occupied by a full-fledged department store operation. Because of its location in a warehouse district and its industrial origins, Eaton's Regina store had an appearance unlike any of the company's other main stores. *Archives of Ontario: T. Eaton Fonds F229. Used with the permission of Sears Canada Ltd.*

I worked first in the grocery department, known then as the Foodateria. It was on the second floor of the building and was a huge operation, at that time, the largest, I would say, under one roof in a building. I began as a stock clerk, keeping the shelves and bins full at all times by bringing up stock in heavy stock trucks from the basement two floors below. It was not too easy because we did not have the type of equipment that is available to make jobs easier today. A railway track along the west side of the store was where shipments came in from the Eaton factories to the east. Rail cars full of bags of sugar, flour, water-softener salt, you name it, would come in regularly, and the work was endless. As you worked on the sales floor, you really got to know the rural and local people who were the regular customers. I either walked to work or rode my bicycle from spring until the September freeze.

We had a staff of twelve or more, with extras coming in for Thursday, Friday and Saturday, our busiest. The meat department alone employed seven people, while five or six worked in fruits and vegetables. Our creamer made and sold butter at three pounds for a dollar, but change was in store. A lot of food was still rationed because of the war, and the store had lots of parking on both sides of it and, even at this date, places to tie up your horse and park a wagon, too.

Regina resident Melva Towne has a history with Eaton's, going back to childhood memories of riding the children's Christmas train set up in the Regina store and of her first work experience with the store—sorting, packing and mailing school textbooks that Eaton's manufactured for many school districts across the country. She treasures memories of meeting comedian Red Skelton when he came in to shop between performances in Regina and admits being "scared to death" when serving one of John David Eaton's sons who was shopping in the store. Still, she remembers the annual Christmas card sent to employees with an Eaton family portrait very fondly.

Yet her most cherished memories are of an event at which she and her colleagues volunteered their time to bring a little joy into the lives of Regina's elderly:

I believe our store was one of the first to host a senior's friendship night. People were brought in by bus after the store closed to see the Christmas decorations. They were from skilled care homes and arrived in wheelchairs and even hospital beds. Not to shop but to enjoy refreshments, goodies, Santa Claus and entertainment groups performing in different areas around the store. They stomped, clapped, danced and sang to the music. Most of us left wiping a tear from our eyes. That's one reason why I wear my beautiful diamond ring for twenty-five years' service with such pride.

The "senior night" is also a fond memory for Maurice Van Buekenhout:

What a sight it was to see! The store was all ready for Christmas, with decorations and Christmas trees with their bright lights ablaze. Residents from all of the nursing homes in town had been sent invitations to come to this event. They came by special buses, by ambulance and by other types of vehicles that could accommodate wheelchairs. The staff all volunteered, including our own retired people, plus members of many other organizations came to assist. There was much home-baking and specially prepared food from the staff, and we had lots of entertainment, too, with choirs singing in the store, and even the Grand Coulee Jug Band came so that the guests could dance. They all went home with a little gift and much happiness in their faces, and in all of our hearts, too.

The Regina store was unique on account of its origins as a warehouse. It housed what was once Canada's longest store aisle, leading from the front entrance to almost the back of the 125- by 500-foot store. The adjacent lot provided convenient parking for customers, and for a time, Eaton's operated a gas station on the site as well.

Rose Cardiff, also of Regina, remembers Eaton's from the perspective of a lifetime customer:

Eaton's was definitely our favourite store when I was young. We would walk from our home in downtown Regina or take the bus. I remember sitting on the cream-coloured benches in the bus shelter on the corner of Broad Street and 7th Avenue waiting for a bus to take us home with our parcels. I will never forget the day I got away from my dad in the hardware department. A kind Eaton's employee lifted this crying five- or six-year-old up so I could see my dad a few rows over. Many years later, my eldest son went wandering—but he thought he wasn't lost, as he was just sitting on the floor watching Mr. Dress-up in the television department! Every year, we'd head off to the Trans Canada Sale. Mom replenished her supply of sheets, Hudson Bay blankets, yard goods and anything else she needed at this sale—"needed" was the operative word for my parents. Yet we spent a lot of time at Eaton's in Regina. I loved it when we got to go to the cafeteria for a treat, like a 7 Up float or chocolate milkshake. It was a rare occurrence, which made it ever so special. The store also had memorable special events—we got to watch the artist Paul Wutlunee paint pictures in the store, and my dad purchased two of them for mom. I also had the honour of meeting Roger Whittaker, who autographed an album I purchased. How I miss that store!

Reverend Kenneth Clarkson's course through life took him away from home during and after World War II, and he spent time in Vancouver before marrying at age forty-four in 1966. Throughout his life's odyssey, Eaton's was a constant, and a cherished one at that:

In 1939, when I had graduated from grade ten, my folks bought my first bicycle, a "Trojan" model from Eaton's. I clearly remember rushing through my noon lunch in order to be at the railroad station to pick up the box that held my bike and carry it home. I rode that bike for many miles around our community before completing grade twelve and heading for the Radio College in Toronto in 1941. Back in its original box it would wait until the end of the war while I served with the RAF ferry command in Montréal and at Gander, Newfoundland. In 1946, I was employed by Trans-Canada Air Lines (later Air Canada) as a radio operator in North Bay, Ontario. I pedaled my way around that city, and, after six years at university in Winnipeg, I became the pastor of a church. I used the bike to do a lot of my pastoral calling, and though I'm now retired that "trusty steed" still serves me well!

A favourite Eaton's story involves his wife Ada's 1989 visit to Regina, where she admired a rug that was on sale at Eaton's but was hesitant to make such a large purchase without her husband's consent. "The sale was over by the time I had a doctor's appointment in Regina the following week," he relates, "but the salesman remembered Ada, and would you believe, he was able to get it for us at the sale price? Did we buy it? You can bet your life we did!"

Maurice Van Buekenhout recalls a special corner of the store, known as the "Assembly Room" and located on the main floor, and describes how this non-revenue-producing space was able to serve customers and the store's staff:

It had chairs and a few Chesterfields in very dark colors and many tables with a small kitchen off to one side in a fair-size room. Many churches and

An interior photo study showing Eaton's Regina warehouse (below) and how the same structure was adapted to the needs of a major department store (top). *Archives of Ontario: T. Eaton Fonds F229. Used with the permission of Sears Canada Ltd.*

different organizations had teas there on Saturday, and for years, a small corner was set up for staff men and women so they could have mixed coffee breaks together. It was a nice gathering place, and many events happened there. Women could have their lunch breaks there, but the men had to go up to a little room high on the roof, called the "Garret." Of course, these things were all done away with in later years as more space was needed for the sales floor, and in 1963, the Regina store closed the Foodateria, so I went to work in many different departments after that.

On August 14, 1968, a new Dominion grocery store and a fifteen-store enclosed mall opened next to the existing store. Known as the Dominion Eaton Centre, it housed a number of shops and provided overflow space for the large existing (207,000 square feet) Eaton store, allowing space for a new beauty salon and a Viking Restaurant.

On November 6, 1928, Eaton's opened another store forty-seven miles west of Regina in the town of Moose Jaw. The handsome, three-storey building at the corner of Main and Stadacona Streets contained fifty-three thousand square feet of selling space on its four levels. In 1940, its main floor was extended to the north by nine thousand square feet, owing to the success Eaton's found there. The store—described by an Eaton's ad in the *Moose Jaw Evening News* as "substantial and enduring: the walls of brick—trimmed with

In later years, Eaton's Regina store received a coat of white paint and a modern sign above its entrance. *Archives of Ontario: T. Eaton Fonds F229. Used with the permission of Sears Canada Ltd.*

white stone—the interior high-ceilinged and airy, with fixtures in polished walnut finish"—brought big-city shopping to Moose Jaw, and what's more, shopping in the Eaton manner to boot, as the ad assured: "The new store, from top to bottom, is planned to serve this city in its vigourous present and prosperous future—to serve it well on principles of courtesy and fairness, assuring full measure of value on every purchase."

In Saskatoon, Saskatchewan's largest city, Eaton's maintained its Avenue D mail-order warehouse for more than ten years, and even expanded it, before assembling property for a retail store in the city's downtown. In 1927, the company bought the business of F.R. MacMillan Limited, a retailer that was located in a four-storey building across the street from the future Eaton location. Frank R. MacMillan was born in Chicago and came to Saskatoon in 1901. After operating a men's wear business for three years, he bought the Second Avenue store of Currie Bros., which he guided through a period of growth culminating in the October 1913 opening of a large new store.

From that time on, MacMillan's was known as "Saskatoon's Greatest Store." Frank MacMillan himself served on the city council from 1913 and was elected mayor in 1919. Before selling to Eaton's, he twice ran unsuccessfully for Parliament, a goal he was unable to achieve until 1930.

A view of the 1928 Moose Jaw store, showing the later one-storey extension to the right. *Archives of Ontario: T. Eaton Fonds F229. Used with the permission of Sears Canada Ltd.*

Eaton's opened a warehouse in Saskatoon in 1916; the building was extended before the store bought the business of F.R. MacMillan in 1927. *Archives of Ontario: T. Eaton Fonds F229. Used with the permission of Sears Canada Ltd.*

On November 14, 1927, after a colossal sale that took more than two full pages of the preceding Saturday's paper to advertise, MacMillan's announced that the business had been sold to the T. Eaton Co. Limited. While Frank MacMillan's letter in the *Saskatoon Phoenix* spoke of his regret at leaving the retail business, he assured his employees and the citizens of Saskatoon that "[t]he enviable reputation of our successors is well

Looking down Saskatoon's Third Avenue, Eaton's gleaming new store stands out against the old MacMillan building across Twenty-first Street. Eaton's operated out of the older store for more than a year until the new one was opened in late 1928. *Archives of Ontario: T. Eaton Fonds F229. Used with the permission of Sears Canada Ltd.*

known and for them we bespeak a most cordial welcome" and added that "[t]he entry of The T. Eaton Company, Limited, into the retail business in Saskatoon affords further striking proof of the general development of Northern Saskatchewan and particularly of the City of Saskatoon."

A little more than a year later, Eaton's was ready to vacate the older building, still owned by Frank MacMillan, for its own newly built home on the corner of Third Avenue South and Twenty-first Street East. Architect Frank Martin of the Montréal firm of Ross and MacDonald (which was responsible for Eaton's huge store in its hometown) created a luxurious, three-storey bijou of a building in what could almost be called the "Eaton Style." The lovely and dignified edifice was faced in Tyndall stone from Manitoba, which was worked elaborately into cartouches, bas-reliefs and twisted ribbon pilasters. Expansive, bronze-framed display windows sat on a base of black marble, and trios of either Roman-arched or flat-topped windows filled in wide bays on the upper floors.

The presence of a more massive treatment with a lone window on the main corner of each upper floor suggests that it was intended to continue the building down both Third Avenue and Twenty-first Street until the block was completely occupied by a symmetrical composition.

In fact, one day before Eaton's 1927 opening in MacMillan's former premises, the Saskatoon City Council received a telegram from the T. Eaton Co. Limited in Toronto requesting a zoning variance to build an eight-storey, 125-foot-high building on its own property. Owing to the unusual width of Saskatoon streets, and the desire to have such a large and prestigious firm build in their city, the aldermen voted to approve the request with little dissent.

While the 1928 building was only three stories in height (though constructed so as to carry five more in the future), it did not disappoint shoppers when its doors formally opened on December 5 of that year. When the approving public came through those doors, it didn't simply mean that there was a big new retailer in town. The real meaning was that Eaton's granted Saskatoon—then a city of forty-two thousand—a full-scale department store much like Canadians in Toronto or Montréal had already enjoyed. Saskatoon had, with the opening of Eaton's, arrived.

The opening was preceded by a gala evening reception in the store, and on the same day, the *Saskatoon Star-Phoenix* carried an announcement, bearing the signature of Robert Young Eaton, that stated:

> *It is a pleasure to announce the opening of this new and larger Store in Saskatoon. The construction of the new building has been a substantial expression of a feeling which this Company shares with the public of Saskatoon—a feeling of confidence, sure and sweeping, in the future of the city. Because of this confidence the store has been planned with a wide "margin of growth" providing for extensions which would more than double its present capacity.*

Elsewhere in the day's paper, Eaton's advertisements proudly presented the store's features, which, they assured customers, "covers, more fully than ever, the wide range of modern department store commodities." In particular, ads drew attention to the store's Algerian Tea Room, "finished in sunny colours which show the Moorish influence, as do the mural decorations by Louis White, distinguished Montréal artist."

In 1941, Eaton's acquired the neighbouring property of the J.H. Early Motor Car Co. Limited, a Dodge dealer, and constructed a one-storey addition to the store that primarily housed the Groceteria, which had previously operated in the basement. A general rearrangement of the store was accomplished at the same time, and a popular coffee bar was installed on the main floor. By this time, Saskatoon's magnificent Bessborough Hotel had

The new Saskatoon store was modern and well lit. It featured stone floors, wood display cases and a sea of white columns bearing plaster capitals (top), and its structure was able to carry five more floors if necessary. *Archives of Ontario: T. Eaton Fonds F229. Used with the permission of Sears Canada Ltd.*

been completed two blocks away, and the vista past Eaton's to the château-like hotel one of the defining features of the city's urban landscape.

In Saskatoon, Eaton's took on the role of one of the city's major department stores and featured typical Eaton sales and promotional activities in its 140,000-square-foot store. Elaine Kozakovich remembers the store from the time she was a child:

> *I do have one very fond memory of the store during its time on Third Avenue—I moved to Saskatoon in 1955. My mother took me to Eaton's, and I had my very first ride on an escalator and an elevator, where a charming lady wore white gloves as she opened and closed the doors. From that moment, for a long time, I wanted to operate an elevator when I grew up (not much demand for that anymore), and even better—I got to see the bones in my feet with the fluoroscope machine! Wow, I was so impressed that the bones of my feet were green! I used that machine more than a few times—I'm surprised that today my feet don't glow in the dark!*

One outstanding, well-remembered event occurred in July 1966, when, during the annual Saskatoon Fair, hockey legend Gordie Howe returned to his hometown to be honoured on July 22, designated by the City of Saskatoon as "Gordie Howe Day." Howe's talent and physical prowess in the game, as well as his accomplishments while playing for the Detroit Red Wings National Hockey League (NHL) hockey team, have led him to become known as "Mr. Hockey" and considered by many to be the greatest hockey player of all time. He was hired by Eaton's to be its official "Sports Advisor" and to promote its Tru-Line range of sporting goods. In that capacity, Howe regularly visited stores and catalogue sales offices to sign autographs and appear in front of an adoring public.

Born in rural Floral, Saskatchewan, in 1928, Howe grew up during the depression and by age eight was playing organized hockey in Saskatoon, where his family had moved. He worked alongside his father as a labourer and construction worker before leaving the city in 1944 to pursue his career. In 1966, it was decided to honour Howe in his hometown during the annual Saskatoon Fair, and in addition to the obligatory autograph session at Eaton's, several days worth of events were designed to show appreciation to the four-time Stanley Cup champion while visiting.

Gordie Howe; his wife (as well as closest friend and supporter), Colleen, herself known as "Mrs. Hockey"; and their four children participated in the Gordie Howe Parade, a children's reception and a tribute program at the Memorial Arena featuring many of Howe's NHL colleagues. The previous night, at a dinner to honour Howe, friend, teacher and mentor Father Athol Murray, co-founder (along with Sister Mary Edith McCullogh of the Sisters of Charity of St. Louis) of the College of Notre Dame of the Prairies in Wilcox, Saskatchewan, paid tribute to the famous "Number 9." The Catholic priest's school became noted as a training ground for Canada's best hockey players, and Père Murray himself was famous for once saying, "I love God, Canada and hockey—and not always in that order!"

The Saskatoon event didn't merely honour a sports hero but also gave an indication of Gordie Howe's true character as a humble and decent man of undeniable humanity. When columnist Vern DeGeer was hired by the *Detroit Times* to write a human-interest story about the great hockey star, he was surprised to find Howe at his parents' modest white Saskatoon bungalow, covered in sawdust, helping his father, Ab, install a new kitchen. Furthermore, DeGeer reported that the home was one "that Gordie bought for his devoted parents with the first monies he had received as a professional hockey player." Perhaps it is speculation, but it would seem that just as

Gordie Howe and his family are treated to a ride in a Pontiac convertible during the 1966 Saskatoon Fair. *Archives of Ontario: T. Eaton Fonds F229. Used with the permission of Sears Canada Ltd.*

Timothy Eaton was a great man who attracted the talented and capable to himself by sheer force of principle and personality, Eaton's, as a store, had the same power to attract the best and brightest, as it did with Gordie Howe.

Eaton's own publicity for the event honoured the hockey star with the following words:

> *Eaton's is happy and proud to have Gordie Howe associated with them in his capacity as sports advisor. It takes more than just hockey prowess to make a man as great as Gordie is, in the eyes of young and old alike. It takes that little something extra. It takes time. It takes liking people. It takes giving of yourself for other people. Successful and sought after as he is, Gordie Howe still finds time to give of himself for others. He devotes spare time to helping with little league baseball, running a hockey school for boys in Detroit at St. Clair Shores, attending youth banquets in both Canada and the U.S., and taking the time to make a youngster in hospital that much happier. Gordie Howe…a great hockey player…a great man!*

Eaton's 1928 store maintained its popularity until proposals were put forth in the 1960s to redevelop the Canadian National Railways station and yards west of the downtown area. Although it was conceived much earlier, Midtown Plaza was not opened until July 29, 1970. From that time on, disused railway and industrial property was transformed into a mixed-use development consisting of a shopping mall, a new office tower for the Canadian National Railway and a civic auditorium, which was completed for Canada's centennial in 1967.

The idea for Midtown Plaza was first voiced in 1960, when Saskatoon mayor Sid Buckwald proposed a relocation of twenty-four acres of CN facilities to the outskirts. Eaton's announced that it would

Gordie Howe, "Mr. Hockey," wearing his red "Eaton's Sporting Goods Adviser" blazer. *Archives of Ontario: T. Eaton Fonds F229. Used with the permission of Sears Canada Ltd.*

build a large new Saskatoon flagship in the plaza in February 1966. When it opened, the Plaza included a shopping mall between the two anchor stores, acres of enclosed parking and a twelve-storey CN Tower office building that closed the Third Avenue vista at the opposite end from the Bessborough Hotel, as once did the 1920s CNR station it replaced.

Eaton's enticed customers with a "We're tickled pink" promotion that took its theme from an ornate pink lamppost, a feature of the modernistic, 200,000-square-foot, three-level store. For the opening, the new Terrace Garden restaurant overlooking Midtown Plaza's mall featured pink lemonade, pink cake and pink ice cream, among other pink delights. Eaton's bade farewell to its longtime location on Third Avenue and Twenty-first Street by featuring, in an advertisement, the older store's well-worn leather-upholstered main floor bench, which had become a meeting place for generations of Saskatonians. Eaton's ad consoled nostalgic customers by saying, "Now the bench is gone. But don't be sad. There's a brand new surprise in store. A new landmark in your life." Midtown Plaza, although it changed the landscape of downtown Saskatoon, was a great and popular success.

Eaton's spread its retail operations throughout Saskatchewan during and after World War II. A forty-thousand-square-foot branch opened on Central Avenue at the corner of Thirteenth Street in Prince Albert on November 18, 1941. Years later, a new, forty-five-thousand-square-foot Eaton branch opened on March 14, 1963, in North Battleford. The latter

In 1970, as a result of a large-scale urban renewal plan, Eaton's opened a modern, new store at Saskatoon's Midtown Plaza. *Archives of Ontario: T. Eaton Fonds F229. Used with the permission of Sears Canada Ltd.*

Eaton's expanded throughout Saskatchewan with city-centre branches in North Battleford (top) and Prince Albert (bottom). *Archives of Ontario: T. Eaton Fonds F229. Used with the permission of Sears Canada Ltd.*

store was a handsome, modern brick building located downtown, rather surprising since it was in actuality well past the dawn of the shopping centre era in Canada.

To the west of Saskatoon, in Edmonton, Alberta, the T. Eaton Co. followed a similar path of expansion into a new market. Advertised as "Edmonton's Greatest Store," James Ramsey Limited was founded by James Ramsey, the so-called merchant prince of Edmonton. Ramsey was born in 1864 in Imlay City, Michigan, but his family moved to Oxford, Ontario, when he was still a child. Gaining valuable business experience in retail stores, he learned of opportunity in Western Canada and relocated to Edmonton, Alberta, where he started his department store business on two floors of the city's landmark Tegler Building, located at 1st Street and 102nd Avenue.

The store's success led it to be expanded on several occasions, first into the 1915 brick-fronted Kelly Block adjacent to the store and later into the purpose-built Ramsey Block, a four-floor commercial structure with a dignified Edwardian commercial façade, built in 1927. The merchant served as an alderman on the Edmonton City Council during 1915 and 1916 and moved on to the provincial legislature in 1917, where he served for four years. Much like Timothy Eaton in Winnipeg, it was Ramsey and his store that broke with local custom and first began accepting the copper penny as payment in the western town.

The Edmonton warehouse's elegant façades, reminiscent of some of the company's most handsome stores, belied the utilitarian function of the building. *Archives of Ontario: T. Eaton Fonds F229. Used with the permission of Sears Canada Ltd.*

By acquiring the Edward Ramsey Co. Limited in Edmonton, Eaton's gained a foothold in the western city, although the store was partially located in a disparate array of structures, including the first two floors of the landmark Tegler building, *Archives of Ontario: T. Eaton Fonds F229. Used with the permission of Sears Canada Ltd.*

Ramsey's store was at the height of fashion, operated its own mail-order division and was planning to expand to Calgary, just as Eaton's was making its march westward in the latter years of the 1920s. On January 17, 1929, Eaton's announced that it had purchased the "stock and goodwill" of James Ramsey Limited, and from that point on, the T. Eaton Co. Limited had another major store in Western Canada. Ramsey himself retired to his vacation home in the Bahamas, where he died in 1939.

Eaton's had already operated a Groceteria in Edmonton, and while keeping the downtown operation at the former location of Ramsey's, it built a large and quite elegant warehouse at 102nd Street and 103rd Avenue. The structure, built of brick with stone trim, carried on the "Eaton Style" of the day with triple arched openings at the second-floor level, as well as a symmetrical design featuring massive corner pavilions.

A handsome warehouse indeed, its heavy goods sales room was popular with Edmonton homeowners.

On August 29, 1939, Eaton's opened a brand-new store at 101st Street and 102nd Avenue, a striking Art Deco–style edifice conceived by architects Northwood and Chivees. The store's wide-open layout stood in contrast to Eaton's former quarters in Edmonton, which consisted of three separate, interconnected buildings with differences of floor level. The cool, light interior was contrasted by rich wood store furnishings in a likewise streamlined style, and its two staircases (reputedly the widest unsupported stairs in Canada at the time) were augmented by Edmonton's first escalators.

Outside, the Tyndall stone and Travertine-faced structure with rounded corners and ribbon windows featured a shiny stainless steel–faced marquee to shade its large display windows and window shoppers alike from the strong western sunlight.

The store's success was such that, after the war, plans were made to increase its area to 267,000 square feet by the 1950 addition of a third floor. Eaton's gradually moved into its expanded quarters without fanfare, but the distinctive streamlined department store was always attraction enough. Downtown Edmonton was the region's powerhouse shopping centre, with large Hudson's Bay Company and Woodward's Department Stores, along with smaller shops like Holt Renfrew, vying for customers in the increasingly prosperous western community.

In 1938, Eaton's vacated its old location for a modern, streamlined store on 102nd Street. *Archives of Ontario: T. Eaton Fonds F229. Used with the permission of Sears Canada Ltd.*

When Eaton's outgrew the two-storey store after the war, a third floor was added in 1950. The store's interior gave off an aura of spaciousness and modernity, expressed in rich materials, in stark contrast to the older store combined in three different buildings. *Archives of Ontario: T. Eaton Fonds F229. Used with the permission of Sears Canada Ltd.*

As Edmonton, flush with wealth from energy-rich Alberta's abundant resources, grew into a large and increasingly sophisticated community, shopping centres developed around the city. On August 8, 1972, Eaton's opened a 125,000-square-foot store in the capacious new Londonderry Mall. The mall was, at the time, the largest shopping centre in Western Canada, and Eaton's promoted its new suburban store with an "Up, Up, and Away" sale enticing customers to Londonderry and its modern branch.

Three hundred kilometres to the south, Eaton's expansion across Canada took a rather different form. The company's fledgling chain of Eaton Groceterias had arrived in Calgary in 1925 and had grown to a two-store operation by May 1927. Fueled by a visit of Harry McGee, Eaton's longtime vice-president in charge of construction, in 1925, as well as by open speculation about the status of a disused city block downtown, rumours proliferated about the possibility of a large new Eaton store in Calgary, already famous for its annual Stampede.

On November 4, 1927, it was announced that the speculation was indeed true; Eaton's not only bought the whole block bounded by Eighth and Seventh Avenues and Third and Fourth Streets but also the adjacent Miriam Block and seventeen lots on Fourth Street directly to the west of the proposed store location. The *Calgary Herald* waxed about the purchase, informing readers that

> *T. Eaton and Co., one of Canada's greatest departmental stores, has purchased an entire city block in Calgary as a site for the erection of a large store…details regarding the building and the amount of money involved have not been announced…Enough is known unofficially here to understand that a series of huge buildings, approaching in importance those of Winnipeg and Toronto, are contemplated.*

The paper went on to say that Eaton's officials, including Harry McGee, were in Western Canada to negotiate the Calgary deal and that an official announcement would be made before long. A few days later, it was announced from Eaton's in Winnipeg that "we have long regarded Calgary as a very desirable point for the location of a company store. Its growth has justified this view." More details would be forthcoming after negotiations to close the alleyway that divided its property were completed with the city.

With all preparations in order, construction on the new Calgary store began in April 1928. In July of that year, Eaton's opened a new order office on the corner of Eighth Avenue and Third Street, just across from the new

At the grand opening of the Calgary store, Lady Eaton poses with the manager and his wife, with her young son Timothy at her side. *Archives of Ontario: T. Eaton Fonds F229. Used with the permission of Sears Canada Ltd.*

store's construction site. The order office augmented the Groceterias and provided direct access to Eaton's merchandise, values and guarantees until the new store was ready to greet retail customers.

The construction of the store was completed in early 1929, and preparations for a gala opening included a visit from Lady Eaton. By this time, it had become traditional for the late Sir John Eaton's wife to pay an inspection visit to each store annually and preside over grand opening ceremonies wherever they occurred. In Calgary, an inspection tour for dignitaries and a luncheon in the new store's third-floor Alhambra Tea Room were held on the day prior to the store's formal opening on February 28, 1929. At the luncheon, both Lady Eaton and her eldest son, Timothy, welcomed Lord Mayor F.E. Osgoode and spoke about Eaton's and Calgary:

> *May I thank all of you for your cordial graciousness. I appreciate this more than I can say. When the company began its expansion, I asked my*

husband the reason for it. I wanted to know if they didn't have enough money or if he desired to have a larger business than the other companies. Sir John's reply was that a big company could not stand still. It had to go forward, or go backward; hence there was only one thing to do—go forward. We do not want all the business in the west; we simply want our share. This applies to Calgary. I am sorry that Mr. R.Y. Eaton could not come here and attend the opening of the store. He has been and will continue to be a tremendous factor in carrying on the business. His has been a colossal accomplishment.

The lord mayor responded with appreciation and recounted that he had met Sir John Eaton earlier when the merchant was in Calgary. Osgoode himself ran a book store in town and asked Sir John if he should be worried about Eaton's opening in Calgary when the noted businessman stopped in Osgoode's store to find a Toronto newspaper. Eaton responded by telling him, "My boy, never mind the T. Eaton Company. Go ahead and give greater attention to your own business!" which the mayor learned, after many years, was very good advice indeed.

The next morning, Lady Eaton and Timothy motored over to the store from the Palliser Hotel, a palatial, E-shaped hostelry built by the Canadian Pacific Railway that had served as their accommodation for the Calgary grand opening. Timothy produced the traditional inscribed gold key with which Lady Eaton opened the door, and a bell was rung indicating that Eaton's was open for business in Calgary. The *Calgary Herald* reported that

As a matter of fact, never in the history of Calgary has the opening of any business establishment caused such a furore. For more than an hour hundreds were lined up on the sidewalk at the four principal entrances to the mammoth building, and when the doors were eventually flung open, there was a wild scramble on the part of hundreds of persons for the honour of being the first to gain admission.

After receiving a bouquet of roses from the store manager, Lady Eaton and her party retreated to the store's fourth-floor reception rooms, where she gave an interview to the press, stating, "The welcome of citizens had been most cordial, and we hope, as in the past, to be worthy of the confidence that has been shown us here." History proved her right, as the store became a dominant anchor in Calgary.

The store introduced to the public that day was indeed a great achievement for the T. Eaton Co. Limited. Designed once again by Ross and MacDonald of Montréal, the four-storey building carried on the theme of earlier Eaton stores in the 1920s expansion program. Like the others, the structure was done in a Renaissance Revival style and was faced in Tyndall stone, which was also used for projecting cornices that divided the façades of the store into a traditional tripartite composition. The base was composed of bronze-framed display windows, over which rose second-floor Roman-arched windows in groups of three, individually separated by twisted pilasters. Above that, the body of the store consisted of rectangular windows in recessed groups carried across two floors to give the effect of height and verticality. A massive cornice capping the whole design met the blue Alberta sky and completed the composition with a flourish.

A contrasting, more massive treatment gave strength and emphasis to the building's corners, but the defining characteristic of the store was its arcade, which paralleled Eighth Avenue and was introduced by wide, two-storey arches on the Third and Fourth Street façades. This amenity, with design details reminiscent of the Louis XIV period, allowed passersby to walk under cover throughout the whole store frontage, with large display cases on either side.

Prior to the opening, the *Calgary Herald* reported on the store's features, giving mention to the "beautiful colour scheme of blue and gold" applied to the arcade ceiling and the space given over to "brilliantly-lit displays" on either side of it. Attention was duly paid to the store's numerous innovations, including Alberta's first escalator, Italian travertine marble flooring, retractable

Entrance to the store's atmospheric Alhambra Tea Room. The colourful, evocative interior design stood out amid the more sober architecture of the store's functional interior. *Archives of Ontario: T. Eaton Fonds F229. Used with the permission of Sears Canada Ltd.*

awnings and modern lighting. Special mention was given to the third-floor "House of Today," a fully-furnished *Moderne* house designed by "Monsieur Ciro, one of the leading architects of Paris." The 155,000-square-foot store incorporated a lunch counter and a full-line Groceteria in its basement, and its 150-seat Alhambra Tea Room was described as having "exotic decorations, the walls and ceilings being finished in gold and aluminum leaf with oriental effects in contrasting and brilliant colourings."

Eaton's advertised the store itself by introducing its policies, such as the "money refunded" guarantee and the D.A. (Deposit Account), as it had in past expansions. On the same day, though, it also produced a magnificently illustrated ad showing the new store over a collage of the company's other western locations. In an archway, in the centre of the ad, reminiscent of the Calgary arcade, the text gave a brief but illustrative history of the T. Eaton Co. and also philosophized about the meaning of such an occasion, noting that with stores from Halifax to Calgary,

[t]*here exists no more enduring testimony to the genius and integrity of the founder which adorns Calgary and which symbolizes the confidence of another great merchandising company in the inevitable development of the Canadian West, and particularly this part of the West. Calgary may well augur favourably from the fact that the greatest institution of its kind in the British Empire, and withal a wholly Canadian organization, has selected this city as the site for one of its handsome, substantial, and best-equipped stores—a building which, four storeys in height and occupying the best part of a big block, is so constructed that its foundations will easily carry an additional six storeys when, in the fullness of time, this additional space shall be required. A virile relationship has been established—a relationship which will tend to make this city a highly important commercial centre. Business attracts business, and it might be accepted that the T. Eaton Company will act as a magnet. Another heavy payroll has been assured, new homes will be erected, more visitors will be drawn here and more money will be put into local circulation. These are not selfish considerations. They*

Opposite: Eaton's in Calgary was a completely new, four-storey building that nevertheless bore a resemblance to the Saskatoon branch (bottom). The dignified, traditional interior was a composition of elegant materials (top). *Archives of Ontario: T. Eaton Fonds F229. Used with the permission of Sears Canada Ltd.*

are the factors which accompany the healthy city. The T. Eaton Company represents another strong asset added to the register of Calgary's sturdy commercial institutions.

When time came to expand the store due to business growth after the Great Depression, it did not come in the form of a vertical expansion, as projected. In 1936, the store's luxuriant arcade was reclaimed as main floor space, and in 1955, a large expansion program was unveiled. In fact, the expansion was front-page news on March 15, 1955, when Eaton's announced that the existing building would be extended across four floors (and the basement) all the way to Seventh Avenue, as well as a large Parkade built to serve shoppers on the existing parking lot across Fourth Street. A tunnel under Fourth Street was planned to connect the four-hundred-car garage and the expanded store. The addition would add 91,000 square feet of space to the existing 176,000-square-foot store and provide new escalators serving all floors, in addition to vastly expanded selections to customers.

The newspaper called the addition, whose plain modernity contrasted with the elaborate façades of the 1929 store, "dignified and modern," while noting that the exterior would be faced in Tyndall stone like the earlier structure; it also reported that the investment of $3 million for the expansion and $500,000 for the parking garage was representative of the confidence Eaton's had in its Calgary operations. The upgraded facility was put into full operation in stages from late 1956 through 1957. The functional 1950s architecture of the new portion was, in the event, softened somewhat by recesses in the façades that mimicked the rhythm of its older neighbour, and display windows gave life and interest to its street level. In the expanded store, a new Valley Room cafeteria became a popular luncheon spot for downtown shoppers.

Like it had in Edmonton in 1972, Eaton's sought the business of suburban customers by joining the Hudson's Bay Company and other nationally known retailers like Birks, Fairweather and Tip Top Tailors by opening a branch store in the new South Centre shopping mall, the first two-level enclosed mall in the Calgary area. Eaton's promoted the opening of its new, 120,000-square-foot location on August 7, 1974, with a "Grow with us" celebration that offered a "tree tag" for the store's first five thousand customers, who could return in the fall and redeem the tag for a fir sapling to plant in their own yard.

The new South Centre store emphasized fashion for the whole family, as was Eaton's custom, but also offered a full selection of home furnishings and complete services, including a Garden Terrace restaurant on the second floor.

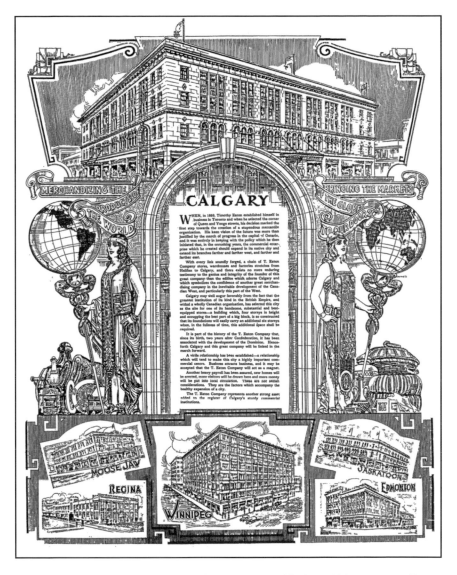

A beautifully illustrated ad introduced Eaton's to the public in a 1929 newspaper. *From and ad, collection of the author.*

In a unique bid to reinforce its Canadian outlook and family orientation, Eaton's South Centre grand opening ads included short biographies and portraits of salespeople hired to operate the new store.

Eaton's presence in Alberta was not limited to its two largest cities. In the late 1920s, the T. Eaton Co. experimented by opening TECO stores in smaller markets. The stores were eventually converted to other nameplates,

Eaton's 1957 addition was in stark, modern contrast to the Neo-Renaissance 1929 Ross and MacDonald creation it augmented. *Archives of Ontario: T. Eaton Fonds F229. Used with the permission of Sears Canada Ltd.*

specifically the Canadian Department Stores in the east and then Eaton's in the west when they were expanded and repositioned to become branch stores of the T. Eaton Co. Western Limited.

Southeast of Calgary, in Medicine Hat, Alberta, Eaton's opened a TECO store in May 1928 in the city's Hull Block at the corner of Third Street and Sixth Avenue. In 1939, the store became a T. Eaton Co. Limited branch store, and in 1941, it was expanded and rebuilt into a full-scale department store. At the same time, the building, known as the Hull Bock, built in 1912, received an elegant stone storefront that bore the Eaton's name. Eaton's grew to became a focal point for shopping in the Medicine Hat, which had acquired the nickname the "Gas City" on account of its huge reserves of natural gas.

In time, the branch, like many smaller Eaton's stores, participated in the special world the retailer created wherever it did business. Archival photographs show window displays dedicated to Quarter-Century Club employees, parade floats, fashion shows and lavish Christmas displays.

Eaton's did not neglect the suburbs as Alberta grew. Shown are the South Centre store in Calgary (1974) and the earlier (1972) branch it built at Edmonton's Londonderry Mall. *Archives of Ontario: T. Eaton Fonds F229. Used with the permission of Sears Canada Ltd.*

To the west, in the city of Lethbridge, at the foot of the Rockies, Eaton's opened a cash-and-carry Groceteria store in the Baalim Block on Fifth Street in December 1926. By April 1929, the store had expanded its lines of merchandise and was advertised as one of the company's TECO units. On December 9, 1939, advertisements proclaimed that in the future, the store would be known as the Lethbridge Branch of the T. Eaton Co. Limited.

Eaton's made a $2.5 million investment in Lethbridge in 1955, demolishing the old premises and filling the block with an up-to-date, modern store in the then current Eaton's style. When it opened on September 22, 1955, the *Lethbridge Herald* summarized Eaton's presence in the Alberta city:

Eaton's to Lethbridge and southern Alberta is like Macy's to New York. For if there is a style to be had, or a price to be met, Southern Alberta shoppers have always counted on Eaton's. Timothy Eaton's foresight and shrewd business calculations and how he passed them on to his successors are as evident in Lethbridge as they are in the rest of Canada. When the store was opened under the presidency of R.Y. Eaton, Fifth Street was "Main Street" in Lethbridge. However, since that time the rest of Lethbridge has built around Eaton's until today it is in the very heart of the city's shopping district. To all shoppers in Lethbridge whether visitors or local residents, it is a part of the city from where you locate your bearings and find your way to the city hall, the gas company or the post office. Ask anyone where something is in downtown Lethbridge and invariably you will receive the answer—it is so many blocks east or west, south or north and so on from Eaton's. In Lethbridge as in the rest of Canada Eaton's has many accredited claims. Here one can purchase a penny button, a broadloom rug, a shoelace or outfit a 30-room mansion.

Lady Eaton dances with her son Gilbert at a gala celebrating the 1955 opening of the new Lethbridge store. *Archives of Ontario: T. Eaton Fonds F229. Used with the permission of Sears Canada Ltd.*

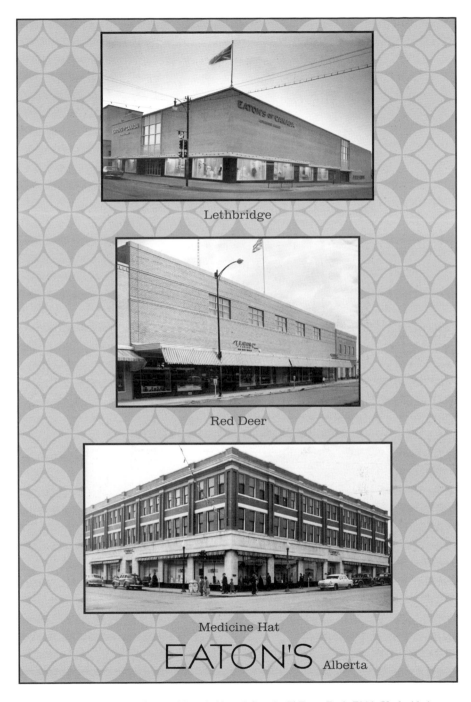

Lethbridge

Red Deer

Medicine Hat

EATON'S Alberta

A trio of Eaton stores in Alberta cities. *Archives of Ontario: T. Eaton Fonds F229. Used with the permission of Sears Canada Ltd.*

The store was constructed in stages, a first portion rising behind the older premises. When the whole construction was ready, it was planned to be opened, as had become the Eaton tradition, by Lady Eaton with a golden key, but owing to bad weather, her plane was grounded at Winnipeg, and she had to take a train to Medicine Hat and continue by car to Lethbridge. As a result, she was unable to be present when the doors were opened, but the "alert, elderly lady," so described by the *Lethbridge Herald*, was able to attend a banquet, where she danced with her son Gilbert, a company director who had accompanied her on the arduous journey to Alberta.

Grand opening customers were treated to a 105,000-square-foot retail store the likes of which Lethbridge had never seen before, and the *Herald* heaped superlatives on Eaton's new home, specifically noting that the escalators connecting all three floors were the first in town and that, in general, it was one of the most comprehensive and modern department stores to have been built in Canada at the time. The facility, which reinforced Eaton's status as an anchor of the Fourth Street shopping district, provided a basement "Coffee Corner" for the convenience of customers and was the work of Winnipeg architects Moody and Moore. The *Herald* commented on the plainness of the modern exterior, which it described as being offset by floor-to-ceiling glass windows on the front and side of the building. One set of these windows allowed light into the store's second-floor "Style Shop," which offered furs and designer fashions to Lethbridge *fashionistas* of the day.

To the north, in Red Deer, Alberta, Eaton's pursued a slightly different path to expansion. The T. Eaton Co. Limited purchased the business of W.E. Lord, which was founded in 1906 and had grown into the town's largest department store by 1911. On July 6, 1928, Eaton's opened a TECO store at the location, known as the Purdy Block, at 111 Gaetz Avenue, between Forty-eighth and Forty-ninth Streets. In October 1939, the whole store was modernized, expanded to two floors and renamed as the Red Deer branch of the T. Eaton Co. Western Limited.

Eaton's prospered in Red Deer, as it did in the rest of Western Canada, but it could not truly become the "Trans-Canada Store" without expanding towards the Atlantic coast as well. As its western expansion came directly to the base of the Rocky Mountains, it also grew farther eastward from its headquarters before it was able to consider crossing the continental divide and dipping its toes into the blue waters of the Pacific Ocean.

Ocean Limited *

Though you refer to us as guests, we came down to be fellow citizens.
—John David Eaton

Just as the mail-order system led the way west for Eaton's, it helped introduce the store to the bucolic and sometimes wildly beautiful provinces that form Canada's east coast. The success of the mail-order trade required ever-larger facilities to handle the business, and in 1917, while returning from his humanitarian mission to help victims of the devastating Halifax Explosion, Sir John Eaton stopped in Moncton, New Brunswick, to look at sites for a proposed catalogue distribution operation, Eaton's first in the east.

Moncton was chosen as a location for the new mail-order distribution centre because of its position at the junction of railroad lines connecting Montréal and Québec to Halifax, Nova Scotia, and Saint John, New Brunswick. As has been mentioned, this reason also led it to be a major location for the repair and car building shops of the Intercolonial (later CN) railway. After its founding in the 1700s, Moncton prospered as a wooden ship-building centre; as the railways arrived, Moncton's prime industry went into decline and had disappeared by the middle of the nineteenth century. The economically devastated city, though, found recovery and resurgence in the form of the railway, which located its head offices there, on its main

---

* The Ocean Limited was a crack overnight luxury train of the CNR that connected Montréal and Halifax daily since its first run in 1904.

line connecting Halifax with Québec. Industry quickly followed, and one of Moncton's leading employers was the Record Foundry and Manufacturing Company, but its facilities were destroyed by fire in February 1916.

Eaton's found that the former location of the foundry, just outside the central business district near the railway and its handsome Victorian terminal building, met its needs perfectly. In 1919, a large six-storey structure rose on the derelict Foundry Street site. The building could be considered a typical example of industrial architecture, similar to countless others all over North America. A sturdy brick edifice of six stories with wide, open bays and large, floor-to-ceiling windows, Eaton's Moncton facility was distinguished by the elegant stone facing of its Foundry Street façade and an elaborately detailed Neo-Renaissance portico at its main entrance.

The building was opened by then president R.Y. Eaton on February 5, 1920, and was visited on opening day by thousands of people. The new enterprise initially hired more than 750 staff and was designed to supply Eaton merchandise to households not only in Eastern Canada but to overseas

Eaton's began construction on a mail-order warehouse in the city of Moncton, New Brunswick, in 1919. It was to serve as a Maritimes hub for the retail giant's catalogue operation. *Archives of Ontario: T. Eaton Fonds F229. Used with the permission of Sears Canada Ltd.*

destinations as well. The grand opening was celebrated later in the day at a banquet for dignitaries held at the Brunswick Hotel, which was located on Main Street, a short way from Eaton's new enterprise, across from the nearby CNR railway station and the landscaped gardens that surrounded it at the time.

Although it was not designed as a retail facility, local customers who ordered merchandise from Eaton's requested a showroom in order to examine goods before committing to purchase, and this feature was opened shortly thereafter. In time, it grew across the building's second floor owing to its popularity. Linda Roach of Moncton describes Eaton's as an "amazing place" and justifies her appraisal by relating her own experience in catalogue sales:

When I started grade ten, I went to Eaton's and applied for a part-time job and I was hired immediately. I was a student, and I worked with mostly older women and men who had their own families. Everyone was polite, friendly and treated me with great respect. You never heard a swear word or an off-colour joke—that just did not happen. I worked in catalogue sales, taking telephone orders from our customers, and soon I was moved to the catalogue sales order pickup desk. Many times I remember taking an order from a customer, and then we would run upstairs to the department and obtain the item and then bring it to the customer. It was fast, and the customers loved the service. It was always fun to go upstairs to the other departments and chat with co-workers (briefly, of course). One evening, I was approached by the catalogue sales manager and asked if I would be interested in another position with credit management for the summer. I was taken and trained to approve or decline purchases made by clients from all over Canada—and I was only in grade eleven. I can still remember sitting in that office surrounded by huge telex machines and answering the telephone from all over Canada and authorizing purchases—it was a great feeling to know that Eaton's trusted me, a student, with such responsibility. When I graduated from high school and left Eaton's, the ladies in catalogue sales gave me a silver charm with the Eaton's logo and the date on it. I still have it, and it never fails to bring back wonderful memories of my three years in a great place. My home life was terrible, but Eaton's was a place where I was treated with respect, given responsibility and I felt my contribution was important. It was awesome!

Within a few years, Eaton's recognized the sales potential at the Moncton site and planned to add a retail store to the complex. The Moncton Eaton store opened on November 27, 1927, and quickly became the top shopping spot in the city. Although it was a full-service department store, and though Eaton's listed it among its "main stores" (as opposed to branch stores), locals for many years referred to it as "the Showroom" on account of its origins. As in western cities, the great store dominated the retail trade in Moncton, and often local businesses had difficulty adjusting to the new retail climate. Lynn Parsons Belliveau recounts the story of her husband's family business as the Great Depression approached:

> *My father-in-law, J.E. Belliveau, wrote about his family history, and that of his father's store, P.A. Belliveau, and I am quoting him: "The T. Eaton Co. opened its major mail-order centre in Moncton in 1920 and, despite early denials of such plans, in a few years set up a large retail store. For many merchants in Moncton, and especially P.A. Belliveau, this competition brought on a serious decline. It had been the custom to extend both short and long-term credit to customers, and especially to the railroad employees, who were a majority in the city and its surroundings. These, like the postal and customs employees, were paid twice a month and on pay days customarily paid instalments on their accounts. When the mail-order business…with its huge buying power capable of under-pricing ordinary merchants…got going there was no credit. All transactions were cash and*

The popularity of "the Showroom" led Eaton's to augment the warehouse in 1927 with a complete retail store. The two-storey department store was considered the company's flagship east of Montréal. *Archives of Ontario: T. Eaton Fonds F229. Used with the permission of Sears Canada Ltd.*

all unsatisfactory goods returnable. This competition hurt P.A. Belliveau's business badly, and substantial debts occurred on the books because it was difficult to refuse credit to people who had so long paid regularly. It seemed as though they were spending their cash with Eaton's and buying from other merchants on credit only when the cash was gone. In the business and in his financial affairs generally, things went downhill quite rapidly after 1927 and reached a climax in 1929, when the business was closed out."

Moncton in the twentieth century became a town dominated by two industries: Eaton's and the CN shops. As a result, Eaton's in Moncton literally became a part of the city's culture in a unique way and is vividly remembered to the present day. Gary Steeves's and his father's recollections show the importance Eaton's held for its Moncton employees, as well as the influence the great store had on their lives:

My father, Earl E. Steeves, worked at Eaton's Moncton store for more than twenty-five years, earning his gold watch and membership into the Quarter Century Club. To me and many Monctonians, he was "Mr. Eaton." I visited the old Eaton store on Foundry Street from a very early age. Whenever I visited the store, I felt like an "insider," not because my dad worked there as a sales clerk but because of the areas of the store I got to visit with him that were not usually seen by the general public. Often, I would accompany Dad into the receiving area at the back of the store, where we would take an elevator to the upper floors of the building. It was especially memorable riding the freight elevator, with its yawning wood-gate doors. The retail space was confined to the first two floors. A main staircase was on the left as you entered the front of the store through big glass doors that separated the large display windows facing Foundry Street. The floors above the retail area housed a different world. Our elevator rides took us to a land of inventories, as well as the Catalogue Division, with its numerous employees busily working, hidden away like ants in an anthill. Eaton's was an intricate part of our family, and for most of the citizens of Moncton in its day. Rare would be the home in the Moncton area that did not have a connection to an employee or a product of this major retail player. The store even became involved in a murder! I remember my father going to court to testify that he had sold a hunting knife to a customer that ended up using the knife to kill someone. My father made the move to the new Eaton's store when it opened at Highfield Square on Main Street. Dad worked in the paint and hardware department in this new location. The new store was modern, of course, but to me it lacked the character and memories of the old store. If nothing else, it was a few steps closer and a shorter walk for my dad's daily ritual. Dad was a dedicated Eaton employee, but above all it was about his customers. He believed in good service and being true and honest to the people he served. If Eaton's could not provide what the customer wanted, Dad was not adverse to sending him to a competitive retailer, often to the chagrin of his supervisor. "A satisfied customer," Dad would say, "will come back to Eaton's." Employees and customers took the store to their hearts, and as a result, the venerable old building became more than a place to work or shop.

The landmark complex was expanded and modernized in the mid-1950s, and the retail store was given an appearance very much like Eaton's new suburban stores of the decade. The modern metal siding applied to the old building, along with new signs proclaiming "Eaton's of Canada," certainly brought the facility up to date, even though it obliterated some of the charming stone features of the structure that had given it character since its appearance in Moncton.

With more than twenty-eight years as a newspaper reporter to his credit, Alan Cochrane of Moncton has been exposed firsthand to the history of Eaton's in Moncton and, consequently, is a fount of knowledge about the store and its service to both the citizens of New Brunswick and those who found themselves in Moncton, especially in times of war:

Moncton was one of the sites for the British Commonwealth Air Training plan, so we had young guys from all over the world (England, Australia, New Zealand, etc.) coming here for their flight training. Eaton's had a bowling alley in its store for employees, and during the war years they held dances and social evenings for the young airmen who were stationed here. Some of them didn't make it, and we have graves of young servicemen who were killed in training accidents before they even got near any real combat missions. I guess my point was that Eaton's was more than a store in Moncton. It was a major employer and part of the social fabric of the city and the entire region. The distribution centre was located downtown next to the railroad tracks, so trains loaded with merchandise would roll up next to the warehouse and unload. In the early days, they would deliver catalogue orders by horse-drawn wagon and it was a big thing for people in rural New Brunswick to get their catalogue orders of everything from shoes to guns and farm supplies.

The two-storey 1927 retail addition featured a sober brick façade with large show windows protected by an overhead canopy along Foundry Street, as well as a well-lit and atmospheric interior (inset). *Archives of Ontario: T. Eaton Fonds F229. Used with the permission of Sears Canada Ltd.*

Eaton's moved to the new Highfield Square development at Main and Highfield Streets in 1969, during the company's centennial year. The new store, in a style similar to the recently opened Anjou branch in Montréal, gave Eaton's a larger, 120,000-square-foot facility, a location directly on Moncton's Main Street and a presence in a dynamic, enclosed retail environment. The mall was adjacent to new CN offices and replaced the venerable old railway station that had graced the site for many years. After the store opened, the older building continued its role as a mail-order facility, and the adjacent retail space was converted into Eaton's Budget Store.

Seeking to expand farther into the Maritime Provinces, Eaton's, in late February 1928, purchased the retail business of Mahon Brothers in Halifax. The store—located in several ancient buildings on the downtown lot bounded by Barrington, Prince and Granville Streets—was founded in 1871 by John C. Mahon. Three years later, the firm became a partnership when Mahon's brother, Edmund, joined him in the business, which was described as specializing in "Dry Goods, Millinery and Mantles."

In 1953, a store modernization hid the elegant old façades behind a modern aluminum skin. In 1969, a new, suburban-style store in Highfield Square, just steps from the warehouse, replaced the older facility. *Archives of Ontario: T. Eaton Fonds F229. Used with the permission of Sears Canada Ltd.*

When it opened, the Halifax store was unique in the Eaton chain because it was the only one that allowed customers to buy on credit. It was felt by the company that it would not be good business in Halifax to tamper with the practice already set in place by Mahon Brothers. The new store still offered Eaton's time-honoured "D.A." (Deposit Account) to customers as an alternate to credit.

Eaton's immediately renamed the business on March 1, 1928, when it took possession, and it proceeded to demolish the old buildings one by one and replace them with portions of what would become an elegant, modern

Heavily clad crowds wait outside Eaton's new Halifax store in March 1928. The signs proclaim the "T. Eaton & Co. Maritimes Limited"; the store was previously known as Mahon Brothers. *Archives of Ontario: T. Eaton Fonds F229. Used with the permission of Sears Canada Ltd.*

new Eaton's store, five stories in height, that became a Halifax landmark. It was situated on the corner of Barrington and Prince Streets in the cente of the downtown shopping district.

To design its store in the Nova Scotian capital, Eaton's engaged Sydney Perry Dumaresq, the second generation of the Haligonian architectural dynasty of the same name. It's clear from the extant work of the Dumaresq architects that the firm did not "impose" a style on clients or locales but rather proffered solutions that were in line with the architectural *mode du jour.* Correspondingly, its landmarks in Halifax range from the 1908 memorial Dingle Tower in Sir Sandford Fleming Park to the Art Deco (and currently threatened) CBC building downtown, as well as varied other works in between. The Eaton store clearly takes cues from the work that architects Ross and Macdonald completed earlier for the company in other cities, notably Montréal, Saskatoon and Calgary, and it also bore a resemblance to the rebuilt Canadian Department Stores branches of the day in various Ontario towns.

The Granville and Prince Street sides of the building show the sloping site that afforded Eaton's street-level entrances on two major thoroughfares, as well as the dividing line (indicated by discolouration of stone) between phases of construction. *Archives of Ontario: T. Eaton Fonds F229. Used with the permission of Sears Canada Ltd.*

Its ground floor facing, deeply dentilled belt course and finely carved window surrounds were executed in a lovely, honey-coloured stone, and the upper floors were clad in a widely variegated earth-tone brick, giving the large commercial structure a lively composition of contrasting materials. The rhythmic pilasters along the building's upper façades also hinted at the more modern style of the 1930s while imparting a vertical emphasis that blended well with the more historic structures neighbouring it on Barrington Street.

The new emporium was completed and fully occupied by 1933, and the starting and stopping points in its path to completion are clearly shown in contemporary photographs due to the aging of its stone veneer. The store itself, which Eaton's advertised as "Your Shopping Centre in Halifax," had, uniquely, two main floors: one, entered from Barrington Street, displayed merchandise traditionally found on the street floor of modern department stores. The other, the so-called Granville Street level, opened to its eponymous thoroughfare on account of the steep slope of the property along Prince Street.

Well before Eaton's replaced its aging Moncton store, pressure for suburban development was felt in Halifax. The downtown store was fairly small at sixty thousand square feet of retail space and was virtually landlocked on its site. Eaton's operated a parking station across Granville Street, but its low capacity of about thirty-five cars did little to satisfy the needs of the growing number of mobile postwar shoppers. After examining the possibilities downtown, and failing to secure enough

Over a number of years, Eaton's pulled down the old buildings it acquired in Halifax and replaced them with this handsome modern store that served Haligonians for more than thirty years. Shown is the Granville and Prince Street corner of the completed store. *Archives of Ontario: T. Eaton Fonds F229. Used with the permission of Sears Canada Ltd.*

property for a meaningful expansion, Eaton's rather boldly decided to leave Barrington Street and relocate its Halifax flagship to the new Halifax Shopping Centre in 1962.

The modern Halifax store, among the first wave of suburban stores that Eaton's was constructing across the country, was a dramatic change from its

Eaton's referred to its new Halifax Shopping Centre store as the "Store for Now People—and that means YOU!" The mall entrance to the 1962 store repeated the same grillwork as the exterior entry and relieved the rather severe nature of the store's design, essentially a brick-clad box. *Archives of Ontario: T. Eaton Fonds F229. Used with the permission of Sears Canada Ltd.*

older downtown predecessor. The store took the form of a crisp, two-storey brick box highlighted by a distinctive white canopy composed of aluminum hexagons, a feature repeated over the store's mall entrance. Eaton's chose the name "Marine Room" for the store's restaurant, as much to echo the success of its luxurious Vancouver restaurant as to honour the seafaring heritage of Eastern Canada.

In 1963, the Halifax Shopping Centre store housed stranded customers and employees who were unable to get home during one the area's brutal winter storms. Since the event predated a similar but larger "sleepover" in the Winnipeg store by three years, Halifax management and employees became fond of chiding the older western store for being jealous of its bravery in the face of Old Man Winter's fury and just waiting for a chance for a comeuppance.

Eaton's later came to serve the community of Dartmouth on the opposite side of Halifax Harbour when it opened a store in the Mic Mac Mall, an enclosed suburban shopping centre on the shores of the lake of the same name. The eighty-thousand-square-foot store, which opened on October 13, 1973, was smaller than the Halifax store but was popular with Dartmouth residents.

Elsewhere in the Maritimes, Eaton's brought its TECO store concept to the smaller cities of Campbellton, New Brunswick, and Glace Bay, Sydney

In 1973, Eaton's opened a new store in Mic Mac Mall to serve the citizens of Dartmouth, whose only options for shopping at Eaton's had been the catalogue or a long trip across the harbour. *Archives of Ontario: T. Eaton Fonds F229. Used with the permission of Sears Canada Ltd.*

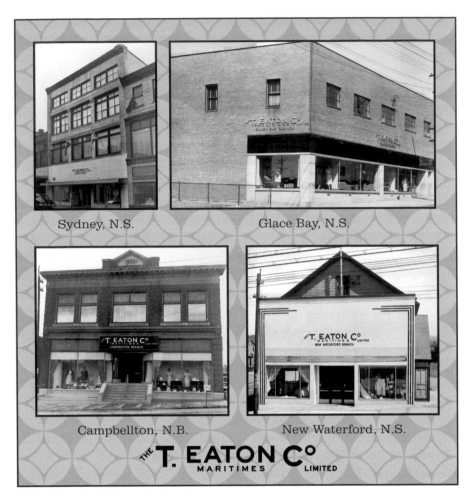

Sydney, N.S.

Glace Bay, N.S.

Campbellton, N.B.

New Waterford, N.S.

™ THE T. EATON C°
MARITIMES   LIMITED

Smaller stores operated by Eaton's in the Maritimes carried the Canadian Department Stores name until 1949, when they became Eaton stores. *Archives of Ontario: T. Eaton Fonds F229. Used with the permission of Sears Canada Ltd.*

Mines and Sydney, Nova Scotia, in 1928. After Eaton's bought the Canadian Department Stores chain, these outlets operated under that name from August 26, 1930, when they were converted, and eventually became T. Eaton Co. Limited branch stores in 1949, when the subsidiary name was retired. Some, like the Glace Bay and Sydney stores, received extensive makeovers at the mid-century point. A positively tiny Eaton's store in New Waterford, Nova Scotia, began life as an Eaton Groceteria before being converted to a branch store of Eaton's. Likewise, a shiny porcelain-paneled front was applied to the ancient wooden building to give it an up-to-date impression.

Newfoundland became the tenth Canadian province in 1949 when residents of the financially struggling island voted to join Canada, having previously been a British possession. Eaton's, shortly afterwards, opened a store in a disused barracks, located behind the station of the narrow-gauge Newfoundland Railway, which became a part of the CNR when the province joined Canada. Gander's international airport was a strategic stopover point for transatlantic aircraft, which, at the time, needed a refueling stop en route. From the moment it established a foothold in Newfoundland, Eaton's could claim to operate from coast to coast in Canada, although it did not yet have stores in every province. The small, makeshift store was the only one that Eaton's called a "Miscellaneous" branch, and it carried, and indeed sold, anything and everything the company's buyers could send there, so starved for mainland merchandise was the new province. It frequently closed after completely selling out its shelves, only to reopen when the next carload of merchandise arrived. The charming character of Newfoundland's populace probably exerted itself more than once in the store, but plausibly never so much as when a Gander customer questioned the "carrying charges added to the monthly statement [by this time Eaton's had relented and developed its own credit card system]…when it's easy to see we're taking the damn packages home ourselves!" After eight years, though, Eaton's felt at home enough in Newfoundland to give up the provisional quarters in Gander.

On June 5, 1957, the store opened a permanent, sixteen-thousand-square-foot location in the Elizabeth Road Shopping Centre in Gander. This relatively small outlet held the distinction for many years as having the highest sales-per-square-foot ratio in the whole Eaton's chain. The figures were partially due to the fact that the jet-setters of the day would seek out the store during the lengthy refueling stop (aided by the Eaton's name placed in large letters on the building's roof, directly in the landing path of transatlantic aircraft and easily visible to passengers). The *Gander Beacon* even once spotted Frank Sinatra buying a tartan skirt for his daughter Nancy in the store during a stopover.

Ludmilla Gvishiani, only daughter of Cold War–era Russian prime minister Alexei Kosygin, cancelled a shopping excursion in Paris after making purchases of clothing and cosmetics at the Gander store. Mistakenly thinking that the store was owned by Canadian-born tycoon Cyrus Eaton—who, in spite of amassing great wealth via the capitalist system, took a sympathetic stance towards communism in the Cold War years—Mrs. Gvishiani, returning from an important diplomatic visit of her father to the United States in 1967, saw the ten-foot letters on the store's roof spelling out "EATONS OF CANADA"

An aerial view of Eaton's 1957 store in Gander shows the effectiveness of the rooftop sign. Insets show the original 1949 store located in a disused barracks (above) and a street-level view of the modern, albeit small store (below). *Archives of Ontario: T. Eaton Fonds F229. Used with the permission of Sears Canada Ltd.*

and decided to go shopping. She later said that her purchases were "as fine as anything I could buy in Paris, and much cheaper!"

Eaton's presence in Canada's newest province was augmented in 1953 when it purchased the Corner Brook Stores Limited of Corner Brook, Newfoundland. Corner Brook, the largest city on Newfoundland's west coast, was a small coastal port and sawmill centre at the mouth of the Humber River, until the construction of an enormous pulp and paper mill in 1923 caused it to experience tremendous industrial and population growth. The mill expanded the town site to accommodate new employees and bankrolled businesses to provide services needed by the influx of workers and their families.

One such business was known as the "Company Store," a retailer set up to serve the shopping needs of Corner Brook residents. The store grew in size even as the Newfoundland Power and Paper Company itself changed hands. In 1928, the mill was purchased by American investors and became known as the International Power and Paper Co. Limited; likewise the store was called the I.P.P. Company Store, and after taking over the location of Fisher's General Store at 67 West Street, it built a completely new building to house its operations, which opened to the public (or at least employees of the mill, who were the only ones authorized to shop there) in November 1937.

When the mill was acquired by the British Bowater firm, the young department store eventually became informally known as Bowater's. A further enlargement in 1944 expanded its operations, and by the late 1940s, when Bowater privatized some of its ancillary businesses, the store was renamed Corner Brook Stores Limited. An advertisement for the thirty-one-thousand-square-foot operation called it "commodious" and noted that all of the various lines carried in the store, from hardware and furniture to groceries and fashions for "young and old," were offered under the store's slogan: "Quality, Style, Service and Satisfaction." A small branch operated since 1940 in nearby Deer Lake was known, appropriately enough, as the Deer Lake Stores Limited.

Solidifying its presence in Newfoundland, Eaton's purchased the business in 1952, and on August 14, 1953, the thirty-one-thousand-square-foot store took the Eaton's name. Almost exactly five years later, the quaint, clapboard-sided building was extensively remodeled, and the *Western Star* newspaper extolled the building's new features, especially its floor-to-ceiling glass display windows, its wide aluminum and glass doorways and the baked enamel panels, which replaced the old store's siding. Overall, the paper told readers that it found that the overall effect of the remodel to be "enhancing and modern."

Paul O'Brien's memories hint at the sizable role played by the store in the lives of the residents of Corner Brook:

My mom, Agnes, worked at Eaton's here in Corner Brook for a number of years. My dad, Walter O'Brien, would take my twin sister, Paula, and me to pick up our mom from her day shift around 5:30 p.m. We would always arrive early, and that would give us a bit of time to search around what seemed to be at that time the biggest store in the world. Mom worked in the cosmetics department, which was characterized by a variety of smells and scents that seemed to entice lots of patrons to that section of the store. There was a well-lit charm bracelet display cabinet that would roll forward or backward depending on which way you pushed the buttons. Mom often spoke about how Eaton's would

The Corner Brook Eaton's store began life as a "company store" of the all-important paper mill in the western Newfoundland town. A few years after the giant retailer purchased the branch, it went through a thorough modernization that replaced the ancient clapboard siding that had covered the store for years. *Archives of Ontario: T. Eaton Fonds F229. Used with the permission of Sears Canada Ltd.*

send their cosmetics personnel on trips to New York for training…and I still have pictures my mom took while on those trips. She has passed on now…but the Eaton's store on West Street here in Corner Brook will certainly be remembered. There was always so much to see at Eaton's.

Most of these memories of Eaton's, although they emanate from a smaller town in a remote location, are indicative of peoples' experiences throughout the Maritimes, where Eaton's relatively small stores became the retail focus for quality and selection. The retail juggernaut also proved that it could merchandise and see profit in tiny places like Corner Brook just as well as in Toronto or Calgary; the store remained a family operation, and local managers and staff knew, understood and valued their customers' needs.

A small but telling detail reflecting Eaton's approach is provided by Hubert Smith, who managed the Corner Brook store from 1972 until 1982, when it closed. He recalls that "the store sold practically everything needed in the household, including groceries, and appliances as well." Eaton's specifically sold appliances that operated on fifty-cycle power, not sixty-cycle, as sold in the rest of Canada. Because Bowater produced electricity for the area, it did so using the British fifty-cycle standard, put in place in Newfoundland long before it became a part of Canada. Until much later, when the generation of power was brought in line with the mainland, Eaton's sold fifty-cycle machines in Newfoundland because, according to Smith, "The problem with sixty-cycle appliances operating on fifty-cycle power was that the timers were not accurate."

That Eaton's was as good with the details as it was with everyday retailing is shown by Ted Cross's memories, dating back to the 1950s:

> *I well remember the original store that still had the grocery section. We wore school uniforms then, with dress shoes, and Eaton's was the only place where I could get a B width. The shoe department would order them especially for me in August before the school year began. I'll never forget the toy section at Christmas, the school section in September and going upstairs to pay the monthly bill at the accounts office, for my parents, as everyone in those days had the monthly account at Eaton's.*

The date of August 16, 1955, was a milestone event in Eaton's history. Although it had operated a Groceteria (from 1928 until 1944) and a catalogue order office (since 1928), the T. Eaton Co. finally opened a retail store in Charlottetown, Prince Edward Island. Islanders, like most people in rural Canada, knew Eaton's merchandise through its catalogue operation, but experienced the stores and their unique atmosphere only if lucky enough to travel. Scott Ryder has just such memories:

> *Oh, how could I have forgotten my earliest memories of Eaton's? It was as a child on a farm in rural Prince Edward Island. Hours were spent*

thumbing through the pages of the Eaton's catalogue—that magical book from which wonderful packages would arrive at our roadside mailbox! And with the cool breezes of fall there was always the countless trips to that mailbox until the Christmas catalogue appeared and the excitement of picking out what you hoped Santa would leave under the tree!

With its entry into Charlottetown, Eaton's didn't just gain a new customer base; it finally achieved the long-held goal of having retail stores in every Canadian province, thus becoming a truly "Trans-Canada Store."

The sixty-eight-thousand-square-foot store proudly carried the sign "Eaton's of Canada" over its Kent Street marquee, signifying its new status as part of a nationwide organization. The opening was deemed important enough that Lady Eaton's son and then president of Eaton's John David Eaton came down from Toronto to preside over the festivities. At a reception held in the town's landmark Charlottetown Hotel, Mayor J. David Stewart presented Eaton with a key to the city, remarking that "it is significant the opening of Eaton's coincided with the Centennial year, and that our next hundred years should start with the opening of such a fine new store." Eaton himself, in accepting the key with gratitude, reminded the mayor that "though you refer to us as guests, we came down to be fellow citizens."

Located at 167–169 Kent Street, the new Eaton store was designed by René Cera, the same Beaux-Arts–trained architect who worked alongside Lady Eaton to create Toronto's famous Georgian Room restaurant. The modern store, perhaps surprisingly, was in complete contrast to Cera's 1924 achievement, but the architect himself hinted at the reason why in an interview with the *Charlottetown Guardian*, saying, "Most stores reflect the architect, but this store was designed to reflect the customer. It might be considered a ladies store in design for it has been found that 90 percent of the shopping done in our store is done by women, so why shouldn't it be?"

The store he designed presented a tall, austere stone façade to Kent Street, outlined by a simple, deep blue-coloured metal cornice that continued down the sides of the building like a frame. A stainless steel–faced marquee cantilevered above what was the radical and distinguishing feature of the store: a continuous floor-to-ceiling glass-fronted vitrine that was broken only by two entrances. Opening day customers made mention, on account of the show windows being open to the interior store at the back, of how light flooded into Eaton's premises; the *Guardian* reported that customers agreed that being in the new branch was "just like being outside."

Eaton's store on Kent Street in Charlottetown, Prince Edward Island, was the work of René Cera, Eaton's chief architect and a graduate of the *École des Beaux-Arts* in Paris. *Archives of Ontario: T. Eaton Fonds F229. Used with the permission of Sears Canada Ltd.*

That effect was probably highlighted by the physical layout of the interior, in which a large, open, two-storey space was surrounded by a mezzanine from which customers could survey the activity on the main floor below. Among departments selling household and utility items, a basement level housed an intimate twenty-two-seat lunch counter, tucked directly under the broad staircase designed to allow access from the main floor. Eaton's acquired property to the rear, on Fitzroy Street, that served as parking, and a waiting room at the rear of the store became a favourite meeting spot over the course of the store's life. Indeed, the ability to pass through the store from street to street made the main aisle a popular thoroughfare in itself, especially in poor weather.

Although the glassy front was designed as a marketing device to draw customers to Eaton's lavishly displayed merchandise, it proved a huge (but thankfully non-fatal) liability one September day in 1959. The *Guardian* remarked that customers and pedestrians "had the unusual experience of seeing a car enter the store—by way of the front window!" A driver from

Nova Scotia, who admitted that she only had three months' experience behind the wheel, hit the gas pedal instead of the brake while trying to park in front of the store, in angled spaces provided for shoppers along Kent Street. Luckily, only manneqquins suffered dismemberment in the "run-in."

In all of these stores, Atlantic Canadians came to appreciate Eaton's throughout the year. Like Eaton stores in other parts of Canada, the holidays were special times and even drew people from small towns into the cities just to experience the special atmosphere the store took on to celebrate Christmas. Wayne Beal, from Midgic, New Brunswick, about forty miles east of Moncton, recalls the magic of Eaton's at Christmas and the impression it made on him:

I first knew about Eaton's from their catalogue, from which my mother ordered all of our back-to-school clothes and Christmas presents. Of course, last year's catalogue ended up in the outhouse, where it was reread and inspired many a young boys' dreams. "Wouldn't it be nice to have that nice new bike or those new skates?"

One day just before Christmas, when I was around thirteen years old, my dad took us all to Moncton to Eaton's. The Christmas decorations and displays thrilled and amazed my sister and brother (who were about seven and eight at the time) and me, too. We spent the biggest part of the day shopping for Christmas presents, while enjoying all those eye-catching displays, bright lights and, of course, all those things on display that we could only dream of owning.

I remember the thing, though, that I found the most intriguing and spent much time watching were those vacuum tubes that the clerks used to send receipts and cash up to the store offices. They were made of clear pipes, and you could see the little shuttles speeding along until they were out of sight. I thought at the time they looked like rats scurrying along through the pipes; such are the thoughts of a thirteen-year-old farm boy. I'm almost seventy-two now, and those memories are as vivid today as when they were enjoyed by a thirteen-year-old lad.

With all these stores, Eaton's easily took on the role of a Canadian retail icon in Atlantic Canada, and significantly, its presence there marked not only early expansion but also the very moment when the T. Eaton Co. truly became the "Trans-Canada Store."

Steel Away

It is our belief that the entry of Eaton's into the Hamilton retail field will help to make this city a still greater shopping centre than it has already become, and will thereby contribute something to the growth and development of business generally.
—R.Y. Eaton

Eaton's came to Hamilton, "Steel Capital of Canada," in 1927, but its involvement in the so-called Bay City at the west end of Lake Ontario began much earlier. Not far from Toronto (actually about seventy kilometres to the southwest), Eaton's was well known in Hamilton due to its catalogue. In 1915, the company opened a factory, the T. Eaton Knitting Co., in Hamilton, and eventually an order office and showroom were added.

Both a teeming metropolis and an industrial powerhouse, Hamilton had already developed a thriving retail core long before Eaton's considered opening a retail store there. Department stores such as the Right House, founded in 1843 as the Thomas C. Watkins Company, and Robinson's, founded by George W. Robinson in 1899, set the tone for the retail district, which was located on South James Street and the Gore Park area of King Street, two major thoroughfares that defined the centre of Hamilton.

A third business, the Arcade Limited, was named after the old office and theatre building it occupied when it opened its door for the first time in 1911. When Hamiltonian J.P. Whalen sought to convert the building into the city's largest department store, he found few investors willing to buy into his vision. In a bold move, he offered shares in his business venture to anyone who could afford to buy them. From the time it opened, the store went from strength to strength because, according to Whalen, it was "[o]wned by Hamiltonians, operated by Hamiltonians, for the benefit of Hamiltonians, and not for the benefit of any private owner."

When the store expanded along James Street in 1915 by acquiring and remodeling the adjacent Griffin Theatre, the *Hamilton Herald* hailed the business, noting that "for an example of what courage, foresight, and energy will do, the people of Hamilton have but to visit The Arcade Limited." A further expansion added a six-storey section along James Street all the way to the corner of Merrick Street. Hamilton's retail district, although it developed primarily south of King Street, was beginning to move northward.

In 1927, the Arcade Limited was put up for sale, and Eaton's wasted no time in purchasing it, on account of the success in the small salesroom at its well-established factory. The sale was announced on June 2, 1927, and

A 1950s view of the Hamilton Eaton's store shows the original Arcade structure and the narrow addition that Eaton's added in 1929 on the right. *Archives of Ontario: T. Eaton Fonds F229. Used with the permission of Sears Canada Ltd.*

the store was converted to the Eaton's nameplate three weeks later, on June 22. Nine months earlier, Eaton's had instituted a citywide delivery service, provided by fine Hackney horses and beautifully liveried wagons, to support the little showroom at the company's knitting mill.

Appropriately enough, the grand opening on that June day was begun with a parade of delivery vehicles, led by three of Eaton's famous Hackneys—Prince Albert, Commander and Knight Commander. Their claim to fame lay in the fact that they had never failed to win first prize at the CNE and the Royal Canadian Winter Fair. More compelling, perhaps, for shoppers was the huge bargain sale held to clear older Arcade merchandise so that the store could be fully restocked with the grade of merchandise long presented in the company's other stores. Eaton's also announced that it would be making major changes in the store to bring it in line with its other operations, such as installing a sporting goods department and opening a catalogue order desk in the building. In addition, the small retail store at the knitting mill would cease operation on account of the new store.

Eaton's lavishly decorated the outside of the building for the event, and the *Hamilton Spectator* reported that "the flags fluttering in the breeze" set the tone for what it called a "gala occasion." The pomp and circumstance of the event was not confined to the exterior, as reported by the newspaper:

> *The inside was gaily decorated with a profusion of flowers, indicative of the lively and sympathetic interest which the Eaton family elsewhere is taking in the new arrival to the Eaton merchandising household here. There were baskets of flowers from the staff of the Toronto store, the Montréal store, the Winnipeg store and western staffs, the Eaton Knitting Company, the Hamilton Spectator, Manager A.E. Carter of the Royal Connaught hotel, and the staff of the Hamilton store. Those of the shoppers to-day who had been regular Arcade patrons must have recognized vast changes in the interior of the store even in the short space of time which has elapsed since the sale to the Eaton Company was consummated, there seems to be a different atmosphere everywhere.*

Reporting that the store was "absolutely jammed" on opening day and that "[i]t is doubtful if such large crowds have ever been seen in a local store," the *Spectator* also informed customers of the changes that Eaton's planned for the future, including extending the retail area of the store to all six floors and basement of the structure, made possible by the downsizing of stockrooms due to the proximity of the Toronto warehouse facilities. It also predicted that the store would benefit Hamilton with increased business in the city, brought about by the "Eaton prestige and reputation" that drew many of the out-of-towners who mingled with Hamiltonians on that day.

Attending the event were Margaret Eaton, Timothy Eaton's eighty-seven-year-old widow, and President R.Y. Eaton, who confirmed that the welcome given to the small store on John Street and the extended delivery service were primary factors in the Eaton's decision to purchase the Arcade Limited and operate a large main store in Hamilton. R.Y. pronounced himself "highly pleased" with the response of Hamiltonians to the store and noted that departmental managers were well satisfied with the sales volume on that busy morning.

Among Hamilton's department stores, all of which remained popular and admired institutions for many years, Eaton's reigned supreme in the "Steel Capital of Canada," enjoying ever-expanding sales and the admiration of its customers for its typically large and wide-ranging selections, special events and its sixth-floor Green Room restaurant. Within a year of opening, Eaton's purchased a strip of land from the City of Hamilton and built a six-floor addition, which extended the store one bay along the city's popular market square, with its open-air stalls. The long, narrow structure, completed in March 1929, added forty thousand square feet to the existing store but featured a Neo-Georgian–style façade whose brick, stone detailing and small, paired windows contrasted with the old structure, which was a Chicago-style commercial building with clear articulation of its structural skeleton and expansive window bays that resulted from it.

When Eaton's acquired the Canadian Department Stores Limited in May 1928, the transaction included a small department store in Hamilton that had been known as T.H. Pratt Limited prior to amalgamating with twenty other retailers to form the failing CDS chain. With its enormous investment in the James Street Eaton's store, the company decided not to continue CDS operations in Hamilton, and the former Pratt store was quietly closed.

Before it celebrated ten years in Hamilton, Eaton's had reconfigured the interior of its store, doubled the number of elevators and replaced the primarily horse-drawn delivery fleet with twenty-one shiny new trucks. The staff of the store had doubled in size during this period, a statistic that supported the growing reputation for fine customer service that came to be a hallmark of Eaton's, not just in Hamilton but across the expanding organization as well. Under the slogan of "Marching Along Together," Eaton's brought its "Goods Satisfactory or Money Refunded" guarantee to

The sliver-like addition to Eaton's faced Hamilton's expansive market to the west, and although the façade was completely out of character with the older parts of the store, it did provide a handsome backdrop for the buying and selling that went on in the sheds and stalls next door. *Archives of Ontario: T. Eaton Fonds F229. Used with the permission of Sears Canada Ltd.*

Hamilton, along with personal service and the dependability for which the store was renowned.

In the 1930s, a defining feature of Hamilton's Eaton store was instituted. As a promotional strategy, Eaton's entered into a forty-week contract with local radio station CKOC to air a children's radio show entitled *Eaton's Good Deed Radio Club*, which began in February 1933. The brainchild of Claude Knapman, who led the club, the show aired on Saturday mornings and encouraged children to

> *Do A Good Deed every day, Obey the golden rule—*
> *Never say an angry word or be unkind or cruel.*
> *Scatter seeds of happiness at home, at play, at school*
> *And you'll find there's sunshine everywhere, Obey the Golden Rule.*

The program, which could be watched live at the station's downtown Hamilton studios as well, encouraged the character growth of its members by focusing on their good deeds and acts of kindness and provided prizes to the children with the most remarkable examples of them. In addition, *Eaton's Good Deed Radio Club* showcased amateur talent and eventually developed its own choral group and orchestra. Special occasions were held for the young crowd at Hamilton's Palace Theatre, which included an annual Halloween Theatre Party, the "Welcome to Santa Theatre Party," Boy Scout Day and an annual birthday extravaganza to celebrate the anniversary of the club's formation. Kite and model airplane contests were well patronized, and memorable activities also sponsored by the club.

Margaret Houghton—distinguished author, historian and archivist of the local history collection of the Hamilton Public Library—considers the *Good Deed Radio Club* to be one of Eaton's most unique retail innovations. "It really was a nice gesture toward children," she says. "Kids got prizes for doing good things, and the program supported efforts of parents to develop their children's character. It was so popular it was eventually exported to Eaton's in Winnipeg, Edmonton, Calgary and Vancouver."

In spite of the original contract with CKOC, the show ran for more than twenty years. During this time, more than 200,000 children became members, and the club awarded 2,700 gold star pins for good deeds. Hollywood star Gale Sherwood (née Jacqueline Nutt) was born in Hamilton and performed on the *Good Deed Radio Club* for more than three years before going to California, where she starred in several television shows and movies and ultimately gained fame by singing with Nelson Eddy for almost fifteen years.

The *Hamilton Spectator* reported that the 20th Anniversary Theatre Party on March 7, 1953, was elaborate and well attended and that the club had fifteen thousand members in its final year; nevertheless, the whole affair had become too expensive to justify its marketing and publicity value. After a memorable, twenty-year run, Eaton's pulled the plug on the *Good Deed Radio Club*.

In September 1938, along with a remodeled third floor, Eaton's opened the Mayfair Shop, which caused a sensation among fashion-conscious shoppers. In a setting that the *Spectator* described as "a shrine of fashion worthy of the lovely things there displayed," high-style fashion was promoted with aplomb. The newspaper reported that the new shop housed "exclusive models in gowns, coats, and accessories," and that "judging from the inquiries already made about the Mayfair Shop, its services will fill a

In 1957, Eaton's opened a new addition to the Hamilton flagship. Part of a larger scheme that never materialized, the addition took into account a desired widening of James Street and bore a thoroughly modern façade. *Archives of Ontario: T. Eaton Fonds F229. Used with the permission of Sears Canada Ltd.*

long-felt need among women of the city." The Mayfair Shop carried the type of exclusive merchandise that Hamiltonians could only obtain by travelling to Toronto in the past, but it was also noted in the *Spectator* article that "numerous [articles of clothing] are ticketed at prices astonishingly moderate." The Mayfair name went on to be used in many other Eaton stores, particularly in Ontario.

The store engaged in a unique improvement program in 1940 when the floor of its ancient basement (that once housed a wine cellar) was lowered to provide a consistent and continuous lower-level salesroom that included a bargain basement. The company also initiated a 140-space customer parking lot on the block north of the store.

In 1956, Eaton's announced an expansion and modernization program that foretold the demolition of the old, four-storey of the portion of the store, to be replaced with a six-storey retail structure and a re-facing of the whole complex to match it, giving Eaton's in Hamilton a modern, windowless appearance. The project envisioned that by 1960, Eaton's 400,000-square-foot store would sprawl along James Street, requiring the demolition of Hamilton's 1890s-era city hall and its familiar clock tower. In the event, only a six-storey addition to the store was built on a small parcel between the original Arcade Building and the old city hall to the south.

The $3 million addition—in a modern, horizontal style set back from James Street, with a wide marquee shading the first floor's expansive show windows—was, according to *Spectator* columnist Milford L. Smith, "a scintillating combination of immaculate Indiana limestone, black granite trim and sweeping panels of alternate light and grey-faced steel." Smith reported on his stroll through the store, and although he admitted that he was "among the City Hall lovers whose sentimental links with the past influenced a desire to see it preserved," he ended the article by admitting that a vision of "Eaton's of the 1960s" caused the well-loved city hall to appear "less haughty, more dingy, and certainly an anachronism in Hamilton's changing downtown."

Although Smith's vision never really materialized, as Eaton's focused on suburban development throughout the 1960s, the old city hall came down in 1961. Ten years later, Eaton's did expand as a first phase of Lloyd D. Jackson Square, the urban renewal project that replaced the well-loved old building, clock tower and all. The store occupied a two-storey "pavilion" that housed expanded men's wear shops, including the new 43 James, a fashion shop named after the pavilion's street address.

While Eaton's conception of a completely new, modern store never actually materialized in Hamilton, it didn't matter—Eaton's was as appreciated as a shopping mecca in the Bay City as it was in any other Canadian town. A special ten-day "Canadiana Showcase," focusing on Canadian-made products, was held at Eaton's in the 1960s. The event, opened by Canadian postmaster general Ellen Fairclough, featured displays of the work of Canadian manufacturers and artisans, fashion shows and a sixth-floor theatre that presented National Film Board productions.

Over the years, Eaton's old store was a familiar landmark in Hamilton, especially with its large, overhanging sign, which could be seen clearly from down the street. *Archives of Ontario: T. Eaton Fonds F229. Used with the permission of Sears Canada Ltd.*

Such one-of-a-kind events undeniably attracted Hamiltonians to the James Street landmark, but Eaton's endeared them on a day-to-day basis with its enormous stocks, high quality and its own inimitable style. Whether because of its lovely Christmas windows, like the five tableaux that presented the story of the Nativity in 1950, or a slice of butterscotch pie in the Green Room, Eaton's became an undeniable favourite in Hamilton.

At Eaton stores all over Canada, though, it wasn't only store-sponsored special events that the public remembers. Margaret Houghton's recollection of the Hamilton store during her time at university in 1972 serves to prove this fact, as well as shed light on a single event the likes of which was probably repeated countless times over in many of the company's stores: "The one distinct memory I have is that I was in Eaton's one day when the loudspeaker came on and announced that Paul Henderson had just scored the winning goal in the Canada-Russia hockey series—of course the whole store cheered."

Likewise, Janice Holden remembers the Hamilton store fondly and enjoys sharing one occasion that stands out for her:

> *I have a memory of shopping at Eaton's in Hamilton in the 1980s. The Eaton brothers, John Craig and Frederik Stefan were in the store during the holiday season to wish the staff a very Merry Christmas. They shook my hand and it was magical. The store was so beautiful, and I could always find what I wanted there.*

As Hamilton expanded, Eaton's did too, opening a 122,000-square-foot store at Eastgate in Stoney Creek on April 4, 1973, and a slightly larger one at the Burlington Mall across the bay in February 1975. Advance publicity for the Burlington store specifically emphasized the fashion focus of the new branch. Speaking at a chamber of commerce luncheon in advance of the store's opening, Ontario stores general manager Hugh Clarkson said, "We have taken the concept of fashion to every possible segment of the selling floor" and also revealed what customers could expect at the new store, from the new Abstract and Attitude shops to the store's Cherry Orchard restaurant.

When it did open, the event was still full of ceremony; John Craig Eaton chose the "first shopper" (Mrs. Leisje Degnaar, accompanied by her five-year-old daughter, Tina), who received a bouquet of roses before Eaton invited the crowd, primarily of "women shoppers with definite tastes who are extremely fashion-conscious" to "come in, everybody, shop!"

Eaton's many stores in Ontario spread the retail operation throughout the province just as the cherished catalogue did for the company in general. In August 1927, Eaton's announced that it had leased space in the Higgins Block in Niagara Falls for a new store. However, establishment of a department store in the famous resort city had to wait until February 1929, when a branch of the Canadian Department Stores was opened on the corner of Victoria and Morrison Streets in a three-storey brick commercial structure.

Eaton's Niagara Falls store opened as a branch of the Canadian Department Stores Limited, but like many other such stores, it eventually took on the Eaton nameplate. *Archives of Ontario: T. Eaton Fonds F229. Used with the permission of Sears Canada Ltd.*

The Victoria Street building, although built of deep red-brown brick with stone accents, resembled the Eaton style of the day, with arched second-floor windows arranged in groups of two and three with similar but flat-topped openings on the floor above. The largest commercial building in Niagara Falls when it opened, the store shared space in the building with an Eaton Groceteria and Walker's Drug Store, but by the time it became an Eaton's store in 1949, the Groceteria had been replaced by a catalogue order office.

Nearby, in St. Catharines, Eaton's acquired the premises of the well-regarded local retailer McLaren & Co. Limited in the 1928 CDS acquisition. McLaren's occupied a group of small, three-storey Italianate commercial buildings at 19–21 St. Paul Street on the corner of William Street, in the area known as the Gore (widening) of St. Paul Street, where commerce flourished from the time of the city's founding. The Canadian Department Stores Limited modernized the store after Eaton's took control, but the whole complex was destroyed by a massive fire in March 1936.

While the ruins, brought about by what the *St. Catharines Standard* called "the most disastrous conflagration in many years," still smouldered, Eaton's, at its Toronto headquarters, quickly made the decision to rebuild at the same site. Residents of the so-called Garden City waited while a new building rose to take the place of the ancient store with which they had become so familiar. On January 27, 1937, the ubiquitous R.Y. Eaton

A streamlined new store executed in brick replaced the burnt-out premises of the Canadian Department Stores in St. Catharines, Ontario, after a disastrous 1936 fire. *Archives of Ontario: T. Eaton Fonds F229. Used with the permission of Sears Canada Ltd.*

was in town to open the store, which itself was a complete break from the past. A glistening, modern, brick-sheathed Art Deco design with a broad, protective marquee, the store was, in its sheer élan and newness, unlike anything else in the area. The newspaper reported that the remarks uttered by the opening day crowd as it flowed through the doors included "beautiful," "how lovely," "something of which St. Catharines can be justly proud" and "a change marking a new era in the city." Furthermore, it informed its readers:

> *The crowds visited every section of the spacious store. They descended to the basement after wandering about the main floor and later ascended to the second floor, finding each a revelation in modern store appointments with a collection of merchandise unsurpassed in the district. The visitors marvelled at the change which has been wrought by modern construction and lighting facilities. It was a delight merely to walk through the store viewing the furnishings and the displays and the fine assortment of merchandise assembled from near and far.*

Like other former CDS stores, the St. Catharines branch was rebranded as an Eaton store in 1949. The forty-thousand-square-foot store served the community well, but the nearby Pen Centre drew customers from downtown

St. Catharines as it expanded from a strip of retail known as the Niagara Peninsula Centre into the fourth-largest shopping centre in Canada. Simpsons-Sears joined the mall in 1966, and in January 1972, when it was announced that it would add yet another anchor store, speculation focused on Eaton's joining the Pen Centre lineup. It was initially expected that the St. Paul Street store, only one-third the size of the new one, would remain in operation as well. Later in the year, though, Eaton's let it be known that it would close the downtown store and operate the suburban location exclusively, but it softened the blow by announcing that the new store would have amenities like a beer garden–style restaurant and a beauty salon.

When the Pen Centre store opened on April 23, 1973, it, like the store it replaced, brought a new world of retail to the Niagara peninsula. Its King's Court restaurant was among the first in the Eaton family to serve beer and wine, although Manager J.D. Gilmour told the *Standard* that the College Street Store's Round Room had been serving alcohol for some time and that the store was "ditching old fashioned taboos" held by Timothy Eaton. He did note, however, that cigarettes and tobacco were still not to be found in any Eaton store. The success of the Pen Centre store was not surprising given the already-popular location. St. Catharines resident Sandra Enskat recounts that "[m]y husband and I have wonderful memories of shopping at Eaton's in the Pen Centre—we were married in September, right around the time that Eaton's would hold its Trans-Canada sale. We have always had a fondness for new towels and bedding, so we would be sure and attend the sale and at least look at all the new things—and we usually ended up treating ourselves to something nice!"

Twenty-five miles west of Hamilton, in Brantford, Ontario, the birthplace of the telephone and former home of Alexander Graham Bell, Eaton's appropriated the firm of Ogilvie-Lochead Limited in the 1928 CDS deal. Founded in 1891, Ogilvie-Lochead occupied a four-storey building in the city's core on Colborne Street. The steep slope to the banks of the Grand River gave the store an additional level fronting on Water Street to the south. As a Canadian Department Store under Eaton management, the business flourished and had to be expanded by taking over the shop to the west of the original building.

Opposite: Eaton's 1973 Pen Centre branch was notable as one of the first Eaton stores to serve beer and wine in its restaurant. Branches near Hamilton were opened in the Eastgate Shopping Centre in Stoney Creek and Burlington Mall in 1975. *Archives of Ontario: T. Eaton Fonds F229. Used with the permission of Sears Canada Ltd.*

Burlington

Eastgate

Pen Centre

EATON'S

After World War II, the anticipation of peacetime prosperity and growth led Eaton's to seek a new home for the store, which it found in the 1916 Arcade Building. The building, in a brick-faced Edwardian commercial style, was located across Colborne Street at the corner of Queen Street. The Arcade had been home to a variety of shops and businesses, including a bowling alley and a "meeting place" known as the "Jungle Room."

Eaton's purchased the building and renovated it with a new corner entrance and a stone façade at ground level. On October 30, 1947, the new CDS opened, but the name was short-lived—like other local outlets of the company, it became a full-fledged Eaton branch in July 1949. Incidentally, the old Ogilvie-Lochead location went on to serve as the Brantford branch of Hamilton's popular Right House for many years.

Around the time that Eaton's purchased the Canadian Department Stores Limited, R.Y. Eaton announced that the store would locate a TECO branch in Kitchener, about forty miles northwest of Hamilton. Commenting on the store's opening in the former premises of the Lang and Treacy Co. Limited at 57 King Street West, R.Y. said that Eaton's hadn't ever considered Kitchener for a branch location until the older store became available. Interestingly, before World War I, Kitchener was known as Berlin, on account of the large population that had relocated there from Germany. Eaton's became aware of the availability of the Lang and Treacy store and, due to its size, decided that its smaller TECO format was more appropriate to the operation. A few years later, in the early 1930s, the store came under the banner of the Canadian Department Stores Limited.

The CDS store in Kitchener was very successful, and after World War II, Eaton's sought out expanded facilities for the operation. When the new store—a modern, three-storey, sixty-thousand-square-foot building at King and Water Streets—opened, it proudly carried the Eaton's name into Kitchener for the first time. In fact, the Canadian Department Stores name was dropped chain-wide, and those locations that hadn't already taken the Eaton name were converted, giving the parent company a number of branch stores in smaller markets all across Ontario.

An ad in the *Ottawa Citizen* around the time of the name change was similar to others across Ontario and the Maritimes. It informed readers

Opposite: The interior of Eaton's 1947 Brantford store (top) gives an idea of what Eaton shopping was like in the former Canadian Department Stores, which changed names in 1949. A new sign on the 1947 Brantford store announced to the world that the four-floor store had become an Eaton's branch. *Archives of Ontario: T. Eaton Fonds F229. Used with the permission of Sears Canada Ltd.*

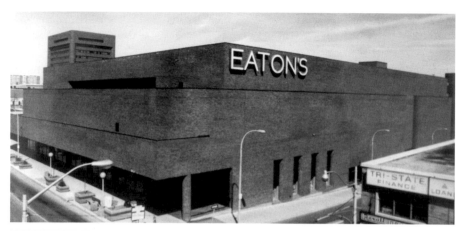

Eatons gave up its modern and popular 1949 store (bottom) on the western side of Kitchener's downtown for a much larger location in the city's new Market Square development in 1973 (top). *Archives of Ontario: T. Eaton Fonds F229. Used with the permission of Sears Canada Ltd.*

that it had been twenty-one years since Eaton's had acquired the Canadian Department Stores Limited, and to celebrate their "coming of age," they would be henceforward known as branches of the T. Eaton Co. During those twenty-one years, the small-town facilities were improved, expanded and brought up to Eaton standards, so by then the name change was mere evidence of a *fait accompli*.

Back in Kitchener, Eaton's became an extremely popular shopping destination and was considered a top performer in the chain. In 1965, $500,000 was spent to remodel the store and bring its merchandising up to date. A bright, white coat of paint and signs sporting the store's new logo beckoned customers, but it soon became undeniable: the store was too small for the market it served. By the 1970s, Eaton's sought larger premises to accommodate the increase in business that it experienced in Kitchener.

After studying alternatives, including a suburban store in Kitchener's Fairview Park mall, Eaton's partnered with Edmonton developer Oxlea Investments Limited to replace Kitchener's ancient but beautiful city hall and popular farmers' market with a modern complex consisting of a shopping mall, new space for the market, a parking garage and a huge, 197,000-square-foot Eaton's store. Opening on October 3, 1973, the big new store was the largest retail outlet in the whole Kitchener-Waterloo region.

Originally designed by architect John Lingwood in concrete, the building was ultimately faced in a red-brown brick as a nod to Kitchener's history and the heritage buildings nearby. The mall's interior was likewise softened by the application of colourful Pennsylvania Dutch hex designs executed by artist Douglas Ratchford. However positive, these adjustments to the design did not erase memories of the handsome old city hall, or its surrounding park, which were regrettably destroyed for the Market Square complex, although fragments of the historic landmark were moved to other locations in town.

It was the Eaton store itself that garnered a great deal of press at the time, due not just to its dimensions but to the amenities provided within, as well as to Eaton's always intriguing merchandising presentations, which were described by the *Kitchener-Waterloo Record*:

> *Although the store is huge by comparison with any other outlet in the vicinity, it will look cosy and intimate through the use of vibrant colour schemes, rich woods, boutique-like departments, room groupings, and props such as gazebos. In the event someone faints or is trampled down at the opening, the management and staff will be ready. The store is equipped with a medical centre on the third floor, complete with two beds and a registered nurse… The store is also equipped with 168 telephones, 10 main trunk lines, and 5 direct lines to Toronto. All under the same roof, customers will be able to buy an airline ticket, obtain insurance or invest in mutual funds, have their eyes examined, have their hair styled (for both sexes) at two different locations, furnish a home from top to bottom, buy a live fish, hamster or bird, and have lunch at a stand-up bar or a sit-down restaurant.*

Five years later, on October 19, 1978, Eaton's opened a smaller branch store in nearby Waterloo's Westmount Place shopping centre. The sixty-three-thousand-square-foot store replaced a vacant Sayvette discount outlet, and the $2 million investment to remodel and reconfigure the store was credited with saving the shopping centre, whose tenants began to flee when Sayvette closed fifteen months earlier. Although relatively small, Eaton's management assured customers that any merchandise that couldn't be found at the new store could be quickly dispatched from the larger one in nearby Kitchener.

The former CDS stores were, in most cases, major anchors of downtown shopping districts throughout Ontario. Chatham, in southwest Ontario, favoured the department store business of Chas. Austin Limited from the time of its founding by Charles Austin in 1895. The store eventually came to be located on the southwest corner of King Street and Market Square, where it occupied five Italianate buildings that took up half a city block. Although it called itself the "Store with the Stock," it was also renowned for its early development of customer services like credit plans, a delivery service and in-store restaurants. Its values were hinted at by its slogan, "It Pays to Trade at Austin's." By the time it became a part of the Canadian Department Stores Limited, Austin's covered more than a half a city block in the historic centre of Chatham. Its success continued under Eaton management, and when the chain-wide name change occurred in 1949, Eaton's wasted no time remodeling the store with a modern façade similar to the then new Kitchener store.

Eaton's was popular and profitable enough in Chatham to escape the 1960s downsizing that saw the T. Eaton Co. close many of its former CDS stores in small Ontario towns, but even that only lasted for about ten years until the store was shuttered in early 1975.

Another branch that remained in the Eaton galaxy for many years (in fact, until 1999) despite its small size was the original Beamish and Smith store in the Muskoka Lakes resort town (and gateway to Algonquin Park), Huntsville, Ontario. Often as busy in July as other Eaton's stores were at Christmastime, the store, on the southwest corner of Main and West Streets, also remained open long after other former CDS stores were deemed anachronistic. Its longevity is often credited to its proximity to the Muskoka retreats of the Eaton family, and this in spite of the fact that the building that housed it once served as the town morgue! Although it was modernized like other small-town Eaton stores, its mid-century façade covered a creaking frame of Douglas fir that served as the structural support for the ancient building.

Eaton's acquired a very popular location in Chatham, Ontario, when it bought the Canadian Department Stores Limited. As an Eaton store, it was later modernized beyond recognition (inset). *Archives of Ontario: T. Eaton Fonds F229. Used with the permission of Sears Canada Ltd.*

The Huntsville store's modern exterior gave no hint of the ancient wooden structure behind the up-to-date 1942 façade. *Archives of Ontario: T. Eaton Fonds F229. Used with the permission of Sears Canada Ltd.*

Eaton's policies, management and merchandising turned the CDS chain around in spite of the depression. It even expanded in Ontario, replacing outmoded facilities with new, variation-on-a-theme Eaton-style stores for CDS outlets in Sault Ste. Marie, North Bay and Peterborough, Ontario, in the early 1930s. The design elements of these buildings take cues from the architecture of Eaton's western expansion into Saskatchewan and Alberta in the late 1920s. North Bay was the first of the former CDS stores to be replaced with a modern branch in the then current Eaton mode.

In April 1929, Canadian Department Stores Limited informed the public in one of its ads in the *North Bay Nugget* that "[i]t won't be long now. In a short time North Bay and district will witness the opening of a store that will be the pride of the North Country," and that they would soon enjoy shopping at "[a] new store in every respect—a handsome new building, new, up-to-date fixtures, and an entirely fresh, new, well-assorted stock of reliable merchandise—all backed by the large purchasing power of The T. Eaton Co. Limited." On April 9, the ancient Beamish and Smith store building was superseded with a new store on Main Street that displayed many architectural elements common to the big Calgary and Saskatoon stores of the same period, but on a much smaller basis. The popularity of the store and its value to North Bay customers is illustrated by its expansion on two occasions after the changeover to the Eaton's nameplate in 1949, first when a large, modern one-floor extension gave the store a presence to the rear on McIntyre Street and, later, when a second floor was added to that annex.

On October 29, 1931, the Canadian Department Stores opened a similar but more capacious branch store in Sault Ste. Marie to replace the premises occupied by its predecessor, Bryans Limited. Located on Queen Street, the new, buff-coloured brick building was designed to carry five additional floors if expansion became necessary. At the time of the opening, Eaton's scored points in the Sault by deeding some of its property back to the city for the widening of March Street, which was improved all the way down to the all-important boat terminals on the city's waterfront.

In Peterborough, Ontario, in 1932, Eaton's vacated the old store once operated by the Cressman Co. Limited and moved to a new building at 312–318 George Street North. The new store, diagonally across from Peterborough's landmark clock tower, mimicked the design of the earlier CDS stores in North Bay and Sault Ste. Marie, but in a much more restrained and austere manner.

The Sudbury store at the corner of Durham and Larch Streets in the "Nickel Capital of Canada" was a place of memories and was a favourite of

The 1929 North Bay store displayed the typical triplets of stone-trimmed Roman-arch windows, while the newer extension to the back was clearly in the 1950s style. *Archives of Ontario: T. Eaton Fonds F229. Used with the permission of Sears Canada Ltd.*

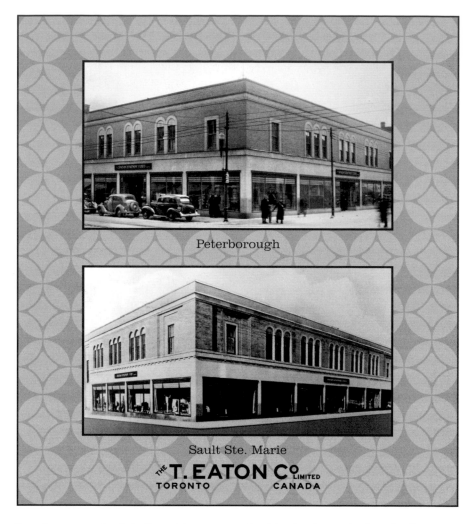

Peterborough

Sault Ste. Marie

Eaton's spent much of the Depression years modernizing local stores in Ontario. Shown are the new 1932 Peterborough (top) and 1931 Sault Ste. Marie (bottom) stores. *Archives of Ontario: T. Eaton Fonds F229. Used with the permission of Sears Canada Ltd.*

the shopping public in the city north of Thunder Bay. Hugh Kruzel shopped at Eaton's in Toronto and Winnipeg, but his fondest recollections surround the old store he grew up with:

> *It was our almost weekly exposure to the Sudbury store that is in my memories most. Toys were down a broad creaking staircase; the department was big enough to entertain and delight with each visit and I lusted after*

models of metal and then plastic. It was the mid- and late '60s—the Vietnam War, rising college unrest and "flower power"—yet my mother was not alone wearing gloves when she took us downtown. What a contrast to the parade of miniskirts and colourful nylons that was creating such a societal stir. The toy section was a treat after dental, doctors' or being dragged to the post office or bank. Do I recall the fragrance of downstairs or the staff? Sadly, no. But my imagination was unleashed as I picked up boxes depicting air battles, ships at sea and an emerging stock of hotrods and spacecraft. The possibility of the Neil Armstrong rising on Gemini above a tail of flame—and maybe even someone reaching towards Luna—was surpassed suddenly by a bulky box of the Enterprise featuring an appropriately alien galaxy. Was I in the store when Kennedy was shot? Perhaps. Certainly, on Remembrance Day at 11:00 a.m., the store stopped. It could just be misty memory, but I think the lights went off, the elevator halted and the floor was silent. It was such an exciting time, and Eaton's was part of it.

Eaton's Sudbury store on the corner of Durham and Larch Streets in Sudbury served as the store of Stafford Limited before becoming a branch of the Canadian Department Stores Limited and, ultimately, an Eaton store before being superseded by the Sudbury City Centre in 1975. *Archives of Ontario: T. Eaton Fonds F229. Used with the permission of Sears Canada Ltd.*

The 1938 replacement for the old, four-storey I.L. Matthews store in Port Arthur (now Thunder Bay), Ontario, was so radical a break with the past that the company chose to convert it to a complete Eaton's store by the time it opened. The first announcement regarding Eaton's plans occurred on January 28, 1938, when it became known that the T. Eaton Co. Limited had purchased the Campbell Block in Port Arthur—bound by Arthur Street, Court Street and Park Avenue—with the intention of razing the existing buildings and constructing a new facility for the Canadian Department Stores Limited branch it operated since 1928.

The next day, Eaton's, from its Toronto headquarters, confirmed in a press release that it would commence work on the new store as soon as the existing properties were vacated and that it hoped to have the store in operation before the end of the year. The first sod was turned on April 19, 1938, and after a remarkable seven-month period of construction, Port Arthur's new Eaton store opened on October 12 of the same year, just as had been promised.

The work of Winnipeg architect Arthur E. Cubbidge, the streamlined store, a startling example of the austere but luxurious Art Deco style of the 1930s, embodied the optimism of a brief era between depression and world war. Eaton's ad in the *Fort William Daily Times-Journal* called attention to the fact that the new store with a new name was able to provide expanded services such as a coffee bar, optical service and watch repair along with merchandise selections hitherto impossible in the older store, all "with Service to Fill Modern Requirements in the Most Modern Manner."

The paper boldly described Eaton's opening, detailing the store's appearance and amenities as if it had just been sent down from heaven:

> *Streamlined—that is the word that leaps to the lips at the first view of the T. Eaton Co. Limited new building in Port Arthur. The same term recurs again and again as a tour of the store is made. The exterior of the building presents an appearance unusual in this area. Plain almost to the point of severity, the walls are composed of black Québec granite topped by white Tyndall stone. A row of display windows takes up almost the entire first story wall facing on Arthur and Court streets. Polished stainless steel frames to the windows as a touch of brightness. The severity of the walls is relieved further by the marquees, faced in stainless steel and lighted, hung over the entrances...A pleasing feature of the design is the rounded corner. A large window at the corner on the second floor, following the line of the curve, is a striking inset in the wall.*

Over the years, the popularity of the Port Arthur (later Thunder Bay) store caused expansions to occur from time to time, but the streamlined, rounded corner remained as a symbol of Eaton's presence on the Canadian Lakehead. *Archives of Ontario: T. Eaton Fonds F229. Used with the permission of Sears Canada Ltd.*

The bright, modern interior was enriched by the use of deep-toned wood fixtures and trim throughout, in contrast with bright white walls and ceilings. The *Journal-Herald* went to similar lengths to describe the noteworthy store's interior, construction and unique features. Among the latter were an innovative air-cleansing system and a completely concealed vacuum-tube system. The store's interior appointments carried on the streamlined theme in terrazzo flooring, plaster ceilings and richly toned wood finishes. The paper noted:

> *Immediately, it is noticed that nothing juts out into aisles. Corners are rounded or cut off. Walls are plain white, and the columns are made as inconspicuous as possible by the use of the same white plaster. Nothing hangs from the ceiling to mar the effect—lighting is indirect...stairways are ample in size, and carry modernistic ornamental iron railings which harmonize with the general design. High ceilings, especially on the main floor, add to the air of spaciousness which the store gives.*

Section locations were identified in Art Deco–style lettering in keeping with the whole store's harmonious conception, and a ground-floor Groceteria replaced the earlier facility across the street. Even though it was in Ontario, the store was administered from Winnipeg, which was closer than the Toronto headquarters, not to mention due to the demographic similarities between the two locations.

Beth Clarkson Chase, a Thunder Bay resident who says, "For us, Eaton's was truly a family shopping experience," relates an amusing story about her mother, Alice: "She worked in the floor covering department in the basement of the store. And when she started, she took a number of phone calls from people asking to speak to a Mr. Clarkson (who was on holiday). My mom often used colourful language and asked a coworker, 'Just who is this Clarkson asshole?' She was duly informed that he was the department manager, and my mom married him in 1953."

She also tells how her mother, after graduating from business college, returned to Eaton's to work in the payroll department, where she personally delivered the pay cheque of a neighbour, who nightly cleaned Eaton's after it closed for business, so he didn't have to get up and travel downtown just to pick up his due. On another occasion, when the payroll was delayed due to a storm, her mom dutifully went into work on Christmas Day to ensure that the staff was paid for the holidays. Beth herself joined Eaton's at age seventeen, eventually wearing the teal, navy blue and white uniform of a server in the store's Marine Room restaurant. Her aunt, Pearl, and cousin, Marge, were also employed at the store, and it is no surprise that she says that "shopping trips that in any other store would have been a half hour were more like two hours at Eaton's because so many employees would ask about my parents, who were their former coworkers and their friends."

The Port Arthur store's extraordinary popularity and its focus as the centre of the shopping district of the Lakehead area led to its expansion on several occasions. In January 1949, Eaton's formally opened a nine-thousand-square-foot extension of the second floor that allowed "vast and modern improvements designed particularly to increase the scope of service to their customers and at the same time fulfill another planned progressive enlargement of certain popular departments," according to the *Journal-Herald*. Fashion departments on the second floor were expanded, and an enlarged china and gift department was moved to the second floor. As a result of the reorganization, the well-liked coffee bar was moved to the basement and enlarged. A completely new feature of the store was a third-floor penthouse accommodating a fur storage vault.

In 1971, after Port Arthur and Fort William amalgamated to form the new city of Thunder Bay, Ontario, it was announced that Eaton's would spend $3 million to expand its store and build a tiered parking structure, the first element in a wide-ranging urban renewal program promoted by the city to improve the former Port Arthur's downtown area. Other components of the plan included an enclosed shopping mall across Park Avenue, a

In Port Arthur, the Canadian Department Stores name was retired in 1938 when the strikingly modern Eaton's store opened on Court Street. *Archives of Ontario: T. Eaton Fonds F229. Used with the permission of Sears Canada Ltd.*

In 1967, Port Arthur employees, including Victor Tuomi (centre) came to work in period costumes to celebrate Canada's centennial. *Courtesy of June Rysinski.*

multistorey hotel and senior citizen housing. Construction continued until the opening of the enlarged and modernized 115,000-square-foot store, which was celebrated on October 29, 1974. The addition, which included a new Marine Room restaurant, filled in the block behind the original store, and the newer section's box-like form was relieved by recessed entrances and chamfered corners.

In Fort William, the second component of today's Thunder Bay, Eaton's operated a Groceteria on Victoria Avenue (remodeled and renamed a "Foodateria" in 1939) but moved the store to South Syndicate Avenue in 1948 when it added appliances and a catalogue office.

Local author Mark Mullo recalls Eaton's in Port Arthur as "an iconic Canadian business housed in a distinctive location," and quite knowingly, since he often walked there from home with his mother as a youngster. He sums up a life of experience with the store by saying, "Timothy Eaton and his empowering vision for this fruitful company had its own special legacy in Port Arthur, and it is noted that legacies last forever. Thank you very much Mr. Eaton!"

In the same era, Eaton's established a store in the northeastern Ontario gold mining centre of Kirkland Lake. Residents of the small town watched the new building rise throughout 1938, and when it opened on March 20, 1939, it was a revelation in spite of its remote location. The *Northern News* pronounced it "completely new in every detail and design":

> *The new Eaton branch, at the corner of Lebel Avenue and Government Road West, is one of the latest designs catering primarily to the convenience of its customers and the attractive showing of the dozens of articles carried in stock by the company. With their high ceilings, ventilation and heating units, and eye-pleasing indirect lighting of the latest invention, the two storeys contained in the building give only the most healthful of surroundings in which to shop or just examine the various counters and stalls of goods.*

In fact, the exterior of the new store resembled the slightly earlier Port Arthur branch to the south. While the exterior sported a similar streamlined style with a rounded corner, on this occasion the whole composition was executed in brick and located on a sloping site. As a result, its shiny marquee wrapped around the corner, sheltering the sidewalk and proudly carrying the store's name. Its entrance resolved the site's steep change in grade by leading into a mid-level foyer from which customers could take stairs to the main floor or descend to the ground-floor Groceteria.

The paper's articles extolled the virtues of the facility, built by what it called the "old established firm" of T. Eaton Co. Limited, and it mentioned many of Eaton's unique features, such as the store's research bureau and its famous guarantee; it also informed residents that the existing Duncan Street catalogue order office would be henceforth located within the new store.

Eaton's brought high-quality retail service to the northern Ontario gold mining town of Kirkland Lake in 1939. Although executed in brick, its streamlined flair and shiny stainless steel marquee distinguished it among its older Government Road neighbours. *Archives of Ontario: T. Eaton Fonds F229. Used with the permission of Sears Canada Ltd.*

Just as the United States did, Canada developed a planned community dedicated to nuclear research. Deep River, Ontario, two hundred kilometres northwest of Ottawa, was designed in 1944 by architect John Bland to house scientists and researchers from the nearby Chalk River Nuclear Research Laboratories. Later, after World War II, the city developed further and dedicated itself to research on the peaceful use of atomic power. Eaton's was there, first as a branch of the Canadian Department Stores in 1946. Later, the store moved to a handsome, modern branch store in the Deep River shopping centre in 1961.

The importance of an Eaton store in such a remote location is illustrated by Lorraine Seguin's thoughts on how Eaton's affected her life:

> *When I was twelve or so, my mother bought me my first downhill skis from Eaton's…red shiny Arlbergs for Christmas! Before that, I skied down the dump hill in Deep River with my boots or pieces of cardboard! Thus began my long skiing career—I have skied all over the world and love it, but without Eaton's in Deep River, we had little access to such luxuries.*

Although the T. Eaton & Co. opened a Canadian Department Stores branch in the new atomic research town of Deep River in 1946, a more convenient shopping centre location replaced it in 1961. *Archives of Ontario: T. Eaton Fonds F229. Used with the permission of Sears Canada Ltd.*

Eaton's became a household word in Canada on account of its merchandise, values and gospel-like policy of "Goods Satisfactory or Money Refunded." Its catalogue operation took the name to practically every location in the vast country, but it would be easy to underestimate the role that these smaller stores played in bringing Eaton's style and service to the public in a tangible way. They stood as examples of how Eaton's adapted itself to the needs of Canadians living in smaller centres of population. Shortly after the purchase of the Canadian Department Stores Limited, though, an immense development rose in its hometown to show that it did not shy away from its status as the "Greatest Retail Institution in the British Empire" either.

The Old College Try

We have imparted to the design sufficient of the modern spirit to make it both intelligible and attractive to those who seek change and the evolution of new ideas.
—Colonel Harry McGee

Nothing in the history of the T. Eaton Co. was as representative of the wealth and optimism of the 1920s as its proposal to build a gigantic new store topped by a soaring tower to house the company headquarters, a short distance to the north of its traditional location at Yonge and Queen Streets in downtown Toronto. Rumours that "something was up" on the blocks bounded by Yonge, College, Bay and Hayter Streets had circulated for years, as Eaton's quietly assembled parcels of land on and around these blocks.

In fact, the property had been acquired and all was ready to proceed with a new store at College and Yonge Streets when Sir John Craig Eaton's edict to "stop the College Street Building until we win the war" was issued. During and after the war, rumours bristled about the disposition of the property. Idle talk within city hall pointed to the fact that Eaton's was behind a proposal to build the store, and the *Toronto Globe* carried a headline predicting "Big Departmental to Be All-Canadian" above a 1916 article about the issue. City hall had received a proposal to build a store on the property, and according to H.H. Williams, who represented the anonymous property owner, it was to be "erected of all-Canadian material, with Canadian capital [to prove] that it is not an American concern coming here."

Williams requested on behalf of his client that the city abandon Buchanan Street, which cut the properties in two, and grant a fixed assessment for the property, on which he estimated that the "actual investment when completed will be in the neighbourhood of $20,000,000." For this, the client would donate twenty feet of its properties along Yonge and College streets to the city of Toronto to facilitate widening the thoroughfares to eighty feet. He also pointed out that one piece of property wasn't acquired because the owner, a resident of Detroit, Michigan, "wants $200,000 for that land and we won't pay that for it."

The aldermen discussed the pros and cons of the deal, according to the *Globe*, and the issue was tabled for further discussion, although one alderman, a Mr. Singer, seemed favourable, saying:

> *They offer us the surface rights of this twenty-foot strip and* [if] *we wanted it, we would have to expropriate not just the land underneath but the buildings above. I met with a man last night who said to me that he heard we were going to sell our birthright for a mess of pottage. You'll hear that kind of talk but the people should be shown that this is a straight and simple proposition.*

News about the development stayed fairly quiet for years until July 1928, and when the *Globe* put a sketch of a completely new building on its front page with the headline, "Great Eaton Store Will Be Last Word in Modern Building," the proverbial cat was out of the bag. The article informed readers that the new Eaton store would rise to seven stories in height and contain more than 450,000 square feet of space dedicated to house furnishings, to be moved from Eaton's 1913 annex at the corner of Albert and James Streets. Furthermore, the paper reported that "a feature of this building that will interest citizens is that it will be set back 20 feet from the street line on Yonge, College, Bay and Buchanan streets, to allow widening of any of the streets when thought necessary," and that "the foundations for the building will go down to bedrock, which will provide the strength to carry additional stories when required."

Globe readers were astonished three months later, on October 14, 1928, when the front page carried an even more stunning image of the same structure, this time enlarged to six times its original size and topped with a soaring, thirty-six-storey tower. The article, below the headline "Eaton's Huge Store to Tower 670 Feet Above Street Level," called the building "colossal" at 4,196,000 square feet of floor space and announced that construction, already underway at the southwestern corner of Yonge and College Streets, reflected only one-sixth of the proposed project. It prophesized that "further units will be added, as may be decided upon from year to year, until finally the last work on the tower, which will be two and a quarter times the height of the City Hall, has been completed."

Newspapers kept abreast of the construction progress of the massive undertaking, and by January 1929, the *Globe* was able to report that Eaton's had finally acquired the final lot on the property for $185,000, even though its assessed value was only $54,000. A major event occurred on September 16 of the same year when Lady Eaton and her two daughters, on an inspection tour of the site, became the first women ever to enter the building. After an "exciting" ride up the open construction elevator to take in the view from the seventh floor, which was at the time no more than a deck, she jokingly asked reporters, "Don't you like our rest room?" pointing to the corner of the store that would soon house a restaurant and lounge.

In spite of the levity, Lady Eaton herself was asked questions of an altogether more serious matter. For some time, a new set of rumours about Eaton's viability had swirled about town and had even made it across the Atlantic to the *Villa Natalia* in Florence, Italy, where she was vacationing. A recent article in the *Financial Times* of Montréal alleged that Eaton's was in financial stress, that its directors were mired in discord and that a syndicate, led by a mysterious financier, was preparing to buy a controlling interest in the company.

In a lengthy discourse, Lady Eaton flatly denied the rumours and recounted how her son Timothy, then at University in England, had been informed of them and nervously cabled his mother to see if they were true. According to the *Financial Post*, she said:

> [The statement by the *Financial Times*] *is false from first to last. To begin with, there have been absolutely no differences of opinion in regard to policy; the directors have been in accord on all important moves. No block of stock large or small has passed into the hands of any investment banking interest…The company is now in the strongest position it has ever been, strongest financially, strongest in volume of business, strongest in buying power; also strongest strategically in having taken the lead in giving quick direct service to hundreds of thousands of its customers in different parts of Canada by serving them through its branch stores in thirty towns and cities in different parts of the Dominion. The idea of some outstanding businessman from outside becoming associated with the business is absurd.*

When all similar businesses are thus dwarfed by comparison, when no outside man or group of men has come within measurable distance of what the Eaton directors have actually achieved, it is evident that there is neither the need of nor the possibility of finding some outside man who could do better. It has long been the company's custom to avoid what might look like boasting, and it is now with the greatest reluctance that these rumours are disposed of in this fashion.

She then added a comment that seems to disprove later speculation that she disliked her husband's cousin, R.Y. Eaton, as an outsider and merely bided her time until he was replaced by one of her sons. She undeviatingly told the press, "Mr. R.Y. Eaton, who is now President, has my greatest confidence and respect. If he has any fault, it is that he is too modest," and she went on to describe his achievements at the helm of the T. Eaton Co. in detail.

In response to her son's cable, she said that she immediately sent back a concise remark, which has gone down in history as one of her more famous pronouncements: "Rumours most malicious and absolutely without foundation...Your syndicate could as easily buy the Bank of England."

Although the facts supporting her statements were subject to change after the onslaught of the Great Depression, Eaton's had the means to complete the store, which opened on a surprisingly cold October 30, 1930. On the day before the doors swung open for the public, a full-page ad proclaimed the arrival of what became known as Eatons–College Street:

Sixty-one years ago Timothy Eaton opened a little two-storey store at the corner of Yonge and Queen Streets to sell crinolines and dolmans to Victorian Toronto....Now EATON's makes another colossal stride forward, with the opening of a great new modern store, to sell to modern Toronto furniture and furnishings, the sinuous dresses and subtly flared coats of 1930, the perfumes and books of today. EATON's–COLLEGE STREET will offer the same good values that Toronto has always expected of EATON stores...It will be opened at 10 a.m. tomorrow, with appropriate ceremony, by the grandson of the founder of the business, second son of the late Sir John Craig Eaton————JOHN DAVID EATON.

The ad not only cemented the family nature of the store as it progressed into the brave new world of the 1930s but also hinted at the fact that Eaton's–College Street was to become much, much more than a replacement for

The proposed new store and Eaton headquarters would have changed the skyline of Toronto had it been completed as envisioned before the Great Depression. A fine white line outlines, more or less, the portion actually completed in 1930. *Archives of Ontario: T. Eaton Fonds F229. Used with the permission of Sears Canada Ltd.*

the 1913 house furnishings annex, including "Specialty Shops" on the first floor for fashions and a basement selling utility items, as well as a restaurant. Furthermore, its projected image as an exclusive luxury store was tempered with adjacent ads offering "Dining-Room Suites $98.50 to $4225.00, Arm Chairs, $14.75 to $175.00, and Oriental Rugs, $11.50 to $5000.00," to make sure that the widest possible market was attracted to the new venture. In fact, another ad reassured Depression-era customers, "We've raised our ceilings but not our prices!"

Corresponding articles in Toronto's papers made front-page news of the opening of the long-anticipated store. The *Globe* showed a photo of the "one of the many batteries of floodlights installed on near-by rooftops for illuminating the mammoth structure at night" and related a story that illustrated, in itself, just how innovative such practices were at the time. Toronto residents in the areas to the north of the city were "startled and puzzled" by a "blaze of lights flashing across the sky." It was explained that a powerful beacon was installed on the roof of the structure to light up the nighttime sky and draw attention to Toronto's new shopping palace. It furthermore enticed its readers with a description of what they'd see on opening day:

> *The store is in itself an example of the most advanced modern architecture. It is a Canadian building throughout, the stone, marble and building materials provided by home industries and manufacturers. At the dignified entrance on Yonge Street, one is impressed with the reserve and simplicity of the lines and decorative features. Height, space, and airiness are suggested. Lights are cleverly hidden and pleasing effects from indirect rays constantly surprise the visitor.*

The newspaper gave a hint of the logistics involved in the moving of merchandise from the old annex to Eaton's–College Street, saying that the operation, which required "eleven hundred men, 60 motor trucks, 400 wheeled hand-trucks [and] 250 skids," continued all night long, as curious onlookers strove to catch a glimpse inside the new store; it concluded that moving night at Eaton's was an "end of the old things and a beginning of the new—for the big store and the big city it serves."

At slightly past 10:00 a.m. on the next day, a limousine arrived at the lofty arched entry to the new store and deposited Lady Eaton and her son John David, who then strutted proudly to the shiny glass doors, where the young man used the traditional golden key to unlock them and then held one open for his mother to make her entry. Once inside, he pushed the button that caused a gong to sound, indicating that the public was welcome to enter. The crowd then swarmed through the store and, having familiarized themselves with its dignified, modern-classical exterior during the months of construction that preceded its opening, submerged itself in the ravishing Art Deco interiors of the new mercantile palace. Later, R.Y. Eaton, among the luminaries present, told reporters:

We wanted to be a source of pride to the city, as well as to ourselves, embodying everything of the best for the convenience and service of the public. To what extent we have succeeded in these aims it will be for the public to judge. While we have kept the idea of beautiful surroundings very much in mind, it is our intention that the character of the business we do, will not lose one iota of the popular and democratic quality for which it has always been known. We do not see why fine and dignified surroundings would be the exclusive privilege of people of great wealth, and it is as much as ever our earnest desire that average people of average means should find this a place to enter, which gives them pleasure and satisfaction, as well as the benefits of moderate costs and unfailing service.

Perhaps one of the proudest attendees of the morning's events was director and senior vice-president Harry McGee, who had been instrumental in the founding of the store's furniture business and had risen from being a six-dollar-per-week clerk forty-seven years earlier to become the man in charge of all of Eaton's construction projects. Two years earlier, R.Y. Eaton had presented him with a Rolls-Royce automobile on the occasion of his forty-fifth year with the company, and it was in many ways McGee's energetic dedication to the company's remarkable physical expansion that was on display on that October morning.

The new Eaton's that first-day customers saw was a revelation, unlike any large purpose-built store in North America at the time. The work of Eaton's favourite architects of the day, Ross and MacDonald of Montréal, in association with Sproatt and Rolph of Toronto, the building presented distinctly ordered, seven-storey façades on the Yonge and College Street corner, along with a two-storey wing extending south to Hayter Street and another, one-storey extension westward to Bay Street. Close examination of the renderings of the completed project show that the wings were planned to support eventual expansion and ultimate completion of the whole block. The entire building, in a modern adaptation of classical styles, so preferred at the time by Canadian architects, was described in florid terms by Eaton's commemorative opening day brochure:

Modern as to-day, with that simplicity of line and grandeur of strength which distinguish the architectural classics of all time…the straight lines, wide flutings, and simple ornaments, the freedom from any touch of the bizarre…This harmony, as much as the sheer majesty of line, gives an exaltation of spirit, akin to that which one feels in the mounting rhythm of one of the great masterpieces of music.

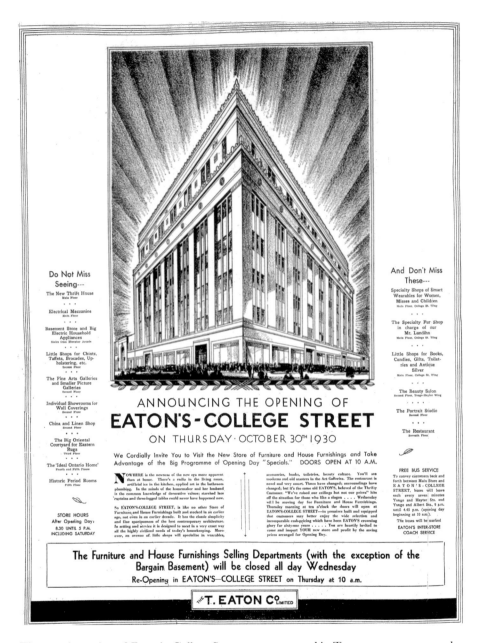

The grand opening of Eaton's–College Street was announced in Toronto newspapers and accompanied by a stunning illustration that captured the imagination of the pre-1930s era. *From an ad, collection of the author.*

The young (twenty-one-year-old) John David Eaton and his mother, Lady Eaton, pause in front of the elabourate Monel-clad doorways of the monumental College Street store. *Archives of Ontario: T. Eaton Fonds F229. Used with the permission of Sears Canada Ltd.*

The exterior was executed in the then traditional limestone from the Tyndall quarries in Manitoba that Eaton's had purchased to ensure the quantity required for completion, and the gleaming white material was worked into the form of cornices, rosettes and broad, fluted rectangular pilasters that sprung from the second floor to support a massive frieze softened by stone rosettes that hid the sixth-floor windows behind it. A recessed seventh floor capped off the composition. At the building's base, broad show windows, broken into three sections by bronze mullions, were surrounded by brown Ganonoque marble enriched with elaborate metal detailing, all sitting on a base of black granite quarried from Mount Johnson in Québec.

Four entrances each on Yonge and College Streets were surrounded by stone worked into a pattern of coffers, and the doors themselves were of glass and richly detailed Monel metal. A central entrance on Yonge Street, clearly a part of the larger composition, was likewise embellished with metal and stone detail work and flanked with oversize lanterns hung from rosettes, scaled to match the substantial new edifice. Eaton's occasional *Story of a*

Although only partially completed, Eaton's–College Street gave a hint of "what might have been" and in itself was one of the most beautiful and elabourate department store buildings ever constructed in North America. *Archives of Ontario: T. Eaton Fonds F229. Used with the permission of Sears Canada Ltd.*

Store publication described the whole thing as having "[g]reat architectural beauty attuned to the modern spirit, a cathedral-like dignity, yet the last word in modern utility," and called it "a place of marble columns, of lofty ceilings, of vast spaces—and above all an Eaton Store."

The substantial difference in elevation from Hayter Street up to College Street was handled in a most ingenious manner by the incorporation of a long, mid-level arcade, floored in Travertine marble and sheathed, like the store's interior pillars, in a French marble known as "Notre Dame 'B,'" one of few materials imported for the store from abroad. Formally called the Plaza, this tall, long and narrow space paralleled Yonge Street and was reached by stairs and an escalator from the lowest, Hayter Street entrance. The Plaza gave access to banks of elevators and, by way of perpendicular flights of stairs flanked by marble-based glass-and-metal vitrines, provided a means of reaching down into the store's basement or up to its main floor.

Electrical items and lamps were featured in the Yonge and Hayter Street wing of the main floor, and a selection of occasional furniture, gifts, pianos, books and the Georgian Room Cake Counter were situated in the

Two photos showing the two-storey extension of Eaton's–College Street to Hayter Street (top) and the one story extension along College Street (bottom). Both of these wings were to serve as a base for the colossal department store and headquarters envisioned before the Great Depression. *Archives of Ontario: T. Eaton Fonds F229. Used with the permission of Sears Canada Ltd.*

tall central block. A special feature of the main floor in this section was the "Thrift House," a replica of a white, shuttered domicile furnished on a budget. Further towards the one-storey Bay Street extension, an array of counters selling accessories, notions, cameras and the like could be found. The Bay Street wing housed the store's "Specialty Shops," featuring fashion apparel for men, women and children. Prominent among these was Eaton's Ensemble Shop, where the best of haute couture was presented to Toronto's

The arcade of the college street store connected Hayter Street to the main seven-storey block and resolved the steep slope of the site. Two views show a view of the arcade looking south from the main store block (left) and the Hayter Sreet entrance foyer (right). *Archives of Ontario: T. Eaton Fonds F229. Used with the permission of Sears Canada Ltd.*

most elite women. Downstairs, shoppers could find a shiny, stainless steel "Soda-Luncheonette" of copious proportions and a full-scale log cabin among departments selling hardware, appliances, sporting goods and other items of a more utilitarian nature.

Throughout the store, the lavish *Moderne* style employed inside differed from the more traditional exterior but in itself contributed to an innovative and harmonious interior of ravishing beauty. Throughout the building, custom fixturing of magnificent craftsmanship provided a backdrop for the huge selection of merchandise on offer. The interior fixtures were designed by Eaton's in-house architectural staff under the direction of René Cera.

Exquisite casework of Ancona Walnut and painstakingly book-matched French Burl was a work of art in itself on the second floor, where drapery fabrics were sold alongside more utilitarian items like paint and wallpaper. Two features also distinguished this floor, the "Regency Room" beauty salon (that Eaton's promised customers to be "the last word in sophisticated comfort") and the Fine Art Galleries.

The latter institution, founded in 1926 by R.Y. Eaton in the 1913 house furnishings annex, was as much a museum as it was a salesroom, housing Eaton's own fine art collection, which included Rembrandt's *Portrait of a Lady*

The entrances to Eaton's–College Street were deeply recessed and beautifully detailed in decorative metal to give a hint of the splendor within. *Archives of Ontario: T. Eaton Fonds F229. Used with the permission of Sears Canada Ltd.*

with a Handkerchief in Her Left Hand, purchased at Christie's in London in 1928 for $165,000. A 1930 opening attraction was a full-size reproduction of Rodin's *Le Penseur*. In time, the Fine Art Galleries became known for its special exhibitions and became an important part of Toronto's (and indeed Canada's) art scene.

Elsewhere, the third floor offered carpets and other floor coverings of a wide variety. A whole section of the floor departed from the *Moderne* scheme to present fine oriental rugs in the atmosphere of a "Saracenic Bazaar." Stucco walls, beamed ceilings, lanterns and tent-like fabric awnings created a rarified atmosphere for the handmade treasures on display.

The other two sales floors at Eaton's–College Street housed a huge display of furniture, but again it was the special attributes of these floors that drew the eye. Prior to opening the store, Eaton's held the "Eaton Model Home Competition" and re-created the winning two-storey design on the building's fourth and fifth floors, labeling it the "Ideal Ontario Home."

The fifth floor sold traditional furniture and housed a "Gallery of Antiques and Reproductions." The most striking attraction of the floor was a series of period rooms either re-created or shipped to the store from historic locations. Among them were the late Jacobean "King Charles Room," a copy of a library from St. John's College, Oxford, and the so-called Oak Panelled Room. Partially taken from a historic home in the Borough of Richmond near London and partially re-created from preserved rooms in the latter city's Victoria and Albert Museum, this room was an example of the early Jacobean style. Others—like the Queen Anne–style "Pine Room," the Georgian-style "Hatton Garden Room," a reproduction of Marie Antoinette's boudoir from the Petit Trianon at Versailles and a reproduction of the King's Gallery at Hampton Court Palace—gave the floor a rarified atmosphere more akin to a museum than a department store.

The sheer jewel in Eaton's–College Street's crown was the suite of rooms consisting of a restaurant and auditorium on the innovative store's seventh floor. Lady Eaton engaged the talents of French architect Jacques Carlu (who also conceived the Montréal store's ninth floor) to create an oasis dedicated to fine dining and the highest-quality entertainment at the very pinnacle of the store. Working in the style that made him famous as a consultant on the interior designs of the era's most lavish ocean liners, Carlu created a broad foyer that connected the banks of elevators on the east and west sides of the building. On the south side of this space, a 1,500-seat concert hall, stage and related service rooms filled the floor. The northeastern corner of the floor was taken up by an astounding restaurant known as the Round Room, on account of its shape and its design theme employing circles at various scales, as well as of differing colours and materials to create a unified composition.

Formally speaking, the restaurant consisted of a domed circular space with four oval alcoves tucked into the corners of the rectangular area it occupied. Carlu, the consummate professional, designed the room down to

Store fixtures carried on the lavish over-the-top modern style of the store itself, often executed in great style utilizing luxurious materials, like these counters for drapery fabrics using exotic wood veneers. *Archives of Ontario: T. Eaton Fonds F229. Used with the permission of Sears Canada Ltd.*

Jacques Carlu's design for the Round Room on the seventh floor was revelatory in its "ocean liner" style, and as a result, it quickly attained status as one of the most effective department store restaurant designs of all time. *Archives of Ontario: T. Eaton Fonds F229. Used with the permission of Sears Canada Ltd.*

the smallest detail, even recommending black as an appropriate colour for waitresses' uniforms. The great domed ceiling, indirectly lit, rose above diners in tiers, from four broad supporting pilasters that formed archways between them that led into the corner alcoves. A soffit finished in black polished glass separated the walls from the dome, in the middle of which was a deep drum, itself bathed in light. In the centre of this expansive cylindrical void hung a very modern chandelier, composed of Monel metal rods supporting discs of Lalique crystal. Uniquely, the chandelier also housed a speaker that provided the room with background music.

On the floor below, circles of coloured linoleum mimicked the ceiling's drum above, and a custom-designed fountain stood at the centre of a small circular pool. The fountain consisted of discs of black glass supported on tubes of Monel metal around a central, fluted cylinder of Lalique crystal. Lighting from below imparted a playful effect on this confection of luxury materials that was further softened by the sound and motion of water.

Everything in the room revolved around this epicentre, like a giant, streamlined carousel, and the gracious and cultivated atmosphere was reinforced by the artwork integrated into it. Four murals by Carlu's wife, Natacha, depicted town life, the forest, the fields and life by the sea, respectively. They were executed in monochromatic earth tones to harmonize with the Round Room's basic colour scheme of silvery beige, grey and banana yellow, strategically accented with black for drama's sake. The murals were located between the pairs of pilasters and framed the room's solitary window (not counting those in the alcoves), its entry doors and its connection to adjacent rooms and the kitchen.

More artwork was supplied in the form of eight sculptures on pedestals housed in tall recesses in the pilasters. Executed by sculptor Denis Gélin, the figures, in an evocative *Moderne* style, were of white enamel, set off by the backlighting of the recesses, which were themselves lined with frames of polished black marble for contrast.

Proclaimed by Eaton's opening brochure as "a domed circle within a square, the corners of which are windowed recesses, this room is a distinguished expression of the aptness, dignity and charm of contemporary architecture and decoration." The Round Room is considered to be not just one of the most beautiful department store tearooms ever built, but one of the world's finest restaurant interiors ever created.

Across the foyer, the Eaton Auditorium opened to the public later, in March 1931, although it was designed as an integral component of the College Street store's seventh floor. It was equipped with a mighty ninety-

The Round Room served as a venue for special events, like the 1939 flower show pictured. At other times, it could be a reception room after concerts in the adjacent auditorium or just a place for the peckish shopper to relax. *Archives of Ontario: T. Eaton Fonds F229. Used with the permission of Sears Canada Ltd.*

stop, 5,804-pipe organ built by the well-regarded firm of Casavant Frères of Ste. Hyacinthe, Québec, designed so as to serve as a backdrop to the room's stage.

The walls and chairs were upholstered in a material called "Fabrikoid" in a pale gold colour, while the stage curtain was of deep gold velour. The prime decorative element in the auditorium was the lighting, integrated into the walls and ceiling. The light sources were installed in two long recesses that rose on either side of the stage and carried across the ceiling towards the rear of the auditorium. Covered with translucent glass to soften the effect of the lighting, the recesses were trimmed in a dentil-like frame constructed of bird's-eye maple and ebonized birch.

The T. Eaton Co. bravely stood behind its investment and even found a way to get traffic to the facility by promoting the lavish auditorium space as a prime performing arts venue. After the Eaton Auditorium opened on March 26, 1931, it soon garnered a reputation as an intimate and welcoming space with superb acoustics; the presence of the spacious foyer and the nearby Round Room set the seal on the prominence of its attractions and made it a centre of Toronto's cultural life. Recitals by Canadian pianist Glenn Gould, opera stars of the calibre of Kirsten Flagstad and Rise Stevens and operatic tenor and Hollywood star Mario Lanza were indicative of the quality of performances offered after hours at Eaton's–College Street.

In the Archives of the T. Eaton Co. can be found file after file of autographed photos presented to the auditorium by the many stars who performed there. From different ends of the musical spectrum, two shall serve here as examples to illustrate what the Eaton Auditorium meant to the cultural life of the city. French actor, singer and entertainer Maurice Chevalier charmed Eaton Auditorium crowds on several occasions. His June 1947 debut garnered a glowing review from the *Toronto Globe*:

> *A good, strong breath of the Folies Bergère blew into Eaton Auditorium last evening, in the person of one, Maurice Chevalier, bon vivant, singer, actor, impressionist and entertainer extraordinary. There are few entertainers who can stage a one-man show and keep audiences interested throughout. Chevalier not only keeps them entertained, he enchants them as well. They just don't want him to stop. With the agility of a man of half his years, he sings, acts, dances, shouts, and scampers about the stage at a great rate. He sings of love most of the time, and mostly in French, with prefaced explanations in a devastating accent. No explanations are needed, however, for his facial and vocal expressions are more than sufficient to convey the*

The clean lines of the Eaton Auditorium were also the result of Carlu's genius, enriched by colour and light, as in the continuous, wood-trimmed lighting fixtures that climbed the front walls and crossed the ceiling to the rear of the room. The slow dimming of these fixtures, as if to suggest a sunset, was an indication to occupants that the concert was about to begin. *Archives of Ontario: T. Eaton Fonds F229. Used with the permission of Sears Canada Ltd.*

spirit, if not the letter, of his songs. They are all new, they are all Chevalier, and they are all wonderful.

The words of Ralph Clarke, the reviewer, conjure up the special atmosphere that must have enfolded at the beautiful showplace that night. Another reviewer, after the next night's performance, quoted Chevalier as saying, "I try to please people. To make them like me. The way to do this is to be natural. I don't work for this. I am as I am. That, in fact is my philosophy: to be as you are. To be frank. To be sincere. To be natural." It would seem that he was completely at home in the exquisitely direct and naturally welcoming place in which he chose to perform.

Russian composer, conductor and pianist Sergei Rachmaninoff, who grew up in Imperial Russia and emigrated after the Russian Revolution, was a star of the North American concert stage for many years before his death in 1943. The autographed photo he left for the Eaton Auditorium shows his famously stern countenance (he was once described as a "six-foot scowl" by fellow Russian composer Igor Stravinsky) that hid his true nature as a kind and generous, if reticent, human being.

Of Rachmaninoff's recital of October 19, 1932, in the Eaton Auditorium, *Globe* reviewer Lawrence Mason wrote, "Rachmaninoff, master-pianist, regaled a great audience in the Eaton Auditorium last night with piano playing such as only a master can command. Enthusiasm ran high, applause was ovational and the inauguration of the Auditorium concert series was in every way a brilliant success." The pianist played four encores after a program that included sonatas by Scriabin, Haydn and Schumann, as well as a fantasia by Franz Liszt. The performances were themselves described by the columnist as "exercises in transcendent virtuosity which won thunderous approval for their incredible dexterity." No doubt, in just one year after its

Sergei Rachmaninoff   Maurice Chevalier

THE EATON AUDITORIUM

Appearances by Russian composer and virtuoso pianist Sergei Rachmaninoff and classic French entertainer Maurice Chevalier serve to illustrate the variety of the Eaton Auditorium's offerings. It was traditional practice for the artist to leave an autographed portrait for the store's archives, and these are but two of the many in Eaton's collection. *Archives of Ontario: T. Eaton Fonds F229. Used with the permission of Sears Canada Ltd.*

debut, the auditorium established itself as a virtuoso space worthy of the highest standards in musicianship of the day.

When it wasn't hosting performances of the utmost quality, the Eaton Auditorium was available for meetings, events and banquets, and the adjacent foyer, Round Room and smaller spaces known as the "Clipper Rooms" contributed distinction and attraction to the store, elevating its status until it became established as a retail destination of a high order, too.

Eaton 100, a special edition of the *Eaton Quarterly* issued in 1969 on the centennial of the T. Eaton Co., relates the experience of Mrs. Gertrude Law, who worked at Queen Street before being transferred to the notions counter of Eaton's–College Street. She recounted her memories of the Depression in Toronto, and turning to her experience at College Street, she said, "I have watched the store take root and grow. They have been happy and interesting years."

Sigrid Wolf, who grew up in Toronto and later became a buyer for Michigan's Jacobson Stores Inc., emphatically disagrees that the store was unsuccessful. "My parents always purchased our household furnishings at the College Street store because my mom totally believed in Eaton's quality for the best value…I don't think they even looked at any other furniture store, ever. If Eaton's College didn't have it, then it must not be worth having, was my parents' belief!"

After the opening of Eaton's–College Street, the former house furnishings annex was remodeled and reconfigured to become Eaton's Budget Annex, connected to the Queen Street store by a tunnel. Eaton's, because of its privately held nature, would not comment on the success of the College Street store. After the initial hubbub of the grand opening, it became obvious that customers were more concerned with surviving the economic malaise that had Canada in its grip over shopping in the rarified atmosphere that the new store provided. Due to the Depression, the uptown location never became the elite shopping mecca that Eaton's hoped for; that distinction was reserved for the intersection of Yonge and Bloor farther to the north. Custom remained with the Queen Street store, and more than one commentator referred to Eaton's–College Street as a "white elephant." For those who wanted to shop for furniture and luxury items, the store provided a free shuttle service between it and its older cousin downtown.

Significant, also, was the fact that Eaton's was perhaps the only department store in North America that for many years had two main stores in the centre of its hometown. Also unique was the fact that after the Toronto Subway opened in 1954, it was possible (because of the stations adjacent

Over time, the Toronto public came to appreciate the atmosphere of the great modern store, but it never replaced its older relative downtown at Queen Street. Sparse traffic in the aisles is an indicator that the Eaton family's dream of moving the downtown retail district northward remained unfulfilled, at least at this location. *Archives of Ontario: T. Eaton Fonds F229. Used with the permission of Sears Canada Ltd.*

to the buildings) to travel from one store to the other blocks away without ever going outside! As the years went on, the College Street store received renovations and alterations that expanded its merchandise range, and it gave traditionally fine service to Toronto shoppers in a uniquely handsome environment throughout its long and quite purposeful life.

All in the Family

It is not yet decided on whom the mantle of Sir John Eaton will fall but I believe my second boy John David has the personality, the ability and temperament to undertake the task.
—Lady Eaton

With R.Y. Eaton firmly at the wheel of the T. Eaton Co., Lady Eaton concentrated on her family and her travels throughout the Depression years, even though she remained a director of the company. Statements she made around the time of the opening of Eaton's–College Street seem to indicate that her son John David was favoured to take on the leadership of the company in 1942, the time specified in her late husband's will. That, however, was some time in the future.

Although the company survived the Great Depression intact, its growth was severely limited in the 1930s, and efforts were concentrated on bringing the Canadian Department Stores to profitability and modernizing or replacing the most outdated of them. The flagship stores, too, stayed up to date, notably in Toronto, where a main floor remodeling brought the innovation of air-conditioning to the store for the first time. Lady Eaton regularly spent winters on the continent and, with her famous 1933 presentation at court behind her, repeated the occasion once more when she introduced her future daughter-in-law, Signy Stefansson, to King George V and Queen Mary in 1933 and again in 1937, when her daughters Florence and Evlyn curtsied in front of King George VI and Queen Elizabeth.

Her primary concern, outside the business, was the fulfillment of a long-held desire to relocate her personal home and family headquarters from Ardwold in Toronto to the farm property that she and Sir John purchased in King City, Ontario. The couple had purchased the farm on the advice of Casa Loma neighbour Sir Henry Pellatt. Lady Eaton's version of the story of how the subject came up throws light on the good-natured friendship between her husband and the fabulously wealthy but ill-fated Sir Henry:

> *Thinking it was a business matter,* [my husband] *left me in the music room and went out to greet his friend in the hall. Presently, the two men joined us, laughing heartily. I asked what was the joke? Sir Henry said, "I told Jack I knew of a beautiful farm near Lake Marie which he should buy. He said he didn't want a farm, so I told him to go to hell, and I'd come talk to you, as you know something of farms!"*

Later, Pellatt showed the property to the Eatons, and before long, they purchased it. The existing stucco-faced farmhouse was expanded, painted pink and renamed *Villa Fiori.* The country home provided a weekend escape for the young family and afforded Sir John the opportunity to relax while

The farm buildings and stables at Eaton Hall Farm were on a scale befitting a large country estate. *Archives of Ontario: T. Eaton Fonds F229. Used with the permission of Sears Canada Ltd.*

fishing on the property's Lake Jonda, which Lady Eaton characterized as a "fine sheet of water." In 1921, they established a herd of dairy cattle at the farm that in 1954 earned Eaton Hall the title of "Master Breeder" from the Holstein Association of Canada.

After her husband's untimely death in 1922, Lady Eaton spent much of her time abroad, and her sons were sent to England or France for schooling. She justified her time away from the business by making her lengthy sojourns to Cannes and Florence work as appropriate meeting places for her far-flung family. As war clouds darkened the skies over Europe, Lady Eaton came back to Canada. Returning permanently to Ardwold was perhaps either too laden with painful memories or just too grand for what she determined to be the needs of her and her family. Furthermore, Toronto's development in the ensuing years since it was constructed raised the value of the property on which it sat quite considerably.

In 1937, Lady Eaton sought her children's approval to sell the older home and construct a new one on their King City farmland. In spite of some objections about the size of the project and its out-of-the-way location, she prevailed and hired local architectural firm Allward & Gouinlock to create her new family headquarters. The result was Eaton Hall, a large home overlooking Lake Jonda, in the style of a Norman Château with turrets, steeply sloped roofs and facing of local Humber Valley stone.

The house, which is often today referred to as simply "the Castle," rivals Casa Loma for ambience, but it is ensconced in a rural as opposed to urban landscape. Beyond the home itself, a broad lawn stretches down to Lake Jonda (now Lake Seneca), giving Eaton Hall a grandiose vista of incomparable beauty across the rippling waters. Beloved artifacts from Ardwold were transferred to Eaton Hall, including a semicircular pergola that found a new home down at the end of the sloping lawn near the lake. Other items like fireplaces, pictures, furniture and two great *torchières* that flank an archway leading to one of the home's expansive spiral staircases gave the new residence a comfortable connection to the Eaton family's past. In fact, Ardwold was sold after the completion of Eaton Hall, demolished and the property developed as an exclusive subdivision, named Ardwold Gate.

Eaton Hall itself, due to its design, was fairly rustic in nature, and its Great Hall, which connects the two wings of the house on the main level, has a floor of polished natural stone and a shallow vaulted ceiling with exposed knotty pine beams, completely in contrast to Ardwold's palatial grandeur. When the house was completed in 1939, it served briefly as a family home

Eaton Hall, pictured here when its lush landscaping was still immature, became, in addition to Lady Eaton's permanent home, an Eaton family headquarters and scene of memorable family events. *Archives of Ontario: T. Eaton Fonds F229. Used with the permission of Sears Canada Ltd.*

and headquarters. Kelly Mathews, who works for Seneca College and is privileged to look across the lake to "the Castle" from her office, is unofficial historian of the house, for which she holds enormous affection: "The history here is so tangible. You can look up at the windows framed in stone, and comparing them with early photographs showing the Eaton family being photographed outside the house, and realize that the faces faintly visible in those very windows were servants who wanted a glimpse of what was going on at the time! I like to think of this house as Canada's *Downton Abbey*—the only difference being that all of the history here is real, not fiction, and actually more compelling for it."

Gilbert Island was given to the Toronto store's recreation department and equipped with facilities for picnics and recreational gatherings. Lady Eaton wrote, "In summertime, even when I happen to be without guests in the house, I am seldom lonely, for I can look across the lake at the energetic groups having fun in the water and hear their shouts around the barbecue." Although she had donated the land, she seldom joined the groups on their outings, so as not to formalize what was meant to be a day of relaxation for them. Kelly Mathews relates her knowledge that "when Lady Eaton came into the store, everybody sat up straight, if you know what I mean, and she didn't want to spoil their day of recreation by inviting that kind of response."

The similarity with the fictional *Downton Abbey* is clear when looking at the home's role in serving Canada during World War II. Lady Eaton writes in *Memory's Wall*:

> *When the Second World War was upon us, it seemed as if Eaton Hall had been completed just in time to be of some service. Having discussed the possibilities with my son, I decided I could help by bringing British children to live there with me during the duration. Mrs. Vincent Massey, wife of our High Commissioner in London, worked very closely with us, keeping us informed and doing everything in her power in those first anxious months to facilitate the passage of children to Canada. So, suddenly my household expanded, and rooms and gardens were full of the laughter and squabbles of youngsters.*

During the war years, Eaton Hall became a hospitable meeting place for servicemen who somehow knew the Eaton family or had letters for them from friends Lady Eaton or her boys had made in Europe. As the war drew to a close, Eaton Hall, as a home for British children, was closed, and Lady Eaton's young guests, who referred to her as "Auntie Flora," returned to their homes, wherever they were, after the conflict was over. Eaton Hall served as a convalescent home for recovering navy personnel after the war, until it could revert back to service once again as Lady Eaton's home and a larger focal point for the retailing family.

The service of Eatonians to their nation during World War II was no less heroic and notable than it had been in the first conflict. Eaton's likewise treated its employees in a similar way, offering to keep jobs open and compensating those serving in the armed forces for the duration. The tangible sacrifice of these men and women was supported at home in many ways, but a seldom-mentioned aspect of life during the conflict involved women doing jobs at Eaton's that were once considered for men only while their brothers or spouses were serving overseas.

Geri Newell remembers that her late mother, Patricia Sipes Newell, was one such woman. She worked as a delivery truck driver in the early 1940s for Eaton's in Winnipeg. "I know that she was proud to do the work at the time, and the other women really enjoyed working together. As a matter of fact, many of them became friends as a result and often socialized together."

After the war, Eaton Hall hosted a huge banquet for returning war employees on September 12, 1946, attended by 1,700 veterans, who received signet rings and war service badges for their service on behalf of Canada (4,000 Eatonians across the country also received the rings locally). The sprawling home was also the scene of an annual buffet soirée for Eaton managers and their wives. The size of the estate and the facilities of the château-like residence allowed it to serve these functions as stylishly as the host family did, with their regal bearing and corresponding concern for the well-being of employees, and hence, their company.

When the construction began on Eaton Hall in 1937, Lady Eaton's son John David was preparing to become president of the company at the time of Robert Young Eaton's retirement. John David Eaton, who was born in 1909, received his primary education at Trinity College Schools in Port

Wartime delivery truck drivers pose for a photo outside of Eaton's Winnipeg complex. Patricia Newell stands on the far right towards the back of the vehicle. The photograph was taken by her husband, Johnny Newell, who was a professional photographer, and they worked together for the National Film Board of Canada after leaving Winnipeg. *Courtesy of Geri Newell.*

Hope, Ontario, and went on to attend Stowe School in England and later matriculated to Corpus Christi College, Cambridge, where he studied foreign languages. Without completing his studies there, he returned to Canada to take a sales job in the men's wear department at the Queen Street store in Toronto. His transfer to Winnipeg four months later had the happy result of meeting his future wife, Signy Stefansson, who was studying art at the University of Manitoba at the time.

Signy Hildur Stefansson, whose father had come to Canada from Iceland in 1876, took an active role in the family business and eventually, as Mrs. John David Eaton, became known as a patroness of the arts. In particular, she became involved in the Art Gallery of Ontario and the Royal Ontario Museum, and in 1961, she was named to the board of governors of York University in Toronto. Two years before that appointment, she was honoured by her father's native country with its highest award—the Order of the Falcon—in thanks for her deep interest, as a Canadian, in her ancestral homeland. Signy and John David Eaton had four sons: John Craig (born 1936), Fredrik Stefan (born 1937), Thor (born 1943) and George Ross (born 1946).

On December 9, 1942, Eaton's officially announced that Robert Young Eaton had resigned from the presidency of the T. Eaton Co. Limited and that the thirty-three-year-old John David Eaton was elected to replace him by the company's directors. The younger Eaton had served as a director himself since 1934, and after a few years overseeing the company's expansion plans in northern Ontario, he returned to Eaton's manufacturing head office in Toronto, for which he was appointed director in 1936 and elected vice-president of the company in 1937.

In thanking the board for its confidence in his leadership, Eaton said that he would carry out his duties "in a manner worthy of the fine example set by those who have presided before me" and acknowledged that "three very remarkable and outstanding men" held the office before him. For the time being, Lady Eaton remained on as vice-president and director, but she relinquished her title not long after her son assumed the presidency. R.Y. Eaton, after more than forty-five years of service to Eaton's, retired, primarily to his home Killyree on Georgian Bay.

John David himself led Eaton's through the last years of the war (when service personnel were again given the same salary benefits as had their World War I predecessors), and the company began expansion anew in the years after 1945. John David Eaton was an avid yachtsman, fisherman and hunter and possessed a droll sense of humour. While the entrance of the

John David Eaton
1909-1973

Signy Hildur Eaton
1913-1992

John David Eaton assumed the helm of the giant organization in 1942 after the retirement of his father's cousin. His beautiful wife, Signy, was of Icelandic ancestry and became known as a patron of charity and the arts. *Archives of Ontario: T. Eaton Fonds F229. Used with the permission of Sears Canada Ltd.*

T. Eaton Co. into British Columbia in 1948 was considered John David's greatest contribution to the company during his tenure as president, in fact, the store already had a mail-order office and small store on Granville Street in Vancouver and was well known because of the reach of its catalogue. In her memoirs, Lady Eaton remarks that while on a trip to Western Canada ("visiting our friends, the Spencers"), John David admired the opportunities for boating on Vancouver's stunningly beautiful harbour and asked aloud, "Mother, why don't we have a business in Vancouver?"

Pamela Bowman has personal recollections of John David Eaton through her family's association with the store:

My father, Donald A. Steeves, was a longtime employee of Eaton's in Moncton. He was a manager in the mail-order department until his death in 1967. Eaton's in those days was truly a full-service store. In addition to the departments typical of the time, there was a cafeteria, a Groceteria (full grocery store) and a post office. Among my dad's other responsibilities, he was also post master, and when we travelled around the Maritimes and beyond, he would always drop in to greet the post masters in various communities. As a child, my life revolved around the store. A big treat was to meet my father in the cafeteria for his coffee break. And of course, since we got an employee's discount, pretty much all our shopping was done there.

In the summer, John David Eaton, then current head of the company, always visited Moncton, and the store manager generally had a garden party to which all managers and their spouses were invited. Eaton's really did feel like family. John David knew my father and his colleagues by name and was interested in knowing about their families. There was a great spirit, and employees enjoyed working there.

When my dad celebrated his twenty-five years with the company, he was presented with his gold Rolex Quarter Century watch. (Instead of the numerals 1–12, it said "1/4 Century" around the dial.) It was a huge celebration, and various groups within the store offered gifts to mark the occasion. I still have the wooden desk with an inlaid leather top that was given to him to commemorate the occasion. My mother was also given two Royal Doulton figurines from two different departments.

In early 1961 my dad was sent to Toronto for four months, along with a man from the Winnipeg store. They were there to learn the new computer system and to implement it in their respective stores afterwards. We went to visit him over the Easter vacation and were taken on a tour of both the Queen Street and College Street stores.

Outside of expansion, one of the hallmarks of John David Eaton's years as president was his advocacy of benefits and privileges for the company's employees. Following the course set by his father and grandfather, for many years John David restated his ongoing opposition to night shopping. Famously, when the Eaton Retirement Annuity Plan was inaugurated, he donated $50 million personally to get the fund started.

In fact, a late-1950s company handbook entitled *Our Company and Its People* is headed by a letter from the president in which he says that *[m]y wish for every person on our staff is that you find both success and happiness in your work here. These two goals are inseparable because happiness in your work and your surroundings is an important element in your success. I sincerely appreciate the fine service and the knowledge that our long-service men and women contribute to their work.*

The booklet goes on to inform employees that

[o]ne of the fascinating things about working for this organization is the diversity of jobs. There is opportunity for you to learn more than one line of work. There is scope for advancement as well as to gain experience. Retailing and all its related operations offer one of the most interesting careers in Canada today…to those truly anxious to get ahead.

While his statements could be easily discounted as corporate hyperbole, the official booklet goes on to describe the standard benefits available to employees, which included the Eaton Retirement Annuity Plan, a Welfare Plan for employees with illnesses, life insurance, a generous employee discount of 10 percent (augmented twice a year to 20 percent) and a vacation policy that gave three weeks' vacation to employees with five years' service and up to six weeks' vacation in the year that they attained membership in the Timothy Eaton Quarter Century Club. Furthermore, the booklet outlines holiday pay, a Wages Savings Plan, payment for useful suggestions and the company's policy on advancement.

Correspondingly, the publication defined employee responsibilities and the firm's merchandising policies of the day, which it said were based on "Timothy Eaton's contract with his first customers in 1869." Several pages were dedicated to the "Goods Satisfactory or Money Refunded" policy and admonished employees to "make exchanges [and adjustments] graciously, willingly, and without delay."

Under John David Eaton's leadership, Eaton's was hit with a serious challenge as the Retail, Wholesale and Department Store Union attempted to organize the Toronto stores of the T. Eaton Co. Limited in 1948. The effort against the company, which was backed by deep pockets of the United Steelworkers of America, began by countering Eaton's image as a benevolent employer but soon turned to criticism of the company's practice of paying female employees less than their male counterparts.

During the organizing drive, John David Eaton countered each of the union's accusations by increasing wages and benefits, and it was during this time that Eaton's adopted its Retirement Annuity Plan. The union eventually resorted to personal attacks on loyal employees, primarily long-term ones, who opposed unionization. Finding this practice distasteful and a foretaste of what they could expect if the union was allowed to represent them to the company that had employed them, the employees voted, in December 1951, in favour of the company, much to management's relief. Tremendous work had to be done at the store to bury the ill will between the opposing factions during the long, four-year ordeal, but before long, Eaton's was back to normal.

Olga Gudz served in the Queen Street store for thirty-two years before she retired from Eaton's in 1988. Born in Winnipeg, of Ukrainian and Polish descent, she moved to Toronto with her family when she was a teenager. Her fascinating life story includes reminiscences of being both an Eaton's customer and an employee. "Did you know that when you ate in the Georgian Room at the Queen Street store, there was a fortune-teller that would come to your table and read your tea leaves?" she asks. "It turned out to be significant for me because she accurately predicted that I would have a boy first and then a girl, but I misunderstood her prophecy that I would be widowed at a young age; I thought she said that I was going to die young, and I just put it out of my mind."

Her husband passed away of a massive heart attack at the age of forty-four, leaving his young wife and two children to continue on without him. She talks about how she got them off to school (which was across the street from her home) and how she had taught her twelve-year-old son to bring his sister home and put out a lunch before they went back in the afternoon. "As soon as they were off to school in the morning, I was on the streetcar downtown, and it was understood that I had to be home by 3:30 p.m., in order to be there when my children got home." Thinking about her life at that time, Olga, who goes familiarly by the name Ollie, remarks:

Thank God for Eaton's and my job there—I worked for several years at Woolworth's on the same block but eventually went to work for Eaton's on Yonge Street. I worked for thirty-two years in the shoe department, and my bosses were all fantastic people. Once, I had a customer, Mrs. Winnifred Taylor, wife of the famous tycoon Edward Plunket Taylor. She was quite a socialite—their family was big in thoroughbred horse racing, and she and her husband were intimate friends of the Royal Family and John F. Kennedy—but she was divorced by the time she became my customer. Some of the other salesladies didn't want to serve her, but I didn't care who you were; I was happy to just do my job. As I waited on her the first time, I

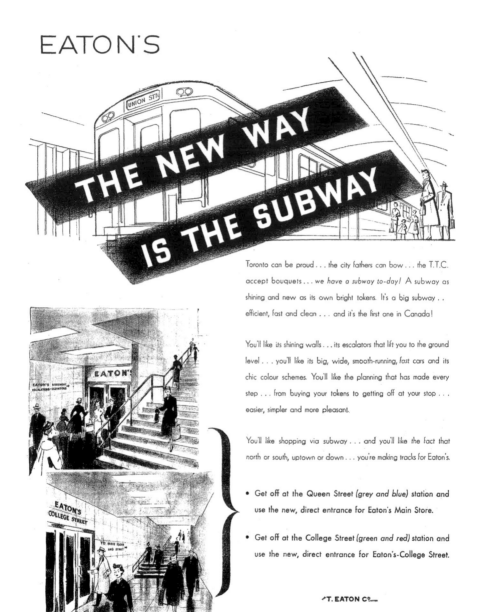

EATON'S

THE NEW WAY IS THE SUBWAY

Toronto can be proud . . . the city fathers can bow . . . the T.T.C. accept bouquets . . . we have a subway to-day! A subway as shining and new as its own bright tokens. It's a big subway . . efficient, fast and clean . . . and it's the first one in Canada!

You'll like its shining walls . . . its escalators that lift you to the ground level . . . you'll like its big, wide, smooth-running, fast cars and its chic colour schemes. You'll like the planning that has made every step . . . from buying your tokens to getting off at your stop . . . easier, simpler and more pleasant.

You'll like shopping via subway . . . and you'll like the fact that north or south, uptown or down . . . you're making tracks for Eaton's.

- Get off at the Queen Street (grey and blue) station and use the new, direct entrance for Eaton's Main Store.

- Get off at the College Street (green and red) station and use the new, direct entrance for Eaton's-College Street.

↗T. EATON C⁰ᴸᴵᴹᴵᵀᴱᴰ

STORE HOURS: 9 a.m. until 5.30 p.m. daily, including Saturday. Telephone Order Service opens at 8.45 a.m. Dial TR. 5111

With the opening of the Toronto subway in 1954, it became possible to transfer from Eaton's main store to Eaton's–College Street without going outside, on account of direct entrances to the adjacent subway stations. *From an ad, collection of the author.*

think at one point I had five handbags on the floor and about ten pairs of shoes out from the stockroom. My manager asked me if I wasn't spending too much time with her, and I just held my hand up as if to tell him "stop." I was only trying to help her with what she needed. In other words, I knew what I was doing, eh? Soon after, she said, "I'll take this…and this… and that"…and her sales check that day was a fabulous amount of money!

Ollie adds that in retrospect, another benefit of her thirty-two years at Eaton's is that "I never, ever had to wait in an unemployment line during that time because my job was secure." "Of course," she adds, "there were crazy things that happened during that time, as is always the case when you are dealing with the public. We had a dirty old man—who turned out to be a Baptist minister of all things—who would always stand under the ladder we'd climb up to get shoes off the upper shelves. Once when I came down and he put his hands on me, I said, 'Oh no you don't' and just shoved him away. Eaton's was a great place to work and it was a wonderful store, but you still had to be strong and look after yourself in situations like that, eh?"

Of her relationships with the Eaton family, Ollie is unequivocal:

The first time I waited on Lady Eaton, I didn't even know it was her. To me, she was just another customer, like any other, but very kind and beautifully attired. When I was done fitting her, she handed me her card and asked if she could call me before she came in again, so I could serve her regularly. We got along very well over time, and I always waited on her. During the time I knew her, she was, to me, a lovely, lovely, lovely lady!

Because she worked during the era of John David Eaton's presidency, Ollie looked forward to his visits to her department. "Mostly, he would just walk through and visit to ask how things were going. At Christmastime, he'd come down to wish us a "Merry Christmas," and I always thought of him… and, in fact, all of the Eatons because I knew their boys, too…just as real, normal people. They treated us very well, and they never, ever acted like big shots or anything like that, eh?"

It was during this era that Eaton's, wherever it traded, came to be considered a timeless Canadian icon, as though it had always been a part of Canadian life and seemingly always would be. Honoured sportsman Gordie Howe continued to visit the stores and catalogue outlets as "Eaton's Sporting Goods Advisor," and his autograph-signing sessions regularly drew enthusiastic crowds. Gordie's son Marty, who himself became a hockey star, remembers that "Gordie toured Canada for Eaton's for a month or six weeks at a time for ten years, signing three-by-five cards for people that would line up to meet him at the store. He would sign a thousand of them every night beforehand and then personalize them when he met the public at the store. This made it faster so he could get to everyone, and no one ever got shuffled out of the way before they got to meet him."

Eaton's locations, particularly the main stores in the big cities, took on roles that extended way past what the words "department store" connoted. Whether it was in the restaurants or food departments offering fine cuisine to customers, at fashion shows, in special events or simply by the arrival, promotion or sale of merchandise that could be either just useful or extremely exotic and anything in between, Eaton's became one with the culture of Canada. The "money back guarantee" built confidence, and people understood that if Eaton's had the merchandise, it must be "right" for them, for the times and, in fact, for Canada itself.

Eaton's was also a bona fide tourist destination for those who came to vacation in Canada's scenic splendor and then enjoy the unique atmosphere of its lively cities and towns. As a result, it was a prolific publisher of promotional city maps that devoted ample space to the attractions of the local Eaton's. Containing information about the souvenirs carried by the store and the wide range of special services offered by this most accommodating of retailers, it also played up Eaton's reputation as the "Big Store with the Small Shops," or, if in Québec, *Eaton vous offer toujours d'avantage*.

A full-page ad in the *Toronto Globe and Mail* published in August 1963, when Toronto was full of visitors for the annual Canadian National Exhibition, enticed shoppers to come and see what the slogan meant. Just like the tourist brochures, it explained what all the fuss was about in Eaton's and why a stop there might just be a good idea for visitors. The areas highlighted in Toronto's two main stores were as follows:

> **The China Shop**—*Where the regal dignity of English bone china, dinnerware and the fragile beauty of imported china are displayed in all their loveliness. Eaton's–Main Store—Basement*
>
> **The Gift Shop**—*A treasure-trove of lovely things for the home, the garden, the cottage…fashioned to delight the eye and charm the taste. Eaton's–College Street, Main Floor*
>
> **The Specialty Fur Shop**—*Where you can choose at leisure—and with confidence—from an exclusive collection of magnificent fur creations. Eaton's–College Street, Main Floor*

The 186 Shop—*Devoted to the finer things in men's furnishings—mostly distinctive imports. A quiet, secluded section, with its own direct entrance from Yonge Street. Eaton's–Main Store, Main Floor*

Seven Seas Gift Shop—*Where you will find the beautiful, the unusual, the unique in gifts, gathered from the four corners of the world. Eaton's–Main Store, Second Floor*

The Fine Art Galleries—*Presenting for exhibition and sale, paintings for virtually every taste; featuring the works of prominent Canadian and European artists. Eaton's–College Street, Second Floor*

The Gallery of Fine Furniture and Reproductions—*Where you will find genuine antiques of classic design and beautiful patina, as well as fine period reproductions. Eaton's–College Street, Fifth Floor*

"Vanity Fair" Beauty Salon—*A wonderful world of charm where you are pampered with personalized service by expert beauticians and stylists. Eaton's–Main Store, Third Floor*

The Silver Shop—*Fine modern sterling, as well as authentic reproductions of Sheffield plate. Eaton's–Main Store, Main Floor*

The Georgian Room—*Gracious pillared dining room in soft green and white décor. Luxurious surroundings and superb Canadian food expertly served. Eaton's–Main Store, Ninth Floor*

The Ensemble Shop—*Exclusive fashions, European imports, couturier creations…and, at little boutique counters, elegant accessories and exquisite lingerie. Eaton's–College Street, Main Floor*

Import Millinery Salon—*A haven of fashion presenting highly individual flattery of beautiful hats from the couture milliners of Europe and New York. Eaton's–Main Store, Fourth Floor*

The Men's Shop—*Fine British clothes and furnishings for men, featuring inherently good quality, distinctive style and competent personal service. Eaton's–College Street, Main Floor*

Trend House—*A completely furnished home showing current fashion trends in furniture and home furnishings interpreted by our "Plan-a-Room" consultants. Eaton's–College Street, Fourth Floor*

The Jewel Shop—*Offering an opportunity for unhurried selection and expert counsel in the purchase of fine diamonds and precious stones. Eaton's–Main Store, Main Floor*

The Viking Room—*Ultra-modern restaurant with free-flow self-servery separated from dining area. Delightful Scandinavian décor. Acoustic tile ceiling for quiet atmosphere. Eaton's–Main Store, Fifth Floor*

Import Shoe Salon—*Shoes created by master-craftsmen throughout the world and assembled in a collection designed to excite the most discriminating. Eaton's–Main Store, Second Floor*

The Crystal Shop—*A glittering pageant of great names in glass and crystal, from England, France, Belgium, Sweden and Czechoslovakia. Eaton's–Main Store, Basement*

Gift Bureau—*Trained shoppers will gladly suggest suitable gifts for you to take home, help you select them and have them gift-wrapped if you wish. Eaton's–Main Store, Second Floor*

The Town House—*The best of New York, London, Paris, Rome, Hong Kong, Montréal…wherever you find high fashion, you'll find a Town House buyer snapping up the cream of the collection for Toronto's best dressed. Eaton's–Main Store, Fourth Floor*

The Hostess Shop—*Where our food advisers can suggest all sorts of native and imported delicacies to add zest to your menus. Eaton's–Main Store, Main and Fifth Floors; Eaton's–College Street—Main Floor*

The Regency Room—*The Powder Box Salon and the Makeup Bar…where the artistry of a staff of beauty experts is enlisted in the cause of loveliness. Eaton's–College Street, Second Floor*

Bath and Boudoir Boutique—*The bathroom is fashion's newest darling and our bath and boudoir boutiques have all the trappings to lift your bathroom out of the commonplace into the rare. Eaton's–Main Store, Second Floor; Eaton's–College Street, Main Floor*

Shopping Service—*A Personal Shopper will be pleased to shop with you or for you, locating merchandise you want without waste of your time. Eaton's–Main Store, Sixth Floor*

In addition, the brochures listed the most important tourist attractions to be found in their respective locations and laid out Eaton's customer service concept by drawing attention to the store's Post Office, Rest Room, Mother's Rest Room, Lost and Found, Coat and Parcel Lockers, Deposit Accounts Office, Travel Service, Service Bureau, Gift Wrap, Public Telephones, Parking Station locations and (in Toronto) the inter-store coach service.

The expansion that brought Eaton's to Canada's Pacific coast is generally considered John David Eaton's greatest accomplishment, but he also ushered the store into the age of the shopping centre. In the period of postwar growth that fueled the expansion of cities, Eaton's continued to improve and expand its stores in Canada's major cities, but the changing retail environment demanded expansion around these cities as well. What's more, the Robert Simpson Co. Limited—which had major stores in Toronto, Montréal, Halifax, London and Regina—partnered in 1952 with Sears, Roebuck and Company of the United States to open Simpsons-Sears stores in areas where Eaton's big Toronto competitor had not been able to expand previously. With the power of the proven Sears catalogue combined with the American retailer's know-how behind it, the Simpsons-Sears combination literally shook Eaton's to its roots.

Eaton's first major response to a changing marketplace occurred to the east of Toronto in Canada's "Automobile Capital" of Oshawa, Ontario, where the company once had a factory but currently only operated a catalogue sales office. A modern shopping centre, which was built just off the 401 expressway at King Street and Stevenson Road, included a sleek, three-level store of 147,000 square feet as the central hub of the complex.

Eaton's described it as "the newest, most modern store in Eaton's Canada-wide organization; an inviting, exciting place to shop—delightfully decorated

Eaton's 1956 branch in Oshawa was its first attempt to build a store in a dedicated suburban shopping centre. Wildly successful, it paved the way for future expansion well into the 1960s. *Archives of Ontario: T. Eaton Fonds F229. Used with the permission of Sears Canada Ltd.*

in gentle pastel tones, spacious and pleasantly air-conditioned, with the latest facilities for customer comfort and pleasure." The ad, however, reserved its boldest lettering for a phrase that was as much a bellwether for shopping centre development as it was for the decline of central business districts: "Parking is plentiful—and FREE!"

The opening festivities were attended by Lady Eaton along with John David and his wife, Signy, who travelled from Toronto to see the company's last word in merchandising and welcome new customers to the store. Eaton's branch itself—designed by the Toronto office of noted retail architects John Graham and Company of Seattle, Washington—was faced in stone panels that bore a more elaborate pattern in the five central bays of the façade, an effect that downplayed any sense of boxiness in the store's appearance. Surprisingly, for its era, the store incorporated entrances from two different levels, guaranteeing good traffic flow through the store.

John David and wife Signy Eaton (left) pose with store executives and the seventy-six-year-old Lady Eaton at the grand opening of the Oshawa store. Lady Eaton made an annual tour of the Eaton stores and, until she was too frail to do so, attended grand openings as an Eaton family figurehead. *Archives of Ontario: T. Eaton Fonds F229. Used with the permission of Sears Canada Ltd.*

Eaton's London store was a successful example of a mid-century downtown department store in an existing retail core. Along with the small, galleria-like Wellington Square, it anchored the east end of London's shopping district. *Archives of Ontario: T. Eaton Fonds F229. Used with the permission of Sears Canada Ltd.*

The little Gander store was Eaton's second shopping centre venture of the era, but in 1960, Eaton's took a different approach to opening a location in the large city of London in southwestern Ontario. Again working with the Graham Company, Toronto, Eaton's partnered with developers Webb and Knapp to build Wellington Square, an enclosed shopping centre in downtown London on the other end of King Street from older anchors Simpson's and Kingsmill's, a locally owned store. The complex included a covered mall housing, a large Woolworth store and a variety of shops, underground parking and a large, 247,000-square-foot Eaton's anchor store that consisted of four floors and a basement.

When it opened on August 11, 1960, it was hailed in the *London Free Press* as "a new experience in shopping in the city," describing the enhanced family shopping possibilities offered by the new development:

> *Customers may buy five-cent plastic toys or a $5,000 mink coat, or stop off for a beauty treatment by experts, while their husbands test the latest fishing rods and the kids sip sodas at the refreshment bar. But women will find the store's attractions not only in the merchandise on display. They will also find it a very pleasant place just to browse. Designed imaginatively by*

architects John Graham and Company, the building adds grace to London's skyline. The new store's builders have thrown up long, clean walls unbroken by windows. The Wellington and York Street walls, for example offer impressive surfaces of plain red bricks. Other walls have areas of ceramic tiles, polished granite, and white marble-faced columns. The surfaces are rich, contrasting, intriguing, and pleasing. The Wellington Street wall pattern is varied by eight decorative show boxes at shoulder height. The two sides of the store have full-sized display windows where Londoners can now admire the attractive and informative displays for which Eaton's stores across the country are known.

Eaton's own ads called the store "the newest, brightest, most modern in a great tradition of Eaton's stores that serve Canadians from the Atlantic to the Pacific" and drew attention to its Mayfair Room restaurant, the work of architect René Cera and luxuriously embellished with a five-panel mural of classical dancers. The ballet theme was reinforced at the restaurant's entry from the store by a striking depiction of the Russian "Firebird." The store promised London's fashionable an array of designer boutiques on the second floor known as the Wellington Shops and informed shoppers that they would find "convenient parking for thousands of cars daily."

As if the large new store wasn't enough, Eaton's constructed a $500,000 service building on London's Highland Avenue to attend to its large new store. Primarily a warehouse, the service building housed the store's new sixteen-vehicle delivery fleet, a heavy goods store and display workshops for the Wellington Square store downtown.

Back in Toronto, though, it would be two years before Eaton's ventured out of the downtown area to build a branch, and that start was tentative at best. Announced the previous October, Shoppers' World opened on May 16, 1962, on Danforth Avenue east of downtown Toronto.

The smaller, sixty-five-thousand-square-foot store at the corner of Danforth Avenue and Victoria Park Avenue was not, at the time, Eaton's best foot forward, but it was a step ahead in the company's Toronto suburban development nonetheless. An Eaton's ad claimed that it was "[o]ne of a series of new stores built or planned to bring Shopping-at-Eaton's within easy access of all our customers in the Toronto area…with merchandise chosen for suburban needs." It went on to mention the store's "wonderful feeling of space," which it attributed to "the full sweep of wide aisles and displays, colourful panels, soft recessed lighting, background music," but it

Eaton's in Shoppers' World was the company's first, somewhat tenuous attempt at serving the outlying Toronto market. The one-storey store's roofline betrays the fact that it was built inside a former factory. *Archives of Ontario: T. Eaton Fonds F229. Used with the permission of Sears Canada Ltd.*

did not mention that the store was, in fact, a disused 1920s-era Ford factory with a strip shopping centre attached.

The garish exterior combined a façade of bold vertical stripes with marquees over the entrances; a small enclosed mall led shoppers to the Eaton store. The presence of angled projections above the roof, which admitted lighting into the factory, belied the store's industrial origins. Its grand opening was notable as the first at which John Craig Eaton, great-grandson of the founder, presided due to his father's inability to attend.

Nonetheless, the Shoppers' World store prospered and grew, serving the east side of Toronto very adequately. In time, it was expanded by thirty thousand square feet as well, although it remained the company's smallest Toronto-area branch for some time.

Later that year, on August 1, 1962, Eaton's unveiled its first new-from-the-ground-up branch store to the suburban Toronto shopper at Don Mills. This time, its store in the Don Mills Shopping Centre, serving the northeast Toronto suburban area, was a stylish modern building with a dramatic

271

recessed entry embellished with colourful modern artwork. The shopping centre had developed in 1955 as a part of a two-thousand-acre "new town" developed on former farmland. It began as a fairly small strip centre, but in the expansion that brought Eaton's in as an anchor, it became an expansive, outdoor mall-like complex in keeping with the guiding principles of the "new town's" development—the separation of vehicular and pedestrian traffic combined with a thoroughly modern, Bauhaus-like aesthetic, as conceived by architects John B. Parkin and Associates.

Eaton's played up the ties of its store to the community it served. In announcing the grand opening of its new Don Mills branch, it called the store

> [a]s *bright, lively and forward looking as the Don Mills Community itself…Eaton's Don Mills was designed specifically for the area it serves. The warm-toned brick and fieldstone building follows the natural contour of the land…and the result is a split-level store with entrances on both levels! The store is spacious, wide, and airy…yet each section preserves its own identity, with the effect of a series of small fashion shops…and…the feeling of space, soft lighting and colours, pleasant music, and the friendly faces of Eaton personnel.*

The Don Mills store, located in a planned community, combined sophisticated modern architecture and art to create a contemporary shopping environment worthy of any large metropolis. *Archives of Ontario: T. Eaton Fonds F229. Used with the permission of Sears Canada Ltd.*

As he had eight years earlier in Oshawa, "Peter the Clown" entertained youngsters who came with their parents to get a glimpse of the new Don Mills store. *Archives of Ontario: T. Eaton Fonds F229. Used with the permission of Sears Canada Ltd.*

A major feature of the store's exterior was an applied mural near the entrance, repeated on the walls of the women's fashion departments. Entitled *Portrait of a Community*, it paid homage to the development of Don Mills and the inherent amenities enjoyed by residents. The shopping centre was enclosed in 1978, and Eaton's store was expanded from its initial size of 110,000 square feet by way of a 45,000-square-foot expansion in 1969. From that time onward, Eaton's Don Mills proffered a new Garden Court restaurant and a beauty salon that it hadn't had during its first seven years.

The two 1962 developments paled in comparison to the 1964 Yorkdale Shopping Centre, developed at the intersection of the new 401 expressway and Dufferin Avenue. The facts made it clear: Eaton's store, at 363,000 square feet in size, was bigger than the Shoppers' World and Don Mills stores combined, and the shopping centre itself topped out at 1.2 million square feet of space, making it not only Canada's first enclosed regional shopping centre but the largest as well.

Eaton's acquired the property in 1955, with a long-term vision to develop a regional centre that would attract development and customers to the site, which was primarily farmland and far outside Toronto's built-up area at the time. As it had done years earlier, the company invited competitor Simpson's to join it in the development, this time convincing its major competitor in the Toronto market that the synergy between the two stores was essential to Yorkdale's success. Construction began in spring of 1962, the shopping centre itself being developed by William Zeckendorf's Trizec Corp. Limited and designed by John Graham and Company (though John B. Parkin designed the Yorkdale Simpson's store).

When it opened on February 26, 1964, crowds of shoppers (requiring fourteen policemen just to direct traffic) poured through the centre's airy, twenty-seven-foot-high malls and marveled at the shopping environment, unlike anything seen in Toronto at the time. The Eaton's store, executed primarily of light brick, consisted of a massive, cross-shaped two-storey enclosure whose ends sported a three-dimensional pattern, imparting detail and human scale to the enormous structure. This mass, softened by curves, appeared to "float" above the store's glassy ground floor.

A two-storey glazed pavilion on the southwest side of the building, where it met the main east–west mall, housed the Eaton court, where a series of pillars flared upward into mushroom-shaped "clouds" that concealed indirect light and supported the Vista Room restaurant above. From the eatery's "pods," shoppers could take a break and dine overlooking the bustling court below or gaze through the pavilion's glass curtain wall to the roof garden, which brought a sense of the outdoors to the interior environment from this vantage point.

Eaton's ads introduced Yorkdale to the public, telling prospective customers that "an exciting new shopping showplace makes its glamorous debut tomorrow…a whole new world of shopping luxury…a whole new

Eaton's Yorkdale, like the enormous and innovative shopping centre it occupied, was the suburban retail prototype *par excellence* when opened in 1964. Its presence at the other end of the shopping centre from rival Simpson's replicated the downtown shopping experience, albeit in a climate-controlled environment. *Archives of Ontario: T. Eaton Fonds F229. Used with the permission of Sears Canada Ltd.*

From the lanes of the Yorkdale shopping centre, Eaton's big new branch was no less striking. Customers entered under stylized "mushrooms" that supported the store's Vista Room restaurant above. *Archives of Ontario: T. Eaton Fonds F229. Used with the permission of Sears Canada Ltd.*

concept of shopping comfort and convenience." To support its claims, it touted the store's special features, among which could be found Canada's first "air curtain" entrance, open escalators and automatic drapes to screen out glare from the restaurant area. It promised a shopping experience to rival the downtown store, most notably with the claim that "[w]ithin the big store, there's a host of 'little shops' where you can enjoy very personal attention."

Yorkdale may have been visionary, but accomplishments in Toronto were not limited to branch development alone. In 1953, Eaton's celebrated the coronation of Queen Elizabeth II as it had traditionally done for the monarchs who preceded her. In addition to placing a focus on British products, which the store reminded customers it had been importing for more than eighty years, Eaton's–Main Store and Eaton's–College Street featured special window displays, including a seventeen-foot-long replica of Buckingham Palace at Queen and Yonge Streets and a model of the Victoria Memorial at College Street.

Eaton's packed a lot of department store into the Yorkdale branch, whose interiors featured elabourate and characterful interiors with custom store fixtures and attractive décor. *Archives of Ontario: T. Eaton Fonds F229. Used with the permission of Sears Canada Ltd.*

As tradition dictated, Eaton's celebrated the 1953 coronation of Queen Elizabeth II by adorning the exterior of its downtown stores with flags, bunting and a huge replica of the Crown of St. Edward over the Queen Street store's entrance. *Archives of Ontario: T. Eaton Fonds F229. Used with the permission of Sears Canada Ltd.*

Both stores were suitably decorated, and lettering on the marquee over the Queen Street store's main entrance proclaimed, "Long Live the Queen—Long May She Reign!" Eaton's own ads vividly described the ceremony of the event:

> *Great masses of Union Jacks and Ensigns fluttering from the buildings... majestic banners in royal scarlet and cloth of gold...a stately canopy bearing a fourteen-foot Saint Edward's crown in sparkling golden crystal. Be sure YOU see the magnificent Coronation decorations featured at Eaton's Main Store and Eaton's–College Street.*

Considerably less fanfare may have accompanied the opening of another Toronto area facility, although its effects were surely more tangible and lasting to the Toronto shopping public. In 1956, Eaton's inaugurated a sprawling warehouse and service centre northwest of Toronto at Sheppard Avenue and Highway 400. The complex served a variety of functions in addition to warehousing heavy goods. A full-scale maintenance facility serviced Eaton's large fleet of trucks, and a whole section of the building housed workrooms dedicated to the production of Eaton's annual Santa Claus Parade. Workshops for items like custom-made draperies and repair shops for rugs and appliances were also housed in the building's 1.1 million square feet of space. Customers could visit the warehouse to shop for hardware, place catalogue orders and jostle for bargain merchandise after a warehouse budget store was opened at the location.

If the 1950s began the era of suburbanization for Eaton's, and the 1960s provided a chance to learn what the suburban customer wanted in their stores, the 1970s saw Eaton's ring Toronto with modern branch stores. After Yorkdale, Eaton's didn't open another store in the Toronto area until February 24, 1971, when it opened a 227,000-square-foot, three-level store in Sherway Gardens west of downtown Toronto. Eaton's branch, a light-brick octagonal container, had five tall glazed arches to break the monotony and denote a mid-level entry and covered outdoor shop location. Retail synergy was again provided by Simpson's, which built an avant-garde cubist structure with an atypical interior curvilinear mall entrance on the other end of the shopping centre's glitzy enclosed promenade.

Eaton's used a stylized butterfly design and the slogan "It's a Sunshine World at Eaton's Sherway" to entice customers to come out to the store, and it even went so far as to give away reusable shopping bags printed with the colourful creature and butterfly kites to youngsters. The store, whose sober

Not long after it opened, Eaton's commissioned this photo of the various modes of transportation needed to transverse its gigantic new warehouse north of Toronto. Notice the illuminated "stop" sign over the corridor intersection. *Archives of Ontario: T. Eaton Fonds F229. Used with the permission of Sears Canada Ltd.*

exterior belied the riot of colour within, offered a wide range of goods, set in elaborate boutique-like alcoves delineated with curvilinear arched openings covered in shiny finishes. Whether the scheme involved blue and yellow for young men, orange for decorative home accessories or hot pink for shoes, the colours were bright and vivid, so much so that the beige-and-grey Town House, set one step up on a beautiful dark wood parquet floor, stood out just as boldly on account of its suave understatement.

The store's Garden Court Restaurant, overlooking its mall entrance, was done up in the ubiquitous 1970s avocado green set off by shades of dark blue and turquoise, and again neutral bas-relief sculptures on opposite side walls became focal points due to their own contrasting lack of pigmentation. Apparently, the store made a great impact, for aerial photos on opening day show parking lots full to the brim and expressway embankments bordering the mall's site taking the overflow of shoppers unable to find parking, in spite of some lingering late-winter snow on their northern faces.

On October 11 of the same year, Eaton's was able to serve Toronto's northwestern suburbs, with a new store at Bramalea Town Centre out past Pearson International Airport. A more conventional concept than Sherway (and smaller at 127,000 square feet), it nonetheless borrowed some of the older branch store's features, including a colourful interior presentation, a Garden Court restaurant and an arched entryway, though this time the arches were limited to three and the store itself was a much simpler rectangular box. Taking into account Eaton's Warehouse store, Bramalea was the ninth in the Toronto area, and the store attracted business to its new location (in an as-yet-unfinished shopping mall) with a "Lucky 9" sale of specially selected items marked down for the opening.

When it opened a new branch east of Toronto in Scarborough, Eaton's likewise announced its coming with unique publicity. Even though Toronto's Pearson International Airport was on the other side of town, the new, 238,000-square-foot store was presented to the public with a flight-themed campaign, and ads announced, "Eaton's is really flying, opening its Seventh-largest store in Canada, Wednesday, May 2nd at the new Town Centre. Study the flight plan to check the best way to get there." It was easy to see the pride Eaton's had in its new stores in the era that saw the debut of the Scarborough branch:

> *Eaton's soars to new heights in modern store design with this latest addition to the family of Eaton's stores. Conveniently located in the recently-built Town Centre, the new Eaton's will be able to serve a wide area and make many more customers happy. Three floors are ready for take-off time. All designed for modern space-age shopping convenience. Boldly-scripted signs point you in the right direction, put you in the desired department. Dramatic displays of merchandise reveal the good things in store for you. Vivid, vibrant colours put a sizzle in your summer shopping. Summer is flying high at the new Eaton's store at Scarborough Town Centre. Come fly with us there!*

In later years, Eaton's opened more stores throughout the Toronto area, and its presence there sustained the idea that Eaton's was more than just a national retailer; it came to be identified as one of Toronto's major

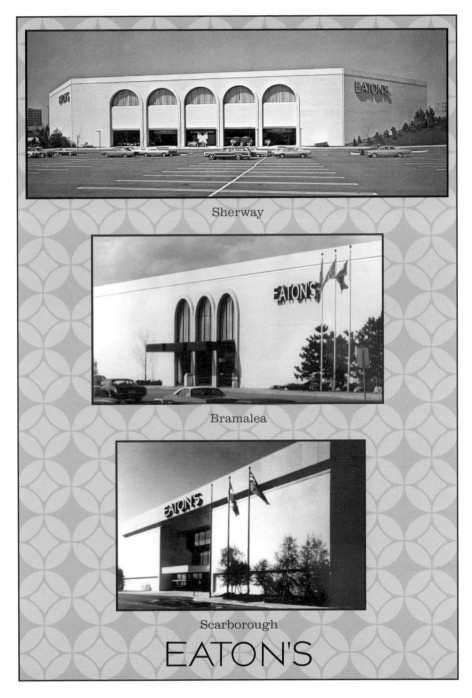

Eaton's opened branches around Toronto in the early 1970s. *From top to bottom*: Sherway Gardens, Bramalea City Centre and Scarborough Town Centre. *Archives of Ontario: T. Eaton Fonds F229. Used with the permission of Sears Canada Ltd.*

Even Eaton's suburban stores proved that it was "the big store with the little shops," as exhibited by the interiors of the Sherway store. *Clockwise from upper left*: the Garden Court restaurant, the Town House, Weather Vane Shop, Like Young Shop, the Executive Shop and the Flame & Flower Shop. *Archives of Ontario: T. Eaton Fonds F229. Used with the permission of Sears Canada Ltd.*

department stores, and brimming with local flavour at that. In Eaton's heyday, the same could be said of its stores in Montréal, Winnipeg and even in smaller markets on the prairies and in the Maritimes.

No doubt Eaton's had to work at creating a presence on Canada's Pacific coast, but by using its time-tested process of acquisition and expansion into new markets, it wasn't long before the store conquered its westernmost geographical market and came to be identified there in the same way as it had all over the rest of the vast and growing nation.

Pacific Heights

If you want to be happy, don't pursue happiness as a goal. Just work hard, think of others as well as yourself, and be human.
—"Mr. Chris" Spencer

Simply put, David Spencer Limited was to British Columbia what the T. Eaton Co. was to Canada in general, and it was no surprise that Eaton's chose to expand to the Pacific coast by purchasing what was arguably the most famous store in the province. That the T. Eaton Co. Limited and David Spencer Limited would one day come together is, from hindsight, practically a foregone conclusion, especially given the similarity between the two businesses, the friendly relationship between both stores' owner-families and Eaton's desire to grow its business into British Columbia.

The latter fact can be illustrated clearly by Eaton's actions before the announcement, in December 1948, of the Spencer purchase. Eight years earlier, in February 1940, Eaton's opened a catalogue office and a small showroom at 526 Granville Street to test the waters in Vancouver. Then, on March 20, 1948, the *Vancouver Sun* reported that Eaton's had paid $1,875,000 for the old Hotel Vancouver site at Georgia, Granville and Howe Streets that was directly across from the Hudson's Bay Company Vancouver store.

A detour from Eaton's story is worthwhile, since the history of the Hotel Vancouver, called "the finest building ever demolished in Vancouver," is itself intriguing if not tragic because of the loss of a great, beloved and representative building. Long a favourite among travellers, and indeed with the Vancouver public, who were fond of dining and dancing in its Panorama Roof and Spanish Grill, the hotel was built in 1916 on the site of a smaller hostelry and was owned from the start by the Canadian Pacific Railway. It looked for all the world like a wedding cake hewn from stone, rising up in setbacks and terraces clothed in elaborate, Italian Renaissance details. Enormous, eight-foot-high gargoyles in the form of moose heads, with impressive racks of antlers, and giant buffalo heads executed in terra cotta graced the fourteenth-floor-level exterior of the structure.

Before the Great Depression, rival Canadian Northern Railway began construction of a massive château-style hotel just one block to the north, but by the time that line's financial problems forced its absorption into the Canadian National Railways, the poor economy had put a halt to the Vancouver hotel project.

As a result, the steel structure of the new hotel dominated Vancouver's skyline for years, a poignant reminder of the optimism of the 1920s laid to waste for all to see. By 1937, construction had restarted, and both the CNR

The atmospheric Hotel Vancouver, demolished in 1949, was an architectural victim of circumstance. Deemed unnecessary by its owner, the Canadian Pacific Railway, when it partnered with rival CNR to operate the "new" Hotel Vancouver a few blocks away, its site served as a parking lot for almost twenty-five years. Eaton's bought it in 1948 for a new department store that never materialized on account of its subsequent purchase of the David Spencer Limited. *From a postcard, collection of the author.*

and CPR partnered to complete the new hotel. Because Canadian Pacific did not want the new lodgings to face competition, it agreed to close the original Hotel Vancouver upon the new one's opening. When it opened on the lot bounded by Hornby, Georgia, Burrard and Robson Streets, it was very well received, but most Vancouverites at the time maintained a deep affection for the old favourite, which got a reprieve due to temporary use as a barracks during World War II.

Servicemen returning from World War II duty found themselves disgruntled over the lack of acceptable housing in Vancouver. As a result, a campaign was formed to occupy the old structure until well over one thousand people, married and single, made their homes in the vacant structure operating as a self-governing hostel. Their protest actions led to the construction of a new, six-hundred-unit housing complex for the veterans and their families, and when the short-term residents left, the once-deluxe hotel again fell into disuse.

Eaton's revealed its plan in early 1948 to demolish the hotel and replace it with a "nine or ten story" store that, according to J. Ross Jenkins, head of Eaton's British Columbia operations, "won't be radical in design, but it will be a credit to the city." He also predicted that the store would include a "roof-garden or pent-house type restaurant above to give a view of the city." However, John David Eaton, when he visited Vancouver that October, cautioned that plans for the store were very vague, in spite of the fact that Eaton's had already sought bids for the demolition of the old Hotel Vancouver from several firms.

Not much else was heard about the project until a bomb was dropped on December 1, 1948, when an ad appeared in the *Vancouver Sun*, signed jointly by John David Eaton and Chris Spencer, the president of David Spencer Limited. This time, the rumours were indeed confirmed: the venerable British Columbia retailer had been bought by the T. Eaton Co. Limited. The Spencer stores would henceforth be operated under the name of the T. Eaton Co. British Columbia Limited.

David Spencer Limited had a long and colourful history from the time of its founding in Victoria, British Columbia, and the store's history reveals many similarities to that of Eaton's. Both founders came to Canada from the British Isles. Both men were devout Christians who practiced the Methodist faith. Both stores became revered, family-owned institutions, and both were known as businesses that possessed a generosity of spirit when dealing with customers, suppliers and employees too. One big difference between the two firms was the fact that Spencer's gladly sold tobacco products, a virtual

John David Eaton, "Mr. Chris" Spencer and J.R. Jenkins, head of the newly formed T. Eaton & Co. British Columbia Limited, share a moment of joviality at the time of the big acquisition, which brought Eaton's to Canada's west coast. *Archives of Ontario: T. Eaton Fonds F229. Used with the permission of Sears Canada Ltd.*

taboo at Eaton's, and a less well known but positively unique aspect of the Spencer organization is that it was possibly the only department store that ever developed from a book and stationery shop.

David Spencer was born at St. Atham, Glamorganshire, Wales, in 1837, during the first year of Queen Victoria's reign. After being educated at the Cowbridge Grammar School, he was apprenticed to a dry goods retailer from 1851 through 1856. By 1858, Spencer, a devoutly religious man, served as a lay preacher in the local Wesleyan Methodist church organization. When he was working in a nearby dry goods shop, a report, in the form of a letter written to his friend Joseph Wilson, describing a gold rush in the Fraser River Valley in British Columbia caught his fancy. Accordingly, he and Wilson left Wales and set sail for the New World in 1862.

Their circuitous westbound route took Spencer first to New York and then south to Panama, where he travelled overland across the isthmus to the Pacific coast. After a stopover in San Francisco, he set foot in Victoria, British Columbia, in December 1863, but by the time of his arrival, the sought-after gold rush had ended. In spite of the arduous journey, Spencer had enough funds in his possession to purchase a business. An article about Spencer's history in the September 30, 1933 *Vancouver Province* noted:

> *By the time they arrived at their destination, the excitement caused by the discovery of gold in the Cariboo had considerably quieted down, and David Spencer, with an almost uncanny sense of business opportunity, decided to locate permanently in Victoria and enter the commercial field, rather than pursue his original plan of prospecting.*

On Friday, January 29, 1864, an ad appeared in the *British Colonist* indicating that the Victoria Library, on Fort Street, would heretofore operate under the ownership of David Spencer. The private circulating library offered "cheap reading" to patrons who either paid a monthly subscription of one dollar or borrowed books for one bit per volume. The business, which also advertised, "Valentines! Valentines!! Sentimental and Comic, New and Beautiful" on that day, expanded its stocks of stationery before long. By 1868, Spencer's library had grown into the city's major bookseller, but a fire in that year destroyed the premises. After rebuilding the store, Spencer sold it to T.N. Hibben & Co., stationers.

A 1941 article in Victoria's *Daily Colonist* about David Spencer and his retail empire shed light on the nature of the man himself:

> *A man respected for his keen sense of what was right in business and private life, Mr. Spencer was among those early pioneers "whose word was as good as his bond." Legal documents were rare things in the early days of Victoria, and a man's worth in the community was judged by his business reputation. David Spencer had the confidence of the citizens of the city, and respect of business and financial institutions. He died in 1920, but left behind him a tradition that has always been maintained by the Spencer Company.*

It was during the time of his ownership of the Victoria Library that David Spencer met his wife, Emma Lazenby. She was known later as a "pioneer woman," and the aptness of the name is illustrated by her arduous, six-month journey from her native Yorkshire to British Columbia, which took her around the Horn of Africa before she arrived in 1864. As she was herself an active and committed member of the Methodist faith, it is perhaps not surprising that she met David Spencer in the choir of the Pandora Avenue Methodist Church. They celebrated their marriage on June 30, 1867, and the union was a fruitful and long-lasting one, as Emma bore Spencer thirteen children—eight girls and five boys.

The actual founding of Spencer's as a retail business can be traced to January 4, 1873, when David Spencer entered into a five-year partnership with William Denny and bought Victoria House, the retail branch of wholesalers Findlay, Durham & Brodie. The one-storey storefront was located at the corner of Douglas and Fort Streets in Victoria and occupied a canopied building thirty feet wide by sixty feet deep. Denny & Spencer announced a mammoth clearance of the existing stock of the business and also proclaimed a policy of cash-only sales because, like Timothy Eaton to the east, "[t]he proprietors have long thought it unfair to the cash buyer to be charged the same Price as those who take long Credit."

The business prospered for the duration of the agreement, but upon its completion in 1878, David Spencer began his own retail venture, leaving Denny to carry on at the old location. The Commerce House, so-called by Spencer himself and located at Government and Fort Streets, opened for business on February 26, 1879, and soon became known as a retailer of dry goods and rugs exclusively imported from England, Europe and the United States. Success-driven expansions followed one after in 1882 and 1885, and in 1886, the store built the two-storey Arcade Building stretching from Government to Broad Street, with Spencer's store occupying the first floor and a YMCA facility and offices above. Item by item, Spencer's added lines like men's and boy's wear, millinery, home decoration, and shoes to its initial dry goods offering. By 1889, it employed forty-one staff and was renowned for the quality of its goods, excellent customer service and a thriving mail-order business.

The first branch was opened in 1890 in Nanaimo, in partnership with William H.S. Perkins, but when this partner retired four years later, it became completely owned by Spencer. Back in Victoria, a disastrous fire in 1901 laid the Arcade Building in Victoria to waste, but it was rebuilt a year later.

Opposite: The two flagship stores of David Spencer Limited in their heyday. *Archives of Ontario: T. Eaton Fonds F229. Used with the permission of Sears Canada Ltd.*

Victoria

Vancouver

 DAVID SPENCER
LIMITED

In 1904, a joint-stock company, David Spencer Limited, was formed, wholly controlled by Spencer and his five sons: Christopher, T.A. (Dean), Victor, David Jr. and J. William Spencer. Having become the premier department store on Vancouver Island, David Spencer set his sights on the mainland, where the city of Vancouver's exponential growth was deemed perfect for a replay of earlier successes. In the 1890s, a property was purchased on Hastings Street in Vancouver in order to facilitate an expansion onto the mainland. The land became superfluous when Spencer's bought out Gordon Drysdale's partner, Charles Stevenson, who had operated the established department store business of Drysdale & Stevenson Limited. In January 1907, Drysdale sold his share to David Spencer, and the store's name changed accordingly. Before long, Spencer's also took over Drysdale & Stevenson's Nanaimo branch and embarked on an expansion program in Vancouver that would see it eventually fill the block bounded by Hastings, Richards, Cordova and Seymour Streets.

By this time, the Victoria store had built or acquired a block-long frontage of two- and four-storey buildings on Broad Street and extended back to Government Street. It was all unceremoniously laid to waste on October 26, 1910, when the whole block went up in flames, causing more than $1 million worth of damage.

On following day, the *British Colonist* reported that the fire, which apparently began in the main aisle of the Spencer store, wiped out a whole block and left about thirty businesses without a home. Only two minor injuries were recorded as a result of the blaze, which mercifully began after business hours and wasn't brought under control until 2:30 a.m. The paper reported that the Driard Hotel across Broad Street was spared the worst, although it was damaged by the inferno, owing to high winds that blew tongues of flame towards it. The paper described the scene vividly:

> *The progress of the fire highly spectacular in every incident was of an appalling character. The spread of flames was remarkable for the fact that the wind carrying them along the top stories of the buildings it was apparently impossible for the fire fighters to locate the best point of vantage on which to concentrate the streams of water. By 11 o'clock it was apparent that the building occupied by David Spencer, Ltd. was doomed. The entire structure was a seething mass of flames. Whirling showers of sparks and flaming debris were borne by the wind in a southerly direction, the thousands of spectators dodging these as they fell to the ground littering the streets.*

After the damage was assessed and the remaining masonry walls toppled for safety, Spencer quickly decided to purchase the Driard Hotel building on the other side of Broad Street, and after a three-week 'round-the-clock remodeling of the exuberant, five-storey Victorian building, Spencer's was back in business, with stocks hustled over from the Vancouver store. Eventually, the Victoria Theatre, dating from 1885, and the Imperial Hotel on the same block were purchased and utilized to expand the Spencer store and give frontage on Douglas Street.

The old buildings, with their dainty Italianate façades, served Spencer's until new structures could be built. A two-storey structure of restrained architectural design, known by Spencer's as "the Arcade," was constructed on the old block, stretching from Government to Broad Street along View Street. This building was constructed to house rental offices and street-level shops, although eventually Spencer's moved its men's store into the Broad Street storefronts as it ran out of space in the makeshift store across the street. The second floor also housed a YMCA and auditorium. When it was completed in 1917, the *British Colonist* was full of announcements for retail stores and professional offices that had "moved to the new Spencer Block."

In late 1917, Spencer's ads announced a rebuilding program and the store removal sales meant to clear merchandise from the old Victoria Theatre and Imperial Hotel buildings. These buildings were ultimately razed, and in their place, Spencer's erected a modern, three-storey commercial block whose central Greek pediments hinted at the design of the former theatre on the site. The new building, characterized by wide, Chicago-style windows separated by piers with applied Neoclassical pilasters, met the sky with an elaborately modeled attic parapet. By January 1919, Spencer's was able to advertise that its new home was fully occupied, and it is this structure, at 1150 Douglas Street, along with the Driard Hotel, that formed the nucleus of Spencer's store in Victoria.

Eventually, Spencer's outgrew the new building and embarked on a program of acquisition and aggrandizement that saw it extend along Broad Street past the Driard Hotel by acquiring, in 1922, the former Kent Hotel and the Wilson Building. Likewise, Spencer's took advantage of the luxuriant Edwardian façade of the two-storey R.V. Winch Building when it bought the property and gained an entrance on Fort Street into the bargain in 1946. Spencer's Arcade provided even more square footage and became the location for the store's home furnishings departments. Even this large building proved inadequate; ultimately the Brown and Melrose Buildings on Broad Street came to become part of the downtown Victoria store. Broad

Street itself separated the two major blocks of the Spencer store, although a well-remembered tunnel, the location of a popular "malt bar," connected them below grade.

In Vancouver, where David Spencer's son Chris (known as "Mr. Chris" to scores of loyal Spencer employees) led the way, the store grew from relatively humble beginnings into a great metropolitan department store able to compete with the best of its well-established rivals the Hudson's Bay Company and Woodward's. In fact, the growth and acceptance of the Vancouver store resulted in its attaining status as Spencer's flagship, and due to its mainland position, it eventually became the head office as well.

When Spencer's changed the name of the former Drysdale-Stevenson Limited store in 1907, it had been operating in the 1880s-era Thompson-Ogle Block, remodeled four years earlier to a more modern storefront of white glazed brick by local architectural firm Parr and Fee. Almost immediately after beginning to operate as David Spencer Limited in Vancouver, the store built a nine-floor addition to the rear at Cordova Street that gave Spencer's a so-called lower main floor just below its main floor fronting on Hastings Street. The tall, narrow block was distinguished less by its austere brick-and-stone commercial style than its rooftop restaurant and roof garden that promised a view of Vancouver's stunning natural harbour. In 1911, a lower and even narrower addition broadened the store's presence eastward along Cordova Street.

On the other side of the block, Spencer's swallowed up the B.C. Saturday Sunset Building on its west side, with its wide and monumental third-floor arch, and the three-storey Standard Furniture building to the east. Spencer's was on a march to take the whole block; eventually the store, under the leadership of Chris Spencer, grew such in volume that it surpassed the original Victoria store and became the flagship for the organization that came to fancy itself as the "Greatest Department Store Organization of the Canadian West." Other acquisitions that were quickly integrated into the greater store included the six-storey Curtis and Wright book and stationery store at the corner of Cordova and Seymour Streets in 1921 and the palazzo-like Molson Bank building to the south on the corner of Hastings Street. This edifice, with a dramatically rusticated first floor, windows surmounted with alternating Greek or rounded pediments at its corners, soaring recesses topped by arches at the fourth-floor level and deep oculus windows supported by carved stone eagles served from its construction in 1898 as a west coast branch of the Molson (of brewery fame) family's Québec-based bank until it was taken over by the Bank of Montréal in 1925.

Around the same time, Spencer's purchased the remaining lots on the block and commissioned Vancouver architects McCarter and Nairn to design a vast new emporium that (had it ever been completed) would have dominated Vancouver's downtown shopping district as much as the store hoped to dominate the market itself. Construction started in 1925 on the expansion, which rose along sloping Richards Street, and extended westward by four bays, while Spencer's continued to operate in its older buildings, except for the Standard Furniture structure, which was demolished to make way for the new building.

When it was completed in late 1926, Spencer's, without much fanfare, simply expanded floor by floor into the structure, obviously anticipating a resumption of construction in the near future to complete the complex. Needless to say, the Great Depression put an end to those lofty plans, and just like Eaton's–College Street, Spencer's had to be satisfied with a variegated physical plant consisting of a truncated yet very deluxe modern store tied to smaller buildings it gobbled up along the way.

Yet the 1926 addition was not without its charms, however incomplete it was. Its modern steel frame was clad in a distinctive yellow brick and

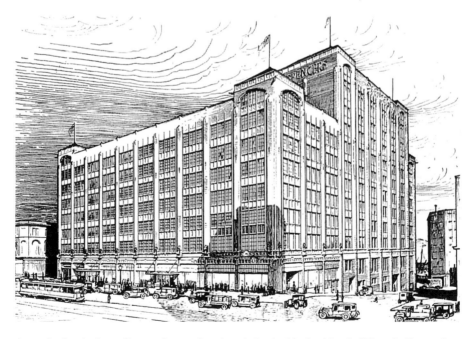

An early sketch shows Spencer's covering the whole city block with a building similar to the 1927 addition. The Depression put an end to such notions. *Archives of Ontario: T. Eaton Fonds F229. Used with the permission of Sears Canada Ltd.*

generously trimmed with stone, and its overall design hinted at corner pavilions that imparted great character to the overall composition. The florid stonework gave the Spencer's a vaguely Gothic appearance, with deep ribs rising up the façades and framing pairs of windows, inevitably inviting the eye to rise up towards the elaborate stone parapet that embellished the roofline. Rhythmic vertical piers enhanced the plasticity of the composition and sprung from brackets integrated into an extravagantly carved belt course of stone above the store's first floor level, punctuating the parapet by culminating in stone carvings in the form of shields, which, along with floral motifs, appeared at other locations along the elevations of this most elegant of department store creations.

Like Eaton's 1929 Calgary store, Spencer's main floor was entered by way of a beautifully detailed arcade of show windows that protected customers from the elements and showcased the store's merchandise to passersby. After making do with inherited properties and haphazard additions, Spencer's made an optimistic and welcoming gesture to the Vancouver public with its expansion.

By the time Spencer's celebrated its Diamond Jubilee in 1933, the store's status as an inseparable part of Vancouver had been well established, and its reputation as a store with a human heart could be gleaned from an article that appeared in the *Vancouver Province* on September 30 of that year:

> *More than 1500 people in Vancouver wake up in the morning, yawn and stretch their lazy muscles. They rush down to 1500 breakfasts, slam 1500 front doors, and are off to just one single destination. Their working lives, their hopes, their ambitions, often even their love affairs are tied up to just one name, "Spencer's." Tall, short, cheerful or grim, tired or chatty, peroxide or brunette, they are 1500 separate individualities, with none other exactly like them. Some have danced into the wee a.m.s' hours of the night before, some have stoically played cribbage until bedtime at 10 p.m. Some have been up with children, others have just taken on a new "steady" who will be forgotten in a fortnight. Here is a scattered city within a city, hundreds of men and women, yielding obedience to just one name: "Spencer"; trained to the one selling philosophy common to all progressive businesses: "The Customer Must Be Satisfied." Yet, with all the bustle and myriad irritations of the day, and of all other days, the store has managed to muster up the one big family feeling.*

Elsewhere, the article paid homage to the store it described as "a mighty business which ties together the people of the world who buy and the people who sell," noting that it incorporated a large welfare department, replete with nurses who dispensed first aid, and a free employees' lending library. The *Province* also noted that the welfare department "has its share of pathos in these times of depression" and that the welfare supervisor "has about 1500 friends in the store." In addition to that department, Spencer's was known for its Jericho Beach Grounds, a recreational facility for employees; its War Aid Volunteers Sports and Social Club; and "Spencer's Remnants," an organization of workers who had served in World War I.

Spencer's also maintained farms in Victoria and Haney, British Columbia, that supplied the store with dairy products and meat. Elsewhere in the province, aside from the aforementioned Nanaimo store, it opened branches in New Westminster and Chilliwack before World War II put a stop to expansion plans. Before being acquired by Eaton's, David Spencer Limited opened branches in Duncan, Courtenay and Mission in its home province.

Chris Spencer, who worked in his father's store from the time he was a youth and moved to Vancouver in 1911, achieved the office of the firm's presidency in 1920 after David Spencer passed away. Margaret Belford interviewed a former waitress from Spencer's dining room, who revealed herself only as "Ivy" but came to know Chris Spencer well in the years before 1948. Writing a 1979 article for the *Daily Colonist* that proclaimed Chris Spencer as "the Merchant Prince of British Columbia," Belford provided clear insight into why the younger Spencer achieved such a sterling reputation in his adopted hometown and among his employees:

> *Throughout his life, "Mr. Chris" did many good works, and travelled far and wide in his work. It has been said that when asked what his line of business was, his inevitable reply would be—"I am a shopkeeper on Hastings Street, Vancouver," and that held good whether he was in London or New York. Also, quite early on, he grew a small goatee beard in an effort to make himself look older than he was. He retained that beard to the end of his life. Christopher Spencer must have been a man of great energy, for besides his philanthropic activities and his stores he was a director of the Pacific Great Eastern Railway, the Bank of Nova Scotia and the Pacific Coast Fire Insurance Co. He was also awarded the CBE by the late King George VI for his war efforts during the Second World War. But all these things were what appeared in the public eye. Thus it was pleasant to sit and talk with one of his employees and to learn what the man had been like to work for. She tells me that one could not wish for a better employer. She recalls that, seeing him on a daily basis for so long, she thought him*

the most even-tempered and kindly of men. "He never forgot a name. Of course, he knew me because I always served him lunch. But it wasn't just me. He knew us all and was interested in us, and he always called us by our names—which he never forgot. And that's not bad when you think of all the hundreds of people who worked for him!"

Chilliwack

Mission

New Westminster

Duncan

Nanaimo

Courtenay

 DAVID SPENCER LIMITED

For Eaton's, the Spencer deal included branch stores that the western store opened, beginning in 1890 with Nanaimo, followed later by New Westminster and Chilliwack until three more stress were added after World War II. *Archives of Ontario: T. Eaton Fonds F229. Used with the permission of Sears Canada Ltd.*

A banquet given on Spencer's eightieth birthday on May 17, 1948, was attended by more than three hundred Spencer employees, for which the store's well-regarded bakery produced a one-hundred-pound cake able to hold eighty candles. In thanking what he referred to as "the great Spencer family" for their loyalty, "Mr. Chris" was quoted as saying, "This business could not have been built up by one man's work, but only by the combined effort of many. I do not know of anything we could have done to be of more use to the province of British Columbia, or to ourselves."

Thus it was that six months later, after closing hours on the night of November 30, 1948, Spencer stood on the store's mezzanine and spoke to his "family" one last time, announcing that David Spencer Limited had been bought by the T. Eaton Co. Limited. For some time, the newspapers had kept quiet about the Eaton-Spencer deal out of respect for "Mr. Chris," who expressed a desire to personally tell his friends and employees about the sale.

Overlooking the store, the largest and most important expression of the organization founded by his father seventy-five years earlier, Spencer spoke of the postwar realities facing the business, noting that burdensome taxes and succession duties made family-owned firms like Spencer's difficult to maintain. The store was faced with either going public or selling out to someone else:

> For many years, the T. Eaton Co. wanted to extend their business in Vancouver. They only put it off because we were great friends. Finally, they couldn't wait any longer. So, we had several meetings, finally came to terms, and tomorrow morning they take over. I think you will consider the present course the natural one and the best for all concerned. You will be wondering how all this will affect you. Our business and that of the T. Eaton Co. are very much alike. I've often been asked by customers originally from Toronto, if we were a branch of Eaton's. Our stores are both family stores. My father and Mr. John David Eaton's grandfather had the same ideas, especially about being of service to their customers, and that can only be done by a loyal and happy staff. I am assured that your jobs are just as safe as they would be if we continued to guide the ship.

With a wave of his hand, and to wild applause from the staff on the main floor below, Chris Spencer concluded his last act as president of David Spencer Limited, saying, "Well, my friends, that's all. You start again Thursday."

Crowds of Spencer employees fill the Vancouver store's aisles in December 1948 to listen to Chris Spencer's announcement that the store had been sold to Eaton's. *Archives of Ontario: T. Eaton Fonds F229. Used with the permission of Sears Canada Ltd.*

John David Eaton also addressed the crowd, stating, "I can only say that the T. Eaton Company has a long-standing reputation for fair dealing both with its customers and its staff and we propose to maintain that reputation in our newly acquired stores in British Columbia. I should like to welcome you as new additions to the Eaton staff family, and express the thought that you will enjoy working with us, and that the customers you serve will like shopping with us, too." He also introduced J. Ross Jenkins, vice-president and general manager of the new T. Eaton Co. British Columbia Limited. On December 1, 1948, a full-page ad appeared in the *Vancouver Sun*, announcing to the public the same news shared with employees the night before.

Although it refrained from changing the names on the stores until after the holiday to avoid confusion to longstanding customers, Eaton's wasted no time in integrating its acquisition to the larger company. Of course, it was neither easy for the company or the store to avoid controversy, and in some cases resentment, after such a change was first rumoured and then so suddenly announced. In time, though, statements such as, "It will always be Spencer's to me!" were voiced with less frequency as Eaton's invested heavily in the store buildings, and customers became familiar with Eaton policies and merchandise.

In Vancouver, as the controversy over the occupation of the old Hotel Vancouver died down, the company did indeed demolish the landmark, but only to turn the property into a parking lot, and most inconveniently at that, since it was five blocks from the store on Hastings Street. Talk of a new store died down as Eaton's slowly renovated Spencer's former flagship with a consistent street-level storefront and modern marquee. Inside, new construction brightened and reorganized the interior while maintaining some of the former owner's traditions. Thus, the British Columbia stores never featured the Ensemble Shop or Town House like its eastern cousins; for many years, these shops for high fashion apparel were named the French Room and Regency Room, in deference to Spencer tradition.

One of the biggest changes instituted by Eaton's was the new Marine Room, which replaced Spencer's matter-of-fact restaurant. The new eatery, again designed by René Cera, was located on the sixth floor and offered the quality of food and service pioneered by Lady Eaton in Toronto's Georgian

Eaton's unified the façade of Spencer's Hastings Street store at ground level, with a new store front and a block-long marquee. *Archives of Ontario: T. Eaton Fonds F229. Used with the permission of Sears Canada Ltd.*

Eaton's French Room was the west coast equivalent of the Toronto and Montréal stores' Ensemble Shop. *Archives of Ontario: T. Eaton Fonds F229. Used with the permission of Sears Canada Ltd.*

Room, this time enhanced beyond imagination by the view: a broad and dramatic panorama of Vancouver's splendid Burrard Inlet, with a backdrop of the dramatic Coast Mountains rising in the distance.

Cera's design divided the five-hundred-seat restaurant into a series of rooms incorporating vivid and colourful fabrics, decorative accents that carried out the marine theme, light wood furniture and natural greenery. Screens composed of deeply framed replicas of indigenous fish served as dividers between the rooms, and the whole installation was tied together by a ceiling consisting of a deep grid that related to the bold plaid upholstery on chairs and banquettes. One of Cera's thoughtful innovations was the cladding of the massive piers between the store's windows with mirrors, effectively making them "go away" and enhancing the spectacular vista they framed. The restaurant, opened in 1949, quickly became a destination that effortlessly drew shoppers and visitors upward through Eaton's to enjoy its many charms.

In Victoria, Eaton's renovated its store as well, most dramatically on the interior, where a great deal of money was spent imparting an elegant,

The luxurious appointments and stunning panoramic view from the Marine Room created an appropriate setting for fine food served in the Eaton tradition. *Archives of Ontario: T. Eaton Fonds F229. Used with the permission of Sears Canada Ltd.*

modern atmosphere to the main floor and updating areas throughout the various buildings that occupied parts of two city blocks. In deference to tradition, Eaton's budget store retained the time-honored name "Bargain Highway," as established by David Spencer Limited many years earlier and embraced by the Victoria public. Eventually, the tunnel that joined the original store's building to the home furnishings departments in the Arcade Building was augmented by a bridge across Broad Street at the second-floor level. Food and hospitality played a major role in Victoria, where the fourth-floor Victoria Room became a favourite shoppers' rendezvous, while the malt bar adjacent to the tunnel under Broad Street gained renown as an attraction for the younger set.

Eaton's then looked to the outlying stores it acquired when it came to British Columbia and sought to replace or modify the branch stores to better support the company's business model. The first change occurred on March 16, 1949, when Eaton's opened a thoroughly modern new store in the so-called Royal City of New Westminster just east of Vancouver. The eighty-four-thousand-square-foot store, about a block to the east

Eaton's updated the Victoria store's exterior and created a handsome modern shopping environment on Douglas Street in the provincial capital. *Archives of Ontario: T. Eaton Fonds F229. Used with the permission of Sears Canada Ltd.*

of the old, four-storey Spencer store that had operated for years at the corner of Columbia and Sixth Streets, caused quite a stir on account of its innovative modern appearance.

The *Vancouver Sun*, informing readers about the store, noted, "The store provides every possible convenience for the shopper, one feature being an

Among the first of Spencer's branches to be replaced was the New Westminster location, opened in 1949. *Archives of Ontario: T. Eaton Fonds F229. Used with the permission of Sears Canada Ltd.*

escalator which carries customers from the Front Street level to the lower main level and then to the main floor. Majestic glass doors and eye-catching show windows, designed to show merchandise to the best advantage, front the building. Not a single item in the design and construction of the 'modern shopper's paradise' has been left to chance, say Eaton officials."

Eaton's celebrated the modernization of the former Spencer store in the Vancouver Island town of Duncan, British Columbia, on July 28, 1950, and then turned its sights on the old store in the Fraser Valley town of Chilliwack. A large new replacement, proudly proclaiming "Eaton's of Canada—Chilliwack Branch" above its broad storefront on Wellington Avenue, opened on April 24, 1952. The new Eaton's bore a resemblance to the New Westminster store of three years earlier but was, in fact, about half its size. The austere, stone-faced store followed a design that became standard for Eaton's small-town stores in the 1950s that became a familiar sight in Canada.

Eaton's added the Kootenay mountain town of Trail, British Columbia, to its list of locations on January 5, 1953, when it acquired Trail Mercantile, the company store of the Consolidated Mining & Smelting Company Limited (CM&S), which operated what is still the world's largest lead and zinc smelter, located on the banks of the Columbia River. Like the Corner Brook store way across Canada in Newfoundland, Eaton's upgraded the operation to provide the type of merchandise and service customers came to expect wherever the Eaton name graced a department store.

Next, Eaton's rebuilt the Nanaimo store, location of the oldest Spencer branch, in operation since 1890. This time, the characteristic stone-faced façade was set back from its property lines on Victoria Crescent and Albert Street, in this harbour city on the middle point of Vancouver Island's east coast. The resulting plaza in front of Eaton's sixty-three-thousand-square-foot store, which opened on April 10, 1958, was large enough to prominently display a magnificent totem pole, paying homage to the area's ethnic heritage. Variegated fieldstone walls between the store's show windows imparted character to the store's first floor.

In 1959, Eaton's built its first new branch store in British Columbia, in the wealthy Okanagan Valley town of Vernon. This time, the forty-six-thousand-square-foot store, at 3401 Thirtieth Avenue in Vernon's central business district, broke the pattern set by the earlier stores by featuring vertical ribs and reveals on its façade above the now traditional wide marquee shading the store's inviting show windows.

Above: North of Victoria, the port city of Nanaimo got a completely new and modern Eaton branch in 1959. The totem pole displayed on the store's entrance plaza is visible to the left. *Archives of Ontario: T. Eaton Fonds F229. Used with the permission of Sears Canada Ltd.*

Opposite: Eaton's made its presence known in British Columbia in the 1950s, opening new stores in Chilliwack, Trail and Vernon. *Archives of Ontario: T. Eaton Fonds F229. Used with the permission of Sears Canada Ltd.*

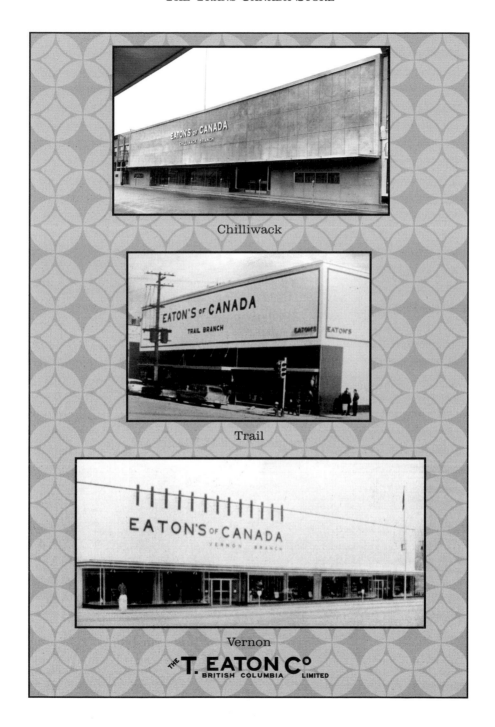

Chilliwack

Trail

Vernon

During the time it built or improved branch stores throughout British Columbia, Eaton's didn't neglect the flagship store in Vancouver either. Initially, the problem of the remote parking facility on the site of the 1916 Hotel Vancouver was solved by providing a shuttle service to shoppers arriving downtown by car. In 1953, though, Eaton's sought to improve access to the store by building a $600,000 parking garage along Cordova Street, just across Richards Street from the store. The parking lot on the site had become inadequate, and cars waiting to get in regularly caused backups around the store.

When the five-hundred-car garage opened in July 1958, it was considered one of the most modern and best-designed in Canada. Wide-span construction eliminated the obstacle of support columns between parking spaces, and the garage was connected to the store by an underground tunnel and a bridge that went directly into Eaton's second floor. The *Vancouver Sun*, along with the help of local Eaton officials, made a great deal about these conveniences, saying that the garage "was designed with the woman shopper in mind—so much so…that milady can now go downtown and do her shopping in her bedroom slippers!"

With so much construction at the branch stores and on the garage downtown, Eaton's was late in expanding into Vancouver's growing suburban areas. Competitor Woodward's, which, like Spencer's, had stores in Victoria and other British Columbia towns, as well as in Edmonton, Alberta, got the ball rolling in 1955 with its branch store in the lovely Park Royal Shopping Centre in West Vancouver, "in the shadow of the Lion's Gate bridge." Eaton's didn't budge from downtown until August 1961, when on the sixteenth of that month it opened a 192,000-square-foot store in the Brentwood Centre in suburban Burnaby.

Being the first big suburban department store south of the Burrard Inlet was probably enough to generate publicity, but Eaton's made sure that customers knew this three-level showplace offered more than just merchandise for sale. Grand opening ads touted the store's Pioneer Room restaurant, its Mayfair Beauty Salon and other services, like an optical salon, a photographic studio and a catalogue order desk. The *Vancouver Sun*, dedicating page after page to reports about and descriptions of Eaton's Brentwood, extolled the company's achievement as "one of Canada's most functional shopping marts as well as a building of beauty."

Tellingly, an article describing the store's décor and amenities put it succinctly: Eaton's, which, at the time, often advertised itself as the "Store for Young Canada," planned and designed its newest expression of its retail philosophy to appeal to "progressive young people who eye both budget and style." The article went on to describe how it came to be that way:

> *Shopping appeal for young families will be stressed at Eaton's new store in Brentwood Shopping Centre. It's the result of surveys undertaken in the neighbourhood two years ago when [Eaton's] decided to locate in the centre. They showed the community in the Burnaby area to be one of up-and-coming young people with growing school children and infants. Taking this into consideration, Eaton's has given a large proportion of its Brentwood store over to the needs of Young Canada. Size ranges are vast. Price ranges are suited to economy or higher bracket. Up and down to all three levels of Eaton's Brentwood run escalators of the newest design. Satin bronze finish with gold-tone porcelain enamel is the décor on both sides. Balustrades on the fashion floor and upper levels are enclosed with coloured glass and act as display fixtures for seasonal merchandise. High above the escalator is a fascinating light well in the roof of the store. This borders a sky-line insert which features star-like indirect lighting. Adding more excitement to the feeling of spaciousness created by this treatment is a hanging planter area.*

About the design of the innovative new store, the *Sun* reported that "the colour has been scientifically researched and selected, artistically applied and interpreted, to create a mood, and to provide appropriate backgrounds for both merchandise and customer," while explaining that colour "in the women's fashion departments is pastel to flatter the complexion or vivid to stir the imagination…Bold, rich red creates the background for the men's departments," and children's departments "arc cosy in coral and the nursery set rejoices in forsythia yellow." It concluded the analysis saying that "each colour chosen adds interest and beauty to the overall decorative effect."

Two months before the opening of Brentwood, Eaton's broke ground for another store, this time in West Vancouver at the existing Park Royal Shopping Centre. Occupying the South Mall expansion area of the popular retail rendezvous at the northern end of Vancouver's iconic Lion's Gate Bridge, the store was distinguished by a stained wooden screen that embellished its façade and lent the box-like building a warm, indigenous character. Telling prospective customers that the new store was "Ready and Eager to Serve You," Eaton's two-page grand opening spread enticed customers:

> *Tomorrow morning EATON'S PARK ROYAL will open its doors so that our West and North Vancouver customers can have more convenient shopping*

Large, modern branch stores serving the outlying areas of Vancouver in the 1960s included Brentwood in Burnaby and Park Royal in West Vancouver. *Archives of Ontario: T. Eaton Fonds F229. Used with the permission of Sears Canada Ltd.*

right NOW. Come Wednesday at 9:30 a.m. and see for yourself this brightest, newest member of EATON's family of stores. It is designed specifically for the area it serves. It is spacious and has easy access from ample parking lots or from the Shopping Mall. It has two floors plus an outdoor shop...It is a building of natural British Columbia fieldstone, brick, and timber beams...architecturally blending with its beautiful nature-given setting. Everywhere in the new store you will have the feeling of space...free flowing aisles, soft lighting and warm colours, pleasant music and friendly EATON's personnel.

On October 3, 1962, John David Eaton himself turned the traditional golden key and the 123,000-square-foot store opened to the public. The opening was conspicuous owing to the presence of John David Eaton's sons

John Craig and Fredrik Stefan, who were employed by the company in Toronto and Victoria, respectively. Eaton's opened in advance of the rest of the shopping centre's expansion, which came online two weeks later, but as beaming store manager F. Emerson West explained, "We couldn't wait for the completion of the rest of the centre—we had to show the store." The *Vancouver Sun* described the scene, saying, "Eaton's gave the assembled crowd of more than 1,000 something to see. Situated between groves of trees, bright with autumn colours that line the banks of the Capilano River and Burrard Inlet and the North Shore mountains, the store has undoubtedly one of the most beautiful settings in Canada."

It was not until 1972 that Eaton's opened another store in the Vancouver area. On May 3 of that year, an attractive, precast-concrete structure, housing Eaton's new store in the Surrey, British Columbia's 1966 Guildford Town Centre, flung open its doors. By the 1970s, the opening of suburban branch stores had become much more commonplace than it had been at the dawn of the shopping-centre era, and the 122,000-square-foot store in Surrey was no exception, with the opening celebrations more geared towards sales, sweepstakes and giveaways (free dogwood seedlings were given to opening day patrons), although Eaton's did advertise "Beautiful store, beautiful area, beautiful savings."

By the time of the Guildford Town Centre opening, John David Eaton was ailing, and his son John Craig Eaton presided over the event. Speaking to the press, the younger Eaton hinted at changes Canada might expect to see over the coming years. While he complimented historic districts like Vancouver's Gastown, saying, "There's room for all of us; I think Gastown is unique in Canada. They sell a different type of merchandise…some unusual and avant-garde fashions, and there's a place for that," he warned Torontonians that their beloved Queen Street Eaton's was not long for this world when he added, "I think if old warehouses are not revenue-producing, they should be torn down. I suppose our store in downtown Toronto might be considered a landmark, but I'd rather have a new building."

Although John Craig Eaton chose to mention Toronto at the Surrey opening, Vancouver itself was preparing for a major change in its downtown retail environment in 1973. For years since the 1948 purchase of the old Hotel Vancouver, the development of the property had been surrounded by controversy. In *The Store that Timothy Built*, the book commissioned for the 100th anniversary of the T. Eaton Co., John David Eaton was quoted as saying that his greatest failure as Eaton's president had been his dealings with city governments over downtown redevelopment. Although he was quoted as speaking about Toronto, Vancouver was no exception. Eaton's waited while the politicians argued over the disposition of Block 42, adjacent to Eaton's parking. John David's actual quote, according to author William Stephenson, was, "City Hall has consistently thwarted us, even though it would mean that we'd pay far more taxes than we do now. How the hell does a storekeeper combat that kind of mentality?"

Nonetheless, the Pacific Centre project eventually became a reality, composed of a shopping mall, a Four Seasons hotel and offices on Block 42, across Granville Street from Hudson's Bay Company's elegant Vancouver flagship store, the thirty-storey Toronto-Dominion Bank tower and a new Eaton's store on Block 41. Conceived by well-known retail specialist and Gruen Associates' chief designer, Cesar Pelli, the Eaton store was a minimalistic, five-storey block faced in white aggregate stone panels and punctuated by black glass curtain walls at its entries. These features, the largest of which was a rotunda set back from Georgia Street and facing the elegant, columned façades of the Bay across the intersection, were an attempt to animate the building and give it scale, as were the small chamfers at its corners. The tower that sat astride Eaton's was likewise clad in a sheer dark curtain wall, an homage to pioneering German modernist architect Ludwig Mies van der Rohe. Its own beveled corners mimicked those on the department store in scale but were executed in glass and aluminum.

Although its design concept was concisely expressed, the ensemble met with fairly severe criticism, mainly centering on the inhospitable nature of Eaton's sheer façades and the unfriendly way in which they met the sidewalk at pedestrian level. In particular, the Granville Street side, which lacked show windows, was said by critics to "make the city's main street [look] like a back lane adjacent to the store" according to the *Vancouver Sun*. The Toronto-Dominion bank building itself was not immune from criticism and acquired the pejorative nickname of "the Dark Tower" before long. The most intense scorn was reserved for years later, when the Pacific Centre Eaton's store acquired two more floors in 1981, designed as a bulbous "crown" of curvilinear panels hovering over a deep reveal of dark glass. Unfortunately, to many observers, the top floor looked like the edge of a toilet seat, and the building was dubbed "the Great White Toilet" by unkind critics.

The plaza in front of the store was graced by a gossamer bird-like sculpture, *Untitled*, by sculptor George Norris, who gained notoriety for his similarly untitled crab installed at the Museum of Vancouver. The flowing lines of *Untitled*, executed in shiny stainless steel, evoked, from various perspectives, a crane, a dragonfly or a ballerina and were a

EATON'S
Pacific Centre

Eaton's finally built a store on the old Hotel Vancouver site, and although it had some fairly dramatic design elements, like a glassy rotunda and a landscaped plaza at its entry, its architecture was not universally well received. *Archives of Ontario: T. Eaton Fonds F229. Used with the permission of Sears Canada Ltd.*

welcome contrast to the geometric and unadorned severity of the Pacific Centre's architecture.

Yet when it opened, Eaton's and the Pacific Centre nonetheless gleamed with all that was contemporary and new. Newspaper reports called the store a "showcase," and Eaton's took full advantage of the opportunity to reposition its image and shed any memories as heir to the Spencer tradition dating back to 1873. The press, interviewing Eaton executives about the store, focused on the store's fashion orientation and singled out its rotunda for praise. Flanked by entrances and housing an innovative, glassed-in jewelry salon, the rotunda rose up to provide a two-storey ceiling on the main floor, with a second-floor balcony overlooking the space. Above, the curved walls and ample light enhanced the "Like Young" shop on the third floor and a gallery of lamps on the fourth.

On February 8, 1973, Vancouver mayor Art Phillips gathered at 701 Granville Street along with Eaton executives, Signy Eaton, her sons John Craig and Fredrik Stefan and Eileen Fisher, the Eaton employee with the longest service in Vancouver, to pull a cord that released hundreds of balloons upward and sent colourful streamers down the face of the dark, shiny Rotunda, announcing the opening of the 490,000-square-foot store. Later, Mrs. Eaton served the mayor as he made the store's historic first transaction, selecting cufflinks from Eaton's wide choice. Conspicuously absent was John David Eaton, who was ill and unable to travel to the event.

The general interior design of the Pacific Centre store was a revelation to customers used to the simultaneously staid yet haphazardly organized store inherited from David Spencer Limited. Colourful, bold and modern, an Eaton spokesman said of the store:

> We already have been getting many favourable comments from those who have had the opportunity of a pre-opening visit to the store, and we expect that most favourable comments will be general as the general public sees and admires our new setting. The goods we had in our old store (on Hastings) with its different levels on each floor would have looked much better in this new centre downtown. Not only will the public look at us differently than it has since we located here by taking over Spencer's store on Hastings in 1948, but members of the staff are getting a lift out of the change already. We feel that people will look at us in a different light after they have seen us in our new home. Now, with our new showcase, we are enlarging our vista. We are continuing to offer the standard items that over a period of more than 100 years have made Eaton's name a synonym for economy and

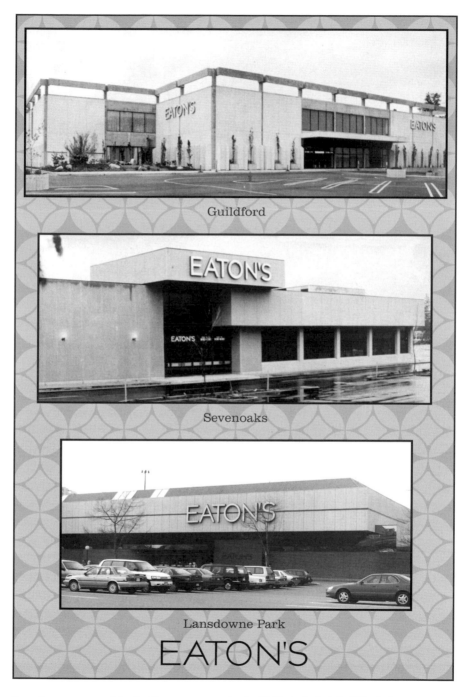

Guildford

Sevenoaks

Lansdowne Park

EATON'S

Branch stores opened in the Vancouver area in the 1970s included Guildford, Sevenoaks and Lansdowne Park in Richmond, British Columbia. *Photos courtesy of Darrell Bateman.*

value, but in addition, we have decided to become more fashion oriented. That's a trend in our own company, Eaton's on St. Catherine Street in Montréal has one of the best fashion images of any retailer, and it is a trend in department stores generally.

The *Vancouver Sun* described the new store's "Big Store Look," characterizing the vivid interior composed of "strong forms and bold colours" softened by the introduction of greenery that "should also assist in the overall attractiveness of the store's impression." The newspaper singled out the fashion floor for its intimate boutiques, arranged along strongly defined aisles, as examples of thoughtful, customer-oriented store design. The special "Pacific Lights" chandelier hanging in Eaton's Rotunda was a focal point meant to give a dramatic first impression of the new west coast flagship, while the popular-priced mall level, which connected across the street to the Pacific Centre Mall, had "the stepped-down fashion look with slightly louder colouring and more definite departmental areas." The new store also featured a reinvention of the Marine Room restaurant, but the location smack-dab in the centre of Vancouver's expanding downtown skyline precluded the view that was such a special feature of its predecessor.

Eaton's, diagonally across from Vancouver's well-established Hudson's Bay Company store, suddenly found itself at the proverbial "100 percent" corner of the city's downtown. The new dynamic left Eaton's former location on Hastings Street somewhat in the lurch and further isolated Vancouver's other well-loved department store, Woodward's, located far to the east in the old Gastown area that was nonetheless in the process of rejuvenation. Soon after the Pacific Centre opened, plans were announced for the new Harbour Centre development on the Hastings Street site. The project replaced the oldest parts of the Spencer store with a modern office tower topped by a revolving restaurant that made the most of the view made famous by the 1949 Marine Room. The 1927 portion of the store was integrated into the development, and Sears opened a major branch in the development as well.

In subsequent years, Eaton's cemented its position as a major force in British Columbia retailing by opening an 84,000-square-foot store at Sevenoaks in Clearbrook on October 15, 1975, and followed that on September 14, 1977, with a large 190,000-square-foot store at Lansdowne Park in Richmond, British Columbia, before the dawn of the 1980s—when the winds of changed caused anything but smooth sailing for the juggernaut that was Eaton's.

I Love a Parade!

It's bound to be one of the happiest shows of the year...a feast of sounds and sights in glorious colour. And it's all brought to you by EATON'S.
—1968 ad promoting the Santa Claus Parade

Canada's traditional Thanksgiving Day is celebrated during the first half of October, and unlike its counterpart south of its borders, the day does not carry any symbolism as the beginning of the Christmas shopping season. For many years, in Canada, the season began with the opening of Toyland (Toyville in Montréal) at Eaton's and the arrival of Santa Claus from the North Pole to listen to the wishes of eager children as they paid him a visit. As the arrival of St. Nick developed into Eaton's Santa Claus Parade, the event became inseparable from the great retailer, just as Eaton's was an integral part of Canadian life.

The parade itself had its beginnings in 1905, when it was determined that Santa Claus should have an appropriate arrival from the North Pole before being escorted to Eaton's Toyland, fully stocked in anticipation of Christmastime traffic. Eaton's pioneered the Christmas parade, an event later copied by Gimbel Brothers of Philadelphia (1920) and both Macy's and the J.L. Hudson Company in 1924. The three American parades gained great notoriety in the United States and were broadcast first by radio and then later, at the dawn of the television age, on the CBS network on Thanksgiving Day. Gimbels' Santa thrilled Philadelphians by climbing up a fire ladder to the store's fifth-floor Toyland, Macy's had its enormous balloons and Hudson's gave Santa the key to the city of Detroit as he arrived at his castle perched on the giant red-brick store's marquee. Yet it was the sheer beauty, creativity and style of Eaton's Santa Claus Parade that made it famous, and in the 1950s, after gaining a place in CBC television broadcasts, it joined its younger American counterparts as one of the "Big Four" Christmas parades of North America.

A 1950 full-page advertisement announced Eaton's famous Santa Claus Parade with a very jolly image of St. Nick himself and preview images of the major floats in the parade. *From an ad, collection of the author.*

The brainchild of Timothy Eaton, and put into practice by his son John Craig Eaton, the parade began as a simple arrival for Santa Claus, signaling Eaton's readiness for the Christmas shopping season. In Toronto, after an imaginary journey from the North Pole, a suitably dressed Santa emerged from the portals of the monumental, Neoclassical Toronto Union Station, boarded a horse-drawn wagon and was conveyed northward to Eaton's on Yonge Street. Along the way, he tossed candy, nuts and trinkets to the assembled crowds.

As the parade developed, it grew in size, and its route changed over time. In 1909, the terminus of the parade was switched to Massey Hall, filled with children awaiting Santa's arrival. The first float appeared in 1910, and costumed characters marched the parade route for the first time in the next year. Starting in 1917, Santa came directly to Eaton's, where he alighted from his carriage to a platform above an entrance canopy, from which he entered the store for direct access to his throne in the store's Toyland, ready for the coming shopping rush. This ceremonial entrance

An artist in the employ of Eaton's Merchandise Display Department puts the finishing touches on a mask for use in the Santa Claus Parade. Note the figure of Punkinhead on the table to the left. *Archives of Ontario: T. Eaton Fonds F229. Used with the permission of Sears Canada Ltd.*

and its regular repetition is what probably led to the general belief among Canadian shoppers that any store could have *a* Santa in residence, but Eaton's was the *real* Santa.

When Eaton's opened the big Winnipeg store in 1905, a similar event took place before Christmas, and the Manitoba capital came to love its own store-sponsored Santa Claus Parade. Montréal gained its own parade 1925, and it came to be staged a week after the Toronto affair. The Toronto parade typically continued past Eaton's store directly to railroad yards on Toronto's waterfront, where the floats were loaded onto freight cars and immediately shipped to Québec, where they could be used again. Parade uniforms were shipped eastward later after they were cleaned and packed for Montréal's *Grand Défilé du Père Noel.* From time to time, Santa Claus Parades were held in other cities where Eaton's had major stores.

By 1969, Eaton's centennial year, the parade stretched one and a half miles, involved five hundred musicians and 1,100 children in costume and cost more than $100,000 to produce. What's more, the Santa Claus Parade differed from other parades, whose sponsors contracted outside firms to create the needed props. Every costume, float and papier-mâché head used in the parade was the product of the store's Merchandise Display Department, which worked out of the old factory buildings north of Albert Street before moving to a fifteen-thousand-square-foot space in the Sheppard Avenue service building in 1956. The craftsmen at work there used no blueprints but created the parade's props, large or small, from the designer's sketches.

A further difference was Eaton's involvement of local children to march in the parade, wearing costumes fitted for them before the beginning of the event. Participation was so popular that at one time there was a waiting list of children eager to be a part of the parade. Youngsters were paid a nominal fee for the day and were rewarded with hot chocolate and cookies afterwards in one of the delivery garages near the store.

The thoughtful composition and timing of the parade was the brainchild of Jack Brockie, who from 1928 until 1963 was Eaton's special events manager. Brockie introduced new technologies to the parade and saw to it that the balance between floats, marching bands and parade characters never conflicted with one another, as well as that the whole thing built up step by step to the crescendo of Santa's arrival, while as many as 500,000 people along the route fell under the spell of the famous event.

Under Brockie's guidance, each year the parade developed a new theme. In 1957, the parade depicted "The Parade of Merry Times," in 1958 "The Royal Road to Toyland" and 1954's memorable parade provided

The Santa Claus Parade passes Toronto's old city hall on James Street, with the venerable store on the right. One of the James Street entrance canopies is ready to receive Santa when he arrives. *Archives of Ontario: T. Eaton Fonds F229. Used with the permission of Sears Canada Ltd.*

onlookers with a panorama of "Rhymes and Fairytales from Distant Lands." While each parade differed in theme, floats were reused from year to year because of their popularity and because of the expense involved in creating them. Among the most popular characters involved in the parade were Cinderella, Mother Goose, Gulliver, Sleeping Beauty, Snow White and the Fairy Queen.

Similarly, the bands and music of Eaton's Santa Claus Parade repeated their performances again and again to the delight of crowds and TV viewers alike, playing Christmas favourites appropriate to the time of year. Frank McEachren, head of Eaton's public relations department (and incidentally, husband of Lady Eaton's daughter Florence), once admitted that the crowd favourite in Toronto was always "Jingle Bells" and that it was usually played just as Santa arrived at his destination.

Santa's conveyance was often the largest and most elaborate of the floats. In earlier years, his float bore him in a sleigh behind his team of reindeer over snow-covered rooftops. Later, Santa arrived behind an animated team of white reindeer, leaping and galloping as the parade made its way down

The climax of the parade was always Santa's arrival at Eaton's. His fanciful conveyance, for many years, was an elabourate float topped by animated galloping reindeer. *Archives of Ontario: T. Eaton Fonds F229. Used with the permission of Sears Canada Ltd.*

An integral part of Christmas at Eaton's was the animated and artistically decorated display windows of the Queen Street store. This image shows a magnificent crèche that would have surely pleased the devoutly religious Timothy Eaton. *Archives of Ontario: T. Eaton Fonds F229. Used with the permission of Sears Canada Ltd.*

Bloor and either University or, later, Yonge Street before depositing Santa on either the James or Albert Street side of the store. It was discovered, after experimentation, that the best method of animating the reindeer was to pay high school boys to ride, concealed, inside the float, pedaling a bicycle mechanism that gave the reindeer their characteristic brio.

A dark-blue and red Eaton's van following Santa carried a second Santa, in case of a problem, along with a nurse and doctor should the excitement of the day overwhelm the parade's celebrity. In most cases, the backups were not needed, but mishaps during the parade were not unknown, ranging from an alcohol-soaked Santa who announced, "Merry Christmas, you little bastards!" when greeting the crowd assembled to receive him to the sober but no less comical one whose "jolly" stomach, padded out with a feather pillow, had become soaked by rain, causing his pants to drop as he ascended the ladder to the store.

Eaton's events at Christmas were not limited to its historic and unforgettable parade but merely started a season in which the store pulled out all the stops to attract customers. Elaborate Christmas windows, notably in Toronto but at all main stores, attracted crowds of onlookers, who came downtown just to see them. Given the religious foundation of the business under Timothy Eaton, one window (at least) was usually dedicated to a beautiful crèche scene depicting the Nativity. The Toronto windows were produced in the same display studios that created the parade floats as well.

Inside the stores, in addition to decorations that turned their interiors into a fairyland of lights, trees and colourful ornaments, many featured a "Toyland Train" for children in the seasonally expanded toy departments to an actual "Christmasland," where Santa held court and received children eager to tell him what they'd like to find under their family's Christmas tree.

In fact, from 1948, a ride on the "Toyland Train" concluded with a souvenir gift of a book featuring Punkinhead, the "Sad Little Bear" who became a famous and famously loved mascot for the store's holiday celebrations. Punkinhead was the creation of Charles "Cartoon Charlie" Thorson, of Winnipeg, the son of Icelandic immigrants. Thorson's life was wracked with pain over the death of his first wife and two infants, as well as the breakup of his second marriage, and he left Canada in 1935 to pursue a career in Hollywood, where he spent two tempestuous years at the Walt Disney Studios. Although disputed by Disney, Thorson claimed to have created the cartoon character Snow White. After Leaving Disney, Thorson worked for Warner Bros., where he originated the character Bugs Bunny for the studio.

Punkinhead, the "Sad Little Bear," was created for Eaton's in 1947 and soon became a beloved symbol of Christmas at Eaton's. *From an ad, collection of the author.*

In 1947, back in Winnipeg, Thorson was asked to create a character for Eaton's at the dawn of the "baby boomer" era. Punkinhead, a bear with an unruly shock of orange hair atop his head, appeared in the Santa Claus Parade. In 1948, he became the subject of books provided by Eaton's for children, and his popularity led, in 1953, to the creation of a wide variety of Punkinhead merchandise, which became immensely popular. The name Punkinhead was a favourite nickname of Thorson's for his own redheaded son.

From 1948, books in which the character featured included *Punkinhead, the Sad Little Bear, Punkinhead and the Snow Fairy, Punkinhead in Santa's Workshop, Punkinhead and the Magic Wishes, How Punkinhead Came to Toyland, Punkinhead and the Christmas Party* and eight others. The artist unwisely sold his rights to the character for a pittance and retired to British Columbia, where he died in 1966. Punkinhead bears, manufactured to high standards set by firms like Steiff of Giengen, Germany, were initially made by Merrythought of Shropshire, England. After 1956, they were produced in Canada and remain highly sought-after collectibles.

Food played a part of holiday celebrations in Eaton's restaurants. Ads announcing the time, date and route of the Santa Claus Parade in Montréal also invited customers to enjoy a "delicious turkey dinner" in *Le 9e* restaurant. The dinner came with all of the trimmings, including a (non-alcoholic) beverage and dessert for a family-friendly price. Eaton's food departments produced a famously rich dark fruit cake that became a holiday standard from coast to coast in Canada. A Christmas meal in the Georgian Room, Grill Room, *Le 9e*, Marine Room, Green Room or any one of the many Eaton food service outlets was an integral and time-honored part of a Christmas shopping trip for generations of Canadians.

For many girls, to receive a gift of one of the famous "Eaton's Beauty Dolls" was the highlight of Christmas celebrations. The dolls—originally manufactured in Germany, featuring bisque heads, sleep eyes and elaborate costumes—were introduced in the 1900 edition of *Eaton's Catalogue*. Production shifted to Canada during World War I and then back to Germany again during peacetime. Canadian manufacture was again introduced during the depression, and plastic dolls debuted in the 1950s.

Darlene Lawson, a freelance writer from New Brunswick, wrote a short narrative explaining the significance of the dolls to the life of a young girl growing up in Canada with Eaton's:

> *Long after Christmas was over and the cold months of winter settled around our little country home, the Eaton's catalogue was my source of entertainment. As the light from the oil lamp burned brightly, Mom sat with her knitting needles, Dad read the daily newspaper or played Solitaire, and I cut paper dolls from the Eaton's catalogue. My favourite was the Eaton's Beauty Doll, and my little girl heart yearned to hold one of the beautiful dolls.*
>
> *As entertaining as my paper dolls were, they were not my only source of inspiration. I had a real live "Eaton's Beauty." Her name was Delta*

Campbell, a friend of my parents who had grown up in Bass River, Kent Co., and had gone off to work in the big city of Moncton. Delta looked like the models in the catalogue. When she came to visit, she arrived in a fancy car. She wore gold and silver bangles, carried a leather handbag, wore bright red lipstick and nail polish and she smoked cigarettes from a long fancy holder. Best of all she worked in the Toy Department of the T. Eaton Co. When Delta came to visit, I would show her my paper dolls and she would let me look at her bracelets. As we talked, she would tell me how she sat those pretty dolls out on the shelves of the Toy Department at Christmas. By the time the next fall rolled around, I waited anxiously for the arrival of the new Eaton's Christmas Catalogue, daydreaming once again about the beautiful dolls.

One Christmas Eve Delta made a quick visit to our home, and, wonder of wonders, Christmas morning, under the tree stood an Eaton's Beauty Doll. She wore a beautiful gown and had long blonde hair. At that moment, I wasn't sure which I loved more, the doll or Delta! For two more years, a beautiful doll appeared under the tree.

Years passed. I graduated from high school and Delta became the Manager of Eaton's Toy Department. With September approaching, I wondered what I would do in the fall. Delta showed up and made me an offer, saying, "Come to Moncton with me and help me prepare the Toy Department for Christmas." From September until December, I worked with Delta and her staff as we sat out trucks, trains, books, teddy bears… and beautiful dolls, transforming the Toy Department into the famous Eaton's Christmas Toyland.

Many Christmas seasons have passed since my first job at Eaton's Toyland. I've had the opportunity to see the five-story Eaton's Centre in downtown Toronto dressed up for Christmas, and watch the Eaton's Santa Claus parade maneuver its way down Yonge Street. I've watched my own daughter's delight as she found a treasured doll under the Christmas tree. I've soared above the beautiful decorations in the glass elevator at Market Square in Saint John with my granddaughter by my side. But every time I see that first display of Christmas dolls…I stop and smile. Caught up in their whimsical look, I remember the magic feeling of packaging a beautiful Eaton's doll, under the watchful eye of Delta, and realizing the thrill some little girl would feel on Christmas morning. Standing there, I am almost certain they smile back. Almost certain they know the mystery, and wonder of love, that is the miracle of Christmas. And I'm grateful, ever so grateful for the memories and inspiration of my "Eaton's Beauties!"

It was the mutual interaction of people with Eaton's during the Christmas holiday that brought joy to so many. It could occur among the crowds in the store itself or while standing on a frigid street watching Santa Claus pass, but the memories left by these events are of the most personal nature. Dr. Mary Jarratt, of Rothesay, New Brunswick, relates how a random pre-Christmas stop at Eaton's by her father on the way home has remained in her memory for many years:

> *My parents, Bill and Mary Jarratt, were married in 1956 and lived in Bathurst, New Brunswick. It's on the north shore of New Brunswick, about a two-hour drive from Moncton. My father was a civil engineer with the Province of New Brunswick, so he often worked in Moncton. He was also a World War II veteran, and when he returned after the war, all of his family had passed on. So the Christmas of 1956 was his first real family Christmas in many years. My mother recalled him coming home a few days before Christmas, bearing Christmas tree ornaments that he had purchased at Eaton's in Moncton. He was as excited as a child, and of course spending money on something as frivolous as Christmas tree ornaments was not something one did every day! We still have one or two of them all these years later. I will always cherish this story about my dear father and Eaton's, for it illustrates the place that it held in people's lives many years ago.*

Of course, Scrooges, Grinches and nonbelievers could negatively, and even correctly, point out that Christmas was the most profitable time of year for Eaton's. Yet taken as a part of Canadian history and culture, which itself has developed from the shared and combined memory of its people, Eaton's contributions to the holiday were mostly free for the asking and warmly remembered again and again by those who experienced them.

Plus ça Change...

They'll have a tough row to hoe, but they'll have lots of help and a hundred years
of experience to draw on. They'll get by.
—John David Eaton

Even in the Eaton 100th anniversary publication, *The Store that Timothy Built*, it seems that author William Stephenson went out of his way to write about the transformation of Eaton's over the 1960s and what customers might be able to expect in the coming years. Under the heading of "The New Challenges of a New Age," the book gave an insight into what was going on in the corporate mind of Eaton's as it looked at itself during the years leading up to its centennial celebration. Although the mood was upbeat, and Eaton's itself seemed to be facing changes head-on, the book ominously let the truth slip in a quote about Eaton's that said the company was (emphasis added) "looking back at its first century and forward, *possibly*, to a second."

Eaton's was, at the time, clearly a traditional, slow-to-change business in a world undergoing a vast metamorphosis. Postwar prosperity fueled the growth of cities and pushed them out far beyond their downtown cores. A "baby boomer" generation was coming of age, and it found interest in everything that was new (that is, groovy or far-out) more so than it did in tradition, no matter how charming, valuable or worthwhile that tradition might be. Central business districts, even though Canada's were probably healthier than those in the United States, had become slightly seedy.

John David Eaton watched it all transpire from his position as the heir to the retailing empire wrought from nothing by Timothy Eaton and built up by his father and his father's cousin. Shy and reticent when not in his downtown Toronto office, he was more apt to be found on a six-week yachting excursion or at home early in his Bauhaus-style mansion on Dunvegan Road having a drink with a friend. Although he most often drove a tiny Volkswagen in Toronto, he also possessed a large yacht, the *Hildur*, and a beautiful Lockheed Jetstar corporate airplane in traditional "Eaton's of Canada" colours, and he even flew his own helicopter to his Georgian Bay retreat.

Even though in poor condition physically, he managed to make regular visits to the stores throughout the 1950s and 1960s, and his own company's centennial book recounted an anecdote about a time when, prepared to give a speech at a dinner honoring longtime employees in Winnipeg, he stood up, became flustered and "sat down without uttering a word."

For day-to-day operations, John David Eaton had come to rely on others to manage the huge retail operation. J. Ross Jenkins, who gained notoriety as the general manager of the newly formed T. Eaton Co. British Columbia from the time of the 1948 Spencer purchase, rose to the office of chief executive officer and kept Eaton's on track during the 1950s. When he retired in 1965, he was replaced by David Kinnear, a longtime Eaton's employee who, like Timothy Eaton himself, was born in Northern Ireland. His career closely followed that of the previous CEO, from Toronto to British Columbia and back again.

With John David Eaton operating the tradition-bound company in a "hands-off" manner, store executives sought methods to bring Eaton's into the brave new world facing it. The new generation could be satisfied by procuring the right merchandise and presenting it in a way attractive to customers, something that Eaton's knew how to do. New stores could be built where necessary to follow the customers. The problem occurred, though, when someone else had already begun to do it quicker and better.

In 1952, Eaton's rival on the other side of Queen Street, the Robert Simpson Company Limited, partnered with Sears, Roebuck and Company of the United States to create a new entity, Simpsons-Sears Limited. The new organization would open stores in Canada in Sears' chain-store format and take over the operation of Simpson's catalogue division nationwide. A rule was in force until 1972 that forbade the opening of any new Simpsons-Sears store in the communities where the Robert Simpson Company already operated, while Simpson's would transfer its entire catalogue operation to the new Simpsons-Sears.

The first Simpsons-Sears store opened in 1953, and within a few years, the new company was running away with sales and profits in Canada. The Simpsons-Sears catalogue, although it did not carry the history or affection attached to Eaton's version, was a hit throughout Canada. The context in which Simpsons-Sears' (later just Sears) growth occurred was, unfortunately, an era also characterized by the chronic loss of market share by Eaton's and its catalogue.

Eaton's management faced the '60s and this loss of market share to Simpsons-Sears with a two-pronged approach. Finding that its operation was top-heavy with management, it sought to hire young, new personnel from outside to "shake up" its operations. Secondly, it somewhat belatedly recognized that the days when Eaton's could just show up and open the doors and effortlessly attract loyal customers to itself were over. Modern stores in enclosed shopping centres were the development path Eaton's had to follow if it were to really compete for its market share.

Any change in such a large organization is bound to be wrought with problems, but Eaton's growing pains in the 1960s were more difficult than most. Computerization of customer billing, successfully introduced by Simpson's several years earlier, became a debacle that caused more than 10 percent of Eaton's credit card holders to cancel their accounts. The factories were shut down or sold, leaving acres of vacant property in the heart of Toronto, one of North America's most dynamic cities.

Most of the Eaton branches acquired in the 1928 acquisition of the Canadian Department Stores Limited were sold off or closed by 1966 and replaced with freestanding catalogue order offices. In most cases, the stores were not unprofitable, but they simply didn't fit the shopping centre formula the company wished to follow in the future. The business lost by closing these stores simply went elsewhere. The hoped-for outcome, that customers would use the order offices as much as the stores that closed, was complicated by the fact that a big new state-of-the-art catalogue distribution centre east of Toronto was fraught with problems from the start, slowing delivery times, fouling orders and depleting customer confidence. Interestingly, in this era, Simpsons-Sears pioneered the opening of smaller stores fit for Canada's less populous cities, with the stated goal of having a retail store in every Canadian city with a population of fifty thousand or more.

Eaton's, which took pride in its decentralized nature, operated as a variety of divisions across Canada, including the T. Eaton Co. Limited of Montréal, the T. Eaton Co. Maritimes Limited and so forth. Modern managers introduced (more or less) centralized buying and control, which lowered costs but caused dissention internally and alienated customers. Buyers in Toronto could now dictate merchandise styles and prices anywhere Eaton's operated. Customers had lost a local voice, so to speak, and it all happened in spite of the fact that the most successful department stores had, in the past, given great control to local department managers to order and price merchandise according to the habits of the customers they knew in an almost intimate manner.

Yet Eaton's still had the cachet of being a homegrown and favourite store, and even though it had shed market share, it was still preferred by many customers for its history, tradition and very identity as a Canadian institution. Some of these traditions were beginning to change, though. In 1968, the policy of draping show windows on Sunday, instituted by Timothy Eaton himself, was quietly dropped, and five years later, the first alcoholic drink was served in an Eaton restaurant. Through enticing new shops and youth-oriented advertising, Eaton's put on a "with-it" face in spite of its aging physical plant. The Queen Street store was covered with a coat of white paint in 1968 in order to give it a brighter and more contemporary appearance, and on the other side of Canada, a warm yellow tone was selected to unify the aging and disparate buildings that composed the Victoria, British Columbia store.

Eaton's 100th anniversary year arrived on January 2, 1969, and was celebrated in a style befitting an august institution that still had a place in most Canadians' hearts. On that morning, John David, Signy, their four sons and the grandchildren opened the door to the venerable Queen Street store with a golden key, according to Eaton custom. The centennial ceremony entailed music, fireworks and a speech by the president. Afterwards, the family posed upstairs for an official photo just under a large portrait of the Governor.

The year 1969 was celebrated at Eaton's with special sales, and all of the company's advertising and printed material was adorned with a special mark announcing "Eaton 100." A few years earlier, Eaton's introduced a slim and elegant new logo and redid store bags, boxes and other ephemera using a handsome new quatrefoil design that came to be associated with the store. Eaton's new shopping bags and boxes, done in a monochromatic composition of greys and olive green, identified the store with a sophisticated, modern point of view. The Eaton 100 logo used the design to advantage as well.

The company sponsored two anniversary publications, the official hardcover souvenir book *The Store that Timothy Built* and, at the end of the year, a lavish, beautifully produced centennial edition of *Eaton Quarterly* that

In January 1969, the Eaton family arrives at the Queen Street store to celebrate the centennial of the T. Eaton & Co. Limited. *Archives of Ontario: T. Eaton Fonds F229. Used with the permission of Sears Canada Ltd.*

not only looked back on "10 Decades of Innovations" but also prophesized about the future as well. The book ended with an article entitled "A Hundred Years Ahead" that suggested that by the year 2069, people would be known only by an official identification number, and their access to Eaton's would be via "the new TouchPad" or a visit to Eaton's Central, a "half-mile-tall" store in a mirrored cylinder "pointed straight at distant galaxies" under the dome of the climate-controlled city still named Toronto!

The *Eaton Quarterly* was a publication that grew out of the store's 1960s process of centralization in which employee newsletters, once published separately in each division, were consolidated. Older employees will well remember the *Mari-Times* (Maritimes), *Entre-Nous* (Montréal), *Eaton News* (Toronto), *Bi-Weekly* (Hamilton), *Contacts* (Winnipeg), *Prairie Breezes* (Saskatchewan), *Chinook Winds* (Calgary), *Edmontonian* (Edmonton) and *Coastal Currents* (British Columbia) as sources for information about the store and their fellow employees.

Perhaps the greatest surprise to the public, but not to the Eaton family, was the withdrawal of John David Eaton in August 1969. Plagued by severe arthritis, Eaton took an early retirement at age sixty and spent the next few years in failing health. He was replaced by Robert Butler as president of the company. Butler's appointment itself was a milestone. He was the first non-Eaton to hold the office of president since the company was established in 1869. It was an accepted fact that John David and Signy's two oldest sons, John Craig and Fredrik Stefan, were not yet up to the task of running the company, and Butler, at age forty-eight, had twenty-two years of experience at Eaton's and often accompanied John David on store tours, experiencing firsthand the breadth of the T. Eaton Co., as well as the strengths and weaknesses he would face as its leader.

Although he was not a family member, his words, which appeared in the *Eaton Quarterly*, indicated that he had a thorough grasp of the challenges facing him, as well as the will to deal with them:

> *In a company that serves as many diverse markets, deals in as many products and services, buys in such different parts of Canada and the world, and employs as many different people as ours does, management must be a closely knit, smooth working team of different abilities and different specialized knowledge…we have to keep in mind that shopping is no longer regarded as a chore and we have to respond to this by putting the fun back in shopping. The need to control costs and improve productivity necessarily focused our attention on organizational and operational matters. The shopper, and her requirements, got out of focus.*

With Butler's ascension to the presidency of Eaton's, John Craig Eaton and Fredrik Stefan Eaton were named to the board of Eaton's of Canada Inc., the family-owned holding company that oversaw the whole operation, retail and all. George Eaton remained occupied with his auto racing career, and Thor, the youngest, didn't maintain a strong interest in working at the store.

The even-keeled and personable Frederik Eaton had the best background to manage the company, although Harvard-educated John Craig had gained experience in buying and management as a trainee (even if he earned renown as a man-about-town). Sigrid Wolf, who grew up in Toronto, remembers, "Oh yes, I knew that John Craig Eaton liked to buzz around town in his purple Rolls-Royce…and I was sure game, in my wild and crazy twenties to date him *and* his purple Rolls, but it never happened, much to my chagrin!"

The ultimate event of the centennial celebration was an informal evening reception given by Eaton's on December 8, 1969, exactly one hundred years after Timothy Eaton opened his first store on Yonge Street. The affair was held at the historic St. Lawrence Hall, an ancient landmark that served as Toronto's city hall at the time of the founding of Eaton's. The *Toronto Star* noted that "the 100th Birthday party…featured several festive touches the puritanical founder wouldn't have allowed—cocktails, cigarettes distributed by pretty girls, a band," and reported that the affair, to which executives who were either involved in Eaton's business or were retail competitors in Toronto were invited, was generally quiet and "was pretty well over by 8 p.m." Although John Craig and Frederik Eaton blew out the one hundred candles on a monumental birthday cake, John David Eaton, now retired, was notable by his absence. In fact, his ailments, including severe arthritis, caused him to stay away from his family's store altogether after his retirement.

Another member of the Eaton family was also notably absent from the centennial celebrations. The "irrepressible" Lady Eaton, who by the time of the event had relocated from Eaton Hall to her secondary home on Old Forest Hill Road in Toronto, was unable to attend due to her own failing health. However, she was remembered by the delivery of a symbolic golden key to her home on the same January morning when her son reopened the doors to the Queen Street store. She passed away on July 9, 1970, shortly after her ninety-first birthday.

In a five-column obituary tribute, the *Globe and Mail* listed the accomplishments of this "carpenter's daughter" who rose to become the long-lived matriarch of one of Canada's richest and most well-known

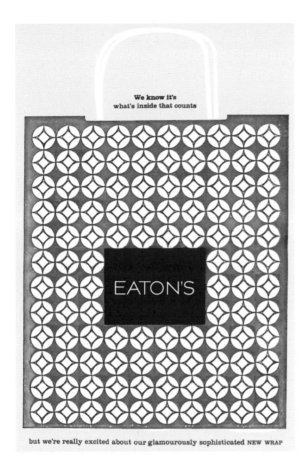

We know it's
what's inside that counts

EATON'S

but we're really excited about our glamourously sophisticated NEW WRAP

Eaton's handsome new design for bags and boxes was considered worthy of a full-page newspaper ad in 1967. *From an ad, collection of the author.*

families. The article recalled her saying in 1951, "I am a traditionalist of the first water. I still say the British Empire. It is still the Dominion of Canada, and the Royal Mail, to me, is still Royal." It summed up her more mundane achievements as well as her numerous contributions to charity and culture. Among the former were her status as the first female motorist in Canada, her journey through Canada's Arctic as an octogenarian and her institution of candlelit carol-singing soirees at Eaton Hall as a family tradition. The latter took paragraph after paragraph to list and showed her interest in medical causes (United Welfare Chest, Canadian National Institute for the Blind and the Canadian Red Cross, among others) and the arts (the Stratford Canadian Players, the Art Gallery of Ontario and the Royal Ontario Museum), as well as her lifelong affection for nature (the Don Valley Conservation Association and the Men of the Trees). The article's statement that "an outspoken individualist, she cut a swath in Canadian history for more than half a century" wasn't just a fact but a profound remembrance of her and what she accomplished.

In 1972, the T. Eaton Co. launched Horizon, a chain of discount, self-service neighbourhood department stores designed to complement Eaton's and compete with discounters like Zellers, Safeway and Kmart of Canada. The project was under the direction of president and CEO-to-be Robert Butler. Initially limited to the Toronto, London and Montréal markets, the stores' early locations were meticulously researched. As a result, the first Horizon store to open, a fifty-two-thousand-square-foot prototype at Victoria Park and Gerrard Avenues in Toronto, sold out of many items not long after John Craig Eaton ceremoniously cut the ribbon on August 16, 1972.

Two London-area stores opened in November of the same year. Children were given buttons that read, "Smile, there's a new Horizon!" at the openings, but the construction program, which anticipated 122 Horizon stores across Canada, was cancelled after just a dozen more stores opened. Most of the locations were not profitable, and the division simply plodded along at a loss until the Ontario units were converted into small Eaton stores starting in October 1978. At the time, Eaton's said that it was remodeling them to have a "softer, more fashionable look," but these mini-Eaton's branches were not terribly successful either, blurring the distinction of the parent company's image.

By 1973, family members who had a direct connection to the great past of Eaton's, as well as its success built on innovative merchandising and a focus on the customer, had passed from the scene. The new management put in place over the past years brought new blood and outside experience into the company, but it was, in fact, a gamble—the new managers had no tie with the store's past and potentially did not understand its customers, lacking a long-term relationship with Eaton's public. Furthermore, the store's merchandising and marketing thrust stood to suffer if the new management was weighted towards individuals with a financial, legal or accounting background. Timothy Eaton, for all his talents (and all his accomplishments), was a merchant above all.

During John David Eaton's tenure, the company opened, in autumn of 1967, the aforementioned catalogue distribution centre in Scarborough, just east of Toronto. Meant to help vacate the buildings north of the Queen Street store in advance of future development as much as to help streamline the moribund operations of *Eaton's Catalogue*, the new distribution centre was more than 750,000 square feet in size. With the political turmoil

Eaton's moved its catalogue operation to a new facility in Scarborough, paving the way for the demolition of the industrial complex adjacent to the main store at Queen and Yonge Streets. *Archives of Ontario: T. Eaton Fonds F229. Used with the permission of Sears Canada Ltd.*

surrounding the Eaton Centre plan, there was speculation that a portion of the former catalogue site on Louisa Street could become the location for a new Toronto Post Office building, but Eaton's remained mum on the property's ultimate disposition at the time of the move to the new three-floor facility in Scarborough. Eaton's own press said that the move had been necessary because "catalogue sales are increasing faster in the cities than in rural areas."

In fact, catalogue sales may have been increasing, but income was anything but. In Simpsons-Sears Eaton's faced a strong and aggressive competitor not just in retail stores but in the catalogue operation as well. In 1973, sales at the twenty-one-year-old organization exceeded $1 billion, and its catalogue operation only grew and grew from its inception. In the same period, Eaton's, in spite of the history and downright affection built up over ninety years, could only point to losses, growing to $17 million in 1974. The Simpsons-Sears catalogue grew past Eaton's, and what's more, the operation was profitable and actually sent out more copies than its pioneering competitor. A plan to rescue *Eaton's Catalogue* by creating a Simpsons-Sears type of operation (also involving the thirteen underperforming Horizon stores) in partnership with American retail giant J.C. Penney was hatched in 1974, but it was rejected by Penney's board in New York less than one year later after the details were fully studied. The episode, and its negative impact on Eaton's image, cost Robert Butler his job; after the final verdict on the Penney venture, he was relieved of his duties as president of the T. Eaton Co. Limited and given the more ceremonial job of chairman.

His replacement, Earl H. Orser, had a finance background and had most recently served as vice-president of finance for Air Canada. At the time of his ascension to the role of Eaton's president, Orser told the *Globe and Mail* that his role was to judge and evaluate "the performance and return on the different elements of Eaton's business. There's an opportunity to improve and upgrade its sales per square foot." Later in the interview, he mentioned Eaton's hemorrhaging catalogue:

> *Profitability of the operation is less than satisfactory. I think we have to make an improvement in order to continue to urbanize our market, that is, to increase the proportion of our market that is in the major metropolitan areas. I think our books have to become more productive. Our sales per page have to be improved, and also there's quite a need for improved materials handling and mechanization in our handling facilities. Those are the main challenges.*

In the event, the challenges were never actually met; the board of Eaton's of Canada Inc. instructed Orser to shut down the operation in late 1975. Thus, a secret plan was devised to discontinue the catalogue that began inauspiciously in 1884 and grew to become a revered icon in Canada. The spring/summer 1976 edition would be the last of its kind; details, including the disposition of more than nine thousand employees, most of them in Ontario, Manitoba and New Brunswick, where the largest catalogue operations were located, were worked out before any official announcement was to be made.

One day before the announcement date of January 14, 1976, notices were delivered to catalogue merchandise suppliers in Québec referring to the discontinuance, and shortly thereafter rumours swirled in the press. The *Globe and Mail* in Toronto speculated "Death of a Catalogue?" on its front page and mentioned the news conference called by Eaton's for later in the day, as well as leaks by catalogue employees who said that they were notified that the catalogue would be history by summer. Earlier, Eaton's had hinted that the catalogue was "in a transition stage," but the news still dropped like a bombshell.

The *Montréal Gazette* was even more forthcoming, reporting on the same day that Eaton management was ordered to be available and warned not to speak to the press under any circumstances. An announcement to employees calmly informed, "We recognize the possible effects of this action upon our many loyal employees, customers and suppliers and can assure you that this decision has been made only after intense and thorough review" and quoting Earl Orser as saying that he had "finally been convinced" to authorize a statement and "put an end to all this nonsense." The *Gazette* also opined that "the closing of the catalogue division appears to be radical surgery for a sick patient," referring to rumours that Eaton's had been unprofitable for years and that the act of closing the catalogue was one of desperation. Speculation aside, the paper concluded after examining operating results reported by Simpsons-Sears:

> *Eaton's thus tumbles from the top spot it has occupied for decades. The new leader will be Simpsons-Sears—a comparative newcomer launched in 1954. It reported catalogue and retail sales of $1.3 billion in 1974, and is thought to have exceeded $1.5 billion last year. Eaton's descent must be particularly unsettling to the company, reputed to be one of the largest family-owned concerns anywhere. For about 100 years Eaton's and Simpsons have done battle, and except at the beginning, Simpsons has been far behind. Now the retailing giant has been knocked off its pedestal by Simpsons-Sears, an upstart hardly out of short pants, and a child of Simpsons.*

The bulletin was also sent to Simpsons-Sears, which did not respond with glee to the news. Recognizing that it now held a monopoly on catalogue sales in Canada, an official, as reported in the *Gazette*, said, "I am personally sorry it's come to this. We still have to work to earn our customers' confidence, and to maintain our growth." Simpsons-Sears also recognized that competition between the two catalogues had been a healthy thing for Canada's economy and that the country's retail landscape had forever changed because of the closure.

At the announcement of the catalogue's demise, Eaton's officials were quick to dispel rumours about the company's other operations. Earl Orser

Three sons of John David and Signy Eaton pose for an official company shot around the time of the centennial. Pictured are Frederik Stefan, John Craig and George Ross Eaton. *Archives of Ontario: T. Eaton Fonds F229. Used with the permission of Sears Canada Ltd.*

was quoted in the *Globe and Mail* as emphatically stating that 1976 sales were running 17 percent over the previous year through the Christmas shopping season and that the department store operation was more profitable than it had been five years previously. He also stated that the closure of four hundred catalogue sales offices and the termination of 4,500 full-time and an equal number of part-time employees was "by far the most difficult part of the decision."

At the same meeting, Frederik Eaton spoke for his family and on behalf of Eaton's unanimous board of directors, saying that "we are quite convinced there is no alternative action than to phase out the catalogue operation, an action we deeply regret." The speculative gamble by Eaton's was that one-third of the catalogue's annual sales would be picked up by Eaton stores and that the rest would go to Simpsons-Sears.

In fact, Eaton's had simply handed over $300 million in sales to its greatest rival. In the five years from 1973 to 1975, Simpsons-Sears went from breaking the $1 billion mark in sales to more than double that amount. The *Toronto Globe and Mail* predicted as much on the same day as Eaton's announcement, calling the younger company "the big winner" in the catalogue closure. Although Eaton's worked to minimize the pain, the paper mentioned suppliers whose orders were swiftly cancelled and laid-off employees as the victims of the situation. The chairman of Simpsons-Sears at the time, J.C. Barrow, said, "I'm as surprised as anyone. I suppose if you're Canadian, the Eaton's catalogue is just like the Anglican Church," but in the same statement, he warned that Sears was not in a position to hire any affected Eaton's employees. Its operation could easily handle the increased volume coming over the horizon—and profitably at that.

Marketing analysts noted Eaton's unaggressive approach to catalogue retailing, sheer marketing blunders (like deemphasizing hard-lines and heavy goods in which it had a distinct advantage, for a fashion emphasis that was hard to market in an inflationary and changing environment) and cost-control issues relating but not limited to the new Scarborough distribution centre as challenges facing the company. One very hard-hit entity as a result of Eaton's action was Southam Murray, the firm that printed and bound the eight-hundred-page catalogues. Southam Murray laid off more than two hundred employees and cancelled an order for new printing presses within days of the catalogue closure announcement, and its leadership speculated that it would be a full five years before the company could rebuild its business to previous levels.

In Winnipeg, the *Free Press* placed a large picture of the latest edition of *Eaton's Catalogue* on its front page, obliterated by a large "X." Winnipeg being a major catalogue distribution centre for Eaton's, the paper reported that 670 permanent employees and 900 part-timers would lose their jobs. The catalogue buildings, like in Toronto, were adjacent to the main store. On a more positive note, it also carried a report that the historic structures across Graham Avenue from the stores could be enlarged and remodeled into a mixed-use complex that would be a plus for downtown Winnipeg.

In Moncton, New Brunswick, where the situation was similar to that in the Manitoba capital, the government promised assistance to laid-off catalogue workers. Mayor Gary Wheeler, after the announcement, proclaimed that "the closing of Eaton's catalogue office in Moncton is the most dramatic blow to the city's economy since the Great Depression."

Reaction among the public was one of nostalgia and sadness rather than anger. By this time, Eaton's, although it was still a representative Canadian institution, had become weakened in the marketplace. Yet many Canadians speculated about what it would be like without the catalogue. Although the reliance of rural Canadians had certainly become lessened as the country grew and modernized, it still held affection in the hearts of those who flipped its pages. An editorial by Peter Whelan in the *Globe and Mail* was particularly eloquent, calling *Eaton's Catalogue* a book of dreams:

Think of achieved dreams: a boy's first wrist watch, a girl's first prom dress, toys that Santa somehow knew about had most young eyes intent on the magic book (fall and winter version). And unachieved dreams: of sitting in a winter-bound kitchen closing the pages reluctantly on—what was it, a suit or dress, something for loved ones—something with a price tag too big. But, having the dream warmed the cold pressing in from outside. These are the personal dreams. Leaf through the memories of older Canadians—or of older Eaton catalogues, and see, dimly, Timothy Eaton's vast impact on national dreams.

Elsewhere Whelan quoted a newspaper editor in rural Ontario who said that "[i]f it were not for the services rendered [by the catalogue] in pioneer days—and they run past the First World War—I don't know how people would have got along." Dr. H.T. Huebert of Winnipeg, in a long letter to chairman Robert Butler, wrote with delicious sarcasm:

I was greatly distressed to read a news release coming out of Toronto. It appears that the T. Eaton Co. is considering the closing of its catalogue sales division. In today's newspaper I read of difficulties in Manitoba—the doctors and the government are having differences of opinion. The transit workers may go on strike. International waters are stormy—Iceland moves to sever ties with Britain and there are troubles in Spain. But surely, the mainstay of Canadian life as we know it, cannot be allowed to succumb without every man, woman and child in Canada being involved in the decision. Just think of it—no more Eaton's catalogue. Absolutely unthinkable! Have the Eaton executives turned a completely deaf ear to the thousands of anguished cries which will emanate from the rural areas of our great nation? Nothing, absolutely nothing could adequately replace the Eaton's catalogue as an unending supply of interesting, high quality paper for outdoor biffies all the way from Newfoundland to Vancouver Island.

As if it wasn't bad enough that Eaton's severed a proud and long-established relationship with its customers by closing the catalogue, the new world of the 1960s and 1970s brought to bear other troubles on the store and its owner dynasty. On the night of June 15, 1976, a gunman broke into John Craig Eaton's home in Toronto's Rosedale neighbourhood and attempted to kidnap his teenage daughter, Signy, who was living with him and his second wife at the time. A neighbour saw the intruder and called the Toronto police. In the meantime, John Craig and his wife, Sherrill, were overpowered and bound, and young Signy was abducted. She managed to escape the intruder, whom John Craig Eaton described as "wearing a Castro hat," when the police arrived. Shots were exchanged, but the suspect, Jean Caron, a native of France who had been twice expelled from Canada in the past, was apprehended nearby.

Earlier, both in 1967 and 1968, John David and Signy's home on Dunvegan Road had been burglarized, but the attempted kidnapping of John Craig's daughter brought the Eaton family into a world where, owing to their wealth and position, such a high-profile existence could prove dangerous. From that time on, the Eaton family employed bodyguards and security forces for protection.

Apparently nothing could protect the Montréal store from terrorism, either. In the early morning hours of November 22, 1968, a bomb exploded on the Metro level of the gigantic store on St. Catherine Street. No one was injured, but more than $25,000 worth of damage was done. Later in the day, a suspicious package was discovered in a stairway, and the bomb found within was disarmed off-site after a heroic extraction by Montréal police; the whole store had to be evacuated. The work of the *Front de Liberation de Québec*, a separatist organization, the bombs were the latest in a series planted in the city. The two men who were responsible for placing the bombs (aged nineteen and twenty years old when the crimes occurred) were apprehended and admitted their actions three years later, but their trials went on for years.

Surprisingly, Eaton's Santa Claus Parade was scheduled for the next day and went off without a hitch, to the delight of thousands of Montréal children and, it must be assumed, Eaton's worried management. In 1969, however, the Montréal parade was unceremoniously cancelled for security reasons. These events proved conclusively that the world around Eaton's had changed, and the big department store, icon or not, had no choice but to follow suit. It did so by reinvigourating the city settings where it had traded for more than one hundred years.

Where All the Lights Are Bright

We needed one word—one happy word—to describe the new Eaton experience to you. We couldn't find it, so we invented it! And here it is: Downtowning!
—Eaton's advertisement, 1977

Through the turmoil of the 1960s and 1970s, Eaton's still strove to present a fashionable and up-to-date face to the public, while behind the scenes, it battled the competition that ate away at its market share and rattled its very structure to its foundations. Management under John David Eaton stepped up suburban expansion across Canada and exerted a great deal of effort to replace Eaton's historic and vaunted Queen Street store. Eaton's 1968 edition of its promotional publication *The Story of a Store* described Eaton's–Main Store as a historic landmark, and its sales per square foot were healthy, but it, like many of the company's downtown stores, did show its age:

> *As the birthplace of The T. Eaton Co. Limited, the Toronto Queen St. Store has a striking atmosphere of community appeal—colourful and captivating—that has become characteristic of Eaton stores elsewhere. It is the true centre of busy downtown Toronto. This store is a famous shopping place and it is a place where people can come to browse around, to see the latest fashion, to meet for luncheon and to spend a day sightseeing. A bronze statue of the founder occupies a place of honour in this store, where originated so many of the merchandising ideas and*

principles which have been woven into the fabric of Eaton business in Canada. The oldest of the Company's places of business, it nevertheless maintains a contemporary outlook.

To Eaton's management, the old flagship, parts of which were more than seventy-five years old, was out of touch with the merchandising image Eaton's should portray. Furthermore, the operation of two large stores in proximity of each other on Yonge Street was an expensive inefficiency that could be solved only by the construction of one large, up-to-date main store. From 1958 through 1966, Eaton's mulled over six different versions of what (though it was initially called "Project Viking") ultimately came to be known as the Eaton Centre.

The final 1960s scheme for the development was mentioned to the public by a Toronto official, speaking at a planning conference in late March 1965. The development, which had been rumoured in the press for months, involved twenty-two acres of city blocks bordered by Yonge, Queen, Bay and Dundas Streets, meaning that it would replace Eaton's Queen Street store; the former mail-order, annex and factory buildings north and west of the store; the Church of the Holy Trinity; and Toronto's landmark old city hall, which was superseded by the attractive and well-received new city hall of 1965, designed by Finnish architect Viljo Revell. The redevelopment, as proposed, required the city to sell or lease the old city hall property at Queen and Bay Streets to Eaton's so the Romanesque Revival sandstone structure could be demolished to accommodate the new complex.

On September 15, 1965, representatives of Eaton's met with Toronto officials and unveiled the plan as designed by architect Mathers & Haldenby, with noted American architects Skidmore, Owings & Merrill as consultants. The $300 million plan would provide a new 1.3-million-square-foot flagship for Eaton's; an adjacent, four-level shopping court; and two levels of underground concourses as its retail component, above a 2,700-car parking garage. Three office towers of fifty-seven and thirty-two stories, a sixty-nine-storey office and apartment tower and a twenty-storey, five-hundred-room circular hotel were arranged around the historic Trinity Church, providing open plazas far in excess of anything that ever existed on the site. The plans also indicated that a few blocks of historic storefront façades along Yonge Street were to be left in place as a part of the program.

The design's gently tapering towers, deeply recessed windowed façades and rectangular Eaton's store resting on polygonal columns with elegant stainless steel details bore resemblance to the current work of Skidmore, Owings &

Merrill's design team. Canadian laws at the time would only allow foreign-based architects a role as associate architects, no matter to what extent they were involved in the design of a project. In this case, Mathers & Haldenby were selected as architects of record; they had earlier designed the 1937 Dunvegan Road home of John David and Signy Eaton in a streamlined Art Deco style not unlike some of the company's stores of the era.

In a photo-article about urban redevelopment schemes, the eminent architectural journal *Architectural Record* voiced an opinion about the Eaton Centre proposal:

> *The idea of selling the old city hall to a private developer naturally became quite a political issue, but Eaton's proposal turned out to be an attractive one to the city, and the Council agreed to lease the old building subject to further negotiation of terms, despite its character as a landmark. Architecturally, however, the juxtaposition of the New City Hall and a series of much larger towers is not particularly fortunate…and it is difficult to imagine how the problems involved in the juxtaposition can be fully resolved. The problem is certainly not of the architects' own making: The Eaton Centre represents development at a scale which makes the greatest economic sense.*

Although Mayor Phillip Givens told the *Globe and Mail*, "We would be stupid to reject the first overtures of such a gigantic proposal, and I am certain any plan they present will exceed, if not rival Rockefeller Centre," no sooner did the plan hit the street than opposition mounted to the demolition of all but the main tower of the old city hall, a familiar and well-loved part of Toronto's historical urban landscape that many Torontonians did not want to lose. It didn't matter that earlier architects' proposals even suggested getting rid of Trinity Church as well, but Eaton's reconsidered, and the church's preservation was an integral part of the latest plan.

While more specifics of the Eaton Centre plan (including the retention of the old city hall's clock tower) were revealed at an earlier meeting, the first "shot across the bow" occurred at a meeting of the Metro Toronto Council on December 10, 1965, before detailed plans, artist's renderings and models were presented. David Owen, hired by the Eaton Centre Limited to head the project for Eaton's, met face to face for the first time with the project's most vociferous critics. Owen was no stranger to comprehensive urban renewal projects, having given up a position of vice-president at Webb and Knapp (Canada) Limited, developer of Montréal's Place Ville-Marie and a subsidiary of successful American developer William Zeckendorff.

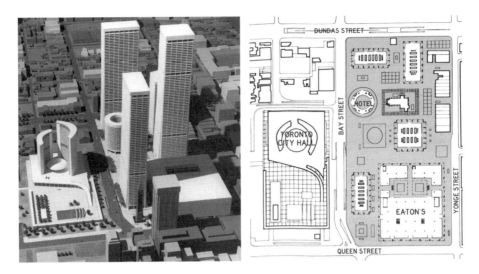

Eaton's proposed an ill-fated plan to radically alter downtown Toronto in 1966. A victim of the scheme was the city's old city hall. *Archives of Ontario: T. Eaton Fonds F229. Used with the permission of Sears Canada Ltd.*

Chief among the critics was Professor James Acland of the University of Toronto School of Architecture. He produced his own rough sketches showing how the old city hall could be incorporated into the Eaton Centre and noted, "This structure is a national monument and to destroy it would be an act of vandalism." Others asked, "Do we have to fill every inch of downtown with skyscrapers?" and added, "What is at stake is not a building but a principle of history." For its part, the *Globe and Mail* reported on the meeting by reminding readers that in 1942, 1949 and 1957, grand jury investigations called the conditions in the building "deplorable," "a fire hazard" and "cockroach infested" and its detention cells "revolting." Around the same time, former governor-general of Canada Vincent Massey sent a letter to the Metro Executive Committee in opposition to the demolition of the old building, calling it "not only a landmark but a symbol of Toronto." Writing from his retirement home, the first Canadian-born governor-general also said that merely retaining the building's tall, slender clock tower was an "unsatisfactory compromise."

The response of Eaton Centre Limited, and thus of Eaton's itself, was that the old city hall presented a barrier to underground connections vital to the Centre's concept. The new city hall was fronted by an expansive plaza on Queen Street, Nathan Phillips Square, under which was a large parking garage. The old city hall bordered the square and formed a barrier between it and the proposed Eaton Centre. However, it was recognized that the exposure of the Bay Street façade of the old city hall as a strong boundary to the east side of Nathan Phillips Square was considered an unexpected but wholly delightful aspect of the city hall and it's forecourt-like square's composition.

Through the spring of 1966, the Eaton Centre became a political conflict, portrayed almost daily in the press. Opposition to the destruction of the old city hall had by this time formed into a citizens group, Friends of the Old City Hall. Previously, the City of Toronto had sold the old building for $4.5 million to the Metro Executive Council, which was responsible for its disposition. To make the Eaton Centre happen, Eaton's publicly offered Metro almost twice as much for the building.

On March 2, 1966, Eaton's unveiled detailed plans for the spectacular complex and informed the public that its new store at Yonge and Queen Streets, as well as the fifty-seven-storey tower facing Nathan Phillips square, would comprise the first phase of the project, due to be completed by 1971, and that the rest of the development would continue until the early 1980s. Upon receiving the necessary approvals, Eaton's forecast that construction could begin as early as summer. According to newspaper reports, both the Metro and Toronto Councils were enthusiastic but could not grant approval until various departments had prepared their reports on the project and after criticism from groups such as the Friends had been heard. Within a few weeks, another damning letter came from Vincent Massey, this time adding criticism of the project's tall buildings in addition to reinforcing his opposition to the razing of the old city hall. He reminded decision makers that "[t]he problem involves many difficulties, but may I suggest that a courageous decision in such matters rarely goes unrewarded, and if this is achieved, coming generations will have reason for gratitude."

The politics grew more intensive as the weather grew warmer. The proposal went back and forth from the Toronto City Council to the Metro Council without a firm a decision in either direction, and the whole process was exacerbated by the fact that 1966 was a mayoral election year. Eaton's dug in; when it was suggested that the fifty-seven-storey tower facing Nathan Phillips Square was too tall, the company offered to lower it by fifteen stories. It warned, though, that in order to make the height reduction economically feasible, the building's footprint had to be increased, making it impossible to preserve even the clock tower of the old city hall. The Metro Council responded by raising the purchase price for the old building. The question arose as to whether the old city hall should be sold or leased, and the matter bounced back and forth between the two councils involved. The project's approval process slowed to a snail's pace; the urgency sought by Eaton's became unachievable.

The mayoral election was won by William Dennison, Toronto city comptroller, who had opposed the removal of the historic city hall from the onset; early in 1967, David Owen resigned as managing director of Eaton Centre Limited, just as a revised design for the Eaton store and Bay Street office tower was unveiled by the company. Although the *Globe and Mail* called the design one "of great strength," the crude sketches that accompanied it seemed anything but—they showed four truncated pyramids supporting a two-storey glass box housing a trade centre on top of the store. The sudden change in design and the departure of Owen from the Eaton Centre team caused speculation about how serious Eaton's was about the development in the first place. The situation also fueled criticism of Eaton's earlier design and the store's insistence that the problematic elements had to be agreed on in order to fulfill the project.

By May, John David Eaton had pulled the plug on the Eaton Centre, citing "civic red tape and financial demands" that made the development unfeasible. Politicians pointed fingers at one another and at John David Eaton himself, suggesting that Eaton's had "bitten off more than it could chew" with the Eaton Centre proposal and had probably recently determined that the whole prospect was uneconomic from the start.

The *Globe and Mail* reported that John David Eaton's letter to both councils said that Eaton's "is still convinced that a comprehensive redevelopment plan for the entire area is required to underwrite Toronto's future as one of the world's great cities. The T. Eaton Co. Limited does not presume to judge for the citizens of Toronto what they want the city to be. The plan represented Eaton's conception of a revitalized downtown core that would inspire and stimulate the growth and development of the city."

The ink on Eaton's letter was barely dry when New York developer Zeckendorff contacted Mayor Dennison offering to develop the property, but his approaches were not taken seriously by the press or politicians. For the time being, Eaton's large and historical physical plant remained intact, yet it also remained an aging complex of underused structures that was seen as an anachronism and, even worse, an obstacle to Toronto's natural northward development.

It was this very episode that led to John David Eaton's comment about being disappointed with his dealings with municipal authorities. For the time being, Eaton's had to content itself with its success in handling downtown developments in Moncton and Saskatoon. By the time the Pacific Centre opened in Vancouver, John David Eaton was far too ill to take part in any company activities; he passed away at his home on August 4, 1973. Newspaper eulogies remembered his involvement in Eaton's growth across Canada, as well as his contributions to charity and to Eaton's generous employee benefits scheme, advanced during his tenure at the store founded by his grandfather.

Despite the Eaton Centre debacle, Eaton's attempts at downtown renewal bore fruit in two Ontario towns, although John David Eaton didn't live to see them completed. It was revealed in the press in July 1973 that Eaton's would participate in the Sudbury City Centre, an urban renewal project in the city of Sudbury that would replace Eaton's traditional store (operated since May 1928) with a two-level store in an urban shopping and office complex on Elm Street. The project was the culmination of eight years of work by the city's urban renewal commission.

When it opened in April 1975, an Eaton's executive said that the company felt that the 126,000-square-foot branch could be considered a "department store because we're still offering the wide variety of goods and services...and 'specialty store' because the accent will be on commodities and shops which are designed to accommodate the specific needs of the Sudbury area." A grand opening sale announced the store to the public, describing it as "where the buys are really beautiful," and ads invited the public to visit the aptly named Copper and Pine Restaurant, which brought Eaton's food service traditions to the new store.

Calling it "A Sudbury Kind of Place" in headlines, Sudbury's *Northern Lights* noted:

> *Eaton's is about to make its mark on an expectant Sudbury in a big way. Your first glimpse inside the big mall doors is one of fashion...and it's a glimpse that takes on panoramic proportions as you wend your way from one shop to the next. Fashion: in a Gourmet Shop that presents shiny enamel cookware against a background of rough-hewn pine. Fashion: in a Bath Shop that "rainbows" the velour towels in dozens and dozens of colours. Fashion: in furniture presentations that coordinate furnishings and accessories right down to flowers in a vase and books on a shelf. Because of Sudbury's sport orientation, Eaton's Sports Shop is a dandy: large, central, and well-equipped. Store décor accents the warmth of natural materials like oak, pine, cedar, suede and copper combined with super-bright*

colours delineating the many little "shops." In total, [it] comes across as a comfortable combination of Toronto influence and Sudbury experience.

Far to the south, one month later, a smaller, eighty-one-thousand-square-foot store opened in the city of Peterborough, where Eaton's had closed its 1930s-era store in the mid-1960s. In 1972, approval by Peterborough City Council of a three-block redevelopment of property directly on the Otonabee River was contingent on a commitment from Eaton's to build a

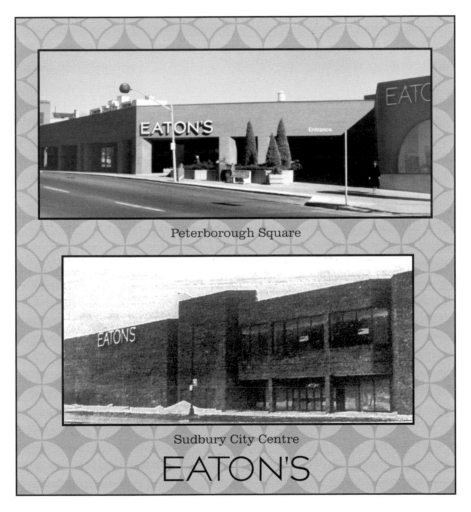

Peterborough Square

Sudbury City Centre

EATON'S

Surprisingly, during the Eaton Centre controversy, downtown redevelopment was more easily accomplished in places like Peterborough and Sudbury. *Archives of Ontario: T. Eaton Fonds F229. Used with the permission of Sears Canada Ltd.*

store. The idea for Peterborough Square, under consideration over a period of ten years, called for a five-storey office building, a hotel, a garage, a riverside marina and a two-level shopping concourse. Significant to the plans were the preservation of Peterborough's notable Market Square building and its landmark clock tower on the corner of George and Charlotte Streets. The development was promoted by the Canadian Pacific Railway, at the time known as CP Rail.

The design of the store fit the pattern set in Sudbury, a simple brown-brick building with glass entrances and a colourful and rich interior meant to illustrate Eaton's fashion emphasis and establish an enthusiastic customer base in Peterborough. The multi-use nature of Peterborough Square was, in its day, extremely innovative, and the attached Red Oak Inn was a luxury hotel that, while thoroughly modern in conception, carried on the tradition of the great railway hotels that were a part of Canada's cultural and historical landscape.

The opening of Eaton's in Peterborough Square was an important event for the city of Peterborough. It was striving to preserve the life of its handsome downtown, and the return of the department store was met with rejoicing; opening day employees later told *Peterborough This Week* that people were so happy with the store that they "came in with champagne and sandwiches for us!"

Back in Toronto, the Eaton Centre sprang to life again in spring of 1970, when newspapers reported that Eaton's was working with Cemp Investments' real estate subsidiary Fairview Corporation to revive the Eaton Centre idea, albeit with a completely different formula, this time avoiding the old city hall altogether. It was speculated that this time, Eaton's would construct a new store at Yonge and Dundas Streets. A multi-level shopping mall would connect Eaton's with Simpson's, stretching all the way to Queen Street. By 1970, the preferred format for a shopping centre, with two department stores "anchoring" a concourse of shops, had become *de rigueur* for the traffic (and profits) it produced.

Over the next few years, both Eaton's and Fairview confirmed that a new plan was under consideration and being privately discussed with Toronto officials. Robert Butler confirmed that "the company's desire to carry out a significant downtown redevelopment is as great as ever," adding a seal of authority to the idea that the store had not given up after the earlier controversy. Lacking a formal unveiling of plans, rumours swirled about the proposal, and in particular, the press speculated that the church of the Holy Trinity would be demolished and that delays were due to the fact that

Eaton's did not wish to leave its traditional location at Yonge and Queen for the Dundas Street site several blocks to the north. Furthermore, the proposed new department store location caused speculation about the ultimate disposition of the College Street store as well.

This time, the developer sought the closure of streets internal to the property and in return would give the city property around the perimeter to facilitate widening of the streets leading to it. Trinity Church let it be known that it would not give up any of its property for purely commercial reasons and hired an architect to propose its own improvements. From this point on, the project became another political fight, and opinions were tossed back and forth in the press for months until Fairview announced in April 1972 that the project was in serious danger of being cancelled.

The political fighting made it impossible to keep to the timeline agreed to earlier with the T. Eaton Co. In a letter to Toronto's development commissioner, Fairview representative Neil Wood blamed the inability to come to agreement on both the city and Trinity Church, citing "a wide difference of opinion" and increased land assembly cost as the reasons the project was on the brink of failure. The letter ended by noting, "Under these circumstances and in view of the wide difference of opinion with respect to the terms of street closure, we feel that there is no point in continuing negotiations at the present time. We will be contacting you again in due course."

The letter stunned the city government, and aldermen took sides, with some demanding that the city appropriate the property for its own development and others demanding that it cooperate in order to get the development off the ground. When a new schedule was agreed to between Eaton's and Fairview, the project was revived again and appeared to have clear sailing ahead of it. In article in the *Globe and Mail*, Alderman John Sewell wrote that the letter "saved Toronto from a fate worse than death. We were wrong: Eaton Centre has revived itself." He also noted that it was his preference that, though the area was "less than pleasant," something could be done to improve it and take advantage of what he called its "charming aspects." Among these he listed "a theatre, shops and restaurants, a pleasant grassed area by the Holy Trinity Church" and the "old and distinguished" buildings along Yonge Street.

In spite of two more years of controversy (even after approvals were granted by the city) and an agreement reached to preserve Holy Trinity Church, the Eaton Centre prevailed. Approval was granted on November 23, 1973, and construction began the following summer. The historic Queen

Street store's days were truly numbered at this point. The first phase of the centre would consist of a 1-million-square-foot Eaton's and a lofty shopping galleria reaching down to the old store. An office tower on Dundas Street, one of three planned, was meant to house the displaced offices of the T. Eaton Co. Once the first phase was completed, the Queen Street store would be demolished, the galleria extended to Simpson's and another office tower constructed. The property to the west along Bay Street was left for future development. The whole complex was the work of architects Bregmann and Hammann of Toronto, along with the Zeidler Roberts Partnership.

Speculation also surrounded the disposition of Eaton's–College Street. If the store was indeed a "white elephant" several blocks north of the nerve centre that was Eaton's–Main Store, it would be without any justification at all once the new Dundas Street store opened for business. The property was sold to the London Life Insurance Co. in December 1973, and Eaton's assured customers that the College Street store would stay open for at least three more years. The *Globe and Mail*, retrospectively calling the dignified building "Eaton's most adventurous merchandising gamble since old Timothy opened for business in 1869," predicted that Eaton's would raze the building and that "when [the doors] close for the last time it will be just another building site." Fortunately, it was redeveloped into an office and retail complex called College Park. Although the building's seventh floor sat vacant for several years, the heritage value of the Eaton Auditorium and the Round Room restaurant were ultimately recognized and reopened as the appropriately named The Carlu, an events centre set in the sensitively restored space.

When the February 1977 opening date for the Eaton Centre approached, Eaton's prepared to close its historic flagship locations. Special menus were served in the Georgian Room at Queen Street and the Round Room at College Street, and for a few weeks prior to the closing, a "Hail and Farewell" clearance was held to wind down business in the stores most Torontonians had known for so long. It was a bittersweet time; while excitement over the flashy new development built, the thought of a Toronto without such comfortable and familiar surroundings did cause sentimental feelings among the public. Timothy Eaton's famous statue was moved from the main Yonge Street entrance of the old store and placed in the lofty greenhouse-style entrance of the new Eaton's overlooking a small plaza at the Yonge and Dundas Street corner of the shiny new store.

When the two older stores came to the end of their useful lives on February 7, 1977, the scene was a mixture of dream and reality. Crowds rushed into

You're invited to discover Toronto's extraordinary new downtown shopping experience...Eaton's Toronto Eaton Centre...a department store unlike any other, anywhere. Getting to the new Eaton's is so easy. Subway travellers can enter on three levels via the Yonge Street line / Dundas station...without going outdoors.

The Galleria offers three enclosed mall level entrances. From the street level there are 4 convenient entrances on Yonge and 1 on Dundas West. If you're driving downtown, our multi-level on-site parking facilities accommodate over 1000 cars. Inside Eaton's you'll find nine shopping floors each with a

separate personality and everything is backed by The Eaton Guarantee— "Goods Satisfactory or Money Refunded." While at Eaton's choose from a host of restaurants to suit your mood, your time. Get ready to smile when you see Eaton's.

We built the store of the future on the best of our past.

Eaton's boasted that "we built the store of the future on the best of our past" for its shiny new flagship. *Collection of the author.*

the stores and fought for bargains. Sales clerks near the doors were told by their managers to "stay behind the counters" when the doors opened, and escalators and stairs became choked with bargain-hunters. The scene at College Street was surreal on account of a prop sale that was held to coincide with the closing. Customers carried artificial plants, display racks, parade costumes and even mannequins out of the store and onto the street or

EATON'S

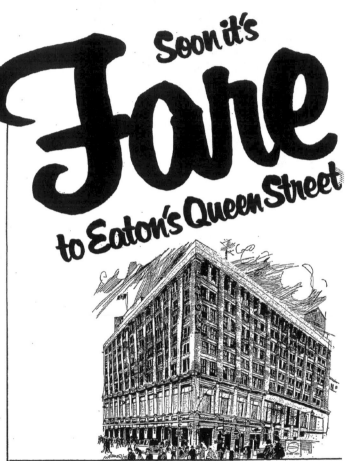

Never a dull moment at Eaton's Queen Street

By 1924, the Queen Street store had reached the size and shape we know today — and that was the year the Georgian Room opened in all its splendour. Crystal chandeliers added sparkle to rich brocade hangings in blue and gold. Thick blue carpet cushioned the grey Italian stone floor. An orchestra played in the musicians' gallery, over the gentle clatter of luncheons and teas.

More exciting times were ahead. In 1933, the first demonstration of television in Canada took place at Eaton's Queen Street with Foster Hewitt as Master of Ceremonies. Huge crowds gathered to watch the flickering black-and-white screens. Nobody thought it could ever be done in colour.

Gloria Swanson, Robert Taylor and other celebrities appeared on the Main Floor during the war years to help the sale of War Savings Stamps. In 1943, Elsie the Cow spent two weeks on the 5th floor on behalf of the Milk-for-Britain Fund. Toronto youngsters had their first ride on the CNR Toyland Train at Christmas, 1945 — perhaps you were one of them. Import Fairs became a regular feature at Queen Street, introducing shoppers to unusual merchandise, foods and exhibits from other countries. During one British promotion, London newspapers and fresh Devon violets were flown in daily. October, 1961, saw the Commonwealth saluted royally on every floor, right down to the Subway Level where Mohan, a charming baby elephant from India, held court in his sturdy palace. A recent Italian gala included a tableau of elegant Medici costumes. What with fashion shows, cooking demonstrations, needlework fairs and beauty clinics, Queen Street has always been a fun place to shop. Do we intend to continue these special events at the new Eaton's? We do indeed. Constantly. Just wait till you see what we have planned for you in the months ahead!

P.S. Even as you read this, Queen Street is gearing up for a farewell you'll never forget. Our buyers have begun to slash prices in every department. Our suppliers have joined in with enthusiasm, bringing in all sorts of special goodies priced to make your eyes sparkle. It's supposed to be a big surprise, but we just can't hold all the activity. So come and see for yourself!

EATON'S

Soon it's *Fare* to Eaton's Queen Street

Hail to Eaton's—Toronto Eaton Centre—opening Feb. 10th. **Farewell** to Eaton's Queen Street and College Street stores. It's been fun!

The end of an era. The start of

Eaton's put a positive spin on the closing of the hallowed Queen Street store and its art-décor companion prior to the opening of the new Toronto Eaton Centre. *From an ad, collection of the author.*

down into the subway. At Queen Street, although most of the departments were picked bare, some shoppers just came to say one last goodbye to the familiar old store and perhaps get a souvenir that would help them jog their memories in years to come—years that would have been unthinkable just a decade ago, years without "their" Eaton store. One shopper remarked to the *Globe and Mail*, "I've been shopping here since 1939, and it's a sad day." Even John Craig Eaton took part, standing in the main entrance vestibule for hours thanking customers for their patronage.

Across the street, competitor Simpson's had been busy planning sales and events to capture the crowds that would come downtown for the February 10 opening. Simpson's president E.G. Burton anticipated that the Eaton Centre would propel his flagship store to surpass even New York's huge Macy's store to hold the highest volume of sales for a single store in North America. A week before the Eaton Centre opening, Simpson's announced a $6 million renovation to its structure, the oldest portion of which was designed by architect Edmund Burke as a Chicago-style commercial building, nonetheless embellished with wide arches and deeply executed details in light-brown sandstone. The familiar building had recently been designated as a heritage site by the Ontario Heritage Foundation.

A grand opening ceremony, attended by public dignitaries and, representing the Eaton family, Signy Eaton and her four sons was held on the morning of Thursday, February 10, 1977. It was a grand affair, with the Forty-eighth Highlanders pipes descending, in full dress, the halted escalators that served as a twentieth-century grand staircase, followed by Lieutenant Governor Pauline McGibbon and John Craig Eaton. After speeches and introductions, a ceremonial ribbon was cut, someone yelled "Okay, let 'em in!" and the sea of humanity assembled to inspect the new Eaton's floor by floor surged through the mall entrance like an incoming tide. Toronto had waited a dozen years since the Eaton Centre proposal was revealed to the public.

The store itself (the work of company architect E.L. Hankinson) was a contemporary, seven-storey structure covered in prefinished panels in a buff golden colour. A rounded tower, taller and more dramatic than the one featured on the 1973 Pacific Centre store in Vancouver, added a point of emphasis near the building's northernmost entrance.

The main floor was recessed to form an arcade along Yonge Street, and the building's huge mass, deeply notched at two locations to minimize the sense of bulkiness, was carried on muscular columns that rose from the sidewalk. Above these columns, the second floor was treated in panels of a bright white colour and punctured with circular openings. The seventh floor, largely of glass, was recessed beyond the main façades, minimizing the apparent height of the store.

Inside, the expansive Eaton store had a lofty ceiling (with large-scale illuminated panels outlined with aluminum trim in Eaton's familiar quatrefoil design) and twin banks of escalators rising up through a three-level atrium that also looked down one level to its "Level 2 Subway," predominately dedicated to men's wear. There were six places for shoppers to eat, ranging from the sit-down Dundas Room and Patio just inside the entrance to a Sir John's pub in the men's store, Bites 'n Nibbles in the Gourmet Marketplace, Pizza and Subs in the basement and a large cafeteria called the Marine Room on the sixth floor.

The Queen Street store did eventually come down, to be replaced by the remainder of the shopping galleria and the Cadillac Fairview Tower, standing like a shiny exclamation point at the southern end of the project where a second-level bridge connected to Simpson's venerable store on the other side of Queen Street. After the 1979 opening of the completed Eaton Centre galleria, the shopping mecca became one of Canada's prime tourist attractions. Snapshots of wide-eyed tourists standing in front of *Flight Stop*, a dramatic sculpture of Canada geese suspended in flight below the arched skylight, soon found their way into countless photo albums. The Eaton family maintained that their new flagship store was a magnificent generator of income.

Yet for all of its newness and shiny modernity, some maintained the opinion that Eaton's in its new home lacked the charm and certainly the familiarity of the older stores that had served Toronto so well for more than one hundred years. Sigrid Wolf, who worked in the expansive cosmetics department in 1977, recalls that it was hard for people to get their bearings in the big store, and not just when it opened. Although the floors above the main floor were numbered logically, those below were called "Level 2 Subway," "Level 1 Subway" (essentially a second basement) and, below that, "3 Below," a youth-oriented floor. Her words convey her impressions characteristically:

> So many customers would ask me for directions, since I was stationed right next to the escalators, and so many of those people were super-cranky about the mega-size downtown mall! At that time, Eaton's boasted that their fabulous new store had three levels of shopping below ground and seven levels of shopping above ground. My Gosh, how that frustrated and confused everyone...especially the old, established Eaton's clients. It was

The new Eaton Centre store was a complete break from the past, from its greenhouse entry to its cylindrical tower executed in chamois-colour panels and butt-glazed glass. *Archives of Ontario: T. Eaton Fonds F229. Used with the permission of Sears Canada Ltd.*

a tad overwhelming, and I'd have to deal comments like "3 floors below! What is that supposed to mean? Are we shopping in the dungeon now?" and "How am I ever going to remember what is on which floor?" Of course, I answered offering my biggest smile, but lordy, lordy, I was so busy explaining everything to everyone, I barely could focus on selling any fragrances! There were loads of complaints, too, that Eaton's was now too far removed from Simpson's (they had been directly across from one another, on Queen Street, for ages), as it was now positioned a whole city block away on Dundas Street. The last outrage was that the mall was too big, for heaven's sake, with its three levels of shops. Yikes! I guess all the tourists and events had something to do with people finally getting used to it.

For her part, Ollie Gudz, who worked for twenty-one years in the Queen Street store, transferred to the shoe departments on the 1977 store's main floor. "It was a mistake. I think they knew it was just too big. What was worse, our stockroom was on the second floor, so we spent a lot of time going up and down the stairs. I don't think it had the flavour that made the Queen Street Eaton's so special, and were my feet ever sore when I went home, eh?"

With the Eaton Centre finally in operation, and an apparent success at that, the company wasted no time applying the same formula to other downtown locations in Canada. During the time Eaton's was struggling to get the Eaton Centre out of the ground in Toronto, it proposed, along with development partner First National Property Corporation, an ambitions redevelopment of twenty acres adjacent to the long-established Montréal store on St. Catherine Street. By 1968, though, the project had been cancelled. In 1977, a part of the plan was finally completed by Rousse Development Limitée. Known as *Les Terrasses*, the mixed-use complex featured a Brutalist-style, L-shaped office building on Boulevard Maisonneuve, while Victoria Street between Eaton's and Montréal's main Kresge store was closed and occupied by a narrow shopping mall set back from St. Catherine Street.

From the entrance plaza, the building rose up in a series of landscaped terraces, topped by a restaurant. Inside, a triangular shopping concourse

The interior of the Eaton Centre store was a revelation, conveying a sense of openness heretofore unseen in the older stores. *Archives of Ontario: T. Eaton Fonds F229. Used with the permission of Sears Canada Ltd.*

housed 115 stores and spiraled up three colour-coded levels. Since *Les Terrasses* shared a wall of the Eaton store, entrances allowed shoppers to move from the mall to the store at different levels. When it opened on February 19, 1977, the press was enthusiastic about this addition to Montréal's network of pedestrian malls, citing the atrium at the Maisonneuve entrance and the elabourate landscaping and planting throughout the space, as well as the innovative "Metro Marché" that connected *Les Terrasses* with the adjacent subway station.

Les Terrasses, however, was only a limited success. The layout, compromised by stairways and spiraling levels, made the centre difficult to negotiate. In late 1985, York-Hanover properties announced that it would rebuild the property, which it acquired in 1978. The revised mall opened in 1991, replacing the recessed plaza and terraced entry (as well as the well-loved Art Deco Kresge Store that was its neighbour on St. Catherine Street) with a four-storey galleria.

Around the same time, Toronto-Dominion square opened next to the 1929 Eaton store in Calgary. The three-level shopping mall beneath the pentagonal dark-bronze glass Home Oil and Dome Towers was topped off with the Devonian Gardens, the world's largest indoor garden at two and a half acres in floor area. The shopping mall at TD Square did connect to the well-established Eaton store across Third Street via a bridge to the mall.

A transformation in 1990 saw the construction of a new Eaton's store one block west of its original location. The original store was demolished and replaced by a multi-floor Eaton Centre shopping mall. Nine bays of the 1929 façade of Tyndall limestone were salvaged and reinstalled on three of the new structure's elevations, providing a hint of the history that took place on the site, surrounded by the modern buildings of an archetypal energy boomtown.

One of the best and most sensitive of the downtown Eaton projects opened on October 11, 1979, in Winnipeg. Just as had been foretold in the press at the time of the closing of *Eaton's Catalogue*, the heritage buildings housing the catalogue operation in Winnipeg were adapted to retail use. Known as Eaton Place, the development housed offices on the upper floors and 120 shops and restaurants. The new retail centre connected to the Eaton store on the basement and main levels, and a shop-lined bridge spanned Graham Street at the second-floor level.

Inside the cavernous building, an atrium was carved out of the structure in order to create the shopping gallery and lower-level Gourmet Market. The connection to the 1905-era Eaton store on Portage Avenue was

A comparison of the Toronto streetscape before (bottom) and after (top) the construction of the Eaton Centre does not show off the new building's industrially inspired architecture to advantage when compared with the traditional warmth of the well-loved Queen Street Eaton's store. *Archives of Ontario: T. Eaton Fonds F229. Used with the permission of Sears Canada Ltd.*

accomplished by razing the Donald and Hargrave Annexes and extending the first two floors of the store towards Eaton Place.

The *Winnipeg Free Press* described the building's transformation from warehouse to public use in detail and editorialized that

> [t]*he architects of Eaton Place have retained the old building, which has its share of historical and architectural significance. Although it is now cast in a new role, it will remain as a reminder to future generations of the time when the arrival of the Eaton's catalogue was a sure sign of a change of season. The advent of a downtown, enclosed shopping mall in Winnipeg will not be without its difficulties, as surrounding stores flock to where they believe the customers will be, and leave other premises vacant. But, as has been demonstrated elsewhere, enclosed downtown shopping is as good a guarantee as can be made that the downtown part of the city will remain alive, vibrant, and most important, competitive with suburban shopping centres.*

Two years later, a project opened in Regina that located a major downtown shopping mall on the north side of Eleventh Avenue between Lorne and Hamilton Streets. The development's name, Cornwall Centre, was taken from Cornwall Street, which connected it to the city's beautiful Victoria Park and its Regina Cenotaph along a north–south axis. Although its construction required the removal of many heritage buildings, its exterior design happily preserved the façade of the Merchants Bank building and left the Imperial Bank and the Western Trust Co. buildings in place. Inside the Mall, the relocated façades of the Bank of Ottawa and the 1900 Canadian Bank of Commerce served as set-pieces against the shops located there.

When the three-storey Eaton store in the Cornwall Centre opened on August 19, 1981, it superseded the old one on Seventh Avenue at Broad Street. A boxy structure of deeply textured buff-coloured brick, it was uncompromisingly modern, with a recessed street floor characterized by round columns and large windows; John Craig Eaton cut the ribbon that opened it. The Cornwall Centre, in spite of criticism, quickly became the dominant shopping centre in Regina, no mean feat in an era that previously saw such long-term retailers as Simpson's (originally the R.H. Williams and Sons store) leave the downtown shopping scene.

In the 1980s frenzy to develop stores in central business districts, Eaton's didn't focus only on large markets. In partnership with the Ontario Downtown Redevelopment Programme, Eaton's actually moved back to

The towers and greenhouse enclosure of the new TD Square rise above the traditional Eaton store in Calgary late in its life. *Archives of Ontario: T. Eaton Fonds F229. Used with the permission of Sears Canada Ltd.*

Winnipeg's Eaton Place created new spaces from the disused Mail Order buildings adjacent to the traditional downtown Eaton store. *From an ad, collection of the author.*

some locations in Ontario that it abandoned in the 1960s and opened stores in the downtowns of others.

The Sarnia Eaton Centre opened in 1982 and immediately brought some of the "Downtown is the happening place" sense to the town across the blue waters (unlike the Danube, really blue!) of the St. Clair River from neighbouring Michigan. Surprisingly, Eaton's rehabilitated an older store once operated by the Hudson's Bay Company, an eastern outpost of the predominately western company, on account of Sarnia's location at the terminus of pipelines from oil-rich western provinces and Hudson's Bay Company's ownership of mineral rights on its landholdings. The new mall roughly paralleled Christina Street, Sarnia's traditional north–south axis, and even preserved a few of the city's historical storefronts. Yet the mall, for all of its newness, was inward-looking.

The year 1984 saw the opening of an Eaton Centre in Guelph, Ontario, where several blocks of the "Royal City's" downtown were replaced with an indoor shopping mall following the gentle curve of Québec Street that led to a new Eaton downtown store. Two years later, a similar development, the Eaton Market Square, opened in Brantford, Ontario. In this case, another inward-looking mall ran along history-rich Dalhousie and Colborne Streets in the "Telephone City." The galleria's Y-shaped configuration allowed small entrance plazas at its western side, and the shopping centre terminated at an Eaton store on the western end. Although the whole complex was executed in a red-coloured brick to harmonize with some of Brantford's landmarks, the Eaton store itself was a fairly unadorned box that certainly focused inward on itself. Ironically, the original Canadian Department Stores location on Colborne Street and the 1947 Eaton store were only blocks from this new development.

The largest project of the early 1980s was located in the national capital of Ottawa. It was supremely ironic that Eaton's, as a Canadian institution and a store that fancied itself as the "Greatest Retail Organization in the British Empire," did not have a strong presence in Canada's federal capital. In the 1970s, Eaton's acquired property on Ottawa's Sparks Street for a development known as Canada Centre that would combine a new Eaton's store with a Four Seasons Hotel, a Holt Renfrew store and a mall of about one hundred shops.

The city of Ottawa and the National Capital Commission, along with the federal government, fearing the impact the development might have on the nearby Rideau Street shopping district, got involved in order to exert influence over the development and revitalization of Ottawa's central business district. Eaton's agreed to swap its Sparks Street properties for the right to develop a commercial centre on Rideau Street.

Eaton's formed the Viking-Rideau Corporation for this very purpose, and ten years of planning and negotiations followed. The final plan involved a large Eaton store, a three-level shopping mall and connections to the Hudson's Bay Company store across the street, as well as the adjacent Charles Ogilvy Limited store, a hotel and a new Capital Convention Centre located on the part of the site covered with disused railway tracks. The Rideau Centre, as it came to be known, also included parking, a rooftop garden and the preservation of the historic National Capital Commission building as office space.

In an *Ottawa Citizen* interview with Toronto architects James Crang and George Boake, the two spoke of the rigors of ten years of planning for the Rideau Centre, drawing attention to the 760 meetings they attended during the lengthy process and calling it a "bureaucratic hornet's nest." Their design, with intimate, skylit malls traversing the site diagonally, was much less monumental than the Toronto Eaton Centre, to which it was often compared, and Crang added that "we believe we've succeeded in designing a complex which reflects the character of Ottawa." The Eaton store itself, though large at 247,000 square feet and elaborate in its interior finishes, was fairly plain in its exterior design, the chamfered corners and some skylit entrances being the only elements adorning the concrete-paneled box.

The Rideau Centre store brought a modern, full-scale Eaton store into Canada's capital city for the first time, but its appearance was decidedly suburban in character. *Archives of Ontario: T. Eaton Fonds F229. Used with the permission of Sears Canada Ltd.*

Both Ogilvy's and the Hudson's Bay Company remodeled and expanded their adjacent Rideau Street stores. The Bay developed an enclosed public space, the Freiman Mall (an homage to A.J. Freiman, founder of the store acquired by the Bay in 1972), which bisected its property and formed a link to Ottawa's historic and popular ByWard Market.

The Rideau Centre's own publicity at the time of the grand opening on March 16, 1983, avoided talk of controversy and drew attention to the its most positive attributes:

> *Ten years in the planning, 21 months in construction, and at a total cost which will approach $1.4 billion when fully completed, Rideau Centre's grand opening...marks a day of proud achievement for many dedicated professionals. The flagship Eaton store is the glittering centrepoint for an unparalleled range of independent stores offering a very wide range of products and services. Arranged throughout an innovative network of pedestrian concourses and boulevards and linked by open, skylit courtyards and malls, Rideau Centre is perfectly suited for shoppers and businesspeople alike. Its cinemas, restaurants, and landscaped roof garden reflect a genuine concern for the quality of the downtown shopping environment. Its forward-looking design planning links the Rideau Centre with the surrounding area through imaginative features such as the fully enclosed and security controlled skywalks which link the complex with the Byward Market via the Freiman Mall. Improved transport facilities were integral to the overall design concept and the Rideau Street Transit Mall is now one of the most efficient public transport corridors on the continent. As an added benefit, Rideau Street is now a far more attractive pedestrian facility and, despite the dramatic re-vamping of the area, the traditional features and character of this section of Ottawa have been preserved, and in some cases, improved through refurbishment.*

It took seven pairs of scissors to cut the opening day ribbon, given the number of government dignitaries attending, and Mayor Marion Dewar couldn't resist taking a subtle dig at Frederik Eaton by saying, "The people of Ottawa have already claimed ownership and called it their own" in her speech. The remark was a reference to political turmoil four months earlier, when Viking Eaton announced that the Centre would be known as the Rideau Eaton Centre. Both public and political reaction to adding the Eaton name were negative until the proposal was withdrawn, but not before acid-tongued debate flew back and forth in the press. The *Ottawa*

Citizen even printed a sarcastic letter from a reader suggesting billboards that announced "Eaton's and over 200 fine stores" showed that Eaton's was admitting it was below par!

Crowds swarmed the long-awaited Rideau Centre on its opening, and the shopping centre carried its success far beyond the opening; it became, as its planners envisioned, a true part of the city. The criticism, however, of Eaton's at the time of its name change proposal ominously marked a point in time when public opinion would no longer go with the store simply because of its well-established name and position in Canada's history.

On the other side of the country, in Edmonton, Alberta, Eaton's watched major competitor Woodward's open a modern new store in the Edmonton City Centre in late April 1974. By the time the massive West Edmonton Mall opened in September 1981, Eaton's had stores all around Edmonton, including Heritage Mall, opened in 1980.

The downtown store, in spite of renovations and its Art Deco styling, seemed out of step with the times, and Eaton's found a solution by partnering with the Ghermazian family (who developed the West Edmonton Mall) and their Triple-Five Group to propose a giant multi-use Eaton Centre. With hyperbole similar to their suburban colossus, the Ghermazians' plan, announced in July 1980, was forecast to include an enormous, 465,000-square-foot Eaton's, a three-level shopping mall and five office and residential towers.

From that point on, on account of the demands of the developer for tax concessions, the Edmonton Eaton Centre project became a political hot potato. At one point, Eaton's pulled out, and the project seemed moribund, but eventually a scaled-down version of the downtown mall was built. Eaton's opened its new store on August 19, 1987, vacating the handsome streamlined structure that had served Edmonton for almost fifty years. Once in its new home, a four-storey, precast-concrete-faced inverted ziggurat with oval-shaped stair towers at its corners, Eaton's unceremoniously pulled down its old store for an expansion of the mirrored, skylit shopping mall within.

If the Edmonton Eaton Centre was more than plagued by its share of controversy, the Victoria Eaton Centre project was an outright battle. When Eaton's and Cadillac Fairview proposed a new, five-storey department store and adjacent shopping mall in the downtown area of the historic capital city of British Columbia in 1986, they did address citizens' concerns by proposing a postmodern aesthetic, with fanciful new façades reminiscent of Victoria's historic buildings, in addition to the reconstruction or replication of four actual historic storefronts. The new Eaton store was designed to look

The Eaton Centre in Edmonton had a multi-level interior of glass, mirrors and shiny metals, but its exterior, uncomfortably overhanging the street and slamming into the sidewalk with blank stair towers, did not erase memories of the delicate streamlined store of 1938 that it replaced. *Courtesy of Darrell Bateman.*

like a larger version of the historic Driard Hotel, which had served as a part of the store since the Spencer days, way back in 1910.

Another part of the plan that became a bone of contention was the proposed vacation of Broad Street, a one-block-long thoroughfare that separated the two main parts of the existing Eaton store. The street was closed in 1969 and turned into a pedestrian promenade popular with shoppers, nearby office workers and Eaton's employees alike. The design of the new Eaton Centre called for a new Eaton's to be built on the Government Street side of the property, site of the two-storey Arcade Building.

As soon as that phase was completed, a new shopping mall would extend all the way to Douglas Street, replacing the main block and Driard Hotel buildings of the old Eaton's store. To realize this plan, Eaton's would buy Broad Street from the city.

After a public unveiling, the project received preliminary approval, but criticism mounted, especially regarding the loss of heritage buildings on the two-square-block area to be razed for the Eaton Centre. Victoria's *Monday Magazine* printed a detailed inventory of the area's historic structures, explaining that whatever the large-scale urban planning aspects of the

Eaton Centre, "Victorians are most impatient for a penetrating look at the more concretely physical heritage and design ramifications of what could be a substantial refiguring of the face of their downtown":

> *What distinguishes downtown Victoria now is the high proportion of buildings that have survived, their cohesiveness, their acutely picturesque grouping around the harbour and, to a degree, their cosmopolitan diversity in historic styles. Also exceptional is the fine scale of buildings, streets, and squares. Match this with our specialized local climate and beautiful natural setting, and indeed Victoria can rank herself a rare commodity.*

For its part, the *Victoria Times-Colonist* chimed in early in 1987 reporting that the "biggest bone of contention has been the process council followed" and that "[c]harges of secret deals, selling public land to a private developer at closed meetings and ignoring recommendations from

The Victoria Eaton Centre, as envisioned by its architect, was a combination of re-created historical façades and new buildings. The tall Eaton store in the style of the old Driard Hotel is seen in the background, while the lower structure on Douglas Street in the foreground was meant to evoke the original Spencer store of 1919. *Courtesy of Ross Crockford.*

advisory committees have abounded." Citizens groups, among them the Hallmark Society, pointed out the fact that ten individual structures on the property were on Victoria's official Heritage Registry. The paper summed up the controversy:

> *On the whole most agree a new Eaton's store is needed and downtown redevelopment is essential, the burning issues have become the scale of the proposed project, fear that heritage buildings will be lost, negative economic effects on established city business, the project's style and council's method of dealing with the plans.*

One of the most vocal opponents to the plan was former Victoria resident and heritage specialist Pierre Berton, who was actively involved when Victoria's much-loved Crystal Gardens swimming pool was threatened with demolition. Writing from Ontario, he told the city council that it was "going to replace the very heart of your city with an ersatz tin and stucco heritage-style envelope. This is sheer vandalism." Berton concluded his missive by telling the city council, "Think it over carefully. Remember that you can't replace heritage. Once it is destroyed it is gone forever."

Attempting to resolve the issue, Mayor Gretchen Brewin on January 19, 1987, appointed a special-development commissioner, Gwyn Symmons, to conduct a five-week review of the project and put forth recommendations that would ultimately form an agreement between the Victoria government and Cadillac Fairview. The *Times-Colonist* called Symmons's job "Herculean—to chart compromises which will satisfy council, the corporation and the citizens and voters," and the final report bears out this judgment. Symmons met with more than 1,500 people in the course of five weeks and stated that opinion "ranges from unquestioning support to uncompromising rejection." He summarized his findings by stating that he could recommend approval of the project, but only subject to modifications (included in the review) to effect a compromise acceptable to project critics and to the developer seeking to build it.

Among the recommendations was the retention of four of the ten heritage façades, the creation of a secondary galleria following the outline of the former Broad Street and two recessed plazas at either end of it to retain at least some of the street's former character as an outdoor space. Regarding the new Eaton's store design, the report had only praise, and it further pointed out that the references to the old Driard Hotel building in its design were appropriate because "the architectural tradition of the City is full of examples of buildings designed to styles from a previous era." In general, Symmons's report also warned the City of Victoria that it should immediately move to develop stronger guidelines for downtown development if it wished to prevent incremental destruction of its architectural heritage and unique atmosphere.

In general, Cadillac Fairview and Eaton's agreed with the proposals, and the council gave the Eaton Centre approval; a building permit was in hand by the end of June 1987, but the project faced one more hurdle in the form of an alternate proposal by University of Victoria chancellor William Gibson and businessman Keith Cowan in January 1988 called "A Civic Square." After demolition of the Government Street block for the new Eaton store was completed, the view of the historic façades around the vacant block inspired the men to propose that the property be turned into a European-style square with landscaping, kiosks and a monumental fountain at its centre, while retaining the underground parking garage already under construction.

Although the idea was popular with Victorians who relished the idea of a planned open space in their densely packed town, the proposal was doomed without funds to buy the property (and to recover the cost already spent in developing it), and Cadillac Fairview stated that the chances of it giving up on the development, at such a late point in the process, in order to turn the property into a civic square were "less than nil."

The new Victoria Eaton's store opened on March 1, 1989, and after the demolition of the Driard Hotel and former Spencer Store facing Douglas Street, the remainder of the Eaton Centre rose over the old Broad Street location and spread north to Douglas Street. The centre, with its elaborate, historicist façades and preserved and re-created heritage fragments, was completed in June 1990.

In Hamilton, Ontario, Eaton's simultaneously followed a similar course, this time acquiring the location of the city's historic market square next to its classic downtown store and building a new, four-level store that would serve the company while the older structure was razed in preparation for a 130-store Eaton Centre on its James Street site. Although the actual purchase of the property was a source of political scandal, the plan to build a new store was met with enthusiasm, especially since longtime Hamilton department store Robinson's left downtown in the 1980s, and Eaton's plans were considered a shot in the arm for Hamilton's retail centre.

When the old store closed, there was, expressed in the press and among Eaton's employees and customers, a sense of nostalgia for the historic premises that had served Hamilton for such a long time. The new Eaton's would be an upscale retail beacon for downtown, but it wouldn't have the famous elevator operators who had become a familiar aspect of shopping on James Street, nor would the new store have historic artifacts like the embossed griffins above the elevators that were holdovers from the days when parts of the building housed the Griffin Theatre.

Nonetheless, when it opened on May 3, 1989, and later, when it was joined by the Eaton Centre Mall, Eaton's new store replaced the old one lingering in customers' memories and offered, according to the *Hamilton Spectator*, a "spacious, bright, skillfully designed new department store with wide aisles, skylights, and modern displays."

The new Eaton stores in downtown shopping centres represented a genuine effort to help Canadian downtowns compete with suburban shopping centres, as well as retain the primacy of the cities as business and cultural magnets, though there was often of necessity a regrettable loss of heritage and tradition that was a byproduct of these developments.

During this era, Eaton's replaced its longstanding Red Deer, Alberta downtown store with a branch in the outlying Bower Place Mall and also built many suburban shopping centre stores, from replacing its long-

Like it did in other cities, Eaton's built a new store in Hamilton and subsequently tore down its old premises to build an adjacent Eaton Centre shopping mall. *Courtesy of Local History & Archives, Hamilton Public Library.*

Lime Ridge Mall

Pickering Town Centre

EATON'S

Eaton's did not neglect the suburbs while reinvigourating the central cores of Canada's cities, but its branch stores became much more generic and certainly lacked the style and excitement of the older branches when they appeared. *Archives of Ontario: T. Eaton Fonds F229. Used with the permission of Sears Canada Ltd.*

established Nanaimo, British Columbia store with one at Woodgrove Centre to constructing stores in Vancouver (Coquitlam), Kamloops (Aberdeen Mall), Edmonton (West Edmonton and Heritage Malls), Calgary (Sunridge Centre), London (Masonville Place), Toronto (Square One, Pickering Town Centre), Ottawa (Les Promenades de l' Outaoais) and Montréal (Carrefour de l'Agrignon, Rockland) among others. The expansion continued to the early 1990s, and Eaton's even acquired some locations that became available when Woodward's Limited went out of business in 1993.

The continuous change that characterized the business in these years was not only confined to store locations. Shortly after the opening of the Toronto Eaton Centre, Earl Orser was let go (although according to the official version, he left voluntarily), and Frederik Eaton was named CEO and president. In fact, the company ownership of John David Eaton was split between his four sons, but it was the decision of the board to grant the title of chairman to Frederik and install his younger brother, George, as deputy chairman. Brother John Craig remained as the chairman of Eaton's of Canada Limited, the family's holding company, and Thor Eaton preferred not to take an active role in retailing. A non-family member of the store's management was Greg Purchase, who had been head of Eaton's Western Division. He came to Toronto to run Eaton's Central Division but soon became executive vice-president and chief operating officer, working closely with George Eaton, who had, at the time, given up his career as a race car driver to take an interest in retailing and his family's company.

In 1991, Frederik gave up his position at the family business to take the post of Canadian high commissioner to the United Kingdom and Northern Ireland. In his absence, George Eaton assumed control of the T. Eaton Co. Limited. George had no retail experience until he joined the store later in life, but having worked with his brother Fred and Chief Operating Officer Greg Purchase in Eaton's day-to-day operations, he felt that he was up to the task.

Signy, the mother of the four Eaton heirs, suffered a stroke at her home in Caledon, Ontario, and passed away on September 10, 1992. She had been on the Eaton's board and was remembered not only for her service to the company that her husband once led but also as a friend and patron of the arts. Her obituary in the *Globe and Mail* noted that the Signy Eaton Gallery and the John David and Signy Eaton Court at the Art Gallery of Ontario were named in her honor, as was a lecture theatre at Trent University in Peterborough, Ontario. The paper referred to her and her husband as "jet-setters before there were jets," and with her passing, one more link with Eaton's magnificent history had been sadly but permanently severed.

The Fall of the House of Eaton

Don't it always seem to go, that you don't know what you've got 'til it's gone?
—Joni Mitchell

It would be accurate to say that from a twenty-first-century perspective, histories of North America's greatest department stores don't conclude happily, and the story of the T. Eaton Co. Limited is, sadly, no exception. Eaton's came through the 1980s, after a period of change and transformation, as a very different organization than it was in the halcyon days after World War II. Eaton's presented a modern and progressive face with shiny new stores in Canada's large cities and a growing number of branches in the suburbs, wherever the customers happened to be.

In its newest shops, like "Signature" for designer women's wear, "Timothy E." for men or its "Peppertree" young women's concept, it presented the so-called designer labels of the day while still fulfilling the role of a large department store with wide-ranging lines of merchandise, from books to power tools and from children's wear to gourmet foods. Eaton's slipping market share rebounded in the 1980s, although loyal customers could no longer stack catalogues in piles at home so that they could order something from it without even leaving the house. Eaton's seemed to remain a historic and popular Canadian icon.

Many analysts claim that Eaton's downward slide towards bankruptcy and eventual failure had its roots earlier in the store's history, as the Eaton family focused on their wealthy lifestyle and let the fortunes of their business wane. Yet looking at Eaton's as it entered the uncertain economic environment of the

1980s, especially from the perspective of urban decay, mass consolidations and closures characteristic of the department store industry south of the border, Eaton's and Canada both seemed to be getting along very well indeed, with handsome and popular downtown areas undergoing continuous and quite innovative renewal. In most large Canadian cities, Eaton's, Simpson's, the Bay and Woodward's in the west gave little indication that they'd dump their flagship stores in a minute as many American retailers did.

In the 1980s, on account of those flashy new downtown stores, and the growing number of outlets to serve suburban shoppers, Eaton's had finally gained the upper hand in halting the slide of its market share that had peaked in the store's "good old days." Yet these years brought their own share of problems to the store's triumvirate management team, consisting of Frederik and George Eaton and Greg Purchase. While the first two concentrated on merchandising and the upgrading of Eaton's image, Purchase was an advocate of continual cost-cutting measures in order to keep Eaton's finances in shape.

In 1982, Eaton's garnered not just poor press but general scorn, too, when it cancelled the Toronto Santa Claus Parade, claiming that the cost to produce it had become too great and that the event had long ago ceased to provide good will and sales impetus for the Eaton stores. On the contrary, though, the millions of people who still lined its route or glued themselves to the television in order to watch the spectacle did associate it with Eaton's, and its cancellation brought bad press and ill will to the store, even though a nonprofit foundation was formed to continue the famous event.

Much like the contentious organization drive of the late 1940s and early 1950s, a new attempt to unionize Eatonians surfaced in 1984. While the store was busy building new outlets across Canada, the recession then plaguing Canada's economy caused a cash flow crisis that the store met with belt-tightening measures that bore heavily on Eaton's employees, whose plight was well reported in the press. Large-scale layoffs and a wage freeze led Eaton's management to realize that department store selling (following the lead of the discount outlets that littered the Canadian landscape) had degenerated into little more than operating a cash register or scanning a barcode. The store came to realize that a staff of part-time workers was, in this environment, just as valuable as the experienced, well-trained and decently cared-for employees on whom it had always relied. This new employer-employee relationship may have helped the company's shrinking bottom line, but it caused dissention among the ranks.

The Retail, Wholesale and Department Store Union began to organize Ontario Eaton stores, this time quite successfully, gaining certification at a number of locations throughout the province. As the process gained strength, the atmosphere in the stores themselves became somewhat contentious, and the whole debacle boiled over during the Christmas rush of 1984, when the employees of six unionized Ontario stores voted to strike.

Eaton's hired part-time staff to minimize inconvenience to its customers during the strike, but the flames were well and truly fanned in March 1985 when a group of three thousand protesters attending an International Women's Day Parade entered the (non-unionized) flagship store in the Toronto Eaton Centre and disrupted business by hurling insults at customers and employees, affixing anti-Eaton stickers to store fixtures and releasing mice inside the cavernous store. Like his grandmother before him, Frederik Eaton became active in the support of loyal Eatonians, braving the scorn of picket lines to man counters in the stores themselves, and Eaton's began offering regular raises to employees in order to counter the urge to organize across the country. When the strike dragged on, and workers returned to their jobs on their own initiative, the union eventually accepted Eaton's wage and salary offers, and the organization drive went no further.

Although it achieved victory against the union in this circumstance, another challenge rose over Eaton's horizon. Many Canadians believed that Canada had settled the issue of reciprocity in 1911 with the defeat of pro–free trade prime minister Wilfred Laurier. In the mid-1980s, at the instigation of popular and respected American president Ronald Reagan, the issue came to the forefront once again. In Canada, this time, the debate was reversed, with the Progressive-Conservative candidate Brian Mulroney arguing for the so-called North American Free Trade Agreement and Liberal Party leader John Turner arguing against it.

Those in favour of Canada doing an about-face on the issue projected that adoption of the agreement would have immense financial benefits for the country, while those opposed focused on a much less easily quantified concern: that Canada's own sovereignty and cultural heritage and the future thereof were in danger if the agreement were adopted. Furthermore, they claimed, the issue had been settled once and for all in 1911 and should not be reopened since Canadians had already spoken on the issue.

In the event, the thrilling elections of 1988, known as the "Free Trade Election," pitted a skeptical John Turner against Brian Mulroney (sarcastically called "Branch Office Brian" by his opponents for his willingness to sell out Canada to its enormously powerful and influential southern neighbour), but it ended in victory for the Free Trade Agreement.

Even from the hindsight of a quarter of a century, it is difficult to determine who was right in their assessment of the agreement. It is not unreasonable to speculate, though, that with its imposition, some aspects of Canada that were absolutely unique when compared to the United States have indeed gone by the wayside. With the introduction of aggressive American retailers like Walmart into the Canadian retail landscape, homegrown stores suffered. Canadian cities, especially those within less an hour or two of Canada's border with the United States, lost local business traffic in an era characterized by rampant "cross-border shopping," mainly Canadians making purchases at the "big box" retailers that grew up on the outskirts of American cities, and drove the last nail in the coffin of the traditional and well-loved American department stores that had been a part of the country's social and cultural landscape for so long.

Eaton's didn't flourish in the light of these developments. On the eve of the elections, market share had begun to rebound, on account of its new downtown stores and revived marketing storewide, and the company's share of the Canadian retail market never grew again. Received wisdom claims that the store made a huge mistake partnering with the Ontario government in developing the downtown malls that both parties hoped would stem the decline of the province's smaller cities (not to mention that Eaton's once operated well-established branches in some of these towns before abandoning them in the 1960s). In fact, the malls were fairly successful upon their debut, but when nothing could stem the tide of American-style "big box" retailers in the outskirts of small cities, Canadian shoppers generally switched ranks and abandoned the sophisticated and lively but more expensive malls and their Eaton anchors.

Eaton's management made several bad judgments as well. After the departure of Frederik Eaton for Great Britain in 1991, leaving George Eaton in charge of the company, an American retail consultant recommended the adoption of an "Everyday Value Pricing" policy akin to that of discount retailer Walmart. Eaton's, under George Eaton's watch, enforced the policy with a vengeance, cancelling all promotional sales, including the enormously popular and highly anticipated Trans-Canada Sale. Canadians didn't accept the strategy, unwilling to believe that Eaton's "low price" was actually the best possible, and at any rate the pricing policy wasn't credible when commodity items (though perhaps cheap China-made articles) were available at lower prices at one of the "big boxes." Even worse for Eaton's was the fact that customers preferred fashion shopping at specialty retailers that knew their patrons better than Eaton's had since purchasing was again recentralized in the 1980s, and they delivered more personal service at the time to boot.

In fact, "Everyday Value Pricing" was a failure in the face of increased competition and the recession of the early 1990s. A cash flow crisis put store renovations out of the question, and Eaton's physical plant suffered as stores became dowdy and tired in appearance. The once flush Eaton Centre store was by then more than fifteen years old, and sales at the company's flagship had dropped to less than two-thirds the level of five years earlier. Other sales figures showed that Eaton's lost its premier position in several markets across Canada where it once held the lead—not just in sales but customer appreciation as well.

Speaking to the *Toronto Star* in 1994, the year in which Eaton's celebrated its 125th anniversary, Frederick Eaton, who had by then returned from the UK and was sitting on the board of Eaton's of Canada, said that contrary to rumours, the T. Eaton Co. Limited was not for sale to Americans or anyone else for that matter, and he added that in spite of the "serious hardship" of a "prolonged and humanly painful recession," "I can assure you we will be in business for another 125 years." In his remarks, he alluded positively to the store's strategy, including the problematic "Everyday Value Pricing" policy.

Red ink mounted at the retailer, which had by then grown to ninety stores and twenty-six thousand employees. Eaton's soon scrapped the "no sales" policy and brought out promotions like "Eaton's Uncrates the Sun" to stimulate business. By 1996, it used self-mocking ads with slogans like "Just to prove Eaton's does have sales, we're having a sale" and "We want to be your store—unfortunately so does everybody else." The public was not amused, even when the Trans-Canada Sale was reinstated in 1996. The new strategy incongruously combined low-price promotion with an attempt to garner more high-end designer fashion business for the store and further confused traditional customers when it engaged a controversial "grunge" music celebrity to promote the store. With customers thus completely perplexed, Eaton's losses amounted to $190 million in that year alone.

Much-needed renovations were financed by a sale of Eaton's real estate assets at bargain prices. Enough money came in to initiate the program in 1995, but it was too late: losses mounted until the company was in outright crisis. An advertisement announcing renovations at three Toronto stores in the *Globe and Mail* on January 7, 1997, touted "A new kind of Eaton's" and urged customers to "Come try us on. You won't want to shop anywhere else." Stating that "[t]here's so much that's different—Maybe that's why other department stores are so quiet these days," the small, reticent and utterly unremarkable ad practically begged customers to come to the store and laid bare the fact the T. Eaton Co. Limited promoted on that day was clearly a far cry from the store Canadians easily and willingly took to their hearts over its long history.

Late in 1996, two of Canada's largest financial institutions, the Toronto-Dominion Bank and the Bank of Nova Scotia, questioned their practices of providing credit to the retailer, and Eaton's began looking elsewhere for the necessary credit to keep it operating. On February 27, 1997, after a disastrous Christmas season, George Eaton appeared at a press conference to announce that Eaton's had filed for protection under Canada's Companies' Creditors Arrangement Act. Except for George Eaton, all of the store's board members stepped down with the announcement.

The filing revealed that Eaton's had lost $250 million in the five preceding years, that sales had fallen more than 30 percent during that time and that 60 percent of its stores were either losing money outright or barely breaking even. To his great credit, though, George Eaton's statements at the press conference came across as sincere and honest. Although he thanked Canadians for their continued support and admonished them to "come in and shop," the reaction in the press did betray a great deal of scorn for the wealthy brothers who had seemingly led their family's company, a Canadian icon that went miraculously from rags to riches, unbelievably, back to rags again.

The filing under the CCAA required Eaton's to develop a restructuring program, and as the year played out, it appeared that, along with all of the gloom and doom that surrounded the saga of the retailer, there were positives as well. The company had secured interim financing with GE Capital of Canada to help it remain in operation during the crisis, and an agreement was reached in June 1997 to share a $291 million surplus in Eaton's pension fund between employees and the struggling store. These monies, savings from the planned closing of twenty-one of Eaton's eighty-five stores, and new financing allowed the company to proceed with the restructuring plan required under the terms of the CCAA.

One negative hurdle that had to be overcome was the fact that so-called vulture funds, generally American, had bought up $100 million in debt owed by Eaton's. Hoping to get the best returns on their dollar, the funds could foreseeably block the restructuring plan and force Eaton's into full-blown bankruptcy if they believed it was in their own best interest.

On June 5, Eaton's announced that George Kosich, former CEO of the Bay, had come out of retirement to replace George Eaton at the helm of the beleaguered company. Kosich guided the Hudson's Bay Company through recessionary times and brought it back to profitability in the early 1990s. He came on board just as Eaton's restructuring plan was being formed. On August 15, the plan was submitted, and at a rally held in the atrium entrance to the Toronto Eaton Centre Store, a band played "Happy Days Are Here Again" as a crowd of executives and employees chanted, "We've got the plan!" Later, George Eaton, speaking on behalf of the family,

A small, nondescript ad beckoned customers to return to three newly remodeled stores in the Toronto area in 1997. In fact, Eaton's promotional advertising of the day conveyed little excitement and was derided for begging customers to try shopping at the failing retailer. *From an ad, collection of the author.*

thanked Eaton's supporters for bearing with the company through its troubles. He also noted the value of the pension surplus deal in the context of the restructuring plan and expressed satisfaction that the $419 million deal offered "our creditors full recovery" of debts owed them by Eaton's.

The plan was accepted by the courts in the autumn, in spite of a number of hurdles involving landlords and the vulture funds. In June 1998, the company, in spite of Sir John Craig Eaton's famous admonition that "there is not enough money in the world to buy my father's name," issued an Initial Public Offering of its stock and for the first time became a publicly traded company on the Toronto Stock Exchange. Shares sold for $15 (and rose quickly to $16 each), with the Eaton family retaining about 52 percent ownership. The offering netted the company $17 million in funds.

By this time, too, George Kosich was able to lay out his own plan for the future of Eaton's. After having closed twenty-one of its remaining eighty-five stores, Eaton's would narrow its focus and transform itself from a "general department store" to "a leading fashion department store in Canada," said company spokeswoman Sigi Brough at the time. Eaton's planned, like many failed department stores in the United States, to phase out lower-margin lines such as furniture, appliances and electronics and severely limit floor space given over to sporting goods and health and beauty aids.

Forecasting a $58 million profit in 1998, George Kosich emphasized:

> *As we have indicated on many occasions, our merchandising strategy is focused on establishing a dominant presence in Canadian retailing in such higher-margin areas as men's and women's fashions, accessories, cosmetics and soft home fashion merchandise. We have already introduced a number of measures to accelerate the replacement of lower-margin hard goods from our merchandise offering. These measures include the renovation and re-merchandising of stores, plus a reduced presence in appliances and electronics.*

In an article about the Kosich's new direction for Eaton's, the *Globe and Mail* called it a complete "break from the past." Noting that Eaton's was one of Canada's most recognizable names, it mentioned, somewhat prophetically, that Eaton's traditional strength was to "supply Canadians with a wide variety of merchandise ever since Timothy Eaton started selling dry goods in Toronto in 1869" and noted that much of Eaton's success and one-time dominance of the Canadian market was a result of its consistent broadening of opportunities to satisfy the Canadian public. An even more ominous byproduct of the new direction was the loss of six hundred jobs company-wide on account of the elimination of departments.

After the restructuring plan was approved, Eaton's launched a new advertising campaign and a revised identity program featuring a new logo and related materials such as shopping bags. Replacing a fairly nondescript late '80s logo and unattractive white bags with red and blue stripes, the new concept featured a blocky "Eaton's" identifier in yellow on a dark blue background. The heavy new design was a far cry from the elegant quatrefoil symbol of 1967 and the beautifully simple identifier that graced both stores and printed items so well that Eaton's called them "glamorously sophisticated" when unveiled so long ago. The similarity between the 1997 logo and colours to that used by Walmart may or may not have been intentional, but the two were undeniably related.

Embarrassingly for Eaton's, when the new bags were distributed in local newspapers in order to show off the store's new image, many noted that they had "made in the U.S.A." stamped on them. Customers criticized the store for its lack of loyalty to Canadian manufacturers, but Eaton's countered that it simply went shopping for the best deal it could in order to procure the bags.

If Eaton's new logo threw a nod to bargain-basement rival Walmart, the whole restructuring plan brought to mind a similar (and similarly unsuccessful) strategy employed by the venerable Woodward's stores that disappeared in 1993 after thriving in British Columbia and Alberta since the late 1890s. Faced with crippling losses in the 1980s, Kip and John Woodward, grandsons of founder Charles Woodward, sold off the company's remaining profitable assets, took the store upscale and discontinued the lines of merchandise (such as groceries, hardware and sporting goods) on which its famous slogan "Woodward's Has It All!" was once based.

Customers never returned to the radically changed store, and after filing for bankruptcy, competitor and rival Hudson's Bay Company put Woodward's, a store that once occupied legendary status in Western Canada, out of its misery by acquiring its remaining assets in 1993.

Of course, history does repeat itself, and before long, it became obvious that Eaton's predictions of profits were not sustainable, especially as the Canadian economy began to weaken and consumer confidence began to slip. Another problem facing the store's recovery was the alienation of traditional customers as Eaton's went after the youth market. Older customers, many of whom harboured loyal and nostalgic feelings for Eaton's, scratched their heads when it began using what one critic called "pouty-faced, spike-haired delinquents" in advertising to help update its image. Unbelievably, new shops for teens, this time using the politically correct buzzword "Diversity" as a name, weren't even ready for business by the time that the store began showing the ads.

Relating her experiences in Montréal, writer Jan Wong contributed a piece to the *Globe and Mail* that underscored the problem facing Eaton's:

> *When I got older and was allowed to go downtown alone, I always went to Eaton's for my Christmas shopping. I trusted them. Don't get me started on the new Eaton's. In Toronto it's now targeting pierced mall-rats. The teen section has cement floors and piped-in rap music. Oh, and across Canada management recently watered down Timothy Eaton's hallowed money-back guarantee.*
>
> *The advertising now has a hip, anti-mom message. "We know what you must be thinking, Eaton's? That's where mom shops…Heck, that's where her mom shops…Well, we're about to change all that. Brace yourself," says one ad for a $550 Mongolian-lamb designer jacket.*
>
> *Pardon me for not being trendy, but I like my mother. And she's probably spent more at Eaton's over the decades than most Canadians.*

Never mind; the young stayed away in droves, and those regulars who still spent money there felt alienated. In a modern world where a gulf exists between generations, and youth are encouraged to harbour negative

A study of Eaton's shopping bags and credit cards shows how the store's graphic identifier changed over the years. Compare the slim and elegant logo on the bag featuring the memorable quatrefoil pattern with the bulky 1997 design executed in bright yellow on blue. *Courtesy of Martin Pelletier.*

attitudes towards their parents and any generation that preceded them, going to Eaton's to shop was tantamount to collaborating with the enemy.

Another stumbling block for the company was a subtle shift in buying habits that became apparent in U.S. markets since the dawn of the 1980s. With the advent of so-called designer merchandise and increasing entertainment and sports celebrity endorsement of products, customers shifted from trusting the retailer that sold the goods towards a more intensive preference for the brands themselves. As time went on, the fact that an established local (or, in the case of Canada, a Canadian-owned) retailer was trusted, or preferred due to traditional shopping habits of families, meant much less than wearing the "right" logo. Traditional department stores carried the merchandise in order to compete, but shoppers could go anywhere, and often did, for the "right" label. They frequently did so even if the merchandise was not of exemplary quality, or even worse, a cheap knockoff.

Even though the all-important Christmas shopping season was in full swing, George Kosich abruptly left Eaton's in November 1998, but both sides officially stated that the departure was planned all along. Eaton's stock was trading at $5.25 per share, almost one-third its initial value. Earlier in the year, most analysts agreed that Eaton's had done a good job coming out of the bankruptcy, but it still had a ways to go before its survival was ensured. A senior bond analyst for the Canadian Bond Rating Service told the *Globe and Mail*, "If you just walk into an Eaton's store, you'll see what kind of disarray some of the departments are in."

After the departure of George Kosich, the company was left in the hands of board chairman Brent Ballantyne, a financial turnaround specialist who had come to Eaton's after filling the same role at Beatrice Foods and Maple Leaf Foods of Canada. Upon taking over as CEO from Kosich, he reiterated that his predecessor did not leave under pressure, saying, "We knew at the time George joined us that it wasn't going to be a long-term proposition," and he repeated Eaton's contention that its new direction was "working where it has been implemented."

By early in 1999, the cat was completely out of the bag. Instead of the forecast $58 million profit, Eaton's lost $72 million in 1998. Its stock, once rising to $16 per share, had now fallen drastically and was blasted as "one of the worst investments of the 1990s" by the business press. Eaton's wasn't just struggling; it was literally hemorrhaging money, and its efforts to stop the bleeding were an unmitigated failure.

Speaking via phone to analysts in December 1998, Ballantyne appeared to be overcome by emotion when explaining Eaton's mounting red ink, but he later explained that his stumbling voice was due to a sore throat he had at the time. One of the participants revealed to the press that "his voice was shaking, there was no question." The *Globe and Mail* led into its article about the incident by speculating that "[c]orporate executives who engage in conference calls with analysts would do well to stock up on lozenges."

By May 1999, with no way in sight to stem the red ink and the collapse of its stock, Eaton's announced that it was putting itself up for sale. The press speculated that American retail holding company (and promoter of its acquired Macy's brand name as a national department store retailer in the United States) Federated Department Stores of Cincinnati was a prime candidate to buy Eaton's. One-time suitor J.C. Penney and rival Sears Canada were named as alternate potential buyers. Any of these options would mean that the T. Eaton Co. Limited would cease to exist as a wholly Canadian institution, but even more ominous was the speculation that no one wanted Eaton's "lock, stock and barrel." However, there was interest in acquiring some of its prime locations for other retail uses. Earlier, an unidentified retail industry source told the *Globe and Mail*, "A lot of U.S. retailers have been up here and kicked the tires but when they saw the engine under the hood, they went home."

Calling the potential sale a "strategic alternative to maximizing shareholder value," Eaton's management attempted to put a positive spin on the events, but a scornful press prophesized that a piecemeal sale of the company's assets and remaining sixty-four stores would follow.

Although it was never formally confirmed, Federated Department Stores had indeed shown interest in acquiring the company, but when these talks broke down in August 1999, hope for Eaton's completely evaporated. The final, *Titanic*-like plunge commenced on August 21, 1999, when a spokesman for Eaton's announced that it had filed a notice of intent to make a proposal to its creditors under the Bankruptcy and Insolvency Act. The *Globe and Mail* reported:

> *By using federal bankruptcy laws instead of restructuring under court protection under the Companies' Creditors Arrangement Act as it did in 1997, Eaton's appears to have thrown in the towel and will go out of business while trying to sell real estate, inventory, and other assets to pay off its creditors. It expects to start liquidating its inventory early next week. Last night's company news release said the company also intends to "pursue discussions with parties who have expressed interest in purchasing its assets or shares."*

Prior to the cessation of trading, Eaton's shares had tumbled to seventy-one cents and were deemed virtually worthless.

The store that commanded almost 60 percent of Canadian department store sales in 1930 had watched its preeminence dwindle to a point where it barely mustered 10 percent of that market on the eve of its bankruptcy. Likewise, its staff, which numbered seventy thousand in the 1960s, dropped to less than one-sixth that number. Of these, about one-third were full-time employees and the rest part time. In spite of an infusion of cash from the pension-surplus and the sale of profitable assets, nothing could halt the slide, and a 130-year-old Canadian tradition, depleted as it was, had come to the end.

On the day before, Eaton's stores in Québec were shuttered, leaving puzzled customers on the sidewalks outside and workers spreading the disastrous news throughout the empty buildings. Québec law allowed creditors to seize unpaid-for merchandise before a court ruling on a bankruptcy case, and some suppliers had done just that. The Québec closings were an attempt to prevent a full-scale looting of the doomed stores.

Public reaction spanned a gamut of emotions, from sheer sadness among both customers and employees to disdain for the way that the Eaton heirs handled their inheritance. Many customers had left Eaton's long ago as the retailer spiraled into difficulty. The standard reaction was, of course, sadness, but newspapers balanced these reports with stories of shoppers who said, "I really couldn't care less." In Vancouver, the papers reported the comments of an Eaton's shopper there too young to remember Spencer's but old enough to have taken Eaton's to heart: "As long as I have been alive there's been an Eaton's; it's part of our history."

Employees mostly reacted to the news tempered by in-store rumours and valid inside information. Many admitted that they faced an uncertain future because this time, it wasn't just projections of store closings or cutbacks—even the newspaper headlines avoided euphemisms on the subject, saying, "Eaton's to Terminate Staff as Its Liquidation Begins."

Some employees offered their experiences over the last few turbulent years in hindsight. They admitted that the stores became terribly shabby and that they vociferously opposed the "Everyday Value Pricing" strategy as they watched shoppers walk away time and again. Many claimed that it had become customary for Eaton's to ignore one of its best assets—the front-line staff that was on the floor with customers. More than one claimed that Eaton's abandonment of its core customer was critical to its failure. The youth group that the store sought was not only fickle, but it also didn't have tremendous amounts of disposable income, and what's more, it never really identified with Eaton's like its former customers did.

Most of the printed economic analysis of the collapse focused on how such an icon, with an iconic name, could come to so inglorious an end. Some experts blamed customers for staying away from the store that they claimed to hold in high regard, but many more placed the blame directly on the shoulders of Timothy Eaton's heirs. One article in the *Globe and Mail*, under the headline "Rags to Riches to Rags," outlined how difficult it was to keep a business alive through successive generations of family ownership, citing Eaton's and the Eaton family as a classic case in point.

In many of the press articles, TV spots, comments and even books written about Eaton's demise, the criticism was often scathing and personal, indicating on a very deep level how the store and its affairs were ingrained in the Canadian conscience. Negative commentary and speculation on how "the boys," as Timothy Eaton's great-grandsons had become known, could have let the store slip through their hands degenerated into outright disdain.

In the midst of it all, one letter to the editor, published a week after the bankruptcy announcement, stood out:

> *I don't read the newspaper much these days. I'm tired of the untruths and misinterpretations and twisting of the facts that naïve writers seem to think is their God-given right. I am tired of reporters trespassing on my property, attempting to gain access to my home and trying to bribe the loyal young man who works for me for information on my whereabouts.*
>
> *My family is in mourning, not just because of the loss of a magnificent and noble company, but more important, because of the impact on its people, both employees and suppliers. My wife and I have visited most of the stores across the country every year and sometimes twice a year to meet the employees and hear of their business concerns. We are on a first-name basis with many of these spirited, loyal and hard-working people and have met a lot of their families. These are the people who built and maintained Eaton's and they are, without question, the unsung heroes.*
>
> *The sadness we find regarding the impact of recent events on these people's families, careers, income and futures is made even worse by the fact that I can't do anything about it. I can only assure them that they are in my thoughts and prayers. So, reporters and writers, please leave all of us alone to mourn as each of us must and in our own way.*
>
> *—John Craig Eaton, Caledon, Ont.*

From left to right are Millie Shale, Gail Poole, Marilyn Arnold, Claudia Kasian, Patricia Charter and Norma Vadeboncoeur.

What's new in shoes? Plenty, according to Eaton's leading fashion authorities. 1970 is going to be a year with a totally new look in fashion and, the fun is going to be in finding the style that's just right for the individual customer.

Shoes are going to play an important role. The fashion shoe is the platform, the sandal and the clog. The midi or longer look to clothes is incomplete without the boot or higher heel.

When customers buy their first longer length coats or suits, it's important to emphasize the shoe and colour co-ordination of the hosiery. Also, the right heel height has to coincide with the correct skirt length.

The shoe for the midi is going to make leg watching interesting. Wearing a midi makes a woman's walk more gracefully, after the athletic strides mini wearers have been making for the past few seasons.

Fashion is changing as it always does. However, the new new shoe styles of the seventies are going to be more attractive and in a great variety of styles. In the years just ahead, more Eaton people are going to be saying: "There's no business like shoe business."

Happier times at Eaton's. In the 1970s, employees pose for an article in *Contacts*, the Winnipeg store's employee newsletter. *Collection of the author.*

In spite of the criticism of Timothy Eaton's grandsons and their handling of the affair, many Eatonians summoned up their sense of loyalty to "their" store and the family who owned it. Maurice Van Buekenhout, after more than forty-five years with the company, to this day expresses his appreciation:

As a member of the Quarter Century Club, I got a numbered certificate, a diamond ring, six weeks' holidays that year (all at once, if you liked!) and five weeks each year after that. Forty years' service was a $600 cheque, which I managed to get in my time. I met many of the Eaton family over my years; I have always felt privileged to work for them. I always had an income; some years were tough, but I always had a job to go to in order to support my wife and family. Eaton people are very special to work with, just one big family and always there for each other. I am very grateful to have worked for Eaton's; the people I met over my lifetime, and the memories of them, will live in my heart forever.

If it was indeed possible to mourn a historic commercial enterprise as though it were human, the events of late summer 1999 undoubtedly bore out the case. The next few months were the period of Eaton's postmortem and the reading of its last will and testament. Accordingly, the liquidations sales were an odd combination of circus madness and the sobriety of a funeral parlour wake. The latter sentiment can be discerned in Reverend Kenneth Clarkson's words about the store's disappearance from the cultural landscape of Canada: "Now, I'm thinking that the account of my life's experiences with Eaton's will make you understand our sorrow when, in 1999, it was forced to discontinue its service to countless folks like us across Canada. No other store has yet or could ever take its place in our hearts."

By the end of 1999, Eaton's had indeed finally shut down, and a number of its stores were sold. Sears Canada became the owner of the majority of Eaton's and initially sought to convert thirteen of the best locations to Sears stores. Hudson's Bay Company bought ten stores, but the once great Montréal store was sold to developers and would never again carry the Eaton name.

Sears chairman Paul Walters announced in September that it would also retain six to eight of the downtown stores it planned to acquire in the deal and would "consider running the stores under the Eaton's banner, but more upmarket than the suburban Sears stores" and bring back "the departments that Eaton's abandoned in the past few years such as appliances and sporting goods." Walters speculated that the stores could be opened as early as summer of 2000. When the downtown store transaction was concluded one month later, Walters stated that it "gives Sears Canada access to a new market segment where Sears Canada currently has no presence. We can now enter this market with a separate and established brand to serve new customers without compromising the solid mid-market position of the Sears brand in suburban markets."

Industry commentators remarked that even though Eaton's bankruptcy and closure amounted to a dark cloud over the famous, defunct institution, the Eaton name still had much value on which Sears Canada could build. What's more, 2,500 new jobs would be created with the reopening of the Eaton stores in Victoria, Vancouver, Calgary, Winnipeg (Polo Park), Ottawa and Toronto (Eaton Centre and Yorkdale). Sears Canada would also have liked to add the once sensational Montréal store to its lineup, but in time the building was sold to developers for conversion to offices, a mall and a lease space for Québec retailer *Les Ailes de la Mode*.

Summer of 2000 came and went, but it wasn't until November, almost into the Christmas season, that the new stores opened. Introduced by a memorable, though not universally admired, ad campaign that associated it with the colour aubergine, the new venture stripped the Eaton's name of capital letters and its apostrophe, officially to make the store seem more "modern" but also to focus on the brand rather than the name's legacy of family ownership.

When they opened to the public, the stores were well received for their elaborate redesign and fine merchandise presentation. On the occasion of the opening on November 25, 2000, Paul Walters set out his vision for the venture that was at once both new and old, saying, "From the outset our objective has been to offer exceptional stores that meet all of the needs and wants of our primary customer—the time-pressed urban consumer who enjoys shopping, wants the latest styles and trends, demands service expertise and wants an exciting entertaining environment to shop in."

The remodeled Eaton Centre store in Toronto expressed that vision in its handsome and contemporary environment, providing Walters's ideal customer with food service in a basement-level Starbucks, as well as a posh fourth-floor restaurant named Cuiscene. An old criticism of modern downtown developments, that they generally turn their backs on traditional streets, was met within the store with a series of designer boutiques on the ground floor that had their own entrances on Yonge Street and into the big store as well.

When it opened in Toronto, the store prepared customers for a totally new shopping experience by taking out an eight-page ad in the *Star* to entice new customers to experience the store. Beginning with a letter from chairman and CEO Paul Walters and announcing, "Customers today want more and we're gonna give it to them!" the letter went on to state:

If you were to ask today's most demanding shoppers what their ideal wish list for a department store would be, what do you think they would say? We asked that question and to be honest their answers weren't all that surprising. What we truly believe will come as a surprise is the manner in which we went about fulfilling them. On November 25th our new doors will swing open for the first time and frankly, we can't wait to show you all that we've been up to. Get ready to discover a truly unique shopping destination. One with the accent on fun. One that delivers the latest in fashion along with value that is truly unexpected. We're certain that you'll discover, in short order, that the result is a shopping experience in this country. For this and more, you only have yourself to thank. After all, the new Eatons wouldn't be the new Eatons without the opinions and input of thousands of Canadian shoppers across the country. Shoppers just like you.

The "new" Eatons featured fashion "for young, for old" and admonished customers to "think style, think fun." A wide range of services, from complimentary gift wrap to a concierge desk awaited new Eaton shoppers. The Yonge Street Boutiques for DKNY Jeans, Polo Sport, Tommy Hilfiger, Kenneth Cole and BCBG Maxazria were lauded as an attempt to create a Rodeo Drive in the heart of chilly Toronto, but even special emphasis was placed on the home furnishings offerings of the new store in the so-called "e home" offerings. With the ads imploring shoppers to "sit aubergine" and "cook aubergine," the store offered unique new brands developed for Eatons and the shops throughout the store like "e home elements," a "kitchen theatre" and a "fully automated audio-visual presentation room."

Elsewhere, the store offered attractions like "Shades and Pens at Eatons," a "Coast to Coast" Canadian souvenir shop, complete alterations and custom men's shirt-making service and an Atelier Spa. Although the opening day ads included a capsule history of Eaton's as a link with the store's tradition, nothing about the new venture—except, perhaps for the preservation of the historic rooms moved from Eaton's–College Street in 1977—harkened back to the illustrious past of Eaton's as an institution. At the same time, a new *Eatons—The Catalogue* was issued in an attempt to connect with home and Internet shoppers, although it was in reality not much more than a standard Christmas catalogue of the type once issued ceremoniously by most department stores. One wag in the press even mentioned the fact that the new catalogue, due to its slim size, would be useless in protecting the shins of would-be NHL stars.

Just the same, in Toronto, an aubergine ribbon was cut, and the store was back in business. The *Toronto Star* exclaimed, "Wall to wall wows. The Aubergine machine was on a roll yesterday for the long-awaited opening of Toronto's new Eatons flagship." A similar reaction met the new stores across the country. In Victoria, the ten-year-old Eatons store downtown was completely gutted and endowed with luxurious new furnishings. On a store tour for journalists on opening day, Manager Gayle Estabrooks appeared to be "more a proud mom than an employee," according to the *Victoria Times Colonist*, as she gleefully pointed out the features of the store, which included a spa and a newly trained staff hired for enthusiasm and positive attitude.

Opening reviews of the fourth-floor Cuiscene restaurant found the food passable, the atmosphere exciting and the crowds desperately trying to negotiate the self-service "food stations" in need of a traffic cop. Ominously, in her review, critic Cynthia Wine mused:

On my way up to the restaurant in the new eatons, a woman on the elevator says "aren't you glad Eaton's is back?" Boy is she in for a surprise. In these early days, many of its gray-haired customers are wandering forlornly from sushi to goat cheese looking for hot beef sandwiches and red Jell-O. Even though we know that this eatons isn't that Eaton's...we live in hope. Now I'm here to tell you to forget it: This place will never have red Jell-O. This is not just a change in fashion: This is a change in philosophy.

It was, in the end, all for nothing: Sears Canada was itself not immune to the vicissitudes of the new millennium's retail market. With double-digit growth and runaway profits a thing of the past, the retailer took a hard look at the reasons its profit had dropped 58 percent in 2000. The visionary Paul Walters stepped down in January 2001 and was replaced by Mark Cohen of American parent company Sears, Roebuck and Company.

On February 18, 2002, the announcement came: Sears Canada would retire the "Eatons" name and operate five of the stores under the Sears banner. In announcing the change, Cohen said, "The notion that customers see value in a top-drawer, high-priced, somewhat selective assortment is false. They value very high levels of presentation and customer service but don't exhibit any desire to pay for it."

With this act, the history of Eaton's had reached, for all practical purposes, its final dénouement. For the third time in three years, the Eaton name, once revered, was associated with failure. By July, the revitalized stores had transitioned into Sears stores, albeit with some of the upmarket brand names that had done well in the experiment. It was the last time the iconic family name rose proudly over a department store entrance.

In Winnipeg, the great 1905 store on Portage Avenue sat vacant until it was razed and replaced with a sports arena, to the great regret of those who attempted to prevent its demolition. Other Eaton stores, like the original Halifax and Saskatoon stores, now house government offices. In 2013, even Sears threw in the towel at its urban locations in the Toronto Eaton Centre and at the Pacific Centre in Vancouver, among others. Both stores are scheduled to be rebuilt and operated by Seattle-based Nordstrom.

As the winds of change buffet Canada's retail landscape, there is little to remind shoppers and tourists of the noble and dignified store that was once synonymous with Canada. A letter to the *Toronto Star* shortly after the 1999 bankruptcy stated it poignantly:

I am saddened by the loss of Eaton's. The mere mention of Eaton's signified power, stability, comfort, trust, reliability and satisfaction guaranteed or money refunded. I believe the annual Santa Claus parade endeared Eaton's to everyone. As an usher, it was my responsibility to check everyone's clothing before the parade, rush downtown in an Eaton's van and distribute the clothing after the parade. Why is Eaton's gone? I'll let the historians play with that question. But forever etched in my mind will be the magnificent bronze statue of Timothy Eaton, who, wherever he is, must be shedding a tear for a lost Canadian tradition.

In fact, the two statues of Timothy Eaton still exist (shiny left toe and all), at the Royal Ontario Museum in Toronto and in the sports arena that stands on the same site where, in 1905, he helped his grandson Timothy press the button that sounded the gong announcing the opening of the first T. Eaton Co. Limited store in the west.

Ironically, in Montréal, the Eaton store building is now known as *Complexe les Ailes*, while the separately owned shopping mall next door retains the Eaton Centre name. The once glamourous restaurant on the ninth floor sits idle and waiting for a new use, although it has been designated a heritage site by the province of Québec.

In Toronto, the landmark College Street store was shorn of one of its wings, restructured internally for commercial space and connected to office and residential towers to become the mixed-use College Park. The extravagant spaces on the seventh floor remained vacant for a while until they were sensitively restored into a special events center named The Carlu in homage to the genius of their designer.

Out at Yorkdale, the structure of the innovative 1964 Eaton's branch was swallowed up whole by the popular and ever-growing shopping centre, its structure housing mall stores and an upper-level restaurant complex but becoming completely unrecognizable in the process. Elsewhere, Eaton's mall stores carry either the Sears or Hudson's Bay nameplates or have been demolished.

Incredibly, although the great Queen Street and Winnipeg stores are just the stuff of memory, many of the small buildings that housed branches of the Canadian Department Stores Limited are still standing in many Ontario towns, though in varying states of disrepair and alteration. In most cases, there is nothing to remind younger residents of these places that the name of one of the world's greatest retailers graced these old buildings for many years.

Reporter Alan Cochrane monitored the history of Eaton's in Moncton and relates the sad facts of its demise, although the original building was eventually saved from complete demolition and the Highfield Square store was operated for a number of years by the Hudson's Bay Company:

> *In later years, Eaton's was the anchor store in Moncton's first shopping mall, and Fred Eaton promised that it would never close. True to his word (well, almost), the Moncton store was one of the last to shut down after Eaton's went bankrupt. The old distribution centre building fell into disrepair and was about to be demolished when a local developer bought it and gave it new life as a modern office building in the downtown known as Heritage Court.*

Just as the press predicted at the time of the bankruptcy and closing, it was indeed an astonishing fall from grace for a company that was so familiar that it came to be recognized as a part of the Canadian cultural landscape. So many years later, although the Eaton name remains on some downtown shopping centres and the statues of the Governor can still be seen and visited, little of the real Eaton's and its meaning to Canadians is anywhere to be found, except in accumulated memory.

Coming back, full circle, to Timothy Eaton, one wonders what he might have made of the unhappy final days of the retail institution he founded and nourished during his lifetime. Given his passion for his business, his will to succeed through thoughtful analysis of problems and, most of all, his faith and overarching humanity, conjecture is quite possible regarding the way he might have faced the crises Eaton's found itself in at the end of the twentieth century.

In spite of all of the accumulated knowledge about the man, though, the final answer must forever remain a matter of speculation, especially more than a century after his passing. Would he have accepted a diminished position and ultimate liquidation for Eaton's in the face of cutthroat competition? Or would he have used his time, talents, and treasures to steer the organization past (and maybe even above) the conflicts and inconsistencies of the day?

Given his faith, the history of his accomplishments and the legacy he left, sadly now merely history, it's not unreasonable to think that the latter outcome might be just that much more plausible.

> *For the rest, brethren, whatever things are true, whatever honourable, whatever just, whatever holy, whatever of good repute, if there be any virtue, if anything worthy of praise, think upon these things.*
> *—St. Paul (Philippians 4:8)*

Appendix A

Timeline of the T. Eaton Co. Limited

1834 Timothy Eaton is born in Clogher, near Ballymena, Northern Ireland (March)

1841 Margaret Wilson Beattie is born in Ontario (March)

1854 Timothy Eaton sails for Canada

1861 Timothy Eaton establishes a dry goods business in St. Marys, ON

1862 Timothy Eaton marries Margaret Wilson Beattie (May 28)

1863 Edward Young Eaton is born

1869 Timothy Eaton opens at 178 Yonge Street, Toronto (December 9)

1870 Eaton's adopts "Goods Satisfactory or Money Refunded" guarantee

1875 Robert Young Eaton is born in Northern Ireland

1876 John Craig Eaton is born in Toronto (April 11)

1877 Second floor added to Toronto store
First delivery service organized

1880 Flora McCrae is born in Omemee, ON (December 1)

1883 The T. Eaton & Co. moves to 190 Yonge Street (August 22)

1884 First *Eaton's Catalogue* issued

1886 An addition gives Eaton's a presence on Queen Street

1891 Name changed to the T. Eaton Co. Limited, a joint stock company

1893 First overseas buying office opened in London

1900 Edward Young Eaton dies (October 3)

1901 John Craig Eaton marries Flora McCrea (May 8)

1903 Toronto Mail order building on the north side of Albert Street opens

1905 The T. Eaton Co. Winnipeg Limited opens (July 15)

1907 Timothy Eaton dies (January 31)

John Craig Eaton becomes president (March)
Louisa Street Factory (first section) opens in Toronto

1909 The T. Eaton Co. Limited establishes a manufacturing plant in Montréal
Winnipeg store is expanded to seven floors (May 19)
Twelve-storey Louisa Street Factory (second section) opens in Toronto
Mail-order operation becomes a separate entity from the retail store
John David Eaton is born (October 4)

1910 Toronto Factory no. 4 opens in Downey's Lane in Toronto

1911 Mail Order building no. 1 opens at James and Louisa Streets in Toronto

1912 Winnipeg store is expanded to eight floors

1913 Furniture Annex opens at James and Albert Streets (January 31)
Signy Stefansson is born in Winnipeg
Six-storey Louisa Street factory opens in Toronto

1915 John Craig Eaton is knighted in Ottawa (June 3)

1916 Saskatoon Mail Order opened (February 7)
Eaton's Hamilton Factory opens (May 12)
Bloor Street embroidery factory opens in Toronto

1917 Twelve-storey factory no. 5 opens at Alice Street (Teraulay) and Trinity Square
Eaton's factory no. 6 opens at Bay and Teraulay Streets in Toronto

1918 Regina Mail Order opened (August 13)

1919 Mail Order Annex no. 1 opens on Albert Street in Toronto (May 23)
Eaton's celebrates its Golden Jubilee (December 9)

1920 Moncton Mail Order opened (February 5)

1922 Sir John Craig Eaton dies in Toronto (March 30)

1923 Robert Young Eaton becomes president of the T. Eaton Co. Limited

1924 Queen Street Store is completed by an eight-storey addition
The Georgian Room Restaurant opens (March 10)

1925 Eaton's buys Goodwin's of Montréal (March 19)
Eaton's opens new Montréal store (April 14)

1926 Saskatoon Mail Order expanded
Eaton's opens in Regina, SK (November 19)

1927 Eaton's buys the Arcade Limited in Hamilton, ON (June 23)
Eaton's opens in Moncton, NB (November 15)
Eaton's purchases F.R. MacMillan Limited in Saskatoon (November 19)

1928 TECO store opens in Kitchener, ON (February 2)
Eaton's buys Mahon Brothers Ltd. of Halifax (March 1)
TECO store opens in Brandon, MB (March 10)
Eaton's Acquires the Canadian Department Stores Limited (May 2)
TECO store opens in Medicine Hat, AB (May 17)

TECO store opens in Red Deer, AB (July 3)

TECO store opens in Sydney Mines, NS (July 12)

TECO store opens in Sydney, NS (August 16)

Eaton's opens in Moose Jaw, SK—sixty-two thousand square feet (November 6)

New Saskatoon Eaton store opens (December 5)

TECO store opens in Campbellton, NB (December 27)

1929 Eaton's purchases James Ramsey Limited of Edmonton (January 17)

CDS opens in Niagara Falls, ON (February 14)

Calgary Eaton's opens (February 29)

TECO store opens in Lethbridge, AB (March 29)

New CDS opens in North Bay, ON (April 9)

1930 TECO stores in Glace Bay, Waterford, Sydney and Sydney Mines, NS; and Campbellton, NB, become Canadian Department Stores (August 26)

Eaton's–College Street opens (October 10)

Eaton's opens new Halifax store (November 4)

1931 Eaton's Annex store opens (January 19)

Montréal Store expands to nine floors; restaurant opens (January 26)

Eaton Auditorium opens at Eaton's–College Street (March 26)

New Sault Ste. Marie CDS opens (October 29)

1932 New Peterborough CDS opens

1934 Margaret Eaton dies (March)

1937 New St. Catharines CDS opens (January 27)

John Craig Eaton is born (May 30)

1938 Fredrik Stefan Eaton is born (June 26)

Eaton's opens in Port Arthur, ON (October 12)

1939 Eaton's opens in Kirkland Lake, ON (March 20)

New Edmonton Store opens (August 29)

Eaton's opens in Red Deer, AB (October 19)

Eaton's (former TECO) opens in Lethbridge, AB (December 10)

Eaton's (former TECO) opens in Brandon, MB (December 13)

Eaton's (former TECO) opens in Medicine Hat, AB (December 15)

1941 Eaton's expands to fifty-two thousand square feet in the Hull Block in Medicine Hat, AB (October 16)

Eaton's opens in Prince Albert, SK (November 18)

1942 Robert Young Eaton retires (December 9)

John David Eaton becomes president (December 9)

Rebuilt Huntsville, ON store opens

1943 Thor Edgar Eaton is born

George Ross Eaton is born (November 12)

1946 CDS store opened in Deep River, ON

1947 New Brantford Store opens (October, 1930)

1948 Eaton's buys Spencer's of Vancouver, Victoria, Nanaimo, New Westminster, Chilliwack, Courtenay, Duncan and Mission (December 1)

1949 Eaton's opens a temporary store in Gander, Newfoundland

New Kitchener Store opens (August 11)

Former CDS stores are renamed Eaton's (August 20)

New Eaton's store opened in New Westminster, BC (November 17)

1950 Eaton's expands Edmonton store to three floors (August 28)

1951 Eaton's opens parking station in Halifax (July)

Stores in Campbellton, NB, and New Waterford, Glace Bay and Sydney, NS, remodeled (July)

1952 Eaton's new Chilliwack store opens (April 24)

Eaton's Trail (Trail, BC) opens (January 5)

Eaton's Corner Brook (Corner Brook, NF) opens (August 14)

1955 Eaton's new Lethbridge store opens (September 22)

Eaton's Charlottetown (Charlottetown, PEI) opens (April 26)

1956 Robert Young Eaton dies

Service Building at Sheppard Avenue and Highway 401 opens (August)

Rebuilt Brandon store opens (September 13)

Eaton's Oshawa Shopping Centre (Oshawa, ON) opens (November 1)

1957 Eaton's Gander (Gander, NF) opens (June 5)

Hamilton store expanded (August)

Calgary store expanded; adds Parkade (August)

1958 Nanaimo, BC store rebuilt (April 10)

Duncan, BC store rebuilt (July 20)

Glace Bay, NS store rebuilt

1959 Eaton's Vernon, BC opens (September 2)

1960 Eaton's Wellington Square (London, ON) opens on (August 11)

Montréal store expands to Bd. Maisonneuve (January)

1961 Eaton's Brentwood (Burnaby, BC) opens (August 16)

Eaton's in Deep River, ON, rebuilt

Toronto Warehouse Store and Service Centre opens (June 15)

1962 Winnipeg Service Building opened (December)

Eaton's Shoppers' World (Toronto, ON) opens (May 16)

Eaton's Don Mills (Toronto, ON) opens (August 1)

Downtown Halifax store vacated (September 10)

Eaton's Halifax Shopping Centre opens (September 11)

Eaton's Park Royal (West Vancouver, BC) opens (October 3)

1963 Eaton's North Battleford, SK, opens (March 14)

1964 Eaton's Yorkdale (Toronto, ON) opens (February 26)

1965 Eaton's sells Brantford, North Bay, Sault Ste. Marie, Brockville, Lindsay and Belleville (July 5)

Eaton's Fairview Pointe-Claire (Montréal, QC) opens (August 12)

Eaton's sells Ottawa, Picton, Napanee, Woodstock, Stratford and Hanover (November 18)

1966 Eaton's reveals plans for the Eaton Centre in Toronto (March 1)

Eaton's closes Peterborough, Niagara Falls, Midland, Pembroke and Deep River

1967 Centennial Shopping Centre opens at Eaton's in Regina, SK

1968 Eaton's Polo Park (Winnipeg, MB) opens (May 1)

Eaton Centre Plans cancelled

Eaton's Les Galeries d'Anjou (Montréal, QC) opens (August 8)

1969 Eaton's Highfield Square (Moncton, NB) opens (February 29)

John David Eaton retires (August 6)

Eaton's celebrates "Eaton 100" (December 9)

1970 Lady Eaton dies in Toronto (July 9)

Downtown Saskatoon store vacated (July 29)

Eaton's Midtown Mall (Saskatoon, SK) opens (July 30)

1971 Eaton's Sherway Gardens (Toronto, ON) opens (February 24)

Eaton's Hamilton adds two-storey "Pavilion" (November 8)

Eaton's Bramalea City Centre (Toronto, ON) opens (October 11)

1972 Eaton's Guildford Town Centre (Surrey, BC) opens (May 3)

Eaton's Londonderry Mall (Edmonton, AB) opens (August 15)

Horizon discount stores debut in Toronto at Victoria Park and Sheppard (August 16)

Horizon opens in London at Westmount Mall (November 1)

Horizon opens in London at Northland Shopping Centre (November 1)

Horizon Sheridan Mall (Mississauga, ON) opens (November 15)

1973 Hastings Street Vancouver store vacated (February 7)

Eaton's Pacific Centre (Vancouver, BC) opens (February 8)

Eaton's Eastgate Square (Stoney Creek, ON) opens (April 4)

St. Catharines store vacated (April 22)

Eaton's Pen Centre (St. Catharines, ON) opens (April 23)

Eaton's Scarborough Town Centre (Toronto, ON) opens (May 3)

Horizon Yonge-Eglinton Centre (Toronto, ON) opens (June 27)

John David Eaton dies (August 4)
Eaton's Bayshore Mall (Nepean, ON) opens (August 8)
Eaton's Cavendish Mall (Cote St-Luc, QC) opens (August 30)
Eaton's Carrefour de l'Estrie (Sherbrooke, QC) opens (September 24)
Horizon Dufferin Plaza (Toronto, ON) (September 26)
Downtown Kitchener store vacated (October 3)
Eaton's Market Square (Kitchener, ON) opens (October 4)
Eaton's Mic Mac Mall (Dartmouth, NS) opens (October 31)
Horizon Greenfield Park (Montréal, QC) opens (November 15)
Horizon Les Galeries St-Laurent (Montréal, QC) opens (November 15)
Horizon Les Galeries des Mille-Iles (Rosemere, QC) opens (November 15)

1974 Eaton's Carrefour Laval (Montréal, PQ) opens (March 28)
Eaton's South Centre (Calgary, AB) opens (August 7)
Horizon Rexdale Plaza (Toronto, ON) opens (October 2)
Thunder Bay store expanded (October 30)

1975 Eaton's Burlington Mall (Burlington, ON) opens (February 20)
Horizon Place Montenach (Beloil, QC) opens (March 6)
Horizon Domaine Shopping Centre (Montréal, QC) opens (March 6)
Robert Butler is replaced as CEO by Earl Orser (March 12)
Sudbury store vacated (April 2)
Eaton's opens in Sudbury City Centre (Sudbury, ON) opens (April 3)
Eaton's Peterborough Square (Peterborough, ON) opens (May 1)
Horizon at Pape & Gerrard (Toronto, ON) opens (August 14)
Mission, BC store closes (August 30)
Eaton's Sevenoaks (Clearbrook, BC) opens (October 15)
Eaton's Place Ste-Foy (Québec, QC) opens (September 11)

1976 Eaton's closes Catalogue operations (January 15)
Les Terrasses open next to the Montréal store (February 19)
Eaton's Garden City (Winnipeg, MB) opens (August 10)

1977 Chilliwack store closes (January 28)
Toronto Queen Street Store vacated (February 7)
Toronto College Street Store vacated (February 7)
Eaton's opens at Eaton Centre, Toronto, ON (February 10)
Earl Orser leaves Eaton's; Frederik Eaton becomes CEO (May 17)
TD Place opens next to the Calgary store (September 1)
Eaton's Lansdowne Park (Richmond, BC) opens (October 15)

1978 Eaton's Promenades St-Bruno (Montréal, PQ) opens (August 23)
Horizon stores to convert to Eaton's (October 6)
Eaton's Westmount Place (Waterloo, ON) opens (October 19)

1979 Eaton's Coquitlam Centre (Vancouver, BC) opens (August 16)
Eaton Place opens adjacent to the Winnipeg store (October 11)
Eaton's St. Vital Centre (West Kildonan, MB) opens (October 17)

1981 Eaton's Aberdeen Mall (Kamloops, BC) opens
Eaton's Lime Ridge Mall (Hamilton, ON) opens (August 1)
Eaton's Heritage Mall (Edmonton, AB) opens (August 5)
Eaton Les Galeries de la Capitale (Québec, QC) opens (August 9)
Eaton's Red Deer store vacated (August)
Eaton's Bower Place (Red Deer, AB) opens (August)
Eaton's Regina store vacated (August 18)
Eaton's Cornwall Centre (Regina, SK) opens (August 19)
Eaton's Sunridge Mall (Calgary, AB) opens (August 20)
Eaton's West Edmonton Mall, (Edmonton, AB) opens (September 15)
Eaton's closes Nanaimo store (September 14)
Eaton's Woodgrove Centre (Nanaimo, BC) opens (September 30)

1982 Eaton's Markville Center (Markham, ON) opens (March 17)
Eaton's Tillicum Mall (Victoria, BC) opens (April 14)
Eatons Sarnia Eaton Centre (Sarnia, ON) opens

1983 Eaton's Willowbrook Centre (Langley, BC) opens
Eaton Rockland (Montréal, QC) opens (August 24)
Eaton Galeries Chagnon (Levis, QC) opens (September 8)

1984 Eatons Guelph Eaton Centre (Guelph, ON) opens

1985 Eaton's Georgian Mall (Barrie, ON) opens
Eaton's Pickering Town Centre(Pickering, ON) opens (August 7)
Eaton's Masonville Place (London, ON) opens (August 4)

1986 Eaton's closes Moose Jaw store
Eatons Brantford Market Square (Brantford, ON) opens
Eaton's The Promenade (Vaughan, ON) opens (August 4)
Eaton Carrefour Angrignon, (Montréal, QC) opens (Augiust 13)

1987 Eatons Edmonton Eaton Centre (Edmonton, AB) opens (August 19)
Eaton Les Promenades de l'Outaouais (Hull, QC) opens (September)

1988 Eaton's vacates Lethbridge Store (April)
Eaton's Lethbridge Park Place (Lethbridge, AB) opens (April 12)
Eaton's Northland Village (Calgary, AB) opens
Eaton's Square One (Mississauga, ON) opens (September 14)

1989 Eaton's vacates Victoria store (February)
Eaton's Victoria Eaton Centre opens (March 1)
Eaton's closes Hamilton store (May)

Eaton's Hamilton Eaton Centre (Hamilton, ON) opens (May 2)

Eaton's Metrotown Eaton Centre (Vancouver, BC) opens

1990 Eaton's vacates Calgary store

Eaton's Calgary Eaton Centre (Calgary, AB) opens

Eaton's Place d'Orleans (Orleans, ON) opens

Eaton's Upper Canada Mall (Newmarket, ON) opens (March)

Eaton's Mapleview Centre (Burlington, ON) opens (September)

1991 Eaton's closes Medicine Hat, AB store (January)

Frederik Eaton becomes Canadian high commissioner to the UK

George Eaton becomes president of Eaton's

Eaton's adopts "Everyday Value Pricing" strategy

Trans-Canada Sales discontinued

Montréal Eaton Centre opens adjacent to Montréal store

1992 Signy Stefansson Eaton dies (September 10)

1993 Eaton's acquires Millwoods Town Centre store, Edmonton AB

Eaton's acquires Southgate store, Calgary, AB

1994 Eaton's Shoppers' World in Toronto closes (June 22)

Trans-Canada Sales reinstituted

Eaton's Erin Mills Town Centre (Mississauga, ON) opens

1997 Eaton's seeks protection under the Companies' Creditors Arrangement Act of Canada (February 27)

George Kosich becomes Eaton's new CEO (June 5)

Eaton's closes six stores (June 30)

Eaton's negotiates a deal to share pension surplus money with employees

Eaton's closes Thunder Bay store (September 30)

$419 million restructuring plan approved (September)

1998 Brent Ballantyne assumes position as chairman of the board (January 1)

Eaton's closes ten more stores (February 28)

Eaton's goes public with IPO offering of 11.7 million shares selling for fifteen dollars each (June 10)

Eaton's announces elimination of hard-goods departments for more space for fashion merchandise

George Kosich suddenly resigns as CEO (November)

Brent Ballantyne appointed CEO (December 15)

1999 Eaton's reports a $72 million loss for 1998 (March 17)

Eaton's is officially put up for sale (May 18)

Eaton's seeks protection under the Bankruptcy and Insolvency Act (August 20)

Eaton's terminated thousands of employees across Canada (August 24)
Eaton's begins company-wide liquidation (August 25)
Sears Canada announces it plan to acquire the T. Eaton Co. Limited (September 20)
Sears Canada announces purchase of six downtown stores to be operated as new Eaton's store (October 5)
Sears officially takes ownership of Eaton's (December 30)

2000 New "Eatons" officially launched at seven former locations (November 25)

2001 Sears Canada CEO Paul Walters resigns, replaced by Mark Cohen from Sears, Roebuck and Company

2002 Sears Canada reports a drop in profits of 58 percent in 2001 (January 17)
Sears Canada announces the discontinuance of the "Eatons" brand and plans to convert the stores to standard Sears outlets (February 18)
Former "Eatons" stores begin the conversion to Sears (February 26)

Appendix B

The Eaton Family Tree

The Eaton family of Canada can trace their roots back to Scotland, before coming to Ireland in the Ulster Plantation of the seventeenth century. The noble Adair family of Scotland were among the colonists who came to Northern Ireland and were granted land confiscated from Gaelic chiefs in the Plantation scheme who sought to anglicize the Irish and impose the Protestant faith on the land. The Eatons came as tenants of the Adairs and settled on land in Clogher, County Antrim. The size of their acreage and the permanence of their (still-occupied) two-storey home indicates the success the family built over many generations in Northern Ireland.

The family tree on the following page spans from the birth of John Eaton in 1784 to the lives of the four great-grandsons of Timothy Eaton, three of whom were in the employ of the family's department store business when it collapsed in 1999. The diagram also focuses on the family members who led the T. Eaton Co. Limited at its apogee in the twentieth century. As a result, two branches of the Eaton family have prominence: the one representing the offspring of John Eaton—the most important of whom was Timothy Eaton, the founder of the colossal department store empire in Canada—and the branch formed by the sons of Timothy's brother John, who remained in Northern Ireland but whose son Robert Young Eaton played an important managerial role in the store's history.

Question marks have replaced dates where information is nonexistent or contradictory.

JOHN EATON *(1784-1834)* m. Margaret Craig *(1796-1848)*
- **Robert** *(1816-1893)*, **Eliza Jane** *(1819-1861)*, **Mary Anne** *(1821-1841)*, **Margaret** *(1824-1900)*
- **John Eaton** *(1827-1895)* m. Margaret Herbison *(1833-1907)*
  - **William Herbison Eaton** *(1873-?)*
  - **ROBERT YOUNG EATON** *(1875-1956)* m. Hazel Ireland *(1889-1965)*
    - **Margaret Craig Eaton** *(1912-1988)* m. John Hubert Dunn *(1910-?)*
    - **John Wallace "Jack" Eaton** *(1912-1990)* m. Phyllis Finlayson *(1915-1997)*
    - **Edith Elizabeth Eaton** *(1913-2010)* m. Paul Robert van der Stricht *(1908-2004)*
    - **Erskine Robert Eaton** *(1915-1942)*
    - **Alan Young Eaton** *(1916-2000)* m. Diana Fishleigh
- **Nancy** *(1829-?)*, **Sarah** *(1831-?)*, **James** *(1832-1904)*
- **TIMOTHY EATON** *(1843-1907)* m. Margaret Wilson Beattie *(1841-1933)*
  - **Josephine Smyth Eaton** *(1865-1943)* m. Thomas David Burnside *(1835-1900)*
    - **Iris Margaret Burnside** *(1894-1915)*
    - **Allan Eaton Burnside** *(1898-1937)*
  - **Margaret Elizabeth Eaton** *(1867-1952)* m. Charles E. Burden *(1863-?)*
    - **Margaret Beattie Burden** *(1898-?)* m. William Avery Bishop *(1894-1956)*
    - **Henry John Burden** *(1894-1960)*
  - **Kathleen Herbison Eaton** *(1869-1870)*
  - **Edward Young Eaton** *(1871-1900)* m. (1) Tillie Robinson *(1869-1895)* (2) Mabel Eckhardt
    - **Marjorie Tillie Eaton** *(1892-1952)* m. Harold Coulson *(1884-?)*
  - (Baby) **Eaton** *(1872)*
  - **Timothy Wilson Eaton** *(1873-1874)*
  - **William Fletcher Eaton** *(1875-1935)* m. Gertrude Cook *(1877-1942)*
  - **SIR JOHN CRAIG EATON** *(1876-1922)* m. Flora McCrea *(1880-1970)*
    - **Timothy Craig Eaton** *(1903-1986)* m. (1) Martha Waddie, (2) Georgina Kearns, (3) Isabella Manning
    - **JOHN DAVID EATON** *(1909-1973)* m. Signy Hildur Stefansson
      - **John Craig Eaton** *(1937-)* m. (1) Catherine Farr, (2) Sherrill Reid, (3) Sally Horsfall
      - **Fredrik Stephan Eaton** *(1938-)* m. Catherine Martin
      - **Thor Edgar Eaton** *(1942-)* m. Nicole Courtois
      - **George Ross Eaton** *(1945-)* m. Terrie McIntosh
    - **Edgar Allison Eaton** *(1912-1988)* m. Mildred Jarvis Page *(1915-1968)*
    - **Gilbert McCrea Eaton** *(1915-1985)* m. (1), Marjorie Maston (2) Maria Marosi
    - **Florence Mary Eaton** *(1919-2012)* m. Frank F. McEachren *(1918-1995)*
    - **Evlyn Beatrice Eaton**, *(adopted) (1919-1989)* m. Russell Payton *(1915-1976)*

Appendix C

Eaton's Store Directories

TORONTO–QUEEN STREET, *190 Yonge Street*—UN 1-5111 (*December 8, 1869*)

Subway Level

Impulse Shop • Gourmet Market 284, 579 • Cake Counter • Wine Cellar • The Hub Cafeteria • Glassware 252 • Crystal 252 • China 252 • Doulton Shop • The Gift Shop 218 • Bar Shop 218 • Bridal Registry • Flame and Flower 208 • Housewares 254 • Small Electrics 277 • Kitchen Country 254 • Creative Kitchen • Mowers 253 • Snowblowers 253 • Ranges 256 • Washers and Dryers 257 • Dishwashers 256 • Refrigerators and Freezers 259 • Vacuum Cleaners 258 • Personal Care 477 • Furnaces 556 • Plumbing 456 • Sporting Goods 261 • Coins, Stamps 405 • Toys 271 • Hardware 263 • Garden Grove 280 • Potting Shed 480 • Lawn and Garden Furniture 280 • Sporting Goods 261 • Pro Shop • Rod and Gun Shop • Outdoor Shop • Luggage 264 • Open Hearth Shop 276

Subway Level–Tunnel to Annex

Paint and Wallcovering 274

Main Floor

Information and Tourist Bureau • Post Office • Toronto 1 Shop 205, 206, 301 • Eaton's Flower Shop • The Jewel Shop 415 • Jewellery 215 • Silver Holloware 515 • Silver Flatware 515 • Clocks • Cosmetics 216 • Drugs, Soaps, Sundries 212 • Pharmacy 212 • Candy Counters 214 • Notions 222 • Blouses 203 • Hosiery 201 • Handbags 217 • Main Floor Lingerie Bar 209 • Gloves 202 • Fashion Accessories 262 • Wigs 225 • Whatzit Nook 241 •

Cameras 512 • Stationery 208 • Social Expression Shop 208 • Calculators 306 • School and Office Supplies 206 • Auto Accessories 263 • Books 205 • Coins, Stamps 405 • Men's Dress Furnishings 228 • Men's Casual Furnishings 228 • The Man's Corner

186 Yonge Street
186 Shop 228

Second Floor
Men's Clothing 229, 429 • The Pine Room 629 • Timothy E. 329 • Tuxedo Rentals and Formal Wear • Men's Footwear 237 • The Board Room • Men's Sportswear 429 • Men's Casual Clothing 229 • Adam Shop 329 • Pants Plus • Abstract Shop 332 • Made-To-Measure Shop 230 • Seven Seas Gift Shop 270 • Fashion Fabrics 233 • Creative Stitchery 224 • Sewing Machines • Women's Shoes 238 • Shoe Salon • Shoe Repair • Custom Gift Wrapping • The Little Red Basket Shop

Third Floor
Lingerie 609 • Loungewear 609 • At Home • Foundation Garments 609 • Popular Price Sleepwear 209 • Popular Price Loungewear 209 • Popular Price Lingerie 509 • Body Fashions 609 • Slipper Bar 238 • Popular Price Dresses 345 • Popular Price Sportswear 545 • Popular Price Coats 445 • Bed linens 236 • Bath Boutiques 336 • Table Linens 356 • Pictures 276 • Wall Decor 276 • Mirrors 276 • Gallery of Fine Art 271 • Eaton's Travel Service • Beauty Salon • Optical 221 • Hearing Aids 421 • Trim-a-Home Shop 219 **Young World**—Infants' Wear 210 • Nursery Shop • Young Happenings • Children's Wear 210 • Eaton's Juvenile • Children's Shoes 239 • Girls' Wear 211 • Jean Tree 211 • Younger Crowd Shop 211 • Children's Hosiery 201 • Junior Shoes 239 • Motion 3 611 • Boy's Clothing • Students' Clothing 432 • 1-2-3 Boutique • Blue Tube

Fourth Floor
The Colony 744 • Chelsea Place Dresses 341 • Chelsea Place Sportswear 246 • Chelsea Place Coats & Suits 344 • The Weather Vane • Mayfair Place Dresses 541 • Mayfair Place Sportswear 546 • Mayfair Place Coats & Suits 444 • Millinery 264 • Wigs 304 • Fur Salon 248 • Bridal Shop • Fourth Gear 640 • Attitude 646 • No. 1 Shop 442 • Like Young Shop 611 • Hairworks **Young Toronto**—Junior Dresses 241 • Junior Sportswear 346 • Junior Coats 244

Boutiques—The Townhouse 546, 343 • Collectors 441 • Ports International 641, 646 • Premier 242 • Attitude • La Boutique • Signature Shop 678

Fifth Floor

Gallery of Fine Furniture 770 • Furniture 270, 470 • Unfinished Furniture 370 • Colonial Corner • Scandinavian Shop • Studio of Interior Design • Bedding 271 • Lamps 377 • Hostess Shop 579 • Entertainment Centre 248, 460 • Musical Instruments 560 • Records 560 • Steinway 360 • Home Comfort 356 • Draperies 267, 456 • Upholstery Fabrics 267 • Floor Coverings 372, 373, 273, 273 • Home Improvements 353 • Viking Room Cafeteria • Snack Bar

Sixth Floor

Customer Accounts Office • Service Bureau • Eaton's Shopping Service

Seventh Floor

Corporate Offices

Eighth Floor

Corporate Offices • Candy Kitchen

Ninth Floor

The Georgian Room Restaurant

EATON'S LOWER-PRICE ANNEX, James and Albert Streets

Tunnel (to Main Store)

Cleaning Supplies 975 • Electricals 977 • Annex Snack Bar

Basement

Cash and Carry Section 950

Main Floor

Hosiery 901 • Gloves 901 • Toys 903 • Gifts 912 • Garden Shop 913 • Luggage 913 • Candy 914 • Stationery 914 • Jewellery 915 • Handbags 917 • Men's Furnishings 928 • Men's Clothing 929 • Boy's Wear 932 • Linens 933 • Shoes 937

Second Floor

Millinery 904 • Lingerie 909 • Dresses 941 • Coats 944 • Sportswear 946 • Children's Wear 910

Third Floor

Lamps 977 • Drapery Fabrics 967 • Drapes 968 • Blinds 969 • Furniture 970 • Bedding 971 • Rugs 972 • Housewares 973 • Paint and Wall Coverings • Lunch Counter • Annex Beauty Salon

14 Albert Street

Mail Order Showrooms

WINNIPEG, *320 Portage Avenue*—**SU**nset **3-2115** (*July 15, 1905*)

Downstairs

Eaton's Foodateria 284, 379 • Lunch Bar • **Eaton's Basement**

Main Floor

The Souvenir Bar • Eaton's Flower Shop • Jewellery 215 • Silverware 215 • Clocks 215 • Cosmetics 216 • Drugs, Soaps, Sundries 212 • Candy Counters 214 • Notions 222 • Hosiery 201 • Handbags 217 • Main Floor Lingerie Bar 209 • Gloves 202 • Fashion Accessories 262 • Wigs 225 • Whatzit Nook 241 • Cameras 512 • Men's Dress Furnishings 228 • Men's Casual Furnishings 228 • Men's Clothing 229, 429 • The Pine Room 629 • Timothy E. 329 • Tuxedo Rentals and Formal Wear • Men's Footwear 237 • Men's Hats 237 • Men's Sportswear 429 • Men's Casual Clothing 229 • Adam Shop 329 • Made-To-Measure Shop 230

Hargrave South

Stationery 208 • Social Expression Shop 208 • Calculators 306 • School and Office Supplies 206 • Drugs Health and Beauty Aids 212 • Pharmacy 212 • Auto Accessories 263 • Trim-a-Home Shop 219 • The Little Red Basket Shop

Donald Street South

Toyland

234 Donald Street

Eaton's Catalogue Salesroom

Second Floor

Fashion Fabrics 233 • Creative Stitchery 224 • Sewing Machines • Flame and Flower 208 • Popular Price Sleepwear 209 • Popular Price Loungewear 209 • Popular Price Lingerie 209, 509 • Body Fashions 609 • Slipper Bar 238 • Women's Shoes 238 • Popular Price Dresses 345 • Popular Price Sportswear 545 • Popular Price Coats 445 • Shoe Repair • Custom Gift Wrapping

Third Floor

Seven Seas Gift Shop 270 • Impulse Shop • Glassware 252 • Crystal 252 • China 252 • The Gift Shop 218 • Bar Shop 218 • Bridal Registry • Silver Holloware 515 • Silver Flatware 515 • Housewares 254 • Creative Kitchen • The Current Electric 277 • Kitchen Country 254 • The Open Hearth Shop 276 • Mowers 253 • Snowblowers 253 • Ranges 256 • Washers and Dryers 257 • Dishwashers 256 • Refrigerators and Freezers 259 • Vacuum Cleaners 258 • Personal Care 477 • Furnaces 556 • Plumbing 456 • Pet Shop 253 • Sporting Goods 261 • Coins, Stamps 405 • Toys 271 • Third Floor Meats 281 • Fancy Food Shop 579 • Cake Counter 1108K • Char Bar • Grill Room Products

Fourth Floor

The Colony 744, 246 • Colony Dresses 341 • Young Sophisticates 341 • Mayfair Place 444 • Women's Place 446, 546 • Shoe Salon • Millinery 264 • Wigs 304 • Fur Salon 248 • Bridal Shop • Lingerie 609 • At Home • Loungewear 609 • Foundation Garments 609 • Beauty Salon • Fourth Gear 640 • Attitude 646 • No. 1 Shop 442 • Coats and Suits • The Weather Vane • Like Young Shop 611 • Mayfair Place 444 • Beauty Salon • The Trimmers • Junior Dresses 241

Young Winnipeg—Junior Sportswear 346 • Junior Coats 244 • Junior Petite Shop • Junior Dresses 241

Boutiques—The Townhouse 343, 546 • Collectors 441 • Ports International 641, 646 • Premier 242 • Attitude • La Boutique

Fifth Floor

Hostess Shop • Portrait Studio 612 • The Grill Room • The Valley Room • The Soup Kettle

Young World—Infants' Wear 210 • Nursery Shop • Young Happenings • Children's Wear 210 • Eaton's Juvenile • Children's Shoes 239 • Girls' Wear 211 • Jean Tree 211 • Younger Crowd Shop 211 • Children's Hosiery 201 • Junior Shoes 239 • Action 5 611 • Boy's Clothing • Students' Clothing 432 • Abstract Shop 332 • 1-2-3 Boutique • Blue Tube

Sixth Floor
Bed linens 236 • Bath Linens 336 • Bath Boutique • Table Linens 356 • Entertainment Centre 248, 460 • Musical Instruments 560 • Home Comfort 356 • Draperies 267, 456 • Upholstery Fabrics 267 • Home Improvements 353 • Books 205

Seventh Floor
Gallery of Fine Furniture 770 • Accent 7 718 • Furniture 270, 470 • Colonial Corner • Scandinavian Shop • Studio of Interior Design • Pictures 266 • Wall Decor 266 • Gallery of Fine Art 271 • Mattresses • Mirrors 276 • Lamps 377 • Assembly Hall

Eighth Floor
Hardware 263 • Garden Equipment 280 • Potting Shed 480 • Lawn and Garden Furniture 280 • Sporting Goods 261 • Pro Shop • Rod and Gun Shop • Outdoor Shop • Paint and Wallcovering 274 • Unfinshed Furniture 370 • Luggage 264 • Eaton's Travel

MONTRÉAL, *677 Rue Ste-Catherine*—**VI**ctoria **2-9211** *(April 15, 1925)*

Metro Level
Eaton's Metro Level—Basement Luncheonette

Main Floor
Jewellery 215 • Silver Holloware 515 • Silver Flatware 515 • Clocks 515 • Cutlery 515 • Cosmetics 216 • Toilet Sundries 212 • Pharmacy • Notions 222 • Blouses 203 • Hosiery 201 • Handbags 217 • "Felinie" 309 • Foundations 609 • Gloves 202 • Fashion Accessories 262 • Wigs 225 • Hat Bar 304 • Main Floor Sportswear 246 • College Shop 646 • Cameras 512 • Men's Dress Furnishings 228 • Men's Sport Shirts 428 • Men's Hosiery 201 • Men's Casual Clothing 288 • The Marco Polo 528 • Men's Hats 428 • Stationery 208 • Social Expression Shop 208 • Calculators 306 • School and Office Supplies 408 • Candy Counter 214 • The Blue Cake Counter 1104 • Specialty Food Shops 379 • Books 205 • Coins, Stamps 405 • Tourist Bureau

Second Floor
Men's Shoes 237 • The Executive Shop 237 • Men's Suits 229 • Warren K. Cook Shop 229 • South Winds Shop 229 • Men's Clothing 329 • Monsieur

Chez Eaton Distinction Shop 629 • Timothy E. 329 • Men's Sportswear 429 • The Sun Shop • Tuxedo Rentals and Formal Wear • Adam 729 • Abstract Shop 332 • Made-To-Measure Shop 230 • "Four Corners" Gift Shop 270 • Chez Elle Boutique 536 • Fashion Fabrics 233 • Creative Stitchery 224 • Sewing Machines • Bedcoverings 436 • Linens 236 • Bath Boutiques 336 • Table Linens 356 • Women's Shoes 238 • "Le Salon" Shoes 338 • Children's Shoes 239 • Teen's Shoes 239 • Optical Salon 221 • Little Red Basket Shop 208

Third Floor
Chelsea Place Sportswear 246 • The 4 Seasons Shop 246 • The Villager Shop 246 • Beach Shop 246 • Chelsea Place Coats 344 • Suburban Shop 744 • Chelsea Place Dresses 341 • Women's Place 446 • La Colonnade Coats 544 • La Colonnade Dresses 541 • La Colonnade Coats 546 • Millinery 264 • Salon Français 305 • Wigs 304 • Fourth Gear 640 • No. 1 Shop 442 • New Orleans Town House 441 • The Ensemble Shop 242 • Fur Salon 248 • Bridal Shop 341 • Ports International 641, 646 • Premier 242 • Attitude 646 • La Boutique 341/641 • Coach House 446 • Le Grand Boulevard
The Young Montrealer Shop—Junior Dresses 241 • Junior Sportswear 346 • Junior Coats 244 • Scene 3

Fourth Floor
China 252 • Wedgwood Room 252 • Glassware 452 • Housewares 254 • Open Hearth Shop 276 • Small Appliances 271 • Foundations 609 • Loungewear 609 • Lingerie 247 • Mic Mac Shop • Lingerie 209 • Le Boudoir 209 • Maternity Shop • Fourth Floor Sportswear 545 • Fourth Floor Dresses 541 • Fourth Floor Coats 544 • Infants' Wear 210 • Nursery Shop • Young Happenings • Children's Wear 210 • Eaton's Juvenile • Girls' Wear 211 • "Like Young" Shop 611 • Children's Hosiery 201 • Boy's Wear 232 • Students' Clothing 432

Fifth Floor
Special Events Centre • 'Trim-A-Home' Shop • Sporting Goods 227 • La Hutte 227 • Toyville 227 • Science Centre 227 • Ranges 256 • Home Laundry Equipment 257 • Refrigerators and Freezers 259 • Outdoor Living 261 • Hardware 253 • Paint 274 • Garden Shop 260 • Garden Grove 253 • Auto Supplies 263 • Place Élégante • Salon Elysee Beauty Salon • Le Bistro • Post Office • Gift Wrapping • Service Bureau
Music Centre—Televisions 440 • Stereos 260

Sixth Floor

Curtains 268 • Draperies 267 • Custom-Made Draperies 456 • Upholstery Fabrics 267 • Floor Coverings 273 • Rugs 272 • Pictures and Mirrors 276 • Luggage 264 • Eaton Travel • Gift Shop 218 • Table d' Hôte Boutique 218 • Flame and Flower 208 • Eaton's Grape Arbor 208

Seventh Floor

Lamps 377 • Accent 7 718 • Gallery of Fine Furniture 770 • Bedroom and Dining Room Furniture 270 • Living Room Furniture 470 • Kitchen Furniture 370 • Unfinished Furniture 370 • Studio of Interior Design • Slumber Shop 271 • Pianos and Organs 360 • La Maison Rustique • Decorator Showroom 456 • Summer-Furniture Terrace 470 • Holiday Live-In Shop • Customer Accounts Office

Eighth Floor

Executive Offices • Hospital

Ninth Floor

The Ninth Floor Restaurant • The Gold Room • Foyer • The Silver Room • Shopping Service

REGINA, *1230 Broad Street*—525-6311 *(November 19, 1926)*

Main Floor North

Hosiery 201 • Gloves 202 • Blouses 203 • Popular Price Lingerie 509 • Jewellery 215 • Silverware 515 • Clocks 215 • Cosmetics 216 • Handbags 217 • Luggage 264 • Wig Bar 222 • Fashion Accessories 262 • Notions 222 • Eaton's Flower Shop 380 • Candy Counters 214 • Cameras 512 • Stationery 208 • Social Expression Shop 208 • Calculators 306 • School and Office Supplies 206 • Glassware 252 • Crystal 252 • China • 252 • The Gift Shop 218 • The Bar Shop 218 • Flame and Flower 208 • Seven Seas Gift Shop 270, 619 • Bridal Registry 618 • Fashion Fabrics 233 • Sewing Machines 570 • Creative Stitchery 224 • Bed linens 236 • Bedding and Blankets 436 • Table Linens 356 • **Eaton's Bargain Centre**

Main Floor Centre

Popular Price Dresses 345 • Popular Price Sportswear 745 • Popular Price Coats 345 • Misses' Dresses 341 • Misses' Sportswear 246 • Misses' Coats & Suits 344 • Maternity Wear 341 • Women's Dresses 541 • Women's

Sportswear 546 • Women's Coats & Suits 444 • Four Seasons 711,744 • No. 1 Shop 442 • Town House 242, 343, 446 • Attitude Shop 646 • Signature Shop 678 • Fur Salon 248 • Bridal Shop 341 • Millinery 264 • Wigs 304 • Lingerie 209 • Loungewear 209 • Body Fashions 209 • Uniform Centre 509 • College Shop Junior Dresses 241 • College Shop Junior Sportswear 346 • College Shop Junior Coats 241 • Drugs, Soaps, Sundries 212 • Pharmacy 212 • Entertainment Centre 260, 248, 460

Main Floor South

Women's Shoes 238 • Slipper Bar 238 • Shoe Salon 338 • Men's Dress Furnishings 228 • Men's Casual Furnishings 428 • Men's Hats 237 • Men's Clothing 229, 429 • The Pine Room 629 • Timothy E. 329 • Tuxedo Rentals and Formal Wear • Men's Footwear 237 • Men's Casual Clothing 429 • Adam Shop 529 • Abstract Shop 232, 332 • Made-To-Measure Shop 230

Young World—Infants' Wear 210 • Children's Wear 210 • Girls' Wear 211 • Children's Hosiery 201 • Junior Shoes 239 • Students' Clothing 432 • Fourth Gear 640 • Creation 1 611

In the Eaton-Dominion Plaza

Eaton's Maison Antoine Beauty Salon 223 • Viking Restaurant

Top Floor North

Sporting Goods 261 • Ski Lodge • Luggage 264 • Auto Accessories 263 • Hardware 263 • Plumbing 456 • Home Improvements 353 • Pet Supplies 253 • Toys 271 • Artists' Supplies 271 • Paint and Wallcovering 274 • Coins, Stamps 405 • Books 205 • Garden Grove 280 • Potting Shed 180 • Mowers and Snow Blowers 253 • Ranges and Dishwashers 256 • Washers and Dryers 257 • Vacuum Cleaners 258 • Refrigerators and Freezers 259 • Personal Care 477 • Home Comfort 356 • Furnaces 556 • Bath Boutiques 336

Top Floor Centre

Lamps 377 • Wall Decor 276 • Gallery of Fine Art 376 • Housewares 254 • Kitchen Country 254 • Electricals 277 • Unfinished Furniture 370 • Trim-a-Home Shop 219 • The Patio Restaurant • Fancy Foods 579

Top Floor South

Gallery of Fine Furniture 770 • Furniture 270, 470 • Bedding 271 • Accent 718 • Fireplace Accessories 276 • Studio of Interior Design • Draperies 267 • Upholstery Fabrics 267 • Musical Instruments 560 • Records 560 • Steinway 360 • Floor Coverings 272 • Oriental Rugs 373

HAMILTON, *James and King Streets*—525-5111 (*June 23, 1927*)

Basement
Sporting Goods 261 • Auto Accessories 263 • Hardware 263 • Bath Boutiques 336 • Housewares 254 • Kitchen Country 254 • Electricals 277 • The Open Hearth Shop 276 • Unfinished Furniture 370 • Garden Grove 280 • Potting Shed 480 • Mowers and Snow Blowers 253 • Pets and Supplies 253 • Luncheonette
Eaton's Budget Basement

Street Floor
Hosiery 201 • Gloves 202 • Blouses 203 • Casual Sportswear 745 • Popular Price Lingerie 509 • Jewellery 215 • Silverware 515 • Clocks 215 • Cosmetics 216 • Handbags 217 • Wig Bar 222 • Fashion Accessories 262 • Eaton's Flower Shop 380 • Drugs and Sundries 212 • Pharmacy 212 • Candy Counters 214 • Fancy Foods 579 • Cake Counter 1104K • Hostess Shop 1100H • Cameras 512 • Stationery 208 • Social Expression Shop 208 • Calculators 306 • School and Office Supplies 206 • Books 205 • Coins, Stamps 405 • Boys' Clothing 232 • Students' Clothing 432 • Men's Dress Furnishings 228 • Men's Casual Furnishings 428 • Men's Hats 237 • Men's Clothing 229, 429 • The Executive Shop 629 • Timothy E. 329 • Tuxedo Rentals and Formal Wear • Men's Casual Clothing 429 • 43 James 529 • Young Men's Shop 232, 332 • Made-to-Measure Shop 230

Second Floor
Women's Shoes 238 • Slipper Bar 238 • Shoe Salon 338 • Men's Footwear 237 • Junior Shoes 239 • Glassware 252 • Crystal 252 • China 252 • The Gift Shop 218 • The Bar Shop 218 • Flame and Flower 208 • Seven Seas Gift Shop 270, 619 • Red Basket Shop 208 • Bridal Registry 618 • Fashion Fabrics 233 • Creative Stitchery 224 • Notions 222 • Sewing Machines 570 • Bed linens 236 • Bedding and Blankets 436 • Table Linens 356 • Beauty Salon 223 • Optical 221 • Hearing Aids 421

Third Floor
Popular Price Dresses 345 • Popular Price Coats 345 • Chelsea Place Dresses 341 • Chelsea Place Sportswear 246 • Chelsea Place Coats & Suits 344 • Ski Lodge • Maternity Wear 341 • Mayfair Place Dresses 541 • Mayfair Place Sportswear 546 • Mayfair Place Coats & Suits 444 • The Collectors 711 • The Colony 744 • No. 1 Shop 442 • Coach House 446 • Town House 343

• The Ensemble Shop 242 • Attitude Shop 646 • Signature Shop 678 • Fur Salon 248 • Bridal Shop 341 • Millinery 264 • Wigs 304 • Lingerie 209 • Loungewear 209 • Body Fashions 209 • Uniform Centre 509 • Portrait Studio 612

Young Hamilton—Junior Dresses 241 • Junior Sportswear 346 • Junior Coats 241

Young World—Infants' Wear 210 • Children's Wear 210 • Girls' Wear 211 • Children's Hosiery 201 • Third Gear 640 • Like Young Shop 611

Fourth Floor
Luggage 264 • Paint and Wallcovering 274 • Lamps 377 • Wall Decor 276 • Gallery of Fine Art 376 • Ranges and Dishwashers 256 • Washers and Dryers 257 • Vacuum Cleaners 258 • Refrigerators and Freezers 259 • Personal Care 477 • Home Comfort 356 • Furnaces 556 • Plumbing 456 • Home Improvements 353 • Entertainment Centre 260, 248, 460 • Records 560 • Yuletide Trim Shop 219 • Draperies 267 • Upholstery Fabrics 267

Fifth Floor
Toys 271 • Artists' Supplies 271 • Gallery of Fine Furniture 770 • Furniture 270, 470 • Bedding 271 • Accent 718 • Fireplace Shop 276 • Studio of Interior Design • Musical Instruments 560 • Steinway 360 • Floor Coverings 272 • Oriental Rugs 373 • Accounts Office • Service Bureau

Sixth Floor
The Green Room Restaurant • The Auditorium • Executive Offices

MONCTON, *95 Foundry Street (November 15, 1927)*

Basement
Eaton's Bargain Basement
Toyland (in season) • Trim-a-Home Shop 219 205 • Red Basket Shop 208 • Offices

Main Floor
Hosiery 201 • Gloves 202 • Blouses 203 • Jewellery 215 • Silverware 515 • Clocks 215 • Cosmetics 216 • Handbags 217 • Wig Bar 222 • Fashion Accessories 262 • Popular Price Lingerie 509 • Lingerie 209 • Loungewear 209 • Body Fashions 209 • Uniform Centre 509 • Women's Shoes 238 •

Slipper Bar 238 • Shoe Salon 338 • Notions 222 • Eaton's Flower Shop 380 • Drugs, Soaps, Sundries 212 • Pharmacy 212 • Candy Counters 214 • Cameras 512 • Stationery 208 • Social Expression Shop 208 • Calculators 306 • School and Office Supplies 206 • Coins, Stamps 405 • Books • Men's Dress Furnishings 228 • Men's Casual Furnishings 428 • Men's Casual Clothing 429 • Adam Shop 529 • Abstract Shop 232, 332 • Made-To-Measure Shop 230 • Men's Footwear 237 • Men's Hats 237 • Sporting Goods 261 • Ski Lodge 261 • Luggage 264 • Fashion Fabrics 233 • Creative Stitchery 224 • Bed linens 236 • Bedding and Blankets 436 • Table Linens 356 • Draperies 267 • Upholstery Fabrics 267 • Glassware 252 • Crystal 252 • China • 252 • The Gift Shop 218 • The Bar Shop 218 • Flame and Flower 208 • Seven Seas Gift Shop 270, 619 • Bridal Registry 618 • Housewares 254 • Kitchen Country 254 • Fancy Foods 579 • Cake Counter 1104K • Hostess Shop 1100H

Second Floor
Popular Price Dresses 345 • Popular Price Sportswear 745 • Popular Price Coats 345 • Misses' Dresses 341 • Misses' Sportswear 246 • Misses' Coats & Suits 344 • Maternity Wear • Women's Dresses 541 • Women's Sportswear 546 • Women's Coats & Suits 444 • The Collectors 711 • The Colony 744 • No. 1 Shop 442 • The Ensemble Shop 242, 343,446, 678 • Attitude Shop 646 • Fur Salon 248 • Bridal Shop 341 • Millinery 264 • Wigs 304
College and Career Shop—Junior Dresses 241 • Junior Sportswear 346 • Junior Coats 241
Young World—Infants' Wear 210 • Children's Wear 210 • Girls' Wear 211 • Children's Hosiery 201 • Junior Shoes 239 • Students' Clothing 432 • Fourth Gear 640 • Like Young Shop 611 • Men's Clothing 229, 429 • The Pine Room 629 • Timothy E. 329 • Tuxedo Rentals and Formal Wear • Auto Accessories 263 • Hardware 263 • Pet Supplies 253 • Toys 271 • Artists' Supplies 271 • Paint and Wallcovering 274 • Lamps 377 • Wall Decor 276 • Electricals 277 • Unfinished Furniture 370Garden Grove 280 • Potting Shed 480 • Bath Boutiques 336 • Gallery of Fine Art 376 • Gallery of Fine Furniture 770 • Furniture 270, 470 • Bedding 271 • Accent 718 • The Open Hearth Shop 276 • Studio of Interior Design • Mowers and Snow Blowers 253 • Ranges and Dishwashers 256 • Washers and Dryers 257 • Vacuum Cleaners 258 • Refrigerators and Freezers 259 • Personal Care 477 • Home Comfort 356 • Furnaces 556 • Sewing Machines 570 • Entertainment Centre 260, 248, 460 • Musical Instruments 560 • Records 560 • Steinway 360 • Floor Coverings 272 • Oriental Rugs 373 • Plumbing 456 • Home

Improvements 353 • Post Office • Customer Accounts Office • Personnel Office • Beauty Salon 223 • Optical 221 • Hearing Aid Centre 421 • Lunch Counter • Restaurant

SASKATOON, *80–201 Twenty-first Street East*—**CH**erry **2-6051** (*December 5, 1928*)

Lower Floor
Toys 271 • Artists' Supplies 271 • Sporting Goods 261 • Luggage 264 • Auto Accessories 263 • Hardware 263 • Bath Boutiques 336 • Housewares 254 • Kitchen Country 254 • Electricals 277 • The Open Hearth Shop 276 • Unfinished Furniture 370 • Garden Grove 280 • Potting Shed 480 • Mowers and Snow Blowers 253 • Pets and Supplies 253
Eaton's Budget Basement
Foodateria Lower Floor—Snack Bar

Main Floor
Hosiery 201 • Gloves 202 • Blouses 203 • Casual Sportswear 745 • Popular Price Lingerie 509 • Jewellery 215 • Silverware 515 • Clocks 215 • Cosmetics 216 • Handbags 217 • Wig Bar 222 • Fashion Accessories 262 • Fancy Goods 224 • Women's Shoes 238 • Slipper Bar 238 • Shoe Salon 338 • Men's Footwear 237 • Junior Shoes 239 • Gift Bar 270, 619 • Eaton's Flower Shop 380 • Drugs and Sundries 212 • Pharmacy 212 • Candy Counters 214 • Fancy Foods 579 • Cake Counter 1104K • Hostess Shop 1100H • Camera Centre 512 • Stationery 208 • Social Expression Shop 208 • Calculators 306 • School and Office Supplies 206 • Books 205 • Coins, Stamps 405 • Boys' Clothing 232 • Students' Clothing 432 • Men's Dress Furnishings 228 • Men's Casual Furnishings 428 • Men's Hats 237 • Men's Clothing 229, 429 • The Pine Room 629 • Timothy E. 329 • Tuxedo Rentals and Formal Wear • Men's Casual Clothing 429 • Adam Shop 529 • Young Men's Shop 232, 332 • Made-To-Measure Shop 230
Foodateria Main Floor

Second Floor
Glassware 252 • Crystal 252 • China 252 • The Gift Shop 218 • The Bar Shop 218 • Flame and Flower 208 • Red Basket Shop 208 • Bridal Registry 618 • Fashion Fabrics 233 • Notions 222 • Sewing Machines 570 • Bed linens 236 • Bedding and Blankets 436 • Table Linens 356 • Popular Price Dresses 345 • Popular Price Coats 345 • Misses' Dresses 341 • Misses' Sportswear

246 • Misses' Coats & Suits 344 • Ski Lodge • Maternity Wear 341 • Women's Dresses 541 • Women's Sportswear 546 • Women's Coats & Suits 444 • Four Seasons 711, 744 • No. 1 Shop 442 • Town House 242, 343, 446 • Attitude Shop 646 • Signature Shop 678 • Fur Salon 248 • Bridal Shop 341 • Millinery 264 • Wigs 304 • Lingerie 209 • Loungewear 209 • Body Fashions 209 • Uniform Centre 509
The Place—Junior Dresses 241 • Junior Sportswear 346 • Junior Coats 241
Young World—Cradle Crowd 210 • Children's Wear 210 • Girls' Wear 211 • Children's Hosiery 201 • Second Gear 640 • Creation 1 611

Third Floor
Paint and Wallcovering 274 • Lamps 377 • Wall Decor 276 • Gallery of Fine Art 376 • Ranges and Dishwashers 256 • Washers and Dryers 257 • Vacuum Cleaners 258 • Refrigerators and Freezers 259 • Personal Care 477 • Home Comfort 356 • Furnaces 556 • Plumbing 456 • Home Improvements 353 • Entertainment Centre 260, 248, 460 • Records 560 • Yuletide Trim Shop 219 • Draperies 267 • Upholstery Fabrics 267 • Gallery of Fine Furniture 770 • Furniture 270, 470 • Bedding 271 • Accent 718 • Fireplace Shop 276 • Studio of Interior Design • Musical Instruments 560 • Steinway 360 • Floor Coverings 272 • Oriental Rugs 373 • Accounts Office • Optical 221 • Hearing Aids 421 • Algerian Room Restaurant

HALIFAX, *1633 Barrington Street at Prince Street (March 1, 1928)*

Granville Street Lower Level
Sporting Goods 261 • Ski Lodge 261 • Luggage 264 • Auto Accessories 263 • Hardware 263 • Pet Supplies 253 • Toys 271 • Artists' Supplies 271 • Paint and Wallcovering 274 • Lamps 377 • Wall Decor 276

Granville Street Level
Stationery 208 • Social Expression Shop 208 • Calculators 306 • School and Office Supplies 206 • Trim-a-Home Shop 219 • Coins, Stamps 405 • Books 205 • Glassware 252 • Crystal 252 • China • 252 • The Gift Shop 218 • The Bar Shop 218 • Flame and Flower 208 • Seven Seas Gift Shop 270, 619 • Bridal Registry 618 • Housewares 254 • Kitchen Country 254 • Electricals 277 • Unfinished Furniture 370 • Garden Grove 280 • Potting Shed 480 • Foodateria 284 • Fancy Foods 579 • Cake Counter 1104K • Hostess Shop 1100H

Main Floor

Hosiery 201 • Gloves 202 • Blouses 203 • Popular Price Lingerie 509 • Jewellery 215 • Silverware 515 • Clocks 215 • Cosmetics 216 • Handbags 217 • Wig Bar 222 • Fashion Accessories 262 • Notions 222 • Eaton's Flower Shop 380 • Drugs, Soaps, Sundries 212 • Pharmacy 212 • Candy Counters 214 • Cameras 512 • Men's Dress Furnishings 228 • Men's Casual Furnishings 428 • Men's Hats 237 • Men's Clothing 229, 429 • The Pine Room 629 • Timothy E. 329 • Tuxedo Rentals and Formal Wear • Men's Footwear 237 • Men's Casual Clothing 429 • Adam Shop 529 • Abstract Shop 232, 332 • Made-To-Measure Shop 230

Second Floor

Lingerie 209 • Loungewear 209 • Body Fashions 209 • Uniform Centre 509 • Women's Shoes 238 • Slipper Bar 238 • Shoe Salon 338
College and Career Shop—Junior Dresses 241 • Junior Sportswear 346 • Junior Coats 241
Young World—Infants' Wear 210 • Children's Wear 210 • Girls' Wear 211 • Children's Hosiery 201 • Junior Shoes 239 • Students' Clothing 432 • Fourth Gear 640 • Like Young Shop 611

Third Floor

Popular Price Dresses 345 • Popular Price Sportswear 745 • Popular Price Coats 345 • Misses' Dresses 341 • Misses' Sportswear 246 • Misses' Coats & Suits 344 • Maternity Wear • Women's Dresses 541 • Women's Sportswear 546 • Women's Coats & Suits 444 • The Collectors 711 • The Colony 744 • No. 1 Shop 442 • The Ensemble Shop 242, 343,446 • Attitude Shop 646 • Signature Shop 678 • Fur Salon 248 • Bridal Shop 341 • Millinery 264 • Wigs 304

Fourth Floor

Bath Boutiques 336 • Gallery of Fine Art 376 • Gallery of Fine Furniture 770 • Furniture 270, 470 • Bedding 271 • Accent 718 • The Open Hearth Shop 276 • Studio of Interior Design • Mowers and Snow Blowers 253 • Ranges and Dishwashers 256 • Washers and Dryers 257 • Vacuum Cleaners 258 • Refrigerators and Freezers 259 • Personal Care 477 • Home Comfort 356 • Furnaces 556 • Sewing Machines 570 • Entertainment Centre 260, 248, 460 • Musical Instruments 560 • Records 560 • Steinway 360 • Floor Coverings 272 • Oriental Rugs 373 • Plumbing 456 • Home Improvements 353

Fifth Floor
Fashion Fabrics 233 • Creative Stitchery 224 • Bed linens 236 • Bedding and Blankets 436 • Table Linens 356 • Draperies 267 • Upholstery Fabrics 267 • Customer Accounts Office • Service Bureau • Personnel Office • Executive Offices

EDMONTON, *102nd Avenue at 101st Street*—**GA 4-0181** *(August 23, 1939)*

Lower Floor—North
Pet Corner 253 • Glassware 252 • Crystal 252 • China 252 • The Gift Shop 218 • The Bar Shop 218 • Flame and Flower 208 • Bridal Registry 618 • Foodateria 284 • Fancy Foods 579 • Cake Counter 1104K • Hostess Shop 1100H
Lower Floor—East
Foodateria 284 (Fruits & Vegetables)
Eaton's Budget Store
Lower Floor—South
Housewares 254 • Kitchen Country 254 • Electricals 277 • The Open Hearth Shop 276 • Auto Accessories 263 • Hardware 263 • Bath Boutiques 336 • Plumbing 456 • Home Improvements 353 • Toys 271 • Artists' Supplies 271 • Unfinished Furniture 370 • Catalogue Order Desk
Lower Floor—West
Sporting Goods 261 • Ski Lodge 261 • Lunch Counter

Main Floor—North
Creative Stitchery 224 • Notions 222 • Boys' Clothing 232 • Students' Clothing 432 • Fourth Gear 640
Main Floor—East
Jewellery 215 • Silverware 515 • Clocks 215 • Cosmetics 216 • Drugs, Soaps, Sundries 212 • Pharmacy 212 • Handbags 217 • Stationery 208 • Social Expression Shop 208 • Calculators 306 • School and Office Supplies 206 • Coins, Stamps 405 • Books 205 • Seven Seas Gift Shop 270, 619
Main Floor—Centre Aisle
Hosiery 201 • Gloves 202 • Blouses 203 • Fashion Accessories 262 • Popular Price Lingerie 509 • Wig Bar 222 • Cameras 512 • Candy Counters 214
Main Floor—South
Women's Shoes 238 • Slipper Bar 238 • Shoe Salon 338 • Men's Footwear 237

Main Floor—West
Men's Dress Furnishings 228 • Men's Casual Furnishings 428 • Men's Hats 237 • Men's Clothing 229, 429 • The Pine Room 629 • Timothy E. 329 • Tuxedo Rentals and Formal Wear • Men's Casual Clothing 429 • Adam Shop 529 • Abstract Shop 232, 332 • Made-To-Measure Shop 230 • Luggage 264

Second Floor—North
Fashion Fabrics 233 • Lingerie 209 • Loungewear 209 • Body Fashions 209 • Uniform Centre 509 • Fur Salon 248 • Bridal Shop 341 • Popular Price Dresses 345 • Popular Price Sportswear 745 • Popular Price Coats 345
Second Floor—East
Bed linens 236 • Bedding and Blankets 436 • Table Linens 356 • Hearing Aids 421 • Beauty Salon
Second Floor—Centre Aisle
Trim-a-Home Shop 219 • Red Basket Shop 208
Second Floor—South
Misses' Dresses 341 • Misses' Sportswear 246 • Misses' Coats & Suits 344 • Maternity Wear 341 • Women's World 541, 546, 444 • Millinery 264 • Wigs 304 • The Collectors 711 • The Colony 744 • No. 1 Shop • The Ensemble Shop 242, 446, 343 • Attitude Shop 646 • Signature Shop 678 • Trim-a-Home Shop 219
Second Floor—West
Young World—Infants' Wear 210 • Children's Wear 210 • Girls' Wear 211 • Children's Hosiery 201 • Junior Shoes 239 • Like Young Shop 611
Young Flair—Junior Dresses 241 • Junior Sportswear 346 • Junior Coats 241

Third Floor—North
Draperies 267 • Upholstery Fabrics 267 • Washers and Dryers 257 • Customer Accounts Office
Third Floor—East
Entertainment Centre 260, 248, 460 • Record Bar 560 • Piano Salon 360 • Musical Instruments 560 • Lamps 377 • Ranges and Dishwashers 256
Third Floor—Centre Aisle
Sewing Machines 570
Third Floor—South
Floor Coverings 272 • Oriental Rugs 373 • Mowers and Snow Blowers 253 • Vacuum Cleaners 258 • Refrigerators and Freezers 259 • Personal Care 477 • Home Comfort 356 • Furnaces 556 • Furniture 270, 470

Third Floor—West

Gallery of Fine Furniture 770 • Furniture 270, 470 • Bedding 271 • Accent 718 • Fireplace Accessories 276 • Studio of Interior Design • Gallery of Fine Art 376 • Paint and Wallcovering 274 • Wall Decor 276

Outdoor Shop, 102nd Street, across from the store

Eaton's Flower Shop 380 • Garden Grove 280 • Potting Shed 480

CALGARY, *408 Eighth Avenue Southwest*—**AM**herst **6-0234** (*February 28, 1929*)

Lower Level

Sporting Goods 261 • Ski Lodge • Luggage 264 • Auto Accessories 263 • Hardware 263 • Pet Supplies 253 • Toys 271 • Artists' Supplies 271 • Paint and Wallcovering 274 • Lamps 377 • Wall Decor 276 • Trim-a-Home Shop 219 • Coins, Stamps 405 • Books 205 • Housewares 254 • Kitchen Country 254 • Electricals 277 • The Open Hearth Shop 276 • Unfinished Furniture 370 • Garden Grove 280 • Potting Shed 480 • Mowers and Snow Blowers 253 • Ranges and Dishwashers 256 • Washers and Dryers 257 • Vacuum Cleaners 258 • Refrigerators and Freezers 259 • Personal Care 477 • Home Comfort 356 • Furnaces 556 • Sewing Machines 570 • Entertainment Centre 260, 248, 460 • Foodateria 284 • Fancy Foods 579 • Cake Counter 1104K • Hostess Shop 1100H

Eaton's Budget Store

Main Floor

Hosiery 201 • Gloves 202 • Blouses 203 • Popular Price Lingerie 509 • Jewellery 215 • Silverware 515 • Clocks 215 • Cosmetics 216 • Handbags 217 • Wig Bar 222 • Fashion Accessories 262 • Notions 222 • Eaton's Flower Shop 380 • Drugs, Soaps, Sundries 212 • Pharmacy 212 • Candy Counters 214 • Cameras 512 • Stationery 208 • Social Expression Shop 208 • Calculators 306 • School and Office Supplies 206 • Men's Dress Furnishings 228 • Men's Casual Furnishings 428 • Men's Hats 237 • Men's Clothing 229, 429 • The Pine Room 629 • Timothy E. 329 • Tuxedo Rentals and Formal Wear • Men's Footwear 237 • Men's Casual Clothing 429 • Adam Shop 529 • Abstract Shop 232, 332 • Made-To-Measure Shop 230

Second Floor

Popular Price Dresses 345 • Popular Price Sportswear 745 • Popular Price Coats 345 • Misses' Dresses 341 • Misses' Sportswear 246 • Misses' Coats & Suits 344 • Maternity Wear 341 • Women's World 541, 546, 444 • The Collectors 711 • The Colony 744 • No. 1 Shop 442 • Coach House 446 • Town House 343 • The Ensemble Shop 242 • Attitude Shop 646 • Signature Shop 678 • Fur Salon 248 • Bridal Shop 341 • Millinery 264 • Wigs 304 • Lingerie 209 • Loungewear 209 • Body Fashions 209 • Uniform Centre 509 • Women's Shoes 238 • Slipper Bar 238 • Shoe Salon 338
College and Career Shop—Junior Dresses 241 • Junior Sportswear 346 • Junior Coats 241
Young World—Infants' Wear 210 • Children's Wear 210 • Girls' Wear 211 • Children's Hosiery 201 • Junior Shoes 239 • Boys' Clothing 232 • Students' Clothing 432 • Fourth Gear 640 • Like Young Shop 611

Third Floor

Bath Boutiques 336 • Gallery of Fine Art 376 • Gallery of Fine Furniture 770 • Furniture 270, 470 • Bedding 271 • Accent 718 • Fireplace Accessories 276 • Studio of Interior Design • Draperies 267 • Upholstery Fabrics 267 • Musical Instruments 560 • Records 560 • Steinway 360 • Floor Coverings 272 • Oriental Rugs 373 • Plumbing 456 • Home Improvements 353 • Alhambra Tea Room • Beauty Salon 213

Fourth Floor

Glassware 252 • Crystal 252 • China 252 • The Gift Shop 218 • The Bar Shop 218 • Flame and Flower 208 • Seven Seas Gift Shop 270, 619 • Bridal Registry 618 • Fashion Fabrics 233 • Creative Stitchery 224 • Bed linens 236 • Bedding and Blankets 436 • Table Linens 356 • Luggage 264 • Valley Room cafeteria

TORONTO–COLLEGE STREET, *402–448 Yonge Street (October 10, 1930)*

Basement

Soda-Luncheonette • Sporting Goods 261 • Ski Lodge • Luggage 264 • Auto Accessories 263 • Hardware 263 • Pet Supplies 253 • Toys 271 • Artists' Supplies 271 Trim-a-Home Shop 219 • Housewares 254 • Kitchen Country 254 • Electricals 277 • Unfinished Furniture 370 • Garden Grove 280 • Potting Shed 480 • Mowers and Snow Blowers 253 • Ranges and

Dishwashers 256 • Washers and Dryers 257 • Vacuum Cleaners 258 • Refrigerators and Freezers 259 • Personal Care 477 • Home Comfort 356 • Sewing Machines 570 • Furnaces 556 • Bath Boutiques 336 • Plumbing 456 • Home Improvements 353 • The Open Hearth Shop 276

Main Floor
Yonge-Hayter Wing
Lamps 377 • Entertainment Centre 260, 248, 460 • Musical Instruments 560 • Records 560 • Piano Salon 360
Yonge-College Street Wing
Hosiery 201 • Gloves 202 • Blouses 203 • Popular Price Lingerie 509 • Jewellery 215 • Silverware 515 • Clocks 215 • Cosmetics 216 • Handbags 217 • Wig Bar 222 • Fashion Accessories 262 • Notions 222 • Eaton's Flower Shop 380 • Drugs, Soaps, Sundries 212 • Pharmacy 212 • Candy Counters 214 • Cameras 512 • Stationery 208 • Social Expression Shop 208 • Calculators 306 • School and Office Supplies 206 • Seven Seas Gift Shop 270, 619 • Candle Shop 208 • Fancy Foods 579 • Cake Counter 1104K • Hostess Shop 1100H • Coins, Stamps 405 • Books 205
College-Bay Wing
Young Toronto—Junior Dresses 241 • Junior Sportswear 346 • Junior Coats 244
The Specialty Shops
The Little Salon 341, 246, 344, 541, 546, 446, 343 • The Coat Shop 444 • The Sport Shop 246, 546, 711, 744, 646, 678 • No. 1 Shop 442 • The Ensemble Shop 242 • The Specialty Fur Salon 248 • The Bridal Shop 341 • The Millinery Shop 264, 304 • The Lingerie Shop 209, 341 • The Shoe Shop 238, 338
The Men's Shops
The Men's Shop 228, 232, 233, 229, 428, 429, 529, 629, 329 • Men's Shoe Shop 237 • Tuxedo Rentals and Formal Wear • Made-To-Measure Shop 230

Second Floor
Yonge-Hayter Wing
Paint and Wallcovering 274 • Beauty Salon 213 • Dr. Horvath Portrait Studio 612
The Young Canada Shops Infants' Wear 210 • Children's Wear 210 • Girls' Wear 211 • Children's Hosiery 201 • Junior Shoes 239 • Students' Clothing 432 • Fourth Gear 640 • Like Young Shop 611

Yonge-College Street Wing
Glassware 252 • Crystal 252 • China • 252 • The Gift Shop 218 • The Bar Shop 218 • Flame and Flower (208) • Bridal Registry 618 • Fashion Fabrics 233 • Creative Stitchery 224 • Bed linens 236 • Bedding and Blankets 436 • Table Linens 356 • Draperies 267 • Upholstery Fabrics Floor Coverings 272 • Gallery of Fine Art 376 • Wall Decor 276

Third Floor
Oriental Rugs 373 • Floor Coverings 372, 273 • Customer Accounts Office • Service Bureau

Fourth Floor
Furniture 270 • Bedding 271 • Accent 718 • Ideal Canadian Home

Fifth Floor
Furniture 470 • Gallery of Fine Furniture 770 • Interior Design Bureau
Period Rooms—The King Charles Room • The Oak Room • The Pine Room • The Hatton Garden Room • Marie Antoinette's Boudoir • The Hampton Court Room • The Adam Room • The Louis XV Room • The French Provincial Room • The Modern Rooms

Sixth Floor
Executive Offices • Hospital

Seventh Floor
The Foyer • The Round Room • The Clipper • The Eaton Auditorium

VANCOUVER, *515 West Hastings Street (December 1, 1948)*

Food Floor
Foodateria 284 • Fancy Foods 579 • Cake Counter 1104K • Hostess Shop 1100H • Malted Milk Bar
Lower Main Floor
Eaton's Flower Shop 380 • Garden Grove 280 • Potting Shed 480 • Mowers and Snow Blowers 253 • Cafeteria
Eaton's Bargain Centre

Main Floor

Hosiery 201 • Gloves 202 • Blouses 203 • Popular Price Lingerie 509 • Jewellery 215 • Silverware 515 • Clocks 215 • Cosmetics 216 • Luggage 264 • Handbags 217 • Wig Bar 222 • Fashion Accessories 262 • Notions 222 • Drugs, Soaps, Sundries 212 • Pharmacy 212 • Candy Counters 214 • Cameras 512 • Stationery 208 • Social Expression Shop 208 • Calculators 306 • School and Office Supplies 206 • Coins, Stamps 405 • Books 205 • Men's Dress Furnishings 228 • Men's Casual Furnishings 428 • Men's Hats 237 • Men's Clothing 229, 429 • The Pine Room 629 • Timothy E. 329 • Tuxedo Rentals and Formal Wear • Men's Footwear 237 • Men's Casual Clothing 429 • Adam Shop 529 • Abstract Shop 232, 332 • Made-To-Measure Shop 230 • Luggage 264 • Sporting Goods 261 • Ski Lodge 261

Mezzanine

Hearing Aid Centre 421 • Service Bureau • Post Office

Second Floor

Popular Price Dresses 345 • Popular Price Sportswear 745 • Popular Price Coats 345 • Misses' Dresses 341 • Misses' Sportswear 246 • Misses' Coats & Suits 344 • Maternity Wear 341 • Your Size Shop 541, 546, 444 • The Collectors 711 • The Colony 744 • Number One 442 • Caravan Shop 446 • Townhouse 343 • French Room 242 • Attitude Shop 646 • Signature Shop 678 • Fur Salon 248 • Bridal Shop 341 • Millinery 264 • Wigs 304 • Lingerie 209 • Loungewear 209 • Body Fashions 209 • Uniform Centre 509 • Women's Shoes 238 • Slipper Bar 238 • Shoe Salon 338 • Young Flair Junior Dresses 241 • Young Flair Junior Sportswear 346 • Young Flair Junior Coats 241

Young World—Infants' Wear 210 • Children's Wear 210 • Girls' Wear 211 • Children's Hosiery 201 • Junior Shoes 239 • Students' Clothing 432 • Fourth Gear 640 • Like Young Shop 611

Third Floor

Fashion Fabrics 233 • Creative Stitchery 224 • Bed Linens 236 • Bedding and Blankets 436 • Bath Boutiques 336 • Table Linens 356 • Catalogue Order Office

Fourth Floor

Housewares 254 • Kitchen Country 254 • Electricals 277 • The Open Hearth Shop 276 • Gallery of Fine Art 376 • Wall Decor 276 • Plumbing 456 • Ranges and Dishwashers 256 • Washers and Dryers 257 • Vacuum Cleaners 258 • Refrigerators and Freezers 259 • Personal Care 477 • Home

Comfort 356 • Furnaces 556 • Sewing Machines 570 • Hardware 263 • Auto Accessories 263 • Pet Supplies 253 • Toys 271 • Artists' Supplies 271 • Lamps 377 • Trim-a-Home Shop 219 • Unfinished Furniture 370 • Beauty Salon

Fifth Floor
Paint and Wallcovering 274 • Draperies 267 • Upholstery Fabrics 267 • Floor Coverings 272 • Oriental Rugs 373 • Entertainment Centre 260, 248, 460 • Musical Instruments 560 • Records 560 • Steinway 360 • Customer Accounts Office

Sixth Floor
The Marine Room Restaurant • Glassware 252 • Crystal 252 • China 252 • The Bar Shop 218 • Flame and Flower 208 • The Gift Shop 270, 619 • Bridal Registry 618 • Gallery of Fine Furniture 770 • Furniture 270, 470 • Bedding 271 • Redi-Beds 271 • Accent 718 • Studio of Interior Design • Home Improvements 353

Seventh Floor
Executive Offices

VICTORIA, *1150 Douglas Street (December 1, 1948)*

Basement—Douglas Street
Foodateria • Fancy Foods 579 • Malted Milk Bar
Basement—Government Street Annex
Coffee Corner • Auto Accessories 263 • Hardware 263 • Pet Supplies 253 • Toys 271 • Artists' Supplies 271 • Paint and Wallcovering 274 • Furnaces 556 • Plumbing 456 • Home Improvements 353
The Bargain Highway—Eaton's Lower-Price Store

Main Floor—Douglas Street
Hosiery 201 • Gloves 202 • Blouses 203 • Popular Price Lingerie 509 • Jewellery 215 • Clocks 215 • Cosmetics 216 • Handbags 217 • Wig Bar 222 • Fashion Accessories 262 • Stationery 208 • Social Expression Shop 208 • Calculators 306 • School and Office Supplies 206 • Notions 222 • Eaton's Flower Shop 380 • Drugs, Soaps, Sundries 212 • Pharmacy • Cake Counter 1104K • Hostess Shop 1100H • Candy Counters 214 • Cameras 512 • Coins, Stamps 405 • Books 205 212 • Men's Dress Furnishings 228 •

Men's Casual Furnishings 428 • Men's Hats 237 • Men's Clothing 229, 429 • The Pine Room 629 • Timothy E. 329 • Tuxedo Rentals and Formal Wear • Men's Footwear 237 • Men's Casual Clothing 429 • Adam Shop 529 • Abstract Shop 232, 332 • Made-To-Measure Shop 230

Main Floor—Government Street Annex

Silverware 515 • Glassware 252 • Crystal 252 • China 252 • The Gift Shop 218 • The Bar Shop 218 • Flame and Flower 208 • Gift Court 270, 619 • Bridal Registry 618 Shop • Housewares 254 • Kitchen Country 254 • Electricals 277 • Unfinished Furniture 370 • Ranges and Dishwashers 256 • Washers and Dryers 257 • Vacuum Cleaners 258 • Refrigerators and Freezers 259 • Home Comfort 356 • Entertainment Centre 260, 248, 460 • Musical Instruments 560 • Records 560 • Pianos, Organs 360 • Garden Grove 280 • Potting Shed 480 • Mowers and Snow Blowers 253 • Personal Care 477 • Sporting Goods 261 • Ski Lodge 261 • Luggage 264 • Trim-a-Home Shop 219 • Red Basket Shop 208

Second Floor

Misses' Dresses 341 • Misses' Sportswear 246 • Misses' Coats & Suits 344 • Maternity Shop 341 • Your Size Shop 541, 546, 444 • The Collectors 711 • The Colony 744 • Number One 442 • Caravan Shop 446 • Townhouse 343 • The French Room 242 • Attitude Shop 646 • Signature Shop 678 • Fur Salon 248 • Bridal Shop 341, 342 • Millinery 264 • Wigs 304 • Lingerie 209 • Loungewear 209 • Body Fashions 209 • Uniform Centre 509 Young Flair Junior Dresses 241 • Young Flair Junior Sportswear 346 • Young Flair Junior Coats 241 • Popular Price Dresses 345 • Popular Price Sportswear 745 • Popular Price Coats 345 • Women's Shoes 238 • Slipper Bar 238 • Shoe Salon 338

Second Floor—Government Street Annex

Gallery of Fine Furniture 770 • Furniture 270, 470 • Bedding 271 • Bedding 271 • Redi-Beds 271 • Floor Coverings 272 • Oriental Rugs 373Accent 718 • Fireplace Accessories 276 • Studio of Interior Design Lamps 377 • Wall Decor 276 • Gallery of Fine Art 376 • Beauty Salon 223

Third Floor

Draperies 267 • Upholstery Fabrics 267 • Bed linens 236 • Bedding and Blankets 436 • Table Linens 356 • Bath Boutiques 336 • Sewing Machines 570 • Fashion Fabrics 233 • Creative Stitchery 224

Young World—Infants' Wear 210 • Children's Wear 210 • Girls' Wear 211 • Children's Hosiery 201 • Junior Shoes 239 • Boys' Clothing • Students' Clothing 432 • Fourth Gear 640 • Like Young Shop 611

Fourth Floor
Victoria Room Restaurant • Hearing Aid Centre 421 • Optical 221

Fifth Floor
Offices

VANCOUVER PACIFIC CENTRE, *Georgia and Granville Streets (February 7, 1973)*

Mall Level
Popular Price Dresses 345 • Popular Price Sportswear 745 • Popular Price Coats 345 • Women's Shoes 238 • Slipper Bar 238 • Shoe Salon 338 • Candy Counters 214 • Cameras 512 • Coins, Stamps 405 • Books 205 • Luggage 264 • Fancy Foods 579 • Cake Counter 1104K • Hostess Shop 1100H • Snack Bar Counter
Eaton's Budget Store

First Floor
Hosiery 201 • Gloves 202 • Blouses 203 • Popular Price Lingerie 509 • Jewellery 215 • Clocks 215 • Cosmetics 216 • Handbags 217 • Wig Bar 222 • Fashion Accessories 262 • Men's Dress Furnishings 228 • Men's Casual Furnishings 428 • Men's Hats 237 • Men's Clothing 229, 429 • The Pine Room 629 • Timothy E. 329 • Tuxedo Rentals and Formal Wear • Men's Footwear 237 • Men's Casual Clothing 429 • Adam Shop 529 • Abstract Shop 232, 332 • Made-To-Measure Shop 230 • Sporting Goods 261 • Ski Lodge
Young Flair—Junior Dresses 241 • Junior Sportswear 346 • Junior Coats 241

Second Floor
Misses' Dresses 341 • Misses' Sportswear 246 • Misses' Coats & Suits 344 • Maternity Shop 341 • Your Size Shop 541, 546, 444 • The Collectors 711 • The Colony 744 • Number One 442 • Caravan Shop 446 • Townhouse 343 • The French Room 242 • Attitude Shop 646 • Signature Shop 678 • Fur Salon 248 • Bridal Shop 341, 342 • Millinery 264 • Wigs 304 • Lingerie 209 • Loungewear 209 • Body Fashions 209 • Uniform Centre 509

Third Floor
Stationery 208 • Social Expression Shop 208 • Calculators 306 • School and Office Supplies 206 • Notions 222 • Eaton's Flower Shop 380 • Drugs, Soaps, Sundries 212 • Pharmacy 212 • Auto Accessories 263 • Hardware 263 • Pet

Supplies 253 • Toys 271 • Artists' Supplies 271 • Paint and Wallcovering 274 • Trim-a-Home Shop 219 • Red Basket Shop • Housewares 254 • Kitchen Country 254 • Electricals 277 • Unfinished Furniture 370 • Garden Grove 280 • Potting Shed 480 • Mowers and Snow Blowers 253 • Personal Care 477 • Furnaces 556 • Plumbing 456 • Home Improvements 353 • Sewing Machines 570 • Glassware 252 • Crystal 252 • China 252 • The Gift Shop 218 • The Bar Shop 218 • Flame and Flower 208 • Gift Court 270, 619 • Bridal Registry 618 • Fashion Fabrics 233 • Creative Stitchery 224 • Beauty Salon 223 • Hearing Aid Centre 421 • Optical 221
Young World—Infants' Wear 210 • Children's Wear 210 • Girls' Wear 211 • Children's Hosiery 201 • Junior Shoes 239 • Boys' Clothing • Students' Clothing 432 • Fourth Gear 640 • One Step Up Shop 611

Fourth Floor
Lamps 377 • Wall Decor 276 • Gallery of Fine Art 376 • Silverware 515 • Draperies 267 • Upholstery Fabrics 267 • Bed linens 236 • Bedding and Blankets 436 • Table Linens 356 • Bath Boutiques 336 • Floor Coverings 272 • Oriental Rugs 373 • Marine Room Restaurant • Portrait Studio

Fifth Floor
Ranges and Dishwashers 256 • Washers and Dryers 257 • Vacuum Cleaners 258 • Refrigerators and Freezers 259 • Home Comfort 356 • Entertainment Centre 260, 248, 460 • Musical Instruments 560 • Records 560 • Pianos, Organs 360 • Gallery of Fine Furniture 770 • Furniture 270, 470 • Bedding 271 • Bedding 271 • Redi-Beds 271 • Accent 718 • Fireplace Accessories 276 • Studio of Interior Design

TORONTO EATON CENTRE, *Yonge and Dundas Streets (February 10, 1977)*

3 Below
Young Men's Shop • Abstract Shop • Hairworks • Records • Impulse • Miss Selfridge Shop • Pizza 'n' Subs
Young Toronto Shop—Junior Dresses • Junior Sportswear • Junior Coats • Shoes

Level 1, Subway
The Fashion Market—Popular Price Dresses • Popular Price Sportswear • Popular Price Coats • Accessories
Housewares • Plants and Flowers • Housewares • Hardware • Drugs • Repair Centre • Health and Beauty Aids • Fine Food Shops • Bakery • Bites 'n' Nibbles Restaurant

Level 2, Subway
Men's Furnishings • Men's Casual Wear • Men's Clothing • Adam Shop • Timothy E. • Made-to-Measure Shop • The Pine Room • Men's Shoes • Luggage • Headquarters • Stationery • Cameras • Books • Sir John's Restaurant

Main Floor
Cosmetics • Lingerie • Body Fashions • Women's Shoes • Sportswear • Accessories • Handbags • Jewellery • Watches • Marco Polo Gift Shop • The Patio • The Dundas Room Restaurant

Second Floor
Dresses • Sportswear • Coats • Attitude Shop • Hairworks • Number 1 Shop • Ports International • Bridal Salon • Signature • Millinery • Beauty Salon • Elizabeth Arden Red Door Salon • Specialized Sizes • Fur Salon

Third Floor
Infants' Wear • Children's Wear • Girls' Wear • Children's Shoes • Boys' Wear • Fashion Fabrics • Sewing Machines • Art Needlework • Artist Supplies • Adult Games • Toys • Records • Sporting Goods

Fourth Floor
Lamps • Pictures and Mirrors • Art Gallery • Draperies • Upholstery Fabrics • Interior Decorating • Bed Linens • Bedding and Blankets • Table Linens • Bath Boutique • Silverware • China • Glassware • Gift Shop • Clocks • Artificial Flowers • Broadloom • Oriental Rugs • Gift Wrap • Bridal Registry

Fifth Floor
Furniture • Gallery of Fine Furniture • Colonial Furniture • Accent Shop • Sleep Shop

Sixth Floor
Appliances • TV Stereo • Business Centre • Pianos, Organs 360 • Portrait Studio • Post Office • Eaton's Travel Service • Optical and Hearing Aids • Marine Room Restaurant • Staff Restaurant

Seventh Floor
Eaton's Budget Annex (Later) • Offices

Appendix D

More Eaton's Stories

Lifelong Friendships between Four Men Begin at *Eaton's Catalogue* in Moncton, New Brunswick

It was the early sixties when three young men named Ron, Don and John were working at *Eaton's Catalogue* in Moncton, New Brunswick. In the beginning they did not know one another but that soon changed. Eaton's was well known for organizing recreational activities for their employees. One such activity that Eaton's decided to organize was to form a hockey team. Ron, Don and John were all interested in hockey so their paths crossed when they all joined Eaton's hockey team.

Not only did these young men enjoy one another's company in the hockey arenas during that first winter hockey season but they continued their friendships onto the golf course the following summer. They had all decided to take up golf through yet another recreational activity organized through Eaton's. John remembers that his very first golf game was when he participated in an Eaton golf tournament where he played with both Ron and Don.

Within a couple of years another young man named Dave joined the hockey team and soon Ron, Don, John and Dave became a foursome at hockey arenas and golf courses. The Eaton's hockey team joined the Moncton Commercial Hockey League and during the winter of 1966–67 the Eaton's team won the league championship. Ron, Don, John and Dave were all members of that hockey team. One summer John and Dave played golf once per week as a team of two in an Eaton's golf program. As a culminating activity at the end of the summer season Eaton's sponsored a full day golf tournament where prizes were awarded and a banquet was held. Ron, Don, John and Dave continued playing sports together through Eaton's for several years until some of them became employed by other companies.

The four men kept in touch and got together on many occasions while busy working and raising their families. This included going on several fishing trips together over the years. During this time Ron and John also coached minor hockey together for eleven years.

In the late nineties Ron, Don, John and Dave decided to get together and golf at least once a year. This continued until 2012 when Dave, the youngest of the group, began to have health issues. During Dave's illness, Ron, Don, John and Dave became even closer. They regularly went out for coffee as a group and went to hockey games on occasion. At least once per month all four men and their partners met for breakfast. These breakfasts became a popular occasion on everyone's calendar. Throughout this time Ron, Don and John supported Dave with regular visits, driving him to appointments and helping him out as much as possible. Dave passed away in 2013. Ron, Don and John will miss Dave but will cherish the many memories that they share of the times they spent together. Ron, Don and John continue to get together and enjoy one another's company. They also plan to play golf together for as long as possible. Their friendship began almost fifty years ago and to think that it all started at Eaton's with their employee recreational activities!

—John Coates

MY FIRST DAY AT EATON'S

E.C. Masters joined Eaton's staff just a few days before the Moncton Mail Order opened in 1920 and retired after celebrating fifty years with the company. His memoirs of the day he started with Eaton's are a unique portrait of working for the T. Eaton Co. Limited as a young man in the interwar period.

I arrived at the employment office at about 7:40 a.m., dressed in a suit which had knee-length pants, long black stockings and laced boots. My name was called out by the employment man, and he went over the application and said I was to work in the general office as a messenger. I was taken to the time office, given a card and number, and then went to the general office on the second floor.

I reported to a man in the general office and was told what my duties would be. He stressed to me that when a buzzer rang twice, I was to go to the private office to see what was wanted.

During the morning I opened mail and sorted out the letters and invoices and stamped on the back of each one with a stamp showing date and time received in the general office; then handed letters to the correspondence section and invoices to the invoice section.

There was a briefing given by a man from Toronto on "the process of an invoice" from the time it left the supplier until it was filed away in the vault.

I sorted out the mail and telegrams and proceeded to deliver them through the building to the various departments, but I did not know where they all were. Just about the time I was ready to leave for the departments, the buzzer rang twice and the boss said "go to the private office." I went down an aisle, knocked on the door, and a gruff voice said "come in!" I opened the door and was curious as I wondered what a private office looked like inside.

A man sitting behind a big desk said in a loud voice, "where have you been? It has taken you so long to get here." By that time, I was nearly under the carpet on the floor. After I was given the message, I can assure you I went out of that office faster than I went in.

Delivering the mail and the telegrams took up the balance of that morning. We then went to lunch from 12 to 1 p.m.

In the afternoon the invoices were numbered with a machine and all entered in a large book and given to the ledger keepers who in turn sent them back to be delivered to the departments. After all mail was delivered, outgoing mail was stamped and sealed and put in a mail bag to be taken to the Post Office. All mail going to the Company in Toronto was put in a large leather case and when closed, it was sealed with red sealing wax which was imprinted with the Diamond "E" so that the seal would have to be broken in order to get into it. It was my job to carry this bag over to the express office and get a receipt for it after the close of a business day.

That was my first day at Eaton's!

Did you know that:

Eaton's first cafeteria for employees was located on the third floor of the subway block on the North side of Main Street.

Eaton's had their own telegraph operator and direct wire to Toronto which was located on the third floor.

Matches, cigarettes, and pipe tobacco had to be left in your locker with your coat.

Teamsters were not allowed to have a whip when driving horses.

When you were sick and sent home by the nurse, you were taken home in what was called a "messenger car" driven by a uniformed chauffeur.

A man wearing an Eaton uniform opened and closed the doors for customers.

The first lunch room in the main building was in the basement where the supply stockroom is. Lunch was served for customers and employees from 11:30 to 2:00 p.m. and there were no coffee breaks then.

You will recognize that I had a particular liking for the Lunch Room when I mention that, at a later date, I married one of the staff from that department!

My first weekly pay with the company was $10; by 1941 it was $25.

A life insurance policy valued at $1000.00 was provided with the premium paid by the company for the first year.

Employees had to provide their own lead pencils. Ink was supplied by the company. Green ink had very restricted use.

The mode of travel to work was by walking or by street car. Snow shoes were very often used to get through the heavy snow which of course was not ploughed in any way from the streets!

—E.C. Masters (submitted by Margaret [Masters] Fullerton)

MY UNCLE ALBERT

I was born in 1943 on the river which goes by the same name as the Acadian community of Memramcook, 12 miles southeast of Moncton N.B. My mother was Melina Maria Girouard whose only sister was my "Aunt Elsie" (Elise Marie) Girouard born in 1906. In the mid 1930s Elsie married Albert Grey, born in approximately 1901 and named after the late Queen Victoria's consort, Albert.

I knew Uncle Albert more in the period 1949 to 1956 when I would visit him at the Eaton's Department Store. In the 1960s I paid some visits at the couple's Braemar Drive home and sporadically at Eaton's Store. After the Men's Clothing Department moved to Highfield Square in the late 1970s I did visit Uncle Albert at the Store location at least once a year until his retirement from Eaton's employment in the mid 1980s.

Here is my recollection which memory will allow of the T. Eaton Company in Moncton and Uncle Albert's presence there: Albert was always happy with his work environment, which was very clean, well lit, and staff could serve French language clients in their mother tongue. He went to Toronto in the spring of 1939 for training. In the mid-1990s after Aunt Elsie passed away, he called me to his Braemar Dr. home to give me an "authorized" close up picture of the Queen Mother who, together with her husband King George VI, had visited Toronto in June 1939.

Albert was always keen to point out how on price and quality, Eaton's had the best lines of product and excellent customer service.

—Jean-Paul Bourque

At the T. Eaton Catalogue

I thought I would share my fond memories of my time spent at the T. Eaton Catalogue in Moncton. This was my first job right out of High School in 1973.

Thanks to Alvin Warren, the window washer at the time, and a family friend, who kept his eye on the job situation, as he knew I was looking. I started out in the mailroom. We weren't allowed to tie up or use the elevators, so we climbed five flights of stairs every day. The spookiest delivery was to the basement.

After a short time I was promoted to the Accounting Section working under Ms. Buck. We worked on large machines inputting debits and credits for supplier accounts. Some of the suppliers were from exotic places overseas. I also had an opportunity to be trained by Mrs. Rasmussen to work on the "Telex" machine. This was also a large machine that we fed thin strips of paper like ribbon with holes punched with messages that were going to head office in Toronto.

On our breaks we could go the lunchroom provided for us, or go to Woolworth's just around the corner. I still remember how good the tea biscuits were to this day. I loved shopping in the bargain basement where they sold "seconds" which had small damages or old stock. I still have a small orange footstool with the price in marker on the bottom for $10.99. Eaton's always had the reputation for good quality items.

I was there when they closed in 1976. Mr. Lockhart and Mr. Lockwood did their best with job placement for everyone. I thoroughly enjoyed my time there and have never felt the large family feeling with any jobs since then.

—Janice Jones

GOODS SATISFACTORY OR MONEY REFUNDED?

It was in the late 50s, and I was 11 years old. My mother asked me to go to Eaton's to return a pair of boots which were too big for me. I was very happy to run this errand for her because she trusted me with this responsibility and I was allowed to miss an afternoon of school.

So, after lunch I got on the bus and headed for Eaton's. I immediately went to the Shoe Department and stood near a sales clerk and waited for her to serve me. I was small for my age, shy and quiet. When the 1st sales clerk didn't notice me, I went and stood next to another sales clerk, waiting to be served. In the meantime, my attention was captivated by the "whoosh" sound made by the capsules of money being sucked up in the tubes. I moved to my 3rd sales clerk, then tried the first one again. Four hours later, finally a sales clerk came over to me only to tell me that the store was closed and I would have to leave. I was crushed; and needless to say, my mother was not impressed.

—A.G. Gollan

A FEW RECOLLECTIONS

I did not have the opportunity to know my maternal grandfather however my mother told me he moved from Nova Scotia to Moncton to work on the building of the Eaton's store. I believe he was an electrician.

As a child I lived in the downtown area and Eaton's seemed to be a part of my daily life. I would pass it every day on my way to school and would often go in one door, walk through the store and go out the other door to avoid the elements. The first sign of Christmas was the *Eaton's Catalogue*, always very exciting. Eaton's would be the only store back in the fifties to put Santa and his sleigh on the roof and have a Santa to visit in the store. Eaton's Toyland was magical to me. I also remember a constant stream of buses being in front of the store picking up the workers.

The thing I remember the most which would be unimaginable today would be the line-up of baby carriages with babies left in them while parents were inside shopping! Strangers would rock the carriages and feed the babies if they were crying, and a bottle was available. I do not know when this all stopped or if there was a specific reason. I was born in 1950 and remember it well. I moved from the downtown area in 1958 and back again in 1963.

I do not recall if the practice was prevalent then. My mother told me she heard a child had put ink on a baby's face, but I do not know if this was true.

Also, my father told me that he purchased my mother's wedding band from Eaton's. She wore it for the 65 years they were married and never once took it off her finger. I enjoyed many shopping trips to both the old and later the new Eaton's store and, like most Monctonians, was very sad when it closed.

—Sherry Cormier

MY FAMILY AND EATON'S

My grandfather, Jesse F. Parsons, of Nova Scotia, went out to Western Canada about 1908 on the "Harvest Trains" as did so many Maritimers during that time of year. He stayed out there, met his future wife, and worked on the construction of the Provincial Legislature Buildings in Regina, Saskatchewan. In 1919 the opportunity came up to move to Moncton to be a superintendent on the construction of the new Eaton mail-order business. So he moved back east with his young family to start the job. My father Lloyd Parsons was born 1919 during the construction year in Moncton.

Shortly after Eaton's catalogue centre opened, Jesse established his own company Parsons Construction Co. Limited (it started as Parsons & Ede, but the partnership only lasted a year) that was hired to build the Eaton retail store (about 1926). Eaton was a huge employer in the area and most Moncton families have a story that relates to work there. My own mother was a huge fan of the Eaton Bargain Basement needing to clothe six children—and it was the only one of its kind in New Brunswick.

In the 1940s, my father Lloyd began his career with Parsons Construction. He had graduated from Mount Allison University, Nova Scotia Institute of Technology (Civil Engineering), and then was the first Canadian to get a Master of Science in Building Engineering and Construction from Massachusetts Institute of Technology. By the late 1960s there was a desire to update Eaton's, so Parsons Construction Co. (under Lloyd) was contracted to build the "new" Eaton's at Highfield and Main Streets in Moncton.

Eventually the Bay took over that Highfield location, and in 2012 it finally closed. There is no longer an Eaton presence in Moncton physically, but everyone carries the presence of Eaton's with him with many interesting memories.

—Lynn Parsons Belliveau

PETALS THE CLOWN

I have so many fine memories of Eaton's, but I bet mine are unique! Of course, growing up in Regina, I rode the train around Toyland as a child. For 5 cents you got to travel through Christmas scenes, a winter wonderland with penguins, and nursery rhymes, and at the end, you got a present—usually a board game or a book.

However, my favourite memories of Eaton's were as "Petals the Clown." I was hired by the store to entertain children attending the Santa Claus breakfast with a magic show. I got a kick out of strolling the through the store, doing magic tricks, and my favourite was to ask children to help me find a baby reindeer that got lost. I'd get them to look in my big clown-pants pocket, where I had a live rabbit hiding. I could convince them that reindeer had fluffy tails and my rabbits Snowball or Ginger were the baby I was looking for. For the 125th anniversary in 1994, I stood outside on 11th Avenue in front of the Cornwall Centre store with my honker and asked people to "honk for Eaton's." I always went in the back door of Eaton's, being a hired entertainer, but remained good friends with everyone there—that was Eaton's!

—Jim Toth

MEMORIES OF EATON'S

Several years ago I was attending a philanthropic event in Toronto, Ontario at which John Craig Eaton and his wife Sally Horsfall Eaton were being honoured. After the event I had the opportunity to speak with Mrs. Eaton. As always, she was gracious and engaging!

We talked about the Moncton store and without the slightest hesitation, Mrs. Eaton commented that the Moncton store had been very good for them and to them. She spoke highly of the dedication of the employees and the patronage of the public that really went far beyond Moncton to all of New Brunswick, northern Nova Scotia and Prince Edward Island through catalogue sales. She also remarked with a pleasant smile that it was a sad time for the family when the catalogue division and finally the retail store was shut down. Sad because it impacted so many loyal employees and shoppers. A delightful conversation to be sure!

Personally, with the closure of the Eaton's store, although The Bay tried for a time to replace it, but failed, the availability and selection of better quality merchandise in Moncton became a thing of the past for a very long time. Brand name, as well as the very good Eaton private label merchandise, and always at a good price are still missing in Moncton. And let's not forget that Eaton service—second to none!

For as long as I can remember, the same Eaton employees were there to greet me and serve me and always with a smile! In fact, I smile as I remember a particular clerk in ladies cosmetics—always the same up style with her hair that I am sure was stiffer than stiff, the bright red lipstick, and the red rouge on her cheeks—and always the same captivating smile and magnetic personality! Today, several decades after Eaton's in Moncton, one can still find those faithful employees speaking well of the Eaton family, and the shopper still wishing that Eaton's was still around!

—Scott Ryder

DOWNTOWN WILL NEVER BE THE SAME

Eaton's was a much valued store and is missed by those here in Thunder Bay Ont. that still recall its existence. My father only allowed my mother to shop at stores such as Eaton's, Chapple's, and McNulty's—because their products were Canadian or European made. From going down to the basement to the snack bar as a kid, to choosing china and glassware for your wedding registry were examples of the wonderful things one did at Eaton's. There was never any dispute over the quality of the merchandise sold at the Eaton's store.

The window displays, especially at Christmas was always something everyone looked forward to seeing when shopping downtown. Our downtown area is at present being revitalized, but it will never be the same without Eaton's.

—Lee Harris

HOW I BECAME AN EATON'S KID

My father, Bruce Knox, began working in the T. Eaton Co. service station, at 7th Ave & Broad St., in Regina on July 15th, 1929. He was 20 years old. He was a farmer's son but had no interest in farming. His passion was cars and people. He was connected, off and on, in managing the Eaton's service station until December 29, 1943, when he opened up his own station at 9th Ave. & Albert St. I have lots of stories of being an "Eaton's" kid plus I worked in the shoe department on Saturdays when I was going to school.

The glitzy "new" Eaton's store in Regina certainly didn't have the warmth and "down home" feeling the old store had. Alas, times change and so does merchandise. No horse harness or drill bits were ever displayed in the Cornwall Centre store. No x-ray machine to determine whether shoes were the right size either.

—Evelyn Rogers

The Day Eaton's Left Charlottetown

In the 1990s the Charlottetown Eaton's store was a thriving retail outlet. It held a prime space on Kent Street. It stretched back to Fitzroy Street, and was a through traffic lane for anyone walking Downtown. It had a large parking lot, and was just a dandy spot in the downtown area. It also was a must-shop spot for all the business people who had offices in the downtown area and who had noon times to pursue the three levels of goods. Everyone was proud of Eaton's as *our* department store and it was a special place to shop, a busy, busy weekday centre.

While serving on City Council during that time, I remember word coming that Eaton's stores were being closed across the country, and that a team from Eaton's management was coming to Charlottetown to assess the store and decide its future. Because we understood our store was turning a profit when so many other Eaton's branches were having difficult times, we felt sure there would be a decision to keep it open.

The assessment crew arrived early on a Saturday morning and headed to the store. The business crowd was home for the weekend and the town shopping crowd were not yet out. The committee found the store wasn't busy, there were only a few cars in the parking lot, and few people in the store. There may have been other reasons but these factors were their talking points after they visited the site, and then just a few days following this special visit it was announced the Charlottetown store would close.

That was a sad day for the city.

—Sibyl Cutcliffe

Our Dad, the Eaton's Repair Man

The T. Eaton Company opened their store in what was then Port Arthur in 1938. My father took radio repair courses from the Radio College of Canada and started working for Eaton's in 1955 until his retirement in 1987, when televisions were just coming in that could not be repaired.

Dad was the only radio repairman for Eaton's for both Port Arthur and Fort William. He had a repair shop in the Eaton's store and the basement of our home and he was also required to go into people's homes and repair the radios. When television came into being, dad taught himself to repair televisions by buying a kit and building a television for our home. At that time a television was mostly just tubes and wires. We had a motorized aerial on our house and in turning the aerial we could pick up Green Bay, Wisconsin fairly clearly, but other stations would come in snowy and not very clear.

As a young boy, I spent a fair amount of time in the Eaton's store and I remember that for many years, there were no cash registers in the store. When a purchase was made, the clerk would insert the cash she received, along with purchase slip into a glass tube about the size of a pop can that had rubber washers on each end. The clerk would then put this tube into an air tube system and this would be received by office staff upstairs. The office person would then put the correct change back into the tube and return it to the clerk in the right department and this would then be given to the customer.

As I got a bit older I did some work in the Eaton's warehouse, before moving on to other work. The cities of Port Arthur and Fort William amalgamated in 1970 to become what is now The City of Thunder Bay, and the Eaton's store closed in 1997.

—Allan Marshall

The Perils of Being a Delivery Man

I was a delivery driver for the T. Eaton Company in Thunder Bay, Ontario in the mid-1970s. The company had a sale on single beds for $99.00 and we were very busy with deliveries. I had one order with specific instruction in bold red letters to deliver before noon. Of course, due to heavy volume, we arrived at 3:00 pm. The address was familiar to me in some way and kept nagging at me but didn't become clear to me until I rang the doorbell and a blonde woman in a hot pink bathrobe answered and asked me to put the mattress in what in normal circumstances would have been the living room. After I did so, I rushed out to the truck to get the box spring and to tell my 18-year-old helper to come with me. The look on his face when he realized we had delivered the premium T. Eaton Co. Limited special bed to the local house of ill repute was priceless. By the way, we did not receive a tip.

—Jack Wall

MUM'S MEMORIES OF EATON'S

Eaton's held a special bond for my mother, Brenda (MacDougall) Fong. She is now 79 and lives in a nursing home in Halifax, Nova Scotia. She had a stroke but she has learned to write with her left hand.

She was born and raised in MacDougall's Settlement which is sixteen miles north of Moncton near Irishtown. Her father was a farmer, and he and the family would go to Moncton once weekly so that he could sell his produce and wares at the farmer's market. As a treat, she and her younger brother Bill would visit the Eaton's department store each week. Although visiting the city itself was exciting for my Mum, she commented that one of her fondest childhood memories was witnessing the magical display at Eaton's Toyland. One year, there was a travelling exhibit of dolls from the nation of France given to Princess Elizabeth of Great Britain before she became Queen Elizabeth II. The exhibit came to Eaton's in Moncton and my Mum recalls standing behind a long roped off section with a large crowd of children and adults to view the magnificent collection. Mum was in awe of the immaculate detail on the dolls' faces and dresses. She apparently was clutching an informative brochure behind her back when a passerby snatched it out of her hand. He explained that he just wanted to read it to see why such a large crowd of people had gathered. She was relieved when he returned it to her.

Finally, Mum has fond memories of eating lunch at Eaton's. She and her brother would eat at a long counter. Just beyond was a rather fancy dining room with white linen. Within the dining room, she described a special area for the bosses and top officials from various departments.

Mum was quite saddened by the closing of Eaton's. It was a store that left her with vivid pictures of her childhood and the years following.

—Peter M. Fong

I Was a Mystery Shopper

My husband and I live in Surrey, BC but we were both born and raised in Sudbury. We lived there for fifty-odd years and raised both our children there. As a little girl in Sudbury, I recall my mother shopping at Eaton's, especially at Christmas time when she would get off the bus in Garson, loaded down with numerous Eaton's shopping bags. My heart beat rapidly with such excitement! For in those bags were all our gifts (all six kids). She always said you could count on Eaton's for quality and style. She passed this message on to us and therefore we shopped there too.

I must look up what year it was that I was a mystery shopper for Eaton's, and I enjoyed it very much. None of the staff knew I was a mystery shopper, but once a week you could count on me shopping in the store either when it was on Durham Street or in the Sudbury City Centre after 1975. I have kept a copy of their last catalogue in 1976 in my memorabilia, which also includes my old Eaton's charge card, bags, boxes, and even a golf ball!

—Ethel Sabourin

The Treasure that Was Eaton's of Montréal

My mom had only one credit card all her life long, and it was to Eaton's, which she would use every summer to buy her 4 children all their new school clothes annually for years. We lived in Québec and always went to the downtown Montréal Store. I loved the elevators and the attendants who would announce both in English and French which floor we were stopping at. I remember getting many wonderful things there but my first personal purchase was a Rubik's Cube that I bought in the huge toy section.

In the store was a plaque with the names of the WWII family members of employees who were killed in action and I can't tell you how awed I was when I found my great uncle's name there. I don't know where that plaque now resides but I do hope it is treated as the treasure it is.

I am glad that I was able to bring my son there once before it closed (I now live on Cape Cod in Massachusetts). There are so many more treasured memories associated with Eaton's throughout my life. They are that much more special as I age.

—Lori Williams

Velma and Maurice Van Buekenhout celebrate Maurice's retirement from Eaton's in 1992 with their family. *Courtesy of Guy Van Buekenhout.*

HOW I MET MY HUSBAND OF SIXTY-TWO YEARS AT EATON'S

When I was growing up on a farm near Dysart, Saskatchewan, my dad would rent a piece of pasture land in the Qu'Appelle valley near the water where we took the cattle each spring to pasture, and bring them home in the fall. It was a lot of work, but it paid off. When I was old enough to ride a horse, one of my jobs was to go down to the pasture and check on the cattle and make sure they were all there. When I wasn't able to find all of them, I would go to the large hunting lodge that was on the property and ask the people there if they could help me find the cattle.

On most weekends, when I went there, I was greeted by a tall, friendly gentleman by the name of Mr. Harry Maltby, who happened to be the store manager of the T. Eaton Co. Limited store in Regina. Mr. Maltby and his friends would come out on weekends, to rest from work and so some fishing and hunting in the area. My dad and Mr. Maltby became friends when he was asked to be Mr. Maltby's hunting guide in the fall when there were wild geese and ducks in the area. I remember seeing the two of them coming home to the farm with ducks and geese hanging from the lengths of their guns and they were very happy.

Mr. Maltby enjoyed coming to our farm and got to know us children very well. He never left for home before my mom would go and fill a cardboard box full of fresh butter, cream, and eggs for him and his buddies to enjoy. When we'd stop over at the lodge, he would give us treats, but our favourite was when they would leave to go back to the city; we would go to their garbage stand and cut the labels off of all the canned food they had used. It was a novelty to us as we only used food that mom would prepare in glass sealers from our garden. We would paste the labels in our scrapbooks and enjoyed looking at them because they were so colourful.

Our family friendship continued throughout my school years, and when I turned 17, and passed grade 9, my dad told me it was time for me to go to work. One weekend, in November, 1949, dad took me and my suitcase, which my mom had lovingly packed, to Regina, got me settled for room and board at his aunt's place, and drove to Eaton's where he marched me straight into Mr. Maltby's office. I remember being shy, but my dad told me not to be scared as Mr. Maltby knew me very well. My dad said "Well, Harry, here she is, ready to work for you." Mr. Maltby just smiled and said "I have a job for you," and he knew exactly where to put me. He took us way to the back of the store where they sold horse harnesses, barnyard tools, milking pails, and all that good stuff that a farm girl knows very well.

We then went to meet Mr. Jack South, manager of the hardware department. Mr. Maltby said "Jack, this is Velma Mellnick from Dysart and she will start working here for you tomorrow." I was very surprised and happy, as was my dad. I don't remember ever filling out an application form or anything; I just started selling the farm items that I was familiar with, and I did very well. Soon, I was transferred to stationery, then to the stove and fridge department. After a few years, I was transferred to the china department where I became signatory, then section head.

When I was promoted to assistant department manager, I went on buying trips to the Hotel Saskatchewan where I met sales people from all over the world. My manager, Mr. Jack Cant, would let me pick out most of the bone china, which came from England, Germany and Italy. It was fun and exciting to watch the arrival of the big barrels of china as they came to the store and were brought up to the china department for unpacking. I was so proud knowing that I had helped to pick out this fine china that came from so far away to be sold at Eaton's. It was a great feeling for a grade nine farm girl from little Dysart!

On the day before I started, I was leaving the store with my dad and ran into Maurice Van Buekenhout, a handsome, tall guy with a big smile. I told him that I was starting work at Eaton's tomorrow. I met Maurice a month earlier when my cousin Victor, who worked at Eaton's, brought him home for Thanksgiving weekend. Maurice worked in the grocery department right next to me in China, and he would send me many notes asking me to go on a date. After a few refusals, I agreed to go out with him, and in April 1951, we got engaged.

I must tell how it happened. I was hard at work in the china department, cleaning, dusting, and unpacking china to be put out for a big Eaton's sale that was coming up. My manager, Mr. Cant, came bursting into the department and asked what had I done wrong, as Mr. Maltby had called him in and told him to "send that little redhead to my office at once!" I told Mr. Cant that I didn't know why Mr. Maltby would want to see me, but he told me it must be something serious to be called up on the red carpet, and that I should go at once and report to him on my return.

When I got to Mr. Maltby's office, he looked at me and said "I hear your fingers have gone crooked. You and that daddy long-legs Maurice next to you have gotten engaged. Now why have you done this? I promised your dad when you started working here that I would keep an eye on you. Now look what you've done! Your dad is going to be very unhappy about this." I told Mr. Maltby that I was sorry for causing him concern, but that Maurice was a real gentleman, and a kind, hardworking person. What's more, we loved each other and all would be well. I thanked him for caring, and told him that I would call my dad.

I'll never forget my engagement day, and think about it often, with a smile. My dad and Mr. Maltby need not have worried. Maurice and I got married on July 26, 1952, have four wonderful children, 12 grandchildren, two great-grandchildren and have been blessed with many friends and a wonderful life—and we're ready to celebrate our 62nd anniversary this year!

—Velma Van Buekenhout

How I Met My Wife of Sixty-two Years at Eaton's

One very important thing that happened to me when I worked at Eaton's was in October of 1949. An acquaintance at work asked me to go home with him to Dysart, Saskatchewan for the Thanksgiving weekend. I did go, and met this girl at his mom's place on the first day I was there, and again at a social gathering the next day. When I returned to Regina, I thought of her, but I knew I would never see her again.

Early in November of that year, I was rushing back to work, going up the main aisle of Eaton's, but whom should I meet, but Velma, and she said "Guess what? I am starting to work for Eaton's tomorrow!" I could hardly believe that if my friend had not taken me home that Thanksgiving, Velma and I would have never met.

We became engaged in April 1951, and will be married 62 years in July of this year. I had to build a big display of groceries on the main aisle, and it featured a new laundry soap that came in big yellow and purple boxes. It was called "Vel," so ever after her nickname was Vel to most people!

—Maurice Van Buekenhout

Bibliography

Bassett, John M. *Celebrites Canadiennes: Timothy Eaton*. Longeuil, QC: Publications Julienne Inc., 1976.

Chisholm, Barbara, ed. *Castles of the North: Canada's Grand Hotels*. Toronto: Lynx Images Inc., 2003.

Dubin, Arthur. *More Classic Trains*. Milwaukee, WI: Kalmbach Publishing Company, 1974.

Eaton, Flora McRea. *Memory's Wall*. Toronto, ON: Clarke, Irwin & Company Limited, 1956.

Ferry, John William. *A History of the Department Store*. New York: Macmillan Company, 1960.

Gourluck, Ross. *A Store Like No Other: Eaton's of Winnipeg*. Winnipeg, MB: Great Plains Publications, 2008.

Longstreth, Richard. *The American Department Store Transformed, 1920–1960*. New Haven, CT: Yale University Press, 2010.

Macdonald, Edith ("The Scribe"). *Golden Jubilee, 1869–1919*. Toronto, ON: T. Eaton Co. Limited, 1919.

Macpherson, Mary-Etta. *Shopkeepers to a Nation: The Eatons*. Toronto, ON: McClelland and Stewart Limited, 1963.

McQueen, Rod. *The Eatons: The Rise and Fall of Canada's Royal Family*. Toronto, ON: Stoddart Publishing Company Limited, 1998.

Palmer, Alexandra, ed. *Fashion: A Canadian Perspective*. Toronto, ON: University of Toronto Press, 2004.

Phenix, Patricia. *Eatonians: The Story of the Family Behind the Family*. Toronto, ON: McClelland and Stewart Limited, 2002.

Santink, Joy. *Timothy Eaton and the Rise of His Department Store*. Toronto, ON: University of Toronto Press, 1990.

Stephenson, William. *The Store that Timothy Built*. Toronto, ON: McClelland and Stewart Limited, 1969.

The T. Eaton Co. Limited. *Eaton 100: A Special Edition of Eaton Quarterly*. Toronto, ON: self-published, 1969.

————. *Eaton's–College Street*. Toronto, ON: self-published, 1930.

————. *Our Company and Its People*. Toronto, ON: self-published, 1959.

————. *The Story of a Store*. Toronto, ON: self-published, 1925.

————. *The Story of a Store*. Toronto, ON: self-published, 1936.

————. *The Story of a Store*. Toronto, ON: self-published, 1946.

————. *The Story of a Store*. Toronto, ON: self-published, 1968.

Whitaker, Jan. *The World of Department Stores*. New York: Vendome Press, 2011.

Index

About the Author

B ruce Allen Kopytek came to be an author almost accidentally: he was searching for new opportunities when his career as an architect imploded as a result of the Great Recession. Although he figured that one day his status as an admitted and gleefully unrepentant "book-a-holic" would lead him to writing, a completely unexpected offer to write his first book—the award-winning *Jacobson's: I Miss It So!*—focused his attention on another of his favourite subjects: the life and times of North America's great, beloved and long-gone department stores.

Educated and licensed as an architect, Kopytek credits his parents and his close-knit family with his passion for travel, history and art. His parents placed education and their faith on a high pedestal and fostered both of these aspects of their family life through frequent travel and interest in culture in all its aspects. For the Kopytek family, life was experienced together, and on quite a high plane at that.

Taking cues from his past, Kopytek has travelled throughout North America and Europe and happily rediscovered his extended family across the Atlantic as a result. In architecture, he considers himself as a "jack-of-all-trades" who must be ready to fulfill any task that might present itself, whether artistic or practical. Along with a resurgent career, he is also proud of his reinvigourated and long-held religious faith.

Along with his wife, Carole, he enjoys travelling, ballroom dancing, lecturing on topics related to his books, cooking and doing volunteer work through his local Roman Catholic parish, St. Lawrence, in Utica, Michigan.

He cherishes his family and not only remains close with his sister, Mary, and brother, Patrick, as well as their children, but also takes delight in the family he inherited when he married again after living as a widower for ten years. His stepson, Jesse, is not just a support where computer technology is concerned but a partner in deeply felt conversations that both enjoy, and his stepdaughter, Jennifer Goodman, has brought a high level of artistic achievement to his family's life—after spending seventeen years with the Joffrey Ballet and achieving the position of principal dancer, she has gone on, in a freelance career, to grace no less than the stages of the Metropolitan Opera House in New York and the Lyric Opera of Chicago.

All of these things are the *mise en scène* for Kopytek's own pursuits in architecture and writing, and he considers them vital ingredients in life's mission. He lives happily with Carole in a townhouse, far north of his native Hamtramck, Michigan, and in spite of all indicators to the contrary ("That's life," says Frank Sinatra!), he has become enamored of his capricious and mercurial but loving cat, Bella—who, when suspecting he is letting his ego get away with him, simply bites him, out of the blue, and settles the matter to her enormous satisfaction.

Note: The photo shows the author in Lady Eaton's study at Eaton Hall in 2013.